Hitting
First

THE SECURITY CONTINUUM: GLOBAL POLITICS IN THE MODERN AGE

Series Editors: William W. Keller and Simon Reich

A series published in association with the Matthew B. Ridgway Center for International Security Studies and the Ford Institute for Human Security

Hitting First

PREVENTIVE FORCE IN U.S. SECURITY STRATEGY

Edited by

WILLIAM W. KELLER and

GORDON R. MITCHELL

UNIVERSITY OF PITTSBURGH PRESS

Published by the University of Pittsburgh Press, Pittsburgh, Pa., 15260

Library of Congress Cataloging-in-Publication Data

Hitting first : preventive force in US security strategy / edited by William W. Keller and
Gordon R. Mitchell.

    p.   cm.   (The security continuum)

  Includes bibliographical references and index.

   ISBN 0-8229-4290-9 (cloth : alk. paper)   ISBN 0-8229-5936-4 (pbk. : alk. paper)

   1. Preemptive attack (Military science) 2. Military planning   United States.   3. United
States   Military policy.   4. United States   Foreign relations   2001–   5. National
security   United States.   I. Keller, William W. (William Walton), 1950–   II. Mitchell,
Gordon R., 1967- III. Series.

  U163.H58 2006

  355.4 dc22   2006015728

CONTENTS

    Preventive Force   199
    JACQUES E. C. HYMANS

PART 4: OUTLOOK

11. Promoting Practical Alternatives to Preventive Force in the Wake of
    Operation Iraqi Freedom   217
    WILLIAM HARTUNG

12. Preventive Force: Untangling the Discourse   239
    WILLIAM W. KELLER AND GORDON R. MITCHELL

    Notes   265
    References   315
    Contributors   347
    Index   351

ABBREVIATIONS

BWC   Biological Weapons Convention
CIA   Central Intelligence Agency
CNN   Cable News Network
CPD   Committee on the Present Danger
CWC   Chemical Weapons Convention
DCI   Director of Central Intelligence
DIA   Defense Intelligence Agency
DNI   Director of National Intelligence
DOD   Department of Defense
DOE   Department of Energy
EU   European Union
FBI   Federal Bureau of Investigation
FCS   future combat systems
GSAVE   global struggle against violent extremism
GWOT   global war on terror
IAEA   International Atomic Energy Agency
IC   intelligence community
ICBM   intercontinental ballistic missile
ICCJ   International Court of Criminal Justice
IIS   Iraqi Intelligence Service
INC   Iraqi National Congress

INR	Bureau of Intelligence and Research (US Department of State)
ISG	Iraq Survey Group
NATO	North Atlantic Treaty Organization
NBC	nuclear, biological, and/or chemical
NGO	nongovernmental organization
NIC	National Intelligence Council
NIE	National Intelligence Estimate
NSA	National Security Agency
NSC	National Security Council
NSDD	National Security Decision Directive
NSS 2002	2002 National Security Strategy of the United States of America
OAU	Organization for African Unity
OSP	Office of Special Plans
PCTEG	Policy Counterterrorism Evaluation Group
PDB	President's Daily Brief
PMF	private military firm
PNAC	Project for the New American Century
RNEP	robust nuclear earth penetrator
STRATCOM	Strategic Command
UAV	unmanned aerial vehicle
UN	United Nations
UNITAF	Unified Task Force (United Nations)
UNOSOM	United Nations Operation in Somalia
UNSCOM	United Nations Special Commission
WMD	weapons of mass destruction

PART 1

Historical
Context

1

Preemption, Prevention, Prevarication

WILLIAM W. KELLER AND
GORDON R. MITCHELL

ECTION 603 OF THE 1986 Goldwater-Nichols Reorganization Act requires each US president to submit an annual report to Congress
outlining the nation's strategic security objectives. This is usually a
low-key affair that passes quietly under the political radar. An exception was
President George W. Bush's September 2002 submission of the National Security Strategy of the United States of America (NSS 2002). That strategy
document drew special notice, partly because it laid out the Bush administration's strategic thinking on the pressing issue of how to deal with the threat
of mass casualty terrorism after 11 September 2001. NSS 2002 also raised
eyebrows by declaring that the emergent danger posed by the "crossroads of
radicalism and technology" presents "a compelling case for taking anticipatory actions to defend ourselves, *even if uncertainty remains* as to the time and
place of the enemy's attack."[1]

Sympathetic commentators lauded NSS 2002 shortly after its publication, arguing that "acting preemptively"[2] was a shrewd way for the United
States to seize the strategic high ground in the "war on terror."[3] On the other
hand, skeptics cautioned that by asserting a prerogative to hit first against

3

terrorists and states that harbor them, the Bush administration risked unraveling the fabric of international law governing the use of force.[4] In explaining their new strategy, Bush officials emphasized a reminder: "Preemption is not a new concept."[5] Indeed, Article 51 of the United Nations (UN) Charter implicitly recognizes a right to "anticipatory self-defense," one that has been invoked previously by nations facing imminent security threats.[6]

Was the Bush administration's commitment to first-strike defense a rash gambit of historic proportions? Or was it simply a rearticulation of one military option long understood to be implicit in national security strategy? Key ambiguities in the text of NSS 2002 made it difficult to tell. It is one thing to use force in self-defense against an enemy that constitutes an imminent danger—Israel's 1967 preemptive strike against Egyptian forces massing in the Sinai desert is a textbook example.[7] It is another matter to strike a potential enemy who is suspected of plotting an attack at some unspecified time and place—consider Israel's 1981 bombardment of Iraq's nuclear facility at Osiraq. The latter case is more accurately described as preventive—not preemptive—use of military force.[8] Yet as Lieutenant Colonel Arnel Enriquez observes, "the distinction between preemption and prevention is blurred in the NSS."[9] By using the terms "preemptive" and "preventive" almost interchangeably, Secretary of Defense Donald Rumsfeld further clouded this distinction.[10] A follow-on strategy paper released by the White House two months after NSS 2002 did little to clear up precise conditions under which the United States would strike first with "preemptive measures" against adversaries suspected of developing nuclear, biological, or chemical (NBC) arms.[11]

Details regarding the White House's new use-of-force doctrine emerged when the Bush administration pulled NSS 2002 off the shelf and put it to use. In a bracing series of speeches and public appearances during 2002 and 2003, Bush officials castigated Saddam Hussein's regime as posing exactly the sort of threat that makes first use of military force prudent. As the buildup to invasion against Iraq proceeded, it became apparent that the US-led campaign would be a preventive, not preemptive, war. Public arguments advanced to justify Operation Iraqi Freedom revealed that the Bush administration's idea of "acting preemptively" went beyond Article 51's "anticipatory self-defense," drifting into the area of preventive warfare to counter "gathering," not imminent threats.[12]

Outright declaration of the preventive attack option in an official US strategy document challenged established rules of international conduct and raised a host of vexing policy concerns regarding alliance cohesion, intelligence capabilities, and resource trade-offs. Some continue to see assertion of this prerogative as a reckless break from established security doctrine.[13] Others downplay the novelty of this turn in American security strategy, arguing that NSS 2002's version of preventive military action is a timely adaptation of the long-accepted principle of preemptive self-defense.[14]

Hitting First engages this debate by analyzing preventive attack strategies from a multidisciplinary perspective that blends insight from political science, rhetoric, and philosophy with practical knowledge drawn from work in institutional policy settings. This opening chapter frames the study by considering NSS 2002's basic dynamics in more detail, outlining the book's common terms of reference, and previewing contents of the ensuing chapters.

A STRATEGY FOR "THE BOYS IN LUBBOCK"

In the fall of 2002, one year after al-Qaida's devastating suicide airline attacks, the blueprint for a new US security strategy was taking shape. While President Bush used broad strokes to outline the nascent strategy in a series of speeches to American military academies, then national security advisor Condoleezza Rice worked on a document that would express the basic concepts in finer detail. She tapped State Department official Richard Haass to write the first draft, then brought in University of Virginia professor Philip Zelikow and deputy national security advisor Stephen Hadley to help with revisions.[15] The result was NSS 2002, a bold and ambitious twenty-nine-page document that announced the White House's intention to "defeat global terrorism" by strengthening alliances, "igniting" economic growth, spreading democracy, and most notably, "acting preemptively" to hit enemies first, before they could mount attacks on the United States.[16]

Ten days after release of NSS 2002, Rice gave a speech that the White House billed as a discussion of the "President's National Security Strategy." In her introductory comments, it became apparent that she viewed the venue for the address—New York—as symbolically important on multiple levels. First, Rice linked her decision to "venture beyond Washington" for the speech with President Bush's preference that NSS 2002 should contain "plain English, not academic jargon." Regarding the strategy document, Rice quoted Bush as saying, "The boys in Lubbock ought to be able to read it."[17] Second, the New York audience provided an opportunity for the administration to frame NSS 2002 as a direct response to the 11 September attacks: "And after 9/11, there is no longer any doubt that today America faces an existential threat to our security. . . . President Bush's new National Security Strategy offers a bold vision for protecting our Nation that captures today's new realities and new opportunities," said Rice.[18]

As a rhetorical strategy for domestic mobilization, Rice's framing device proved enormously successful. The simple formula 9/11 = NSS 2002 became a ubiquitous theme in public deliberation.[19] It was a compelling notion that played well with "the boys in Lubbock," and also seemed to explain how Bush could transmogrify so dramatically from an advocate of "humble" US foreign policy on the 2000 campaign trail to a determined interventionist in the Oval Office two years later.[20] However, even as this popular narrative illuminated, it also obscured. In the words of Andrew Bacevich, "The grievous losses suffered in the attacks on the World Trade Center and the Pentagon had seemingly rendered all that had gone before irrelevant."[21] By fixing 11 September 2001 as the temporal starting point for discussions about US security strategy, Rice's framing device cultivated mass amnesia about the crucial fact that the lion's share of strategic concepts in NSS 2002 had been pilot-tested long before al-Qaida attacked the US homeland.

In this vein, consider that NSS 2002's bureaucratic lineage can be traced to earlier planning documents, such as a 1992 Pentagon Defense Planning Guidance draft,[22] a 1996 strategy paper prepared for Israeli prime minister Benjamin Netanyahu,[23] a 1998 pressure group letter to President Bill Clinton,[24] and a US think-tank report published in 2000.[25] Each of these boardroom blueprints endorsed first-strike force as a key element of defense strategy and suggested Iraq as prime target for preventive war.[26] However, authors of these reports, such as John Bolton, Stephen Cambone, Lewis Libby, Richard Perle, Donald Rumsfeld, Abram Shulsky, Paul Wolfowitz, David Wurmser, and Dov Zakheim, encountered resistance when, as private citizens, they attempted to translate their ideas into policy with private lobbying during the Clinton administration. Their 2000 Project for the New American Century (PNAC) report, *Rebuilding America's Defenses*, contains a striking metaphor that likens military planners' lack of interest in the PNAC "hit first" strategy during the 1990s to a complacent ring fighter gone soft:

[Some believe] the United States can enjoy a respite from the demands of international leadership. . . . Like a boxer between championship bouts, America can afford to relax and live the good life, certain that there would be enough time to shape up for the next big challenge. . . . But as we have seen over the past decade, there has been no shortage of powers around the world who have taken the collapse of the Soviet empire as an opportunity to expand their own influence and challenge the American-led security order.[27]

After Bush's 2000 election victory ushered them into the corridors of power, Bolton, Cambone, Libby, Perle, Rumsfeld, Shulksy, Wolfowitz, Wurmser, and Zakheim took a big step toward realizing their goals, but obstacles remained. Their sweeping vision of American "dominance" through military "transformation" and "regime change" was blocked by recalcitrant quarters of the entrenched Washington bureaucracy. Yet in their 2000 planning document, the PNAC authors presciently foresaw one scenario that could break the logjam: "Further, the process of transformation, even if it brings revolutionary change, is likely to be a long one, absent some catastrophic and catalyzing event—like a new Pearl Harbor."[28] The fact that the 9/11 attacks provided just this sort of "Pearl Harbor" jolt to the system has fueled the speculation of conspiracy theorists. For example, Claremont University theology professor David Lee Griffin cites the PNAC "new Pearl Harbor" reference as one piece of evidence supporting the theory that Bush administration officials conspired to enable the 9/11 attacks.[29] As *Publishers Weekly* notes in a review of Griffin's book, "Even many Bush opponents will find these charges ridiculous."[30] Yet it is far more difficult to dismiss findings from the National Commission on Terrorist Attacks upon the United States (9/11 Commission) that PNAC-affiliated Bush administration officials such as Rumsfeld seized almost immediately on the 9/11 attacks as triggers for preventive war against Iraq. According to notes taken by Rumsfeld's deputy Cambone, when smoke was still billowing out of the Pentagon at 2:40 P.M. on 11 September 2001, the secretary of defense hunkered down in the operations center, and "[Rumsfeld's] instinct was to hit Saddam Hussein at the same time—not only bin Ladin."[31] Other Bush officials soon followed suit; Bob Woodward reports that days later, at Camp David, Wolfowitz "seized the opportunity" of 9/11 to press his long-standing case for attacking Iraq.[32]

Hitting First explores this episode as an instance of what Frank Baumgartner and Bryan Jones call "policy entrepreneurship," the practice of alert actors responding to windows of opportunity by asserting agency in the policy process.[33] As Chris Mackenzie notes, the policy entrepreneur is "skilled in the art of argument and persuasion, and is able to manipulate how problems and policy issues are defined, so as to mould new 'policy images' and exploit the many 'policy venues' present."[34] Rumsfeld's and Wolfowitz's first round of policy entrepreneurship did not succeed—on 15 September 2001, Bush rebuffed their calls to invade Iraq in the immediate aftermath of 9/11.[35] Yet soon afterward, they regrouped with other former PNAC members to mount a much broader and more coordinated campaign that culminated in NSS 2002 and Operation Iraqi Freedom.[36] This campaign institutionalized key tenets of the 1992 Defense Planning Guidance draft, the 1996 "Clean Break" memorandum, the 1998 PNAC letter to Clinton, and the 2000 PNAC report. It also built public support for preventive war in Iraq through a variety of strategies involving intelligence manipulation, foreign diplomacy, and media influence. Notably, the Bush administration's continuing commitment to preventive warfare is underscored in the National Security Strategy of 2006, which reinforces NSS 2002's assertion of the prerogative to strike first against "gathering" threats. According to National Security Advisor Stephen Hadley, "The President's [2006] strategy affirms that the doctrine of preemption remains sound and must remain an integral part of our National Security Strategy."[37]

THEORETICAL APPROACH

This volume analyzes the role of preventive military force in US security strategy in a narrow sense, exploring the Bush administration's official codification of a preventive first-strike prerogative, and expansively, looking at how NSS 2002 relates to the broader historical record. Several discourse-oriented chapters focus on the fact that much of the Bush administration's definition and legitimation of its preventive warfare strategy was accomplished in official speeches and public statements by cabinet members.[38] While NSS 2002 provided a sketch of the Bush first-strike policy, details that transformed it into a working doctrine came in key public addresses, such as President Bush's West Point graduation speech, Vice President Richard Cheney's address at the Veterans of Foreign Wars, and Secretary of State Colin Powell's presentation to the UN.[39] Analysis of these addresses helps to explain how the White House successfully sold its new military approach to key audiences.

The considerable time lag separating announcement of the proposal to invade Iraq and commencement of Operation Iraqi Freedom opened unprecedented space for US officials and sympathetic advocates to proffer public arguments justifying a specific first-strike venture prior to its execution. In a democratic society, declaratory policy expressing an official commitment to use preventive military force raises burdens of public justification for decisions to implement such policy in given instances. The significance of this process surpasses domestic political considerations, since, as Mohammed Ayoob notes, "Normative justifications, when resorted to repeatedly, lead to the emergence and consolidation of a range of international expectations that, in turn, begin to change the normative framework within which states operate."[40] Some chapters in *Hitting First* take this insight as a point of departure to evaluate the history of preventive military force, its moral status, and its strategic appropriateness, especially in light of alternative security strategies that emphasize nonmilitary means of prevention. Here, study of the wider policy arena builds context necessary to assess NSS 2002's dynamics and future prospects.

The parameters of a shared theoretical approach weaving the contributors' research together emerged during the course of two workshops convened to organize paper drafts around common terms of reference. This task proved somewhat challenging, given that much of the nomenclature relating to the Bush administration's embrace of preventive military strategy is itself ambiguous. As workshop discussions proceeded, it became apparent that the imprecise character of some of the central concepts offered an important window into understanding public debate over NSS 2002, where advocates tend to stretch the meaning of elastic terms and where semantic confusion often fuels controversy. The authors of *Hitting First* adapted to this phenomenon by carefully delineating three of these malleable and contested concepts—one acronym, one distinction, and one spectrum.

"WMD"

The official origin of the phrase "weapons of mass destruction" can be traced to a 1948 resolution passed by the UN Commission for Conventional Armaments.[41] However, the phrase (and its acronym, "WMD") did not become a fixture of Cold War public dialogue until US officials deployed it to dramatize the horror of chemical weapons usage during the Iran-Iraq War. Then came the 11 September 2001 attacks, after which Bush administration officials chose "WMD" as a favored catchphrase. So many followed suit that the American Dialect Society voted "WMD" its "Word of the Year" for 2002.[42] According to a study by Susan Moeller of the University of Maryland's Center for International and Security Studies, "Most journalists accepted the Bush administration's formulation of the 'War on Terror' as a campaign against WMD."[43]

The ubiquity of "WMD" as a term of reference has a significant effect in framing public discussion of NSS 2002, since the acronym enables advocates of preventive war to argue that first-strike force is a necessary response to a syndrome of disparate threats neatly bundled together under the umbrella of "WMD." As Moeller observes, media reportage tended to reinforce this notion during the run-up to the 2003 Iraq War: "Most media outlets represented WMD as a monolithic menace, failing to adequately distinguish between weapons programs and actual weapons or to address the real differences among chemical, biological, nuclear, and radiological weapons."[44] This semantic leveling obscures the fact that each class of weapons falling under the "WMD" umbrella varies significantly with regard to potential lethality and destructive power; the feasibility of protection and defenses; and potential missions.[45] When dimensions of threat are blurred in this fashion, inaccuracies are easy to introduce. For example, the rhetorical flexibility afforded by the omnibus category "weapons of mass destruction" enabled Bush administration officials to support claims of an Iraqi "WMD" threat (replete with ominous "mushroom cloud" imagery) by pointing to evidence of possible Iraqi chemical weapons development. Clearly, chemical weapons lack the capacity for nuclear destruction, yet as Wolfgang Panofsky points out,

"Linking these three classes of weapons in a single WMD category elevates the status of both biological and chemical weapons."[46]

In a study that predates the Bush administration's "WMD"-based justifications for war against Iraq, Carnegie Endowment for International Peace analyst Gert Harigel argues that the term "weapons of mass destruction" is "misleading, politically dangerous, and cannot be justified on grounds of military efficiency."[47] Moeller's more recent study concludes that fresh disclosures detailing misuse of threat intelligence in the Iraq case "have dramatically demonstrated the need for greater public understanding of the role that WMD plays in the formulation of and rhetorical justifications for US security policy."[48]

The chapters in *Hitting First* are crafted to address this need, with authors focusing critical attention on how the conflation of chemical, biological, radiological, and nuclear weaponry enacted by the acronym "WMD" frames public understanding of NSS 2002 and steers deliberation on the topic of preventive military force. This approach highlights, for example, how the relationship between chemical, biological, and nuclear threat categories plays out at the seam connecting the intelligence community (IC) to policy-makers, as well as how the monolithic "WMD" construct works rhetorically to persuade public audiences of the necessity to launch first-strike attacks. To avoid reproducing confusion created by the phrase "weapons of mass destruction," the contributors to this volume follow Greg Thielmann's lead, adopting the standard practice he used at the State Department's Bureau of Intelligence and Research (INR). At the INR, Thielmann directed analysts to eschew the acronym "WMD" when writing reports, and instead either name the specific class of weapons being referenced (for example, chemical, biological, radiological, or nuclear weapons) or, in a pinch, to use the more accurate phrase "unconventional weaponry."

PREEMPTIVE VERSUS PREVENTIVE USE OF FORCE

The distinction between preemptive and preventive use of military force is codified in an official Pentagon document,[49] and recognized as a key tenet of international law.[50] However, as we noted previously, some proponents of NSS 2002 prevaricate by using the terms "preventive" and "preemptive" interchangeably.[51] The resulting fog of semantic confusion facilitates a mix-and-match rhetorical strategy that defends preventive military force by linking it to the more legitimate aspects of preemptive action. As Arthur M. Schlesinger Jr. observes, this tactic has proved quite effective: "Given the disrepute attached to the idea of 'preventive' war, the Bush administration prefers to talk about 'preemptive' war, and too many have followed its example."[52] Unfortunately, as Henry Laver argues, eliding this important distinction not only clouds understanding of the real nature of NSS 2002, it also poses tangible security risks:

Potential allies may perceive such imprecision as an American inability to recognize the subtleties and nuances of diplomacy, resulting in decreased international confidence and hindering the prospect of a united front against terrorism. Indiscriminately swapping terms can also mislead potential enemies, convincing them to accelerate development of deterrent capabilities, namely "WMD," to counter a perceived threat from the United States when none may in fact exist.[53]

In making the preemptive/preventive distinction a common reference point of analysis, authors of *Hitting First* sort out this tangle of nomenclature, revisiting historical episodes and scholarly commentaries that elucidate and rehabilitate the distinction.[54] Conversely, scrutiny of the recent texts and practices that erode the distinction helps show how the Bush White House successfully invoked the parlance of self-defense to legitimize a manifestly offensive military strategy. For example, rhetorical analysis reveals how transmogrification of the term "imminence" enabled Bush officials to execute this persuasive maneuver in official speeches prior to the 2003 Iraq War. Looking ahead, authors analyze the possible fallout that permanent erasure of the preemptive-preventive distinction might have for the US IC, American military readiness, and the morality of US foreign policy.

THE SPECTRUM OF FORCE

Soon after the release of NSS 2002, a US MQ-1B Predator unmanned aerial vehicle (UAV) flew into Yemen, where it tracked a sport utility vehicle (SUV) being driven by suspected al-Qaida terrorists. About an hour later, a US soldier guiding the UAV, in a command center some 350 miles away in Dijibouti, launched an AGM-114 Hellfire air-attack missile that destroyed the SUV and its passengers. Military analyst Bill Yenne calls this episode a "small but important turning point in military history," because it was the first time the United States used a UAV to carry out an offensive strike mission.[55] This application of first-strike force, though less controversial than the 2003 Iraq War, raises a host of questions regarding "low-intensity military confrontations." As Seyom Brown notes, we are "entering a vast unknown" where the maturation of such technology creates capabilities to use preventive force in unique ways that challenge established principles of sovereignty and political accountability.[56] Since these low-intensity attacks raise different issues than full-scale military interventions with regime-change missions, any assessment of preventive military strategy must come to grips with the spectrum of force that can be applied in striking first.

The authors of *Hitting First* engage this issue by adopting preventive military strategy's spectrum of force as a common reference point of analysis. One windfall of this approach is a comprehensive history of all recorded twenty-four preventive attacks against NBC weapons targets, with the attacks sorted at various points along the spectrum, ranging from low-intensity missile strikes to high-intensity regime-change interventions. The analytical flexibility afforded by a commitment to consider different kinds of first-strike force also brings the topic of humanitarian military intervention and peacekeeping under the purview of inquiry. The resulting comparisons between traditionally low-intensity peacekeeping missions and high-intensity preventive attacks yield surprising insights. Finally, the spectrum-of-force approach colors prospective assessments of the intelligence and military capacity to implement first-strike strategies, since obviously, low-intensity warfare tends not only to be less destructive but also less resource intensive than its more elaborate counterparts on the higher end of the use-of-force spectrum.

The remainder of this chapter previews the book's content, which comes in four sections. Section one fills out the historical backdrop framing the debate over NSS 2002. The second section examines public discourse advanced to justify the theory and practice of preventive warfare. The logistical constraints complicating the implementation of NSS 2002 are considered in section three, while section four assesses the future of first-strike force in US security strategy in light of the analyses offered in these pages.

A WIDE ANGLE LENS: PREVENTIVE MILITARY STRATEGY IN HISTORICAL CONTEXT

Public memory of military conflicts is often colored vividly by iconic images that capture telling moments. The photograph of marines valiantly raising the American flag over Iwo Jima became a symbol of US commitment and fighting spirit during World War II, just as the image of naked, nine-year-old Phan Thi Kim Phuc fleeing a napalm attack dramatized the agony of war in Vietnam. On 9 April 2003, an event unfolded in Baghdad's Firdos Square that seemed flush with history-making potential—a statue of ousted Iraqi dictator Saddam Hussein was pulled off its moorings, then smashed to pieces by what appeared to be a jubilant crowd of liberated Iraqis.

Since Firdos Square is adjacent to the Palestine Hotel, which housed many journalists covering the 2003 Iraq War, visual images of Hussein's toppling statue quickly circled the globe. American reporters punctuated "the war's most symbolic piece of video"[57] with breathless commentary. Mark Phillips of CBS News described the scene from Baghdad: "This crowd has been growing. . . . It's a scene to remember. It's not just remarkable. It's not just extraordinary. It is historic."[58] The episode was thick with drama; "Every detail of the toppling dripped with upbeat, telegenic symbolism."[59] News anchors stoked excitement back in US television studios. On the *Today* show, Katie Couric announced, "I think it's safe to say we may be witnessing the lasting symbol of Operation Iraqi Freedom right now."[60] Couric's colleague Tom Brokaw framed the unfolding events in Cold War terms: "It is so reminiscent to me of watching the Berlin Wall coming down."[61]

In a matter of hours, "the images from Firdos Square already had been condensed into easily rerun 10-second bursts: the statue falls, the crowd cheers."[62] In the news cycle that followed, many echoed Brokaw's Cold War framing of the image. On Fox News, correspondent Ceci Connolly said, "It was reminiscent, I think, of the fall of the Berlin Wall. And just sort of that pure emotional expression, not choreographed, not stage-managed, the way so many things these days seem to be. Really breathtaking."[63] Secretary of Defense Rumsfeld struck a similar chord at a news conference later in the day, saying that after watching Hussein's statue tumble, "one cannot help but think of the fall of the Berlin Wall and the collapse of the Iron Curtain."[64]

The most evocative initial images from Firdos Square were close-in shots of excited people crowding around the statue, pulling on a rope attached to the neck of Saddam Hussein's likeness (see figure 1). This tight vantage point seemed to validate the triumphal news narrative that described the statue takedown as a spontaneous outburst of jubilation by scores of liberated Iraqis: "The networks knew we'd be transfixed by the amazing video: This is the sort of flash from the front that plays in Peoria. The rich imagery seemed to speak volumes about the overthrow of the evil dictator."[65]

Less widely circulated photographs told a different story. These images, shot from a wider angle, showed Firdos Square from a more panoramic perspective (see figure 2). From this vantage point, it became apparent that the crowd was much smaller than suggested by the tighter shots, and that Hussein's statue was actually being pulled down by an American M88 recovery vehicle. In fact, Firdos Square itself turned out to be ringed by several US military tanks, causing some to wonder "whether the toppling of the statue of Saddam was as spontaneous as it was made to appear."[66]

More doubts were raised when an internal army study disclosed that the US 305th Psychological Operations Company played a significant role in the event.[67] When this psychological warfare unit arrived at Firdos Square on 9 April 2003, it "started to do some PSYOP [psychological operations] broad-

FIGURE 1. *(left)* Statue of
Saddam Hussein being toppled
in Firdos Square, Baghdad,
9 April 2003. Photo © Patrick
Robert/Corbis.

FIGURE 2. *(below)* Statue of
Saddam Hussein being toppled
in Firdos Square, Baghdad,
9 April 2003.
Photo © REUTERS TV.

casts about bringing about a free Iraq."[68] Soon thereafter, a colonel with the 4th Marine Regiment "saw the Saddam statue as a target of opportunity and decided that the statue must come down."[69] Assessing things with the benefit of hindsight afforded by this broader picture, communication scholar Christopher Simpson notes, "This particular event was more of what you might call a propaganda event. It was a publicity, a photo-op if you will."[70]

Part one of *Hitting First* draws back the analytical lens to cast NSS 2002 in broad historical perspective. Just as a panoramic view elucidates key parts of the 9 April 2003 scene in Firdos Square, a long view of history provides salient background for understanding the strategic, tactical, and political dimensions of preventive military force. In one respect, this approach lends perspective by clarifying NSS 2002's origins. Bush administration strategists did not fashion a post-9/11 military doctrine from whole cloth. Rather, their ideas built on strategies and techniques honed in the Cold War struggle against the Soviet Union, as well as initiatives by several UN General Secretaries to recalibrate the relationship between national sovereignty and the use of force during the 1990s. Analysis of this historical arc sheds light on how the ideas in NSS 2002 evolved, and provides useful reference points that fill out the contextual backdrop framing understanding of the Bush administration's emergent use-of-force doctrine. For example, consider that in 1984, secret authorization for US first-strike attacks on guerrilla forces came from classified National Security Decision Directive (NSDD) 138, entitled, "Preemptive Strikes against Suspected Terrorists."

The still-classified portions of this directive authorized the establishment of secret FBI and CIA paramilitary squads and use of existing Pentagon military units—such as the Green Berets and Navy SEALs—for conducting what amounted to guerrilla warfare against guerrillas. It authorized sabotage, killing (though not "assassination"), preemptive and retaliatory raids, deception, and a significantly expanded intelligence collection program aimed at suspected radicals and people regarded as sympathizers.[71]

As NSDD 138 demonstrates, Secretary Rumsfeld's comparison of a tumbling statue in Baghdad to a crumbling wall in Berlin is not the only dimension of Operation Iraqi Freedom with deep Cold War roots. Since preventive use-of-force strategies have been proposed and implemented before, a close look at these historical correlates is warranted. Chapter 2, Dan Reiter's "Preventive Attacks against Nuclear, Biological and Chemical Weapons Programs: The Track Record," is a companion piece to his 1995 *International Security* article on the oft-misunderstood history of preemptive warfare.[72] Reiter uses a similar approach here to assess the track record of success for the twenty-four preventive attacks that have been launched against

NBC weapons programs from 1942 to 2003. He categorizes these attacks into discrete clusters, including Allied strikes on the German and Japanese unconventional weapons programs in World War II; Israeli and Iranian attacks on the Iraqi nuclear program from 1979 to 1981; Iraq's Scud attacks on Israel's nuclear program (during Operation Desert Storm) and Iran's nuclear and chemical facilities (during the Iran-Iraq War); US and coalition forces cruise missile strikes on al-Qaida NBC weapons facilities in Afghanistan and Sudan; and finally the numerous US and coalition strikes versus Iraq's NBC assets from 1991 to 2003.[73]

Every "track record" assessment contains normative assumptions, and Reiter makes his transparent by engaging openly the question of how one decides whether a given preventive attack "succeeds." The resulting discussion yields valuable insight regarding the selection of criteria for evaluating the effectiveness of preventive attacks on NBC weapons programs. For example, Reiter finds that one key dimension of assessment criteria involves the time horizon for evaluation. A "snapshot" approach that focuses on the immediate aftermath of a preventive attack (for example, the dome of Iraq's Osiraq nuclear facility was blown up by a 1981 Israeli raid) may heighten perception of short-term success, yet obscure the fact that over the longer term, nations often restore weapons facilities damaged in limited preventive attacks that do not achieve regime change. Reiter develops this point in an extended analysis of Israel's strike on the Osiraq reactor. A preview of Reiter's argument appears in his March 2005 letter to the editor, published in the *Atlantic Monthly*. James Fallows's response underscores the salience of Reiter's historical research in the contemporary policy debate regarding the wisdom of using preventive first-strikes to attack Iran's nuclear infrastructure.[74]

In chapter 3, Simon Reich's wide-angle lens for framing understanding of NSS 2002 focuses attention on the erosion of national sovereignty as an operational cornerstone of the international system. Multilateral peacekeeping missions have long relied on preventive military force to achieve humanitarian objectives. Reich shows how relatively recent changes in the operational attributes and broader mandates of peacekeeping missions have steadily diluted the principle of sovereignty.

Reich's analysis traces doctrinal shifts that have unfolded over the past two decades, amid humanitarian crises in Somalia, Rwanda, and Macedonia. Traditional peacekeeping doctrines protected sovereignty by stipulating that peacekeeping forces required consent from affected states before intervening. The rise of the "peace enforcement" paradigm, championed by a series of UN secretary generals, including Kofi Annan, narrowed this stipulation by making sovereignty conditional. Under peace enforcement, which gained adherents in the mid-1990s, states that violate universally accepted principles of behavior—international norms—give up their right to sovereignty and become subject to the application of preventive military force without consent.

The surprising upshot of Reich's analysis is that Annan inadvertently did important spadework that laid a foundation for NSS 2002's frontal assault on the principle of national sovereignty. The doctrines of coercive humanitarian intervention and preventive military intervention are supported by different groups (primarily the UN and the Bush administration), advocate different methods (multilateralism versus unilateralism or a limited coalition), and have different objectives (the relief from ethnic conflict, genocide, or famine versus addressing a clear and present danger of unconventional weaponry or terrorism). However, Reich argues that they share an important root in that they challenge the shibboleth of sovereignty in the new millennium.

In chapter 4, Gordon Mitchell and Robert Newman study other historical precursors to NSS 2002, such as NSC-68, the 1950 planning document known as the "blueprint for Cold War defense."[75] Others have noted how NSC-68's endorsement of "any measures" necessary to fight the Cold War bears a similarity to NSS 2002's assertion of a first-strike prerogative.[76] In "By 'Any Measures' Necessary: NSC-68 and Cold War Roots of the 2002 National Security Strategy," Mitchell and Newman build on this scholarship by reconstructing the political strategies and argumentative maneuvers deployed by Paul Nitze and the Committee on the Present Danger (CPD) to ram NSC-68 through a skeptical national security bureaucracy and translate its ringing alarmism into plans for US preventive warfare against the Soviet Union. Their findings reveal argument patterns that readers may find familiar today, such as deductive logic schemes that convert absence of evidence into positive proof, reliance on defector testimony as a preferred form of intelligence data, and synthesis of disparate data points into monolithic threat constructs.

Another prominent theme of this analysis is that historically, preventive warfare and public deception go hand in hand. As one illustration, Mitchell and Newman point to Operation Northwoods, a 1962 plan by the Joint Chiefs of Staff to trick the US public into supporting a military first strike on Cuba. This plan called for the US government to create pretexts for preventive war by staging bizarre events such as rigged airline hijackings and "remember the *Maine*" incidents at sea, which would then be blamed on Fidel Castro.[77] General Lyman Lemnitzer, mastermind of this deception gambit, went on to join Nitze and Paul Wolfowitz in the influential 1975–1976 "Team B" experiment in competitive intelligence analysis. Mitchell and Newman show how Wolfowitz and others in the George W. Bush White House replicated this Team B strategy sixteen years later to "fix" the "intelligence and facts" around the policy of regime change in Iraq.[78]

ADLAI STEVENSON MOMENTS: PUBLIC DISCOURSE
JUSTIFYING USE OF PREVENTIVE MILITARY FORCE

One factor likely to complicate American military planning in a world of
first-strike warfare is the likelihood that ad hoc coalitions will have to be assembled each time a major operation is contemplated. Allied consent not only
enables US military forces to use foreign bases and gain access to airspace;
it also works as political glue holding together often fragile political coalitions assembled to back particular military missions.[79] This challenge calls on
American officials to rally potential coalition partners to the cause by prof-
fering sufficiently persuasive evidence of a threat. But such evidence is not
always easy to obtain, and interested states and other political entities can
interpret it very differently.

A textbook example of successful persuasion took place in 1962, when
American ambassador Adlai Stevenson shocked the world by presenting to
the UN Security Council dramatic aerial photographs of Soviet nuclear missiles being unloaded in Cuba. Such evidence gave instant legitimacy to the
Kennedy administration's naval blockade in the Cuban missile crisis, and led
commentators to coin the phrase "Adlai Stevenson moment" to describe episodes where US officials present "incontrovertible" evidence justifying use of
force in international crisis situations.[80]

Secretary Powell felt the historical weight of Stevenson's smashing presentation some forty years later, as he prepared his own pivotal UN address
on Iraq in early 2003. "The greatest challenge was knowing that it was going
to be an Adlai Stevenson moment," Powell told an interviewer. "And every
reporter was getting their score sheet out."[81] Powell's address scored quick
political points for the White House and provided a much-needed short-term
boost in public support for Operation Iraqi Freedom. But over time, key elements of his case disintegrated—the probative value of satellite photography
showing alleged Iraqi chemical weapons activity was discounted;[82] a British
dossier on Iraq's terror links proved to be drawn from a plagiarized graduate
student paper;[83] Iraq's aluminum tube imports were judged by International
Atomic Energy Agency (IAEA) scientists not to have nuclear enrichment applications;[84] and the single source for documentation of Iraq's alleged mobile
biological weapons facilities was discredited as a "serial fabricator."[85] Perhaps
this episode calls for coinage of a new locution—the "Colin Powell moment"—to describe instances where high-stakes justifications of US military
force appear initially persuasive, but then erode under subsequent scrutiny.

In the aftermath of Operation Iraqi Freedom, considerable energy has
been spent dissecting the massive intelligence failure that led to Secretary
Powell's UN debacle. But another mystery has received comparatively little

attention—if Powell's evidence was so poor, why did a raft of opinion leaders find his arguments persuasive, and why did public support for the Iraq War surge following his speech?[86] In the second section's opening chapter, "Strategic Doctrine, Public Debate and the Terror War," Tom Goodnight gains purchase on these questions by analyzing how Bush administration officials lowered the rhetorical bar for Powell's speech by articulating details of NSS 2002 in ways that set lax proof standards for justifying use of first-strike force.

Goodnight's analysis focuses on how Bush administration officials shifted the meaning of a pivotal term, "imminence," in public speeches clarifying the dynamics of their new first-strike posture. In American jurisprudence, the origin point of standards for determining the legitimacy of anticipatory self-defense can be traced to an 1842 legal case involving border skirmishes with Canada, where Daniel Webster set forth criteria stipulating conditions under which a threat could be sufficiently "imminent" so as to justify preemptive warfare. Whereas Webster's criteria for assessing a threat's imminence emphasize factors such as the immediacy and unavoidability of impending enemy attack, speeches by Bush, Rumsfeld, and Cheney lay out a subtly different formulation of imminence. Goodnight shows how this reformulated concept of imminence structured public debate on Operation Iraqi Freedom. This analysis not only helps explain the persuasiveness of Powell's UN address, but it also lays bare some of the key working dynamics of NSS 2002. According to Goodnight, the White House's revised imminence standard reverses the burden of proof in public argument by insisting that unless a foreign enemy proves that it does not possess unconventional weapons programs, it can be assumed to pose an imminent threat. Stephen Hartnett and Laura Stengrim classify this maneuver as an argumentative fallacy known as the *argumentum ad ignorantiam*—"the rhetorical trick of manufacturing certainty out of uncertainty."[87]

When Goodnight relates these findings to the distinction between preemptive and preventive warfare, he highlights some thorny dilemmas facing officials who must juggle conflicting political and operational concerns in justifying the use of first-strike force. As an enemy threat becomes more immediate, evidence justifying a preemptive attack grows more convincing, and the political case for use of force becomes easier to make. But if would-be preempters wait too long for threat evidence to mature, they forfeit the element of surprise and give enemies an opportunity to harden their arsenals, lessening the chances that a preemptive first strike will succeed. Here a Hobson's choice between political disrepute and operational failure bedevils first-strike planning. This dilemma takes on a slightly different form for officials contemplating use of preventive military force. In this problematic, the opportunity to neutralize an enemy's nascent arsenal, before it has fully matured, maximizes prospects for operational success. But this in turn introduces political complications, since it may only be possible to justify preventive first-strike missions by wringing maximum proof from speculative data pointing to an enemy's early efforts to develop NBC weapons. Building on this insight, Goodnight notes how NSS 2002 contains an inbuilt impetus to exaggerate threat evidence.

While numerous official investigations have concluded that the American case for preventive war against Iraq was based on exaggerated threat evidence,[88] so far the Bush administration has largely escaped political accountability for these errors by blaming the IC. Rodger Payne's chapter, "Deliberate before Striking First?" revisits the Iraq War timeline and notices something startling—administration officials were exaggerating threat evidence on Iraq *before* the IC completed its National Intelligence Estimate (NIE) in October 2002. This is especially remarkable in light of the fact that key Bush administration officials were saying that Saddam Hussein was "in check" and "living on borrowed time" as late as February 2001. Noting that the "we were given bad intelligence" excuse does not account for the White House's exaggeration of threat evidence from February 2001 to October 2002, Payne searches for other explanations and discovers evidence of a systematic effort by Bush administration officials to manipulate public debate. With this effort, Payne picks up where the Senate Select Intelligence Committee stalled. That committee originally planned to follow up on its July 2004 report of the IC's role in the Iraq prewar intelligence failure with a phase two investigation that would focus on the White House's role in the fiasco. However, that follow-up probe proved difficult to execute, as the second stage of the investigation suffered through postponements, derailments, and restarts.[89] Payne amplifies evidence published in the annex of the committee's phase one report to detail how the White House's "communicative misdeeds" distorted public debate and may have pressured the IC to produce its flawed NIE in October 2002.

Payne frames the significance of this strategic deception campaign by examining how it sharply contradicts portions of NSS 2002 that insist on the importance of public deliberation and debate as safeguards that limit preventive war options. Clearly, US officials were concerned that other nations might cynically adopt NSS 2002's logic and use it as a "pretext for aggression." Payne shows how these concerns led the White House to attach "deliberative caveats" to its assertion of a first-strike prerogative. Drafters of NSS 2002 apparently hoped that abuse of the preventive warfare option by other nations could be curtailed by stipulating a requirement that first-strike force ought to be justified in public spheres of deliberation prior to executing attacks. What are the consequences of the White House violating its own self-imposed deliberative requirement? This question drives the concluding portion of Payne's analysis, where he suggests that one negative security outcome may be a "Chicken Little effect," where world skepticism sown by US strategic deception complicates efforts to persuade audiences of the need to act swiftly when real threats appear on the horizon.[90]

In "On Justifying the First Blow," philosopher Tom Rockmore closes out part two by adding a moral dimension to the discussion of whether and how first-strike force can be justified. Echoing Goodnight, Rockmore uses the preemption-prevention distinction as a point of departure for his analysis. After rehearsing how the distinction plays out in official, scholarly, and commonsense terms, Rockmore considers the moral status of first-strike attacks by comparing how preemptive and preventive uses of military force square with various just war theories. Rockmore's conclusion circles back to Thrasymachus, the character in Plato's dialogues who simplifies moral dilemmas into a tidy axiom: "Might makes right."

FROM BOARDROOM TO BATTLEFIELD: CHALLENGES OF IMPLEMENTING PREVENTIVE WAR STRATEGY

While numerous official studies offered in-depth assessments of the logistical challenges presented by the prospect of forcible regime change in Iraq, Bush administration officials' confidence that US forces would be "greeted as liberators"[91] led them to ignore such advice and publicly deride those who questioned the "cakewalk" formula.[92] As senior White House officials noted around the time that the decision to go to war was being finalized in July 2002, "there was little discussion in Washington of the aftermath after military action."[93]

After sustaining thousands of US military fatalities and hundreds of billions of dollars later, it is apparent that preventive warfare's translation from boardroom to battlefield tends to be more difficult than official planners of Operation Iraqi Freedom foresaw. Part three of *Hitting First* studies this practical issue by analyzing how logistical challenges complicate efforts to pursue first-strike military strategy on three levels: intelligence, military capability, and allied diplomacy. In successive chapters, Greg Thielmann, Peter Dombrowski, and Jacques Hymans assess how material constraints in each of these areas are likely to color future attempts to protect US security through application of preventive military force.

Thielmann begins his chapter, "Intelligence in Preventive Military Strategy," by explaining how the institutional routines of US intelligence tradecraft have evolved in ways that predispose analysts to view the world through a glass darkly. A series of traumatic surprises, ranging from Pearl Harbor to 9/11, have heaped pressure on the IC to provide more accurate warning of looming dangers. Thielmann notes that this pressure, when combined with the tendencies of hostile states to camouflage their real military capabilities and the predilection of US politicians to stretch intelligence data, generates systemic inertia to produce inflated threat assessments. He shows how all three of these factors coalesced in the Iraq case to cause a major intelligence failure. The jettisoning of caveats and official dissents from intelligence reports, conflation of chemical and nuclear threat categories, as well as Saddam Hussein's own "double game of deception" worked to paint an ominous picture of the Iraqi regime that diverged dramatically from reality.

Thielmann's experience as an intelligence insider positions him well to highlight the variegated nature of the IC and show how consensus intelligence assessments, such as the 2002 NIE on Iraq, are woven together in a give-and-take process that brings together the US government's major intelligence agencies for negotiation, and sometimes debate. To illustrate, he points to IC discussions regarding Iraq's alleged development of weaponized UAVs. In 2002, the main US intelligence entities battled over the question of whether Iraq was developing threatening UAV capability. Central Intelligence Agency (CIA) analysts argued that Saddam Hussein had embarked on a developmental program to use UAVs for delivery of deadly biological agents. However, air force intelligence, later joined by the Defense Intelligence Agency (DIA) and army intelligence, disagreed with this assessment, arguing that since Iraqi UAVs were intended primarily for reconnaissance and not attack missions, CIA's ominous analysis should be discounted.

Eventually, public audiences heard only about the CIA's alarming descriptions of Iraq's UAV program. As an explanation for why the substance of the internal IC disagreement was expurgated from declassified versions of the 2002 NIE, Thielmann points to the intense political pressure put on the IC by NSS 2002 to produce actionable intelligence justifying a preventive first-strike against Iraq. In a sobering passage, Thielmann speculates that "a more faithful rendering to the public on the dearth of hard evidence concerning the existence of delivery vehicles for the 'WMD' agents of concern would almost certainly have affected public willingness to wage war."

Looking ahead, Thielmann anticipates that the endemic factors driving threat inflation will persist in the future. This poses serious problems for implementation of NSS 2002, since preventive war strategy depends on the IC to produce "near certain" assessments of incipient threats. The natural response of the IC to these demands, reasons Thielmann, is to further tilt intelligence analysis in a direction that prioritizes warning over prediction, ironically reinforcing the underlying dynamics that produced intelligence failure prior to Operation Iraqi Freedom.

Can this spiraling dynamic be overcome? The stakes are high, especially since reliable intelligence is essential for effective functioning of a wide array of security instruments that have little to do with preventive warfare, such as tracking and containing the spread of fissile materials and enforcement of international nonproliferation regimes. This is why rejection of the preventive war doctrine rates high on Thielmann's list of formulas for positive change. There has already been some hopeful movement toward implementation of other recommendations on his list, such as separation of the positions of CIA director and Director of Central Intelligence (DCI).[94] Whether this move translates into meaningful intelligence reform may depend in large part on how the new Director of National Intelligence (DNI) addresses the remaining vital areas of change that Thielmann isolates in his conclusion.

Thielmann's analysis raises grave doubts about American capability to muster the necessary intelligence resources required to implement successfully NSS 2002. In the section's second chapter, Dombrowski asks whether the Pentagon possesses the requisite military capabilities to pursue preventive military force over time. His study begins with a general assessment of the types of military hardware and personnel necessary to execute preventive strike missions. Dombrowski then identifies Syria and Iran as the most likely targets of future US first-strike attacks. His treatment of hypothetical US campaigns against Syria and Iran focuses on three parameters: geography; military balance and effectiveness; and intensity of resistance to foreign military intervention.

Does the US military have what it takes to prevail against these potential adversaries? Dombrowski is not sanguine on this point, partly because of the fact that US military capabilities seem mismatched to respond to the unique set of contingencies presented by these hypothetical war scenarios. For example, recent investment in high-technology weaponry (such as Predator and Global Hawk) maximizes US long-range strike capability. But this hardware has only limited utility versus Iran, a nation that, as Dan Reiter explains in an earlier chapter, has learned a lesson from Osiraq, dispersing and burying nuclear facilities to reduce substantially their vulnerability to standoff attack. On the other hand, if the United States decides to pursue full-scale regime change via the preventive war option, Dombrowski predicts that its overwhelming conventional firepower would probably produce a quick force-on-force victory over the much smaller Iranian army. The problem is that consolidation of this victory would likely entail substantial postconflict nation building, something the US military is not particularly well equipped or eager to do.

In a conclusion that dovetails with some of Reiter's key findings, Dombrowski notes that the distinction between limited preventive strikes and regime-changing preventive military intervention is crucial for determining the workability and credibility of first-strike strategy. Should US military spending priorities continue to shape a fighting force with capabilities that do not respond well to the resource demands presented by first-strike missions, Dombrowski contends that US military credibility will decline, and American security will be compromised. He ends by exploring possible remedies, including adding more "boots on the ground," integrating civilian capabilities into military planning, and cooperating more with allies.

Interlocking themes enable the Thielmann and Dombrowski chapters to be read as companion pieces. For example, Dombrowski notes that it may be difficult to pursue allied cooperation effectively if Washington continues to alienate security partners by distorting public debate with manipulated intelligence data. Likewise, Thielmann argues that the structural impetus for IC threat inflation will be very difficult to correct if policy-makers continue to push the envelope on NSS 2002's maxim that "our best defense is a good offense."[95]

As the Bush administration learned prior to Operation Iraqi Freedom, the diplomatic challenge of persuading international audiences to accept US justifications for application of preventive military force can be onerous, particularly when powerful allies mount diplomatic counteroffensives designed to frustrate US rhetorical efforts. Jacques Hymans's chapter, "A Sheep in Wolf's Clothing? France's Struggle with Preventive Force," examines the French counterdiplomacy campaign conducted during the run-up to the 2003 Iraq War. The pointed intransigence displayed by France in opposition to US arguments for Operation Iraqi Freedom caused some commentators to wonder whether the arrival of NSS 2002 opened a permanent rift in US–France relations. If correct, such assessments point to a rocky road ahead for US diplomats seeking to broaden international support for future first-strike ventures. Hymans discounts the inevitability of this scenario, using a careful analysis of the influences driving French prewar policy to elucidate factors that cast its diplomatic decision-making in a much more complex light. His approach enables one to see French opposition to Operation Iraqi Freedom less as an instance of principled rejection of US "hyperpower," and more as an approach shaped by specific contingencies, such as unique trends in the German electoral cycle and the French experience in Algeria. Allied reactions to US proposals for application of first-strike force diplomatically constrain US policy options. As a case study of the nascent phenomenon of preventive warfare diplomacy, Hymans's chapter elucidates some of these constraints and suggests how they might be overcome. These insights, which highlight the contingent nature of French foreign policy, may provide succor to those who worry that Washington's diplomatic relationship with France is a lost cause.

THE FUTURE OF FIRST-STRIKE STRATEGY

The 2004 US presidential election campaign provided an occasion for the nation's voters to take stock of the Bush administration's first-strike force strategy. As William Hartung notes in chapter 11, the trajectory of campaign discussion largely skirted the question of whether NSS 2002 offers a sound framework for US security in the future. However, Democrats did offer some preliminary sketches of a competing approach to post-9/11 security, and Hartung uses these as points of departure for discussion of his own "policy of preventive diplomacy," which serves as an alterative to NSS 2002. The Hartung approach stipulates that military force should remain a strategy option, but that it should be used as a last resort. Force is included as part of a "layered defense," where nonmilitary measures of prevention based on diplomacy, treaties, rigorous inspections, intelligence, law enforcement, and economic leverage take precedence. Hartung draws from reports published by prominent study groups and task forces to show how a redoubled commitment to "prevention, not intervention" offers a more promising US security strategy. Finally, Hartung explores how it might be possible to leverage political arguments for such a preventive diplomacy approach. This links the contents of his chapter back into the volume's earlier analyses of rhetorical strategies deployed by the Bush administration to privilege first-strike force at the expense of nonmilitary tools of prevention.

In the volume's concluding chapter, "Preventive Force: Untangling the Discourse," we consider whether Operation Iraqi Freedom may be a dead end for the White House's preventive war ambitions, or perhaps just an unexpected detour. Condoleezza Rice's statement that we "would never want to do another Iraq,"[96] coupled with her rejuvenated approach to diplomacy as secretary of state, seems to indicate that the pendulum of US foreign policy has swung back into a more moderate equilibrium. On the other hand, the operationalization of high-tech "global strike" plans by the Pentagon, along with a recycled round of bellicose rhetoric directed toward "axis of evil" states such as Iran, points to the prospect that the Bush administration may be planning an encore to Operation Iraqi Freedom. If the Bush administration does attempt to give first-strike force a second chance after the strategy's checkered debut in the 2003 invasion of Iraq, a key determinant of policy success will likely be the degree to which the White House and its public interlocutors remedy factors that contributed to mistakes in 2002–2003. During the run-up to Operation Iraqi Freedom, a breakdown in the marketplace of ideas resulted in widespread political support for a preventive war that was legitimated politically as an exercise in self-defense but turned out to be an instance of raw aggression against a phantom enemy. Can this error be avoided in the future? We close the book by considering this question, drawing on analyses in earlier chapters, studies of public opinion, and rhetorical theory, to suggest preliminary answers.

2

Preventive Attacks against Nuclear, Biological, and Chemical Weapons Programs

THE TRACK RECORD

DAN REITER

THE SEPTEMBER 2002 National Security Strategy of the United States of America (NSS 2002) declared a heightened risk of attack by "rogue states and terrorists" against the United States in the twenty-first century, potentially with nuclear, biological, or chemical (NBC) weapons. It stated, "To forestall or prevent such hostile acts by our adversaries, the United States will, if necessary, act preemptively."[1] This doctrinal statement was used to justify the 2003 Iraq War, and may be used to justify future wars against countries such as Iran, North Korea, or Syria.

Will this strategy work? Will preventive/preemptive attacks provide enduring solutions to the threats posed by NBC proliferation? If they will, then even in the face of high costs, they may be attractive policy options, given that NBC attacks against American interests are plausible and potentially catastrophic. If they will not, then their high costs and risks would counsel against launching such attacks.

To answer these questions, the chapter examines all twenty-four preventive attacks against NBC programs that have occurred. The chapter divides the attacks into two categories, more limited preventive attacks that aimed to destroy NBC weapons and production facilities, and broader preventive attacks that aimed to disrupt NBC programs by overthrowing governments that possessed or sought to possess NBC weapons.

Analysis of past preventive attacks against NBC programs yields two conclusions. First, limited attacks such as air strikes almost never work, in that they rarely delay NBC programs significantly. Further, any minor successes in the past are not likely to be repeated in the future, as in anticipation of such attacks regimes are concealing and dispersing their NBC facilities. Second, attacks that change regimes might help remove NBC threats, though even when successful, war does not always change regimes durably. Moreover, the uncertain benefits of such wars must be weighed against very high costs. Resources might be more efficiently spent on counterproliferation and counterterrorism priorities other than preventive attacks against NBC programs.

This chapter's first section discusses and distinguishes between preemptive and preventive attacks. The second section briefly summarizes twenty-four preventive attacks against NBC programs. The third section assesses whether limited preventive strikes against NBC programs substantially delay the acquisition of NBC weapons. The fourth section examines preventive attacks against NBC programs that culminated in regime change. The fifth section examines instances in which states considered launching preventive attacks against NBC programs but did not, finding that in no case would a state have been better off launching such an attack. The final section concludes, weighing the costs and benefits of preventive attacks against NBC programs.

PREEMPTIVE AND PREVENTIVE ACTION

The Bush doctrine makes reference to both "prevent[ion]" and acting "preemptively." Preemptive and preventive attacks both anticipate future threats, the core logic being better to attack now than be attacked later. The critical distinction between them is the immediacy of the threat. Preemptive attacks respond to threats that are imminent, usually taking place in the context of an ongoing crisis; preventive attacks respond to threats that are more distant, occurring when one side perceives that over the longer term, months or usually years, the enemy will grow steadily stronger.[2] Preventive attacks accept the certainty of war now in exchange for avoiding the possibility of a less favorable war in the future, meaning that in some sense, as Otto von Bismarck once put it, "Preventive war is like suicide from fear of death."[3] As a matter of history, preventive attacks are more frequent than preemptive attacks. Since 1816, there have been only three preemptive wars but more than thirty preventive wars.[4] Though it uses the word "preemptive," the Bush administration appears to be laying the groundwork for what is traditionally thought of as preventive. The preemption side is easier to justify, as an immediate threat more strongly indicates the imperative of an attack within decision-making circles and makes the attack more palatable as self-defense to both domestic and international audiences.[5]

Before the 2003 Iraq War, the United States generally avoided preventive attacks, making the NSS 2002 especially salient. Indeed, the United States launched no wars for purely preemptive or preventive motives from its founding up to 2003.[6] The United States participated in some wars in response to direct attacks on American soil or forces (World War II, 2001 Afghanistan War), to protect American friends or allies (Vietnam War, Korean War, 1991 Gulf War, arguably World War I), to protect human rights (arguably Spanish-American War, Kosovo), to protect American commercial interests, especially at sea (War of 1812, Boxer Rebellion, World War I), and to expand American empire (arguably Spanish-American War, Mexican War). The United States has also launched a number of attacks intended to overthrow anti-American governments (examples include Grenada and Panama), though none of those anti-American governments posed a threat anywhere near as direct or severe as that posed by an NBC-armed state.

HISTORICAL BACKGROUND ON PREVENTIVE ATTACKS AGAINST NBC PROGRAMS

Preventive strikes against NBC programs include any use of force that has the intention or effect of substantially degrading or delaying the acquisition of NBC weapons by a state or nonstate actor. This is a very broad definition, but it permits compiling a long and inclusive list of preventive attacks against NBC programs, which is an important task. To date, no one has attempted to compile a list of preventive attacks against NBC programs, and a first cut can best serve future scholarship by providing more raw data rather than confining the list at the outset.[7] Further, even the apparently marginal cases offer lessons—for example, the existence of a number of smaller attacks that failed to degrade substantially NBC programs demonstrates the difficulties of such missions. Intrawar cases are important, both because they offer lessons (such as the failure of massive strikes during the Gulf War because of Iraqi concealment and dispersion) and because intrawar preventive strikes against NBC programs are possible in the future. Last, there are few costs to presenting a more inclusive list. There are no frequency or other statistical tests, meaning there is no risk of biasing the results by "artificially" increasing the size of the population. In total, there have been twenty-four instances

Table 1. Preventive Attacks against NBC Programs, 1942–2003

Year	Attacker	Target	Attack Objective
1942	British commandos	German nuclear program in Norway	Limited
1943	Norwegian commandos	German nuclear program in Norway	Limited
1943	Allied B-17s	German nuclear program in Norway	Limited
1944	Norwegian commando	German nuclear program in Norway	Limited
1945	Allied forces	German nuclear program	Regime change
1945	US aircraft	Japanese nuclear program	Limited
1945	Allied forces	Japanese NBC programs	Regime change
1979	Israeli agents	Iraqi nuclear program in France	Limited
1981	Israeli aircraft	Iraqi nuclear program	Limited
1980	Iranian aircraft	Iraqi nuclear program	Limited
1991	Iraqi Scuds	Israeli nuclear program	Limited
1991	Coalition forces	Iraqi NBC programs	Limited
1993	Coalition forces	Iraqi nuclear program	Limited
1998	Coalition forces	Iraqi NBC programs	Limited
2003	Coalition forces	Iraqi NBC programs	Regime change
1984	Iraqi aircraft	Iranian nuclear program	Limited
1985	Iraqi aircraft	Iranian nuclear program	Limited
1985	Iraqi aircraft	Iranian nuclear program	Limited
1986	Iraqi aircraft	Iranian nuclear program	Limited
1987	Iraqi aircraft	Iranian nuclear program	Limited
1987	Iraqi aircraft	Iranian nuclear program	Limited
1988	Iraqi aircraft	Iranian nuclear program	Limited
1998	US cruise missiles	al-Qaida chemical program in Sudan	Limited
2001	Coalition forces	al-Qaida NBC programs in Afghanistan	Regime change

Note: All attacks took place on the target's homeland, unless otherwise noted.

of preventive strikes against NBC programs, grouped into eight clusters and summarized in table 1.

The first cluster includes five separate Allied attacks against the German nuclear weapons program during World War II. The Allies first sought to disrupt German heavy-water production in Norway. A British raid in occupied Norway in autumn 1942 met with disaster when the commandos involved were all killed either upon crash landing or after capture by German troops. The Allies tried again with a February 1943 attack by Norwegian commandos, who successfully destroyed the heavy-water production installation at Vermork. However, a Swedish report indicated that heavy-water production might have recommenced as early as August, so the Allies followed up in November 1943 with a daylight bombing raid of 200 B-17s, which succeeded in permanently shutting down the plant. In a February 1944 follow-up mission, a single Norwegian commando destroyed the remaining stocks of German heavy water.[8] Last, the D-Day invasion of Europe was in some sense a preventive attack against the German nuclear program, as a special Allied intelligence mission called Alsos sought out German nuclear scientists and facilities as Allied ground forces advanced across Europe. Alsos completely eliminated the German nuclear program in April 1945 when its operatives found and captured the German experimental atomic pile at Haigerloch and Werner Heisenberg's laboratory at Heichingen.[9]

The second cluster concerns the war against Japan in World War II. Japan pursued developing an atomic weapon during World War II, getting as far as uranium separation on a laboratory scale. The Japanese atomic bomb project was destroyed in an April 1945 bombing raid on Tokyo, though the United States was unaware of the program's existence.[10] Aside from the atomic weapons program, Japan also had an active biological weapons program.[11] The entire war, culminating in a Japanese regime change, ended Japan's pursuit of biological weapons.

The third cluster includes two Israeli attacks and one Iranian attack against the Iraqi nuclear program. In April 1979, Israeli operatives detonated explosives at a French production facility near La Seyne-sur-Mer, damaging the cores of two nuclear reactors that were to be shipped to Iraq. In 1981, Israel launched an air strike against the Iraqi nuclear reactor at Osiraq, destroying the reactor dome.[12] Shortly following the Israeli strike, Israel made an announcement that came to be known as the "Begin Doctrine," which, anticipating NSS 2002, stated, "Under no circumstances would we allow the enemy to develop weapons of mass destruction against our nation; we will defend Israel's citizens, in time, with all the means at our disposal." Israel's public commitment to the Begin Doctrine waned by 1984, though some members of the Israeli military supported it into the mid-1990s.[13] The 1981 Israeli attack followed a relatively unsuccessful September 1980 air strike by two Iranian F-4 aircraft, which caused only minor damage.[14]

The fourth cluster includes Iraqi attacks on the Israeli nuclear reactor at Dimona during the 1991 Gulf War. Iraq launched six Scud missiles against Dimona, in retaliation for the 1981 Osiraq raid. None struck the reactor.[15]

The fifth cluster includes four American-led attacks on the Iraqi NBC program. The first of these was Operation Desert Storm in 1991, the primary aim of which was the liberation of Kuwait, though a secondary mission was the substantial disruption of Iraqi NBC facilities. During the war, some 970 strikes were conducted against NBC targets.[16] The second attack was the January 1993 launch of some forty-four cruise missiles against the Iraqi Zaa'faraniyah nuclear complex.[17] The third was Operation Desert Fox, a 1998 wave of air strikes against Iraqi military and NBC targets launched in response to Iraqi refusal to meet its United Nations Special Commission

(UNSCOM) commitments.[18] The last was Operation Iraqi Freedom, the 2003 invasion of Iraq motivated principally by the fear of an enduring threat from Iraqi NBC weapons.[19]

The sixth cluster concerns the Iranian nuclear program. With West German cooperation, Iran began construction of two nuclear reactors at Bushehr in 1974. The shah started a small nuclear weapons program before being deposed; the new Khomeini regime appears to have at first abandoned the nuclear program, but then restarted it in the mid-1980s following Iraqi chemical weapons attacks. During the 1980–1988 Iran-Iraq War, Iraq launched seven separate air strikes on Bushehr.[20]

The seventh cluster is the August 1998 American missile attack against the al Shifa factory in Sudan. In response to terrorist bombings of American embassies in Africa, the Clinton administration decided to strike back against terrorist targets in Sudan and Afghanistan. The target in Sudan was a factory that the American government believed secretly produced chemical weapons for Osama bin Laden's terrorist group, al-Qaida, believed to be responsible for the embassy attacks. The attack destroyed the factory, though the evidence that the factory produced chemical weapons and had links to bin Laden is weak.[21]

The eighth is the 2001 war in Afghanistan, in which American and coalition forces combined with opposition groups to overthrow the Taliban regime, which had allowed al-Qaida to maintain bases in Afghan territory. During the war, coalition forces elected not to bomb buildings suspected of housing chemical and biological weapons facilities.[22] After the Taliban regime had been overthrown, facilities were discovered that al-Qaida might have used to produce NBC weapons. For example, British forces in spring 2002 discovered a centrifuge for liquid separation and an oven for drying slurried agents.[23] Documents pertaining to constructing dirty (radiological) bombs and nuclear weapons were also found.[24]

LIMITED ATTACKS ON NBC PROGRAMS

Most preventive attacks on NBC programs are limited, intended only to destroy NBC weapons or production facilities. Such attacks can be greatly attractive to policy-makers, as they offer the promise of operational success at very low costs either in terms of friendly casualties or collateral damage. The limited nature of the attacks also means the geopolitical fallout is less than for broader regime-change attacks.

Have such attacks worked? Have they substantially delayed or eliminated states' acquisition of NBC weapons? The record of success for limited attacks is weak. The limited attacks against the German nuclear program were insufficient; regime change was necessary to eradicate the program. The bombing raid against the Japanese nuclear laboratory inadvertently destroyed an embryonic program, though the overthrow of the Japanese government was necessary to terminate the biological weapons program. The missile strikes on Sudan likely did little damage to al-Qaida NBC capabilities, as the factory targeted likely did not produce chemical weapons as the Clinton administration claimed.

The limited American raids (1991, 1993, and 1998) on the Iraqi NBC program also inflicted relatively little damage. The 1993 raid was quite small, only a few dozen missiles. The 1998 Desert Fox raids were not trivial, comprising some 1,000 aircraft sorties and cruise missile strikes against an array of targets. However, they caused only marginal damage to Iraqi NBC programs, because concerns for Iraqi civilian casualties encouraged coalition planners to avoid some targets, and more generally because of poor intelligence on target location.[25]

The massive air strikes against Iraqi NBC programs during the 1991 Gulf War were in a narrow sense successful, in that they reached 75 percent of their targets. However, prewar intelligence provided an incomplete picture of the extent of the Iraqi NBC program, meaning that substantial Iraqi NBC assets were left untouched. A General Accounting Office report declared that "the goal of eliminating Iraq's NBC capabilities was not even approximated by the air campaign; very substantial NBC capabilities were left untouched. An intelligence failure to identify NBC targets meant that the air campaign hit only a tiny fraction of the nuclear targets and left intact vast chemical and biological weapons stores."[26] Specifically, though the attacks destroyed perhaps 75 percent of Iraqi chemical weapons production capability, they left standing substantial stocks of the weapons themselves, as 150,000 such munitions were discovered by United Nations (UN) inspectors in 1993. This failure rate is even more disturbing considering that the bulk of preventive strikes targeted chemical munitions capabilities.[27]

The Iraqi biological weapons program also suffered only limited damage. The Department of Defense reported that though some facilities such as at Salman Pak and Al Kindi were destroyed, nearly all of the actual agent production equipment had been relocated, allowing Iraq to "easily renew production of biological agents when intrusive UN inspections are discontinued."[28] Further, the actual biological weapons Iraq possessed during the war, several dozens of warheads and bombs equipped to deliver agents like botulinum and anthrax, were not destroyed.[29]

The attacks also inflicted little damage on the Iraqi nuclear program. The 1981 Israeli raid on Osiraq had convinced the Iraqis to disperse, conceal, and harden their nuclear facilities, making them very difficult to find and

destroy by 1991. Prewar intelligence substantially underestimated the scope
of the program. The attacks destroyed only 15 percent of the program; many
strikes hit empty buildings. A high-level defector reported that only three of
the seven major Iraqi nuclear development sites were destroyed during Desert Storm. The conclusion of the official US government *Gulf War Air Power
Survey* was that "measured against the goal of destroying enough of the Iraqi
nuclear-weapons program to push an Iraqi nuclear weapon out to the end
of the decade or beyond, the bombing was not effective. At best it forced
the Iraqis to disperse and hide the visible elements of the program, thereby
temporarily suspending production of enriched uranium." One American
who participated in the 1991 International Atomic Energy Agency (IAEA)
postwar inspections of Iraq noted that the attacks at best "inconvenienced"
the Iraqi nuclear program.[30]

The 1981 attacks on the Iraqi Osiraq reactor are frequently portrayed
as the prototype of a successful attack on an NBC program. The Israelis
incurred no casualties, achieved operational success, and imposed a minimum of collateral damage. It has been argued that the strikes had a very
real payoff, as Iraq might have used nuclear weapons against Iran during the
Iran-Iraq War, and eventually might have used them against Israel. Further,
some argue that because Iraq in 1990 was engaged in a crash program to
develop a nuclear weapon, it might conceivably have produced a weapon in
as little as one year. Without the Osiraq attacks, Iraq might have completed
a nuclear weapon before it invaded Kuwait, deterring any attempt to liberate
Kuwait and introducing the risk of nuclear escalation in the event of war.[31]

The existing evidence indicates, however, that the benefits of the attack
have been exaggerated.[32] At the time of the attack, Iraq planned to produce
plutonium (rather than enrich uranium) as a route to building a nuclear
weapon. However, there were two impediments to Iraqi plutonium production. First, the French-provided reactor would have been subject to the inspection of both the IAEA and French technicians. The IAEA planned on
sending an inspector as frequently as every two weeks, and it would likely
have installed cameras for constant surveillance before the reactor became
operational. French inspectors, on site continuously, would have filed daily
reports.[33] Notably, the Iraqis had plans to defeat the cameras and elude the
on-site inspections.[34] However, it is uncertain whether such plans would have
succeeded. The French technicians were likely opposed to Iraqi acquisition
of nuclear weapons; there is indirect evidence that they knew beforehand of
the Israeli air strike, and they may have even assisted the strike by providing
intelligence to the Israelis.[35] The French technicians, then, would have been
highly motivated to report any illegal weapons activity. Further, plutonium
production is extremely difficult to conceal, both because the procedures

require shutting down the reactor to insert and withdraw the uranium rods and because the transportation devices that move the plutonium–producing uranium targets cannot be hidden. In short, these activities could "hardly escape observation by the French technicians, visiting International Atomic Energy Agency inspectors, or the IAEA's permanent surveillance cameras at the site." Importantly, the Iraqis were dependent on the French for reactor fuel, so discovery of secret plutonium production and diversion would likely have shut the reactor down.[36] Imad Khadduri, a former Iraqi nuclear physicist, agreed with this assessment, noting,

> The possibility of such an undertaking by Iraq is delusional. The tight refueling schedule for such an endeavor, which is required to prevent "poisonous" plutonium 238 from developing, would be impossible to hide from the French scientists who would have been collaborating with us for years and the IAEA inspectors. Had we even diabolically thought of kicking both out and running the reactors ourselves for such a purpose, the limited fresh fuel that was allowed for us would have aborted any such attempt at the outset.[37]

Second, inspections aside, there were physical barriers. The reactor itself was a light-water-moderated reactor, meaning that it was not designed for efficient plutonium production, rather than a gas–graphite reactor, a more efficient plutonium producer. Further, the French had originally promised to supply 80 percent enriched fuel, but in 1980 they unilaterally renegotiated the terms, declaring they would instead supply 18 percent "caramel" fuel to block the production of weapons-grade plutonium. The Iraqis at first refused the caramel fuel, but by 1981 the French held firm and declared they would only supply the lower grade caramel fuel to a rebuilt reactor. Khadduri noted that "neither would the unique design of the reactor core for the 'Caramel' fuel allow for fuel designs specific for plutonium production." In the opinion of an American physicist who inspected the site, under the best conditions (including assuming that all inspection measures were evaded) the reactor might have given them a one-year advantage in a ten-year program to make atomic bombs.[38]

Khadduri has gone so far as to claim that the Osiraq attack actually initiated Saddam's efforts to acquire an atomic bomb.[39] The veracity of this claim is uncertain; another Iraqi nuclear defector, Khidhir Hamza, had been working on building an Iraqi nuclear weapon since the early 1970s, and was specifically and directly ordered by Saddam in 1979 to build such a device.[40] However, Khadduri does make the interesting point that Jafar Dhia Jafar, a leading Iraqi nuclear scientist arrested and tortured in 1979 for suspicion of collaboration with the political opposition, was rehabilitated and sent to work on the atomic bomb after the Osiraq attack, evidence that the Osiraq attack may have accelerated if not initiated the Iraqi nuclear program. Other observers also speculate that the Osiraq attack may have increased Saddam's commitment to acquiring a nuclear weapon.[41] Hamza has claimed that after the attack, Saddam increased by more than fifteen times the number of scientists devoted to and the amount of money spent on the nuclear weapons programs.[42]

Only under the most generous assumptions, in which the Iraqis eluded for a decade detection of illegal weapons-related activity in a publicly known reactor under the gaze of cameras, daily inspections from French technicians, and perhaps biweekly onsite inspections from the IAEA, and overcame technical limitations inherent to their reactor and fuel, can we project that Iraq might have had an atomic bomb by 1991. Regardless, it is unlikely that that "success" could be replicated. The central lesson of Osiraq for Iraq and other potential proliferants is to keep the location of nuclear facilities secret, lest they attract attacks. The 1981 attack changed the approach of the Iraqi program away from plutonium production and toward uranium enrichment, ironically helping Iraq conceal its program, as it could feign the complete destruction of its nuclear program while still pursuing uranium enrichment secretly. This shift to secrecy is one important reason why the Gulf War coalition underestimated the scope of the Iraq nuclear program in 1991 and why its intelligence on the locations of Iraqi nuclear facilities was scarce and incomplete, leading to a largely unsuccessful attack against Iraqi NBC assets.[43] Other nations learned this same lesson. One factor leading the air force to oppose air strikes against the North Korean nuclear program in 1993 was doubt about whether intelligence about the location of North Korean nuclear facilities was complete.[44] These difficulties have persisted; in 2003 a former Pentagon official commented that "taking out the one facility at Yongbyon with cruise missiles does not shut down the North Korean nuclear program—it's not like Osiraq in Iraq. They may have one to two weapons and a clandestine highly enriched uranium program."[45] Iran has likely concealed and dispersed enough of its nuclear facilities such that a preventive air strike against its facilities would at best marginally delay its nuclear program.[46]

The series of Iraqi attacks on Iranian nuclear facilities during the 1980s are in some ways comparable to the 1981 Israeli attack on Osiraq. They also sought the destruction of an embryonic nuclear program, and ultimately achieved operational success, as they inflicted major damage on the Bushehr site. Absent the attacks, the reactor might have been completed by 1990, and in the wake of the attacks the reactor has not yet been completed.[47]

Interpreting the Iraqi attacks on Bushehr as successful deserves qualification, however. Drawing inferences about the extent of the damage or even the nature of the Iranian program (including the intensity of the Iranian commitment to acquiring nuclear weapons) in the 1980s and 1990s is difficult, as there are "serious gaps in the historical flow of evidence," according to one expert.[48] The fact that Iraq engaged in several attacks across a span of years indicates that the first attacks may have been operationally unsuccessful. More important, Bushehr itself may have had only limited importance for the Iranian nuclear weapons program. Like the Osiraq reactor, Bushehr was subject to IAEA inspection, meaning that diversion of plutonium or enriched uranium for a weapon would have been at best difficult; the reactor also relied on foreign technicians and foreign sources of reactor fuel. It was also a light-water reactor, poorly designed for plutonium production, and it was to be fueled with 3 percent enriched uranium, "totally unsuited as weapons fuel." Though the Bushehr reactor is still not completed, international concern about Iranian proliferation is higher than ever, because of fears both of secret facilities and known facilities such as Esfahan, Aran, and Natanz.[49]

In sum, limited strikes against NBC programs have a very poor record of performance. In even the best examples of such attacks, the 1981 Osiraq raid and the 1980s Iraqi attacks on Bushehr, the net delays of the targeted nuclear programs were minimal. Notably, future attacks will get no easier, as proliferants will likely conceal and disperse their NBC facilities, making limited attacks even less likely to succeed. Last, fear that such attacks would release chemical or biological agents or nuclear radiation into civilian areas may constrain the United States from launching comprehensive air strikes. This concern limited the 1998 Desert Fox attacks and was one of many factors constraining American decision-makers from launching preventive strikes against North Korean nuclear facilities in 1994.[50]

REGIME CHANGE ATTACKS ON NBC PROGRAMS

There are four cases of preventive attacks on NBC programs that culminated in regime change, Germany 1945, Japan 1945, Afghanistan 2001, and Iraq 2003. It is still too early to judge whether regime-change preventive attacks in the last two cases have provided long-term inoculation against NBC programs. Regarding the Afghanistan War, though, experts are doubtful that all of al-Qaida's NBC production facilities were located in Afghanistan, meaning that even under the best-case scenario of al-Qaida and the Taliban being permanently removed from Afghanistan by a peaceful and pro-American Afghan government, the al-Qaida NBC threat remains.[51] The Iraq case is odd, in that denuding Iraq of NBC production facilities may be trivial given its substantial disarmament before the war began.

The German and Japanese cases are more interesting, however. In both cases, defeat effectively eliminated militarism, and neither country has ac-

quired NBC weapons in the decades since. However, speculation about rep-
licating the German and Japanese experiences must confront two sets of concerns. First, facilitating these transitions has been costly. It required gigantic
amounts of economic aid to both countries, and the stationing of hundreds
of thousands of troops abroad for a half century. The Cold War provided
a political context in which the American public supported expenditures of
hundreds of billions of dollars on these missions. Any future preventive attacks must be discussed in the context of the long-term commitment of resources, and (as discussed below) whether there might be more efficient ways
of spending resources to reduce terrorism and NBC weapons proliferation.

Second, there were a number of conditions that lined up in both Germany and Japan to favor success that may not be present elsewhere.[52] Both
countries enjoyed relative ethnic heterogeneity, meaning that the lifting of
a totalitarian government did not encourage ethnic subgroups to fight each
other or secede, as in Lebanon or Yugoslavia. Most important, there was
general harmony between what needed to be done to democratize and de-
militarize these nations, what the occupation forces wanted to do, and what
the people wanted.[53] Notably, when a society does not demand demilitariza-
tion and democratization, regime change may not cure a state of militarism
or the production of NBC weapons in the medium or long term, the collapse
of Germany's Weimar Republic serving as an ominous warning.

More generally, structural factors, such as low per capita income, a reliance on oil or mineral exports, being surrounded by nondemocratic states,
and lacking a strong civil society, may impede successful democratization.[54]
Some have speculated that cultural factors impede democracy, noting the
absence of democracy in the Arab world and the low incidence of democracy
in the Muslim world.[55] Possible targets of future preventive attacks on NBC
programs experience one or more of these factors. Iran is oil-dependent and
Muslim, and it resides in a nondemocratic region; North Korea is quite poor
and has essentially no civil society. This does not mean that democratization
is impossible in these nations, but it does mean that external intervention
should not be seen as a guarantee of successful regime change toward either
democracy or even a pro-American regime. The American experience in the
Western Hemisphere provides ample evidence for caution, where the occasional intervention that has successfully implanted an enduring democracy
(such as in Panama in 1989) must be compared to an array of failures (such
as interventions in Haiti and the Dominican Republic).[56] Attempts by the
UN in the 1990s to democratize through peace-building missions has enjoyed only very spotty success, sometimes failing catastrophically in places
like Angola and Rwanda.[57] As noted, it is too early to declare success or failure
in the democratization efforts in Iraq and Afghanistan, though it is probably

safe to say that in 2006 Iraq looks worse than either Germany or Japan looked in 1947, and Afghanistan looks worse than either Germany or Japan looked in 1949. Importantly, a failed attempt to implant democracy can mean disaster, drawing in more and more American troops and economic resources without establishing stable governance. Such failures may also undermine the war on terror by making American troops attractive targets for attacks and by producing "failed state" environments in which terrorist groups can recruit and establish training facilities.

OPPORTUNITIES MISSED?

The discussion thus far has focused on preventive attacks on NBC programs that have occurred, examining whether they have worked. Conversely, have there been instances in which in hindsight a state should have attacked another state that possessed or was developing NBC weapons? There certainly have been a number of opportunities. The United States considered launching preventive attacks against NBC programs run by the Soviet Union in the 1950s and early 1960s, against China in the early 1960s, against Cuba during the Cuban Missile Crisis, and against North Korea in the 1990s.[58] Elsewhere, India considered launching preventive attacks against Pakistan's nuclear program in the 1980s, the Soviet Union considered attacking China's nuclear program in 1969, and Egypt considered attacking Israel's Dimona nuclear reactor in the 1960s.[59]

Should any of these governments have attacked? Would the benefits have exceeded the costs? In every case in which a nation considered but did not launch an attack, even if one assumes that such an attack would have been operationally successful (an uncertain assumption given the low success rate of those attacks that have actually occurred), that state was better off not attacking. In no case did a potential target acquire NBC weapons and then use them against the potential attacker. Further, in some cases the costs of attacking would have been exorbitant, killing millions.

Consider the specific cases. The United States considered launching preventive attacks against the Soviet Union in the late 1940s and early 1950s, but even as the Soviet Union attained full nuclear parity, neither it nor its allies attacked the United States or its principal allies. Ultimately, internal political change within the Soviet Union transformed Soviet and Cold War politics, reducing the nuclear threat to essentially zero. Had the United States attacked the Soviet Union, this would have meant the deaths of tens of millions of people.

The United States also considered launching preventive attacks, either air strikes or a ground invasion, against Cuba during the Cuban Missile

Crisis. The attacks, of course, proved unnecessary, as the missiles were voluntarily removed in exchange for minimal American concessions, a commitment not to invade Cuba and the removal of obsolete missiles in Turkey. Importantly, the costs of an attack on Cuba were underestimated at the time and could have been extraordinary. When the naval blockade began, most of the intermediate range missiles and their respective warheads were in Cuba and nearly operational,[60] raising the possibility that attacks against the missiles would have put the Soviets and Cubans in a "use them or lose them" situation, perhaps encouraging their use if they came under attack. Additionally, a ground invasion might have invited nuclear escalation through the use of Soviet nuclear torpedoes against American aircraft carriers, or the use of Soviet short-range nuclear missiles against landing American troops.[61]

Averting an American preventive attack against China in the early 1960s also proved to be wise. Since 1960, China has not attacked the United States or any American ally; a preventive attack would have "solved" a problem that never appeared. Occasional belligerent moves like the 1996 missile tests were effectively contained with deterrent moves.[62] Further, China has evolved into being a strategic asset, through Nixon's rapprochement, integration of China into the world economy, and inclusion of China in confronting international challenges like negotiations surrounding North Korea's nuclear program. A preventive attack would have foreclosed these strategic and economic benefits, to say nothing of the massive civilian casualties.

A preventive attack against North Korea has (thus far) proven unnecessary. North Korea has not attacked its neighbors since 1953. Conversely, the costs of war in Korea might have been exorbitant: half a million casualties in the first ninety days; up to a million military and civilian casualties, including as many as 100,000 American dead; financial costs of $100 billion for the war effort; and regional economic costs of $1 trillion.[63] A more limited air strike against North Korean nuclear facilities is not a more attractive option, both because of concealment and dispersion of North Korean nuclear facilities, and because of the possibility of North Korean retaliation in reaction to even a limited air strike. Secretary of Defense William Perry worried about this possibility, and General Gary Luck declared, "If we pull an Osirak, they will be coming south." One high-level North Korean defector estimated that the chances of a limited attack escalating to a general war were about 80 percent. North Korean options for retaliation ranged from launching artillery barrages to attacking South Korean nuclear power plants to invading South Korea.[64]

Other preventive attacks on NBC programs would have been similarly foolish. A Soviet preventive attack against Chinese nuclear facilities would have been gigantically destructive and was ultimately unnecessary, as there were no clashes after the attack was considered in 1969. An Egyptian attack on Israeli nuclear facilities in the 1960s would have been fruitless, as Israeli nuclear weapons had little bearing on Egyptian-Israeli relations. The continued development of the Israeli nuclear program did not deter Egyptian attacks in 1969 or 1973, nor did it stop the Israeli-Egyptian peace agreements in the 1970s, agreements that greatly served Egyptian interests by returning the Sinai Peninsula to Egypt and solidifying American support for Egypt.[65] Lastly, India is better served for foregoing preventive attacks against the Pakistani nuclear program. A principal reason India forewent such an attack is that Indian military leaders could not guarantee that Indian cities could be protected from conventional or even nuclear attacks from Pakistan, and a nuclear war between the two countries could have killed several millions of people.[66] More important, the successful elimination of Pakistan's nuclear weapons would not have improved Indian security, as an Indian nuclear monopoly did not translate into diplomatic advantage in the 1970s and 1980s, and after going nuclear Pakistan did not extract concessions on Kashmir or other issues with its nuclear saber.

WEIGHING THE MERITS OF PREVENTIVE ATTACKS ON NBC PROGRAMS

The historical record of preventive attacks against NBC programs is not very encouraging. Limited attacks short of imposing regime change have been quite unsuccessful at eliminating NBC programs. The episode most often cited as successful is the 1981 Osiraq attack, though close analysis reveals that this attack at most delayed the Iraqi nuclear program marginally. Significantly, the lessons of Osiraq to conceal and disperse NBC facilities learned by potential targets make it unlikely that such attacks will succeed in the future.

The costs of preventive attacks may be paid to destroy NBC programs that do not exist, will not succeed, or are years or decades away from completion. The attacks against German heavy-water production in World War II were ultimately successful, but heavy water itself is a dead end in bomb design.[67] The 1998 missile strikes against Sudan may have destroyed a factory with no connection to the production of chemical weapons. Estimates of the Iraqi NBC program just prior to the 2003 war as well as Iraq's connections to terrorist groups were substantially exaggerated.[68] More generally, the difficulties of intelligence collection on NBC programs are detailed in Greg Thielmann's chapter in this volume. Rodger Payne's chapter lays out the failures of the public debate to assess accurately Iraq's NBC capabilities before the 2003 Iraq War.

Fortunately, there are sound, cost-effective alternatives to preventive attacks that address NBC proliferation; in his chapter in this volume, William Hartung lays out "preventive diplomacy" as an alternative. Most centrally, deterrence is a proven, successful policy. The United States has successfully deterred a number of nuclear-armed, anti-American dictators from using NBC weapons. Soviet, Chinese, and North Korean leaders all refrained from using nuclear weapons in the context of an American promise of retaliation. Iraq elected to launch conventionally armed rather than NBC-armed Scud missiles against Israeli cities during the Gulf War in part because of fears of Israeli and American retaliation.[69] Significantly, the United States successfully deterred Iraq in the 1990s from launching further aggression, and probably could have deterred Iraq into the future without launching a preventive attack.[70]

An important shortcoming of deterrence, however, is that it is substantially less effective against terrorists than against governments. Probably the most prudent scenario for an NBC preventive attack would be some repetition of the 2001 Afghanistan War, where the goal is to overthrow a regime widely known to support potentially NBC-armed terrorists, where the regime is vulnerable to American military action, where the regime is generally hated within the country (increasing the likelihood of transition to a pacific, democratic regime that will cooperate in the war on terror) and internationally (to reduce anti-American backlash), and where the military action is multilateral (defusing anti-Americanism and enabling burden sharing). However, policy-makers must be careful before seeking to replicate the Afghanistan experience. The Taliban and al-Qaida have not been eradicated from Afghanistan, and the nation is nowhere near being a stable democracy. Indeed, two central lessons of Afghanistan are that the costs of (re)building government and society should not be underestimated and that a long-term and sustained commitment will be needed. We do not at this point know if Afghanistan will slide back into the kind of failed state environment that permits terrorist groups to thrive. Further, in a narrow sense the Afghanistan War may have advanced the war on terrorism but had less of an effect on the dangers of NBC proliferation, as al-Qaida NBC operations were not primarily based in Afghanistan.

Deterrence aside, international diplomacy coupled sometimes with internal political change has proven to be a surprisingly successful means by which states have completely and permanently abandoned NBC programs. By one count, some twenty-two countries have tried to attain or have attained nuclear weapons but have abandoned their attempts (or programs) without preventive attacks.[71] These efforts have meant substantial nonproliferation success since the 1960s, when it was feared that by 2000 dozens of nations would have gone nuclear. Economic sanctions, internal political changes, and reduction in international threat pushed South Africa to abandon its nuclear program. Sanctions also pushed Libya to abandon its NBC programs, and the combination of sanctions and international inspections were very effective in stripping Iraq of its NBC programs in the years before the 2003 attack.[72] The collapse of the Soviet Union created three nuclear states, Ukraine, Belarus, and Kazakhstan, and all three gave up their existing nuclear arsenals with international pressure, guidance, and incentives. Argentina and Brazil both abandoned their nuclear programs because of internal changes and international pressures.

Lastly, NBC preventive attacks have significant costs, even if one's only goal is fighting terrorism and NBC proliferation. The Iraq War has increased global anti-Americanism and terrorist recruitment.[73] Even a limited attack against Iranian nuclear facilities would likely stimulate Iranian support for anti-American terrorism. The Central Intelligence Agency (CIA) reported in 2004 that Hezbollah "would react to an attack against it, Syria, or Iran with attacks against U.S. and Israeli targets worldwide."[74]

From a material perspective, to reduce NBC and terrorism risks the resources spent on preventive attacks could be spent more effectively elsewhere. Peter Dombrowski nicely lays out the demands the NSS 2002 will make of US military capabilities in chapter 9 of this volume. More specifically, according to one August 2004 analysis, the $144.4 billion spent on the Iraq War (then; the figure is now in the hundreds of billions) could be spent much more effectively on other counterproliferation and counterterrorism programs, including $7.5 billion to safeguard American ports; $4 billion to modernize the Coast Guard; $2 billion for better cargo security; $10 billion to defend airliners from surface-to-air missiles; $240 million for machines to detect explosives on passengers at airports; $7 billion for another 100,000 police officers; $2.5 billion to aid fire departments; $350 million to integrate police, fire, and other emergency radio networks; $3 billion to improve security on roads and railways; $30.5 billion to secure nuclear materials in the former Soviet Union and elsewhere; $2.25 billion to accelerate the deactivation of 6,000 nuclear warheads through the Nunn-Lugar initiative; $24 billion to create two new army divisions; $15.5 billion to double the number of active special forces troops; $8.6 billion to rebuild Afghanistan; $11 billion to convert Afghan crops away from opium (which finances terrorist operations); $10 billion to increase foreign aid; and $775 million to increase public diplomacy efforts in Arab and Muslim states.[75]

In sum, future opportunities for preventive strikes on NBC programs must be evaluated with great caution. Limited strikes, though lower in cost, are extremely unlikely to work, especially because targets will probably conceal and disperse their NBC facilities. Larger campaigns that successfully change regimes can nullify an NBC threat, though successful regime change and democratization are not easy tasks, and even operational success against one state may increase NBC and terrorism threats if the costs are inflaming anti-Americanism and drawing off funds from other critical priorities.

3

The Curious Case of Kofi Annan, George W. Bush, and the "Preemptive" Military Force Doctrine

SIMON REICH

F POLITICS MAKES strange bedfellows, then few can be more curious than the cast of characters involved in the evolution of the doctrines of preventive and "preemptive" intervention, which extends from United Nations (UN) secretary generals Boutros Boutros-Ghali and Kofi Annan to former Australian and Algerian foreign ministers Gareth Evans and Mohamed Sahnoun, respectively, all of whom promoted the doctrine of preventive intervention. Academics from European, Canadian, and American universities were linked with policy pundits from New York and Washington in advocating this doctrine. Yet, ultimately, what had begun as a doctrine with very specific (and distinct) motives that clearly predated the events of 9/11 contained a thread that eventually wound its way to George W. Bush, Donald Rumsfeld, and Paul Wolfowitz, albeit it in the amended form of the doctrine of preventive intervention, as American troops engaged Iraqi forces in warfare, purportedly motivated by both (simultaneously) the existence of a clear and present danger and the impulse to spread democratic values.

In a stronger form, I contend that what is most striking is that although these two groups might share little in common in terms of motives or political views, they have all contributed—wittingly or otherwise—to the evolution of the doctrine of preventive intervention. They have done so by assisting in the reconstitution of the definition of sovereignty, contributing significantly to the erosion of its standing as the operational cornerstone of the international system, and thus providing the justification for an unprecedented large-scale military action. They have, collectively, done much to denude one of the most foundational of international norms.

Of course, it is not surprising that they did so for very different reasons. Proponents, such as successive secretary generals, fomented the doctrine of preventive intervention in the name of humanitarianism. They advocated multilateral action on the basis of emergent large-scale threats to civilian populations from either their own governments or from contending military-style forces in the context of disintegrating states.[1]

In contrast to the doctrine of preventive intervention, others (notably Richard Haass), in its early stages of evolution, advocated an alternative doctrine. This formulation justified intervention in promoting the cause of self-styled American "imperialism"—albeit, as I discuss, a self-proclaimed unconventional, "enlightened" view of imperialism in which the proclaimed intent was to use American power to extend beyond national interest to, purportedly, a global one. This doctrine defended military and economic action on the basis of a conflict over democratic values and economic liberalism.[2] It was, in that sense, an attempt to operationalize the "liberal peace" argument, predicated on the assumption that creating a world of liberal democracies (even, admittedly, if that was to be achieved through the use of violence) would make the world a safer place in the long term. Liberal states, proponents of this "liberal peace" view argue, are generally more pacifistic and do not fight wars against each other.[3] So the creation of a world order of free trade–oriented democracies would serve American interests but also, hypothetically, the cause of global stability. This doctrine appeared to be popular with what was to subsequently materialize as the new Republican administration in the period predating the 2000 election. But it was ultimately rejected because of its explicit multilateralist leanings in favor of a neoconservative formulation predicated on more explicit national security considerations and a unilateralist process. Richard Haass, his formulation rejected, thus left his position at the Department of State within the first two years of the new administration.

The version eventually advocated by the Bush administration, threading itself from the UN to the United States, was that of the doctrine of "preemptive" intervention. It justified initiating military action on the basis of an emergent clear and present danger to American citizens and property, regardless of whether that threat was to be carried out within the United

States. Humanitarian or "enlightenment" considerations were therefore replaced by strategic ones as the basis for the abrogation of the territorial integrity of another state and the possible replacement of indigenous governments.
What is striking is not simply the differences between the three positions but
also their commonalities.

SOVEREIGNTY DILUTED

A process was set in motion beginning with the debates of the early 1990s
that challenged the old basis for intervention—the prevailing doctrine of
peacekeeping. Peacekeeping respected the concept of sovereignty as sacred, and was reactive, limited in character, and based on the consent of
all parties. In this chapter, I therefore suggest that—despite the differences
in motive stretching from the presiding UN to the US administrations—
advocating preventive intervention in the aftermath of the Cold War challenged a historic shibboleth, that of the preeminence of the concept of sovereignty. Doing so thus facilitated a reconstitution of an international order
in which sovereignty was neither emblematic of nor a guarantor of the status
quo.[4] What began as a limited incursion into sovereignty based on humanitarian grounds had the unintended consequence of generating alternative
justifications, employed for very different reasons, that sought to intervene
in very different ways.

My intent in this chapter is to show that there has been a movement
through these successive stages in the course of the last decade and a half.
The status quo was epitomized by the doctrine of peacekeeping. It represented a benchmark regarding intervention, contingent on a Weberian, Cold
War conception of sovereignty—one defined in terms of territorial integrity
and the right of the domestic autonomy of states.[5] The disassembly of European empires in the two decades after World War II extended the formal state
system, albeit under bipolar management, although the process by which that
retreat from empire took place contributed heavily to the creation of a series
of embryonic failed states. When the inevitable failure of stable governance
materialized, and intrastate conflict ensued, external intervention was predicated on a consensus being reached among belligerents that external forces
had to be invited to provide a dividing line—what William Zartman termed
a condition of "ripeness."[6]

Peacekeeping was the dominant interventionist response of the international community during the Cold War, one that began eroding at the end
of the Cold War. Certainly, the process of simultaneous convergence and
fragmentation in the last two decades of the twentieth century has been well
documented and debated, and the combined accelerating effects of this pro-

cess on conflict needs little elaboration here.[7] But with the reconstitution of the international system, the initial deep and abiding wedge into the Cold War conception of sovereignty blossomed with the development of the doctrine of preventive intervention. This doctrine challenged peacekeeping as the dominant policy response. It has had a humanitarian mission, as does peacekeeping. But fomented by the disintegration of many states and the resulting genocidal activities of many ethnic groups (Serbs and Hutus being only among the most extreme examples), proponents of preventive intervention questioned the preeminence of sovereignty and the notion of territorial integrity in the limited circumstances of state disintegration and ethnic conflict. Proponents of preventive intervention have focused extensively on the human rights of victims and the responsibilities of states to enforce those rights.[8] A shift in focus therefore occurred, from the security of states to that of individuals, with the primary proponents of the doctrine of preventive intervention being moral entrepreneurs located in nongovernmental organizations (NGOs), and their primary instrument being multilateral institutions attempting to employ multilateralist policies.[9]

The issue of the conditions under which intervention could take place had predated the Cold War but had largely been eschewed during the five decades of superpower rivalry. Once the very idea of the abrogation of sovereignty again gained legitimacy, a key debate ensued designed to address the question, Under what conditions could nonconsensual intervention be justified? As Martha Finnemore suggested, in regard to strong states: "What has changed is when it will suit them—not the fact of intervention but its form and meaning. What has changed are state understandings about the purposes to which they can and should use force."[10]

Those proponents within the UN (and related state officials and intellectuals) emphasized humanitarian motives—within the defined parameters of the protection of civilians within failed states, in the context of multilateral processes of decision-making and joint implementation. Imminent danger demanded preventive measures.[11]

Yet unilateralists (or those willing to construct narrow coalitions) within the Bush administration have seized upon this abrogation of the sacred cow of sovereignty to argue in favor of broadening the grounds for initiating action. Two formulations of this argument surfaced in the first two years of the Bush administration, both sharing the belief that action should be focused not so much against failed or disintegrating states but can be invoked against oppositional states—regimes that either (in the first variant) broadly oppose the values, principles, and practices upon which a American-led world order would be constructed or (in the latter) those that present a purported clear and present danger.

Treating the Cold War doctrine of peacekeeping as a benchmark in which the concept of sovereignty is preeminent, this essay compares three countervailing doctrines, and attempts to provide some links in the chain of the evolution of each. I describe the details of the emergence of, as well as comparing, the four doctrines of peacekeeping, prevention, imperialism, and preemption according to four dimensions. These are the nature of sovereignty according to each doctrine, their primary values, their operational attributes, and their broader mandate. Evidence for the characterization of each doctrine will be drawn from UN debates and reports, speeches by UN and US administration officials, and limited materials regarding historic interventions. My goal is to understand the evolution of sovereignty's dilution, through a fluid process that frames and legitimates for policy-makers their intervention in Afghanistan and Iraq—if only for themselves and an American audience.

THE TRADITIONAL DOCTRINE OF PEACEKEEPING

As Martha Finnemore has so cogently and convincingly pointed out, the tradition of intervention, motivated by either debt collection or humanitarian intervention (notably to protect Christians), predated the Cold War.[12] Yet proponents argue that the principle of sovereignty remained resolutely eminent for the duration of the Cold War itself, both in the "normative discourse" of international politics,[13] and in the fabric of international law. The intent was to protect the weak against the strong.[14] This ideal, not surprisingly, did not always materialize. Soviet actions in Hungary and Czechoslovakia were clear episodes of incursions, albeit weakly justified by the superpower. For many colonial states, however, nonintervention was the general practice. To intervene without invitation was illegitimate,[15] and shaped state action.[16] As Finnemore succinctly states, "sovereignty and self-determination norms trumped humanitarian claims during the Cold War."[17]

Certainly, there is an extensive, coherent, and well-formulated literature on peacekeeping, expanded upon at length in the course of the 1990s, one that is too voluminous to detail here. Rather than recapitulate its content at length, I only seek to outline its major attributes in this discussion.

In institutional terms, John Ruggie has argued that there has not been a systematic doctrinal approach adopted toward peacekeeping at the UN. Rather, the organization's understanding has been very poor, notably when it strays into what he describes as "gray area" operations that straddle the terrain between peacekeeping (in its most limited sense) and "war fighting."[18] The term "peacekeeping," Ruggie points out, is not even mentioned in the UN Charter.[19]

Ruggie is content to argue that the limits of peacekeeping's operation-alization as a doctrine is the source of the problem. But the UN's incapacity to form and implement a coherent doctrine does not detract from the notion that such a peacekeeping doctrine (whether explicit or not) exists that guides behavior. Indeed, important to its emergence over four decades was the cen-tral notion that the primary purpose of peacekeeping is to allow antagonists to end aggression in order to generate a possible agreement. Mediation is only of limited interest once both sides have exhausted their desire to fight. As Mats Berdahl suggests: "[Peacekeeping] has traditionally been used to describe various forms of legitimized collective intervention aimed at avoid-ing the outbreak or resurgence of violent conflict between disputants. As a distinctive form of third-party intervention governed by the principles of consent and minimum force, peacekeeping operations have been expressly non-threatening and impartial."[20]

The thirteen UN operations between 1948 and 1988 generated, says Berdahl, a body of principles, procedures, and practices that came to consti-tute a corpus of case law and customary practice. As Sir Marrack Goulding, former UN undersecretary general responsible for peacekeeping operations, has importantly noted, this collection of law and practice sets precedent in the UN and is the primary way in which all future activity is justified.[21]

In effect, this approach is conservative, what Thomas Weiss has referred to as "classicist," because it maintains that politics and humanitarian inter-vention should be completely dissociated. As he states when describing this approach: "Until recently, the two most essential humanitarian principles—neutrality (not taking sides with warring parties) and impartiality (nondis-crimination and proportionality)—have been relatively uncontroversial, as has the key operating procedure of seeking consent from belligerents."[22]

The aim of intervention in the "classicist" position, according to Weiss, is "to do no harm."[23] To this might be added the principle that force is legiti-mate only as a last resort, for defensive purposes, and to be used both with minimal discretion and to the least extent possible.

Unlike realists, who rejected most multilateral peacekeeping or interven-tion in the 1990s on the grounds that the benefits were too low, the costs too high, and the options too few,[24] both classicist and maximalist proponents of peacekeeping therefore favor involvement on humanitarian grounds. The maximalists primarily concur with the realist assumption that the sovereignty of states is sacrosanct. To them, that means that states have rights (in the Westphalian sense). In effect: "The traditional conception of sovereignty as rights attributes to states jurisdictional exclusivity within their own borders and grants very limited and narrowly construed bases of legitimacy for other actors, whether another state or an international institution, to intervene in any form in what in their territorial locus are considered domestic affairs."[25]

Intervention is only justified in extreme situations, with the consent (if not at the initiative) of states, and thus legitimacy is predicated on the assumption that the activities of peacekeepers are by the consent of all antagonists, and impartial in conduct, and that their operations are transparent, nonintrusive, and minimally coercive in character. Thus, says John Ruggie, "[p]eacekeeping is a device to guarantee transparency, to reassure all sides that each is carrying out its promises."[26]

Indeed, the primary purpose of peacekeeping forces is to protect themselves (albeit minimally or unarmed) rather than to enforce the peace or achieve broader humanitarian goals.[27] Strategically, this pushes proponents of peacekeeping toward insulation rather than engagement policies; withdrawal even when on the ground; and the criticism that their universalist belief that they can sustain their contribution to humanitarian fulfillment under most circumstances is badly mistaken.

Some scholars have attempted to develop a comprehensive framework that subdivides peacekeeping operations into their various component parts.[28] Ruggie, however, summarizes the UN peacekeepers' posture and operational assumptions concisely when he states:

> Above all, peacekeeping is predicated on the consent of the parties which, typically, have agreed to cease hostilities before a peacekeeping mission is deployed. Moreover, peacekeepers fight against neither side but play an impartial interpositionary role, monitoring a ceasefire or controlling a buffer zone. Indeed, they do not fight as such. They carry only light arms and are authorized to shoot only in self-defense—and, on occasion, in the defense of their mission if they come under direct attack. Unlike fighting forces, then, peacekeepers are not intended to create the peace they are asked to keep. They accept the balance of forces on the ground and work within it. Ironically, this military weakness may be an advantage in that it reassures all parties that the peacekeeping force cannot alter the prevailing balance to their advantage. In short, peacekeeping is a device to guarantee transparency, to reassure all sides that each is carrying out its promises.[29]

THE DOCTRINE OF PREVENTIVE INTERVENTION

By 1997, the authors of one major report concluded that an alternative doctrine, what some have referred to as a "peace enforcement" approach,[30] was already unfolding. As they remarked: "At the moment there is no specific international legal provision against internal violence (apart from the genocide convention and more general provisions contained in international human rights instruments), nor is there any widely accepted principle that this should be prohibited."[31]

The foundations that undergird the doctrine of preventive intervention are vastly different from that of the peacekeeping one. Rather than drawing from the idea of reaction and limited engagement, preventive intervention starts from the assumption that sovereignty is conditional upon universally acceptable behavior—international norms—and that potential large-scale conflicts with dire humanitarian implications can be identified. The purpose of preventive intervention is to forestall such crises. Timely action to intercede can therefore be successfully undertaken, it assumes, by relevant forces.[32] Rather than being reactive, organizations like the UN must learn to take the initiative.[33] This belief is coupled with another, that "effective preventive strategies rest on three principles: early reaction to signs of trouble; a comprehensive, balanced approach to alleviate the pressures, or risk factors, that trigger violent conflict, and an extended effort to resolve the underlying root causes of violence."[34]

The justification for such action therefore rests on a contrasting definition of sovereignty to the traditional, hitherto hegemonic one employed by proponents of peacekeeping. The traditional view focuses on the rights of states. In this alternative version, states have responsibilities or obligations to their citizenry. One vaunted report summarized this position: "Where a population is suffering serious harm, as a result of internal war, insurgency, repression or state failure, and the state in question is unwilling or unable to halt or alter it, the principle of non-intervention yields to the international responsibility to protect."[35] Thus sovereignty

[d]oes not include any claim of the unlimited power of a state to do what it wants to its own people. . . . It is acknowledged that sovereignty implies a dual responsibility: externally—to respect the sovereignty of other states, and internally, to respect the dignity and basic rights of all the people within the state. In international human rights covenants, in UN practice, and in state practice itself, sovereignty is now understood as embracing this dual responsibility. Sovereignty as responsibility has become the minimum content of good international citizenship.[36]

According to this view, the implication of this perspective is that state authorities are responsible for the functions of protecting the safety and lives of citizens, as well as the promotion of their welfare; that national authorities are responsible to both the national citizenry and international community through the UN; and that the agents of states are responsible for their actions and accountable for acts of commission and omission. In sum, they are accountable where hitherto they benefited from purported impunity.[37] Failure to accept these responsibilities is the foundation for a "just cause" for intervention.[38]

Such claims are made against the backdrop of the development of the concept of human security, with its focus on the security of individuals as being of primary importance rather than the territorial integrity of states. This extends beyond civilian exposure in interstate wars to the physical safety of individuals in all contexts, their economic and social welfare, and the protection of their human rights.[39]

This kind of holistic approach to the definition of human security is consistent with the doctrine of preventive intervention in at least three different respects. First, its proponents move beyond the precipitant causes to consider underlying ones. They do so by distinguishing between structural and operational elements of prevention. Broader structural components (such as the battle against poverty and disease) involve crucial long-term strategies to avoid the conditions that foster intrastate conflict. Operational aspects involve strategies that address the immediate or contingent precipitants of war.[40]

Second, in contrast to peacekeeping, the focus in this doctrine is not exclusively on military intervention. Military intervention is only one form of preventive intervention. Broader strategies can include political and diplomatic initiatives, economic threats or incentives, as well as the threat or use of force. Intervention thus has twin components of sanctions and rewards that extend beyond the threat of imminent duress.[41]

Third, this approach extends "downstream" to include not only conflict resolution but also "peace building," often in the form of the reintegration and reconstruction of fragmented states, comparable to the embryonic process of state building currently under way in Afghanistan and Iraq. Conflict prevention, where appropriate, thus entails an extended, indefinite commitment to a process beyond the immediate use of force and sanctions. William Odom, former director of the National Security Agency, offers a less than enthusiastic, if realistic, comment that one does "have to recognize what successful interventions involve. Simply put, they must provide a surrogate government for a very long time, normally decades, while effective indigenous governmental institutions are created. Interventions inspired only by humanitarian impulses without a concomitant willingness and capacity to provide surrogate government are both politically and morally irresponsible."[42]

So the analysis of causes, the breadth of function, and the degree of time commitment all shift in the context of the doctrine of preventive intervention from that of peacekeeping. Although there is some disagreement over the timing of force, a war-fighting capacity is essential to establish and sustain credibility—and force remains "an appropriate" option. Its use should be "fair but firm."[43]

Yet it would be a mistake to conclude that the only justifications for preventive intervention are idealistic or moralistic. Appealing to rationalist instincts, some commentators on the utility of this doctrine also consider the proposition that "an ounce of prevention is worth a pound of cure." Bruce Jentleson, for example, offers a rationalist riposte to traditional realist approaches by suggesting that the option of preventive intervention saves money because of the huge costs involved in individual peacekeeping operations in the 1990s compared to the estimated costs of a preventive intervention operation.[44] Such claims are always subject to skepticism, given the inherent gap between the known cost of prior peacekeeping operations and the "guesstimates" involved in Jentleson's assertion. But his approach does provide the basis for serious debate amongst rationalists, and thus shifts the emphasis away from a characteristic representation of the argument as being between worldly rationalists and naive idealists.

Tom Farer gives a pragmatic and contemporary face to such realist arguments when he states that advocates of humanitarian intervention have "attempted to show that unremediated butchery in foreign lands adversely affects the interests of people at home. They emphasized material factors like spikes in undocumented immigration caused by persons fleeing persecution and the threat of deadly diseases or international criminal and terrorist organizations able to incubate in anarchic places."[45]

Consistent with my broad argument, the UN's leadership has played a pivotal role in the development of this doctrine since the mid-1980s—in response to the failure of peacekeeping operations to address a succession of humanitarian crises. The doctrine has developed in stages in a dialectic interaction between world events and policy-makers' responses.[46]

THE COLD WAR TRANSITION

A succession of UN peacekeeping failures led critics to conclude that the UN had neither the resources nor the strategy to act effectively.[47] Three cases were pivotal. The first involved military intervention in Macedonia, a very small and otherwise undistinguished operation whose importance lay in the fact that it set a precedent by becoming the first case where the principle of preventive intervention was used to justify UN activities under Resolution 795.[48] The second case was that of Rwanda, which was significant because of the very size of the genocide, the clear signals of impending slaughter, the apparent capacity of the West to intervene at a relatively small cost—and its refusal to do so. More notable therefore for what the UN did not do, Rwanda became inextricably associated with General Roméo Dallaire's attributed claim in April 1994 that the deployment of a relative small number of 5,000 mobile troops could have significantly reduced the slaughter in Rwanda, if not quell it.[49]

The third case was that of Somalia, where the UN made a significant movement away from the traditional peacekeeping paradigm toward something that was far more coercive in operation and broader in intent. Of the three, the importance of Macedonia as a historic precedent cannot be overstated. The role of the Rwandan genocide in illustrating the lack of equity and moral paucity of the West was of enormous importance in promoting the doctrine of preventive intervention. But, having said that, the case of Somalia cannot be underestimated—both because of the way in which the West was extensively involved and because the failure of both the US and UN missions illustrated the need for a more coherent strategy (than peacekeeping) in the context of humanitarian crises.

In this period, it was the secretary-general of the UN, Boutros Boutros-Ghali, who initially became the most vocal proponent of the development of a capacity for preventive intervention. In *An Agenda for Peace*, a 1992 report published relatively soon after his taking office, he described it in terms of being a new technique designed to prevent cross-border or intrastate conflict from erupting.[50] Boutros-Ghali there introduced the concept of "peace enforcement" as one designed to maintain cease-fires. As Edward Luck suggested, Boutros-Ghali stressed "that low-level action, at modest cost and risk, may prevent the need at a later point to choose between doing nothing and intervening forcefully."[51]

Two months later, as Daniel and Hayes point out, Boutros-Ghali characterized preventive intervention as a task beyond a traditional peacekeeping function, entailing deployment beyond the expressed consent of antagonists and in which the UN could use necessary force. "In this way he sanctioned the term 'peace enforcement' and, whatever his intentions, helped advance the view that the international community now had available a continuum of options with peace enforcement in the middle."[52] He saw it as a way of enforcing the peace against all signatories to an agreement who violated its terms. "In such a conception the peace support contingent is somewhat like a policeman on the beat with authority to support community-backed norms against all comers regardless of their affiliation."[53] In a further development of this idea, by 1995 Boutros-Ghali dropped the term "peace enforcement" and instead simply began to refer to "enforcement"—thus further distinguishing between peacekeeping and enforcement in the move toward prevention.[54]

In early 1993, Kofi Annan became the undersecretary general responsible for peacekeeping operations. Prior to his new appointment, he had vocally favored adopting a new paradigm for peace support built around inducements founded on the principle that "inaction in the face of massive violence is mor-

ally indefensible, non-involvement an illusory option."[55] Indeed, Annan had
been outraged by the inequity he perceived in the West's willingness to act to
intervene in Bosnia when Somalia, Sudan, Mozambique, and Liberia all then
ranked markedly higher in terms of the potential magnitude of the human
tragedies. Annan considered such a choice to be motivated more by the location of the war in Europe than consideration of the human implications—a
clear if unpopular point he made during a visit to Sarajevo in 1992.[56]

Certainly, Boutros-Ghali's demands were most immediately stimulated
by events in Somalia, where hundreds of thousands of victims were dying,
yet the Organization of African Unity (OAU) opposed UN intervention because no Somali government had requested assistance.[57] The Organization of
Islamic Conference, however, did press for action, providing Boutros-Ghali
with a justification to visit Somalia. In the midst of the fighting, Boutros-
Ghali prevailed upon the General Assembly, under Resolution 733, to establish a total arms embargo (albeit belated), urge a cease-fire, establish a
humanitarian relief effort, and issue an invitation to all parties in Somalia
to attend a meeting in New York in an attempt to reach a compromise. But
efforts at reconciliation proved unsuccessful, complicated by a history of
personal animosity between Somali warlord Mohamed Aideed and Boutros-
Ghali himself.[58]

The UN and the United States did eventually intervene in Somalia,
an episode chronicled extensively elsewhere.[59] That intervention, according
to critics, proved to be a failure in large part because of the bad faith that
existed between the United States and the UN. The United States was initially intent on pursuing an independent policy through the Unified Task
Force (UNITAF), predicated on the provision of immediate relief to starving
Somalis. Boutros-Ghali's objective was to institute a policy intent on the kind
of nation building that would precipitate a further move toward preventive
intervention. The Americans, according to Stephen John Stedman, were
never going to be interested in such goals.[60] Indeed, they were preparing
for an independent, short-term action before handing the operation over to
the UN.

Commentators have suggested that the American leadership of UNITAF
marked a watershed in the expansion of functions from traditional peacekeeping to broader peace operations. In contrast, it was the initial United Nations
Operation in Somalia (UNOSOM) that constituted a classic peacekeeping
operation there.[61] The UN Security Council passed Resolutions 751 and 767,
which sanctioned the deployment of troops, the airlift of emergency supplies,
and the provision of an advisory team to Somalia.

The US commitment, which extended to the provision of UNITAF
troops, was designed to stabilize the situation and provide a secure environ-

ment for the delivery of humanitarian assistance. This initiative, Resolution 794, was approved by the UN Security Council in December 1992. The UNITAF force, "Operation Restore Hope," would act forcefully and without the consent of locals if necessary. The resolution allowed for a greater use of all necessary force when faced with resistance, the appearance of weaponry, the construction of roadblocks, or evidence of banditry.[62]

Pointedly, the Americans therefore shifted outside the parameters of the traditional peacekeeping approach—pushing the agenda of Boutros-Ghali's peace enforcement paradigm. Notably, it was considered a successful humanitarian operation, effective in securing the distribution of relief supplies and stemming the death of Somalis.

Subsequently, Boutros-Ghali engendered the next move toward the doctrine of preventive intervention. In the wrangling over the second UN-OSOM mission, the United States reiterated its unwillingness to sustain its participation and pressed the UN to begin the transition toward the phased withdrawal of US troops, to be replaced by UN troops in the field. Resolution 814 created UNOSOM II, its mandate being to provide humanitarian intervention, generate a secure environment for economic assistance, and assist in the political reconstitution of a Somali government.[63]

Yet Boutros-Ghali recognized that only the United States could effectively disarm and demobilize the militias. He encouraged the United States to implement a coercive disarmament plan, extending its operations throughout Somalia and not just in the South, where it had primarily operated.

In fact, the Secretary-General did not even want to start planning for UNOSOM II until the United States accepted this broader mandate and began carrying it out. But despite a change in administrations [George H. W. Bush to Clinton], the US course of limiting the geographic scope of the operation, and avoiding general disarmament activities was set and would not change. As a result, Boutros-Ghali continued to insist until late April 1993 that it was premature and dangerous to begin planning for a US takeover. He was so certain that UNITAF could be pressured into implementing a "coercive disarmament" plan that the United Nations never prepared a plan of its own.[64]

Therefore Boutros-Ghali himself demanded further aggression in a move away from peacekeeping and toward greater coercive preemption.[65] Indeed, paradoxically, as the situation in Somalia worsened (and the United States introduced a war-fighting Quick Reaction Force to Somali in search of the warlord Mohamed Aideed), the gap between the US position and that of the UN subsequently widened, For, counterintuitively, it was Boutros-Ghali who advocated that the UN adopt an increasingly aggressive line, even as the US position was softening. Lobbying hard for Security Council Reso-

lution 837, he advocated that UN forces use all necessary means to arrest,
detain, and prosecute those Somalis who had attacked UN forces. As Daniel
and Hayes assert, the successful adoption of Resolution 837 "changed the
entire premise upon which UNOSOM had been operating. The UN was
now at war."[66]

Some contingents, like the Italian and the French, demurred at this
new UN directive, issuing conflicting orders to their troops. Nonetheless,
violence escalated, with the United States intent on locating Aideed, while a
separate UN force operated determined to defeat Aideed's Somali National
Alliance forces, stabilize the environment, and begin the process of nation
building. Neither operation succeeded in attaining its goals.

UNOSOM failed, according to Daniel and Hayes, because it lacked the
doctrine, resources, and political backing to fight a war. Furthermore, according to Stedman, the US refusal to support the UN mission—and the
eventual US withdrawal—doomed the operation to failure.[67] Indeed, Edward
Luck has offered the assessment that the mere US announcement of its intention to withdraw its troops from Somalia and not join the UN operation
was enough to precipitate the unraveling of the UN's efforts.[68]

Nonetheless, despite the mission's evident failure, events in Somalia
proved to be a watershed. They signaled the consolidation of a move away
from peacekeeping to something that was broader in scope and different in
character. Boutros-Ghali's efforts to bring order to Somalia and consolidate
the humanitarian operation there may have failed, but they laid the foundation for the idea of linking enforcement powers to a political mandate. Kofi
Annan may have been correct in suggesting, in a 1994 interview, that it would
be some time before the UN would support a peace enforcement mission of
its own.[69] But the foundation had been laid for the construction of a doctrine
in support of that idea,[70] with the UN the location for discussion.[71]

THE CONSOLIDATION PHASE

The period 1996–2001 was marked by a different kind of conflict and intervention, traceable to the low-level sustained presence in Macedonia into
1999, and the precipitous series of events that marked the North Atlantic
Treaty Organization (NATO) campaign in Kosovo as sanctioned by the UN.
Both could be linked to the principles of preventive intervention. But neither
was precipitated by the same kind of broad-based humanitarian crisis as was
evident in the first half of the 1990s.

Boutros Boutros-Ghali had been the first high-ranking UN official to
so aggressively promulgate the intellectual and emotional development of
the doctrine of preventive intervention. But the appointment of Kofi Annan

as secretary-general of the UN signaled its "takeoff" stage as he emphatically promoted humanitarian intervention through the UN Development Program's yearly reports.[72]

In perhaps his cumulative statement, the UN's millennium report entitled *We the Peoples: The Role of the United Nations in the 21st Century*, Annan offered his views about the major challenges facing humanity in the new century. The central theme in his discussion about poverty, AIDS, debt relief, and conflict prevention was that of a "human-centered" approach to security.[73] He redefined security in terms of demographic, poverty-related, and substantive violent threats to individuals rather than the more traditional conception of security as being a threat to the territorial integrity and sovereignty of states.[74] In that context, Annan thought it necessary to move from being a "culture of reaction" to a "culture of prevention."[75]

Bruce Jentleson suggests that Annan advocated an enormous shift in order to reinterpret a series of UN Articles as being collectively threaded to justify preventive intervention. These include Article 2(7) on sovereign rights; Article 3 on rights regarding life, liberty, and personal security; Article 55 on human rights as a fundamental and universal freedom; and Article 56 that pledges membership action toward promoting these goals. Thus, according to Annan, "even national sovereignty can be set aside if it stands in the way of the Security Council's overriding duty to preserve international peace and security."[76]

Such rhetoric found its way into a series of UN documents sponsored and issued by the secretary-general designed to exhort the Security Council and the General Assembly to accept this interpretation. In attempting to justify a new interpretation of "sovereignty as responsibility," Annan, for example, stated that "conflict prevention is one of the primary obligations of member states set forth in the UN Charter, and UN efforts in conflict prevention must be in conformity with the purposes and principles of the Charter."[77] Military and diplomatic intervention therefore became one of the key elements of this "culture of prevention."

Annan's comments were acute and focused, suggesting that "the time has come to translate the rhetoric of conflict prevention into concrete action."[78] Annan attempted to reorganize the UN institutionally along these lines, focusing his efforts on reorienting the fourteen departments under the umbrella of the Interdepartmental Framework for Coordination in 1998 primarily in order to address the issue of prevention. He also aggressively promoted a series of UN resolutions designed to strengthen peacekeeping and nation-building capacities, and to focus the efforts of the Department of Political Affairs on playing a useful role in such cases.[79]

Annan was not alone in these efforts, being assisted by a series of senior former politicians and high-profile UN officials. The leading members of this group included Lakhdar Brahimi, former Algerian minister for foreign affairs and chair of the Panel on United Nations Peacekeeping Operations; Mohamed Sahnoun, senior Algerian diplomat, OAU and Arab League official, and Brundtland Commission member; and Gareth Evans, former Australian minister and member of Parliament.[80] The latter two served as co-chairs of an NGO, the International Commission on Intervention and State Sovereignty, which produced the 2001 report entitled *The Responsibility to Protect*. That report is arguably the most comprehensive statement of the foundations of a preventive intervention doctrine to date. Not surprisingly, although funded by the Canadian government, the mandate of the commission was to reinforce Annan's rhetoric.

The first phase of the evolution of the doctrine of preventive intervention was therefore primarily developed in the context of African conflicts. The second, however, generally was not. War raged in the former Yugoslavia, as NATO forces brought a dictator to his knees. But this case made UN officials focus increasingly on the cases that predated 1996, and how the genocides of the period could have been avoided.

American reaction to these efforts was sporadic and occasionally hostile. Some exceptional American scholars of this trend, such as Bruce Jentleson (formerly a State Department official and senior adviser on foreign policy to Al Gore), were writing extensively on the normative, political, and policy aspects of what Jentleson preferred to term "coercive prevention."[81] In general, Jentleson provided evidence that contradicted the traditional conservative assessment that claimed that the American public opposed military intervention in addressing the large-scale effects of humanitarian crises.[82]

This period was marked by several cases of "indirect American intervention" (East Timor, Sierra Leone, and Liberia) and one outstanding, contentious case of direct intervention in Kosovo. Critics contended that the NATO bombing in Kosovo might have been illegal under international law (albeit that the bombing was purportedly justified by Belgrade's abrogation of UN Security Council Resolution 1199) because China and Russia refused to sanction the bombing campaign.[83] Others denounced the American position as hypocritical because President Clinton claimed a moralist and collectivist impulse but was in fact unilateralist in action and self-serving in motive.[84] Proponents of the action, in contrast, suggested that it took place without Security Council support, but may have been legal according to a growing volume of humanitarian law by virtue of precedent.[85]

Concerns about international law, however, seemed to play no obvious role in explaining the decision by President Clinton to articulate his "Clinton

Doctrine" on 22 June 1999. Here, in presenting a perspective consistent with and congruent to the doctrine of preventive intervention, Clinton offered "an avowal to stop mass murder everywhere despite the cost to the principle of sovereignty."[86] Seemingly, the Clinton administration's position had become congruent with that of Annan's; sovereignty was conditional, and the use of force legitimate. The "can of worms" that had opened up concerned the condition under which force was applicable.

THE DOCTRINE OF IMPERIAL INTEGRATION

Any chance of continued congruence between the UN position and that of US policy-makers, however, was quickly eclipsed by George W. Bush's presidential triumph. The new president had articulated his explicit hostility to such humanitarian, preventive missions,[87] indefatigably stated during his presidential campaign with the comment, "We should not send our troops to stop ethnic cleansing and genocide in nations outside our strategic interest."[88] Pressed to view American involvement as necessary, conditioned more by American interests in and the structural conditions that others argued necessitated engagement, Bush and his advisers seemed immovable on the issue. Their position echoed the sentiment of some commentators that it was not the American role to prevent each tragedy (nor was it capable of doing so) and that American national interest, not moralism, should be the basis of decision-making.[89]

The American objective as defined by Bush and his advisers was conditioned by two considerations: to avoid being bogged down in the prospect of "nation building" ("the Vietnam syndrome") and to avoid taking casualties as the foremost goal (the "zero casualties syndrome"). Humanitarian intervention, many such as influential columnist Charles Krauthammer argued, would clearly transgress both of these primary policy goals.[90] Bush, in effect, was echoing and responding to the policies and events of his father's administration.[91] Only later were events in Iraq to reflect how far George W. Bush had reversed course on both of these issues.

American commitment to the development of the doctrine of preventive intervention therefore stalled. Within the White House, however, two alternative doctrines were being contested. Both concurred with the UN's and the Clinton administration's view that sovereignty was conditional, yet these two views were driven by contrasting impulses.

The first doctrine was articulated by Richard Haass, who then held the post of director of the Policy Planning Staff at the US State Department. In a speech before the Foreign Policy Association, Haass dramatically outlined his views, which were reflective of an imperial notion of America's role in the world. Haass spoke of the paucity of, and confusion about, both the goals and the instruments of policy. This confusion, he suggested, engulfs the way in which Americans respond to a series of transnational threats, including mass destruction, terrorism, infectious diseases, and environmental degradation. In the aftermath of 9/11, according to Haass, there is a need to develop a new doctrine that fuses the "transnational and the traditional" and to provide a coherent rationale for addressing a series of threatening situations across Latin America, Asia, and the Middle East.

Such a doctrine, Haass suggested at the time, "not only gives overall direction to policy, but it also helps establish basic priorities. It can help shape, size, and direct the allocation of resources, while allowing policy-makers to conserve that most precious of all resources, their time." Furthermore, suggested Haass, "a doctrine offers strategic clarity."[92] He labeled his a "doctrine of integration." Haass outlined the central rudiments of such a doctrine when he stated:

In the 21st century, the principal aim of American foreign policy is to integrate other countries and organizations into arrangements that will sustain a world consistent with U.S. interests and values, and thereby promote peace, prosperity, and justice as widely as possible. Integration of new partners into our efforts will help us deal with traditional challenges of maintaining peace in divided regions as well as with transnational threats such as international terrorism and the proliferation of weapons of mass destruction. It will also help bring into the globalized world those who have previously been left out. In this era, our fate is intertwined with the fate of others, so our success must be shared success. We are doing this by persuading more and more governments and, at a deeper level, people to sign on to certain key ideas as to how the world should operate for our mutual benefit. Integration is about bringing nations together and then building frameworks of cooperation and, where feasible, institutions that reinforce and sustain them even more.[93]

The values reflective of this doctrine are predictable—the rule of law; limited state power; and a respect for women, private property, equal access to justice, and religious tolerance. All were depicted as universal values, although many are arguably predominantly American in character. In sum, Haass claimed that these values "are captured by the idea of integration," a "profoundly optimistic approach to international relations" in which (through a process of consultation and cooperation) power can be pooled.[94]

Integration should be applied to both relationships (between the United States, on the one hand, and both developed and developing countries, on the other) and to institutions (multilateral and regional). The purpose should be to create "an architecture for this new global era that will sustain the co-operative pursuit of shared global interests." In addressing the concerns of humanitarian crises that have more commonly been associated with preventive intervention, Haass commented:

Some nations and their people cannot now tap into the benefits of the globalized economy because of these countries' institutional and economic weaknesses. It would be morally repugnant—and defy our nation's deepest values—to ignore the plight of the citizens of such countries. And, as Afghanistan taught us all too well, it would also be unwise to look away when states begin to fail. Today's humanitarian problem can all too easily become tomorrow's strategic threat. It is for reasons such as these that the United States is pressing for fundamental reforms in how the World Bank handles development assistance. And, that is why President Bush announced last month his bold initiative to dramatically increase American foreign assistance by 50% over the next three years. The Millennium Challenge Account, moreover, will be allocated according to criteria that stress the mutually reinforcing connections among good governance, the rule of law, investment in people, open markets, and poverty reduction. Establishing new norms for this new era will be equally important to our success. The right to self-defense is an international norm that none deny. But over the past decade, we have seen an evolution in how the international community views sovereignty. Simply put, sovereignty does not grant governments a blank check to do whatever they like within their own borders. Instead, the principle that sovereignty carries responsibilities is gaining ground. We saw this in the humanitarian interventions of the past decade, such as in Kosovo. When governments violate the rights of their people on a large scale—be it as an act of conscious policy or the byproduct of a loss of control—the international community has the right and sometimes even obligation to act. Since September 11, behind President Bush's leadership, we have seen similar changes in how the international community views states' responsibilities vis-à-vis terrorism. Countries affected by states that abet, support, or harbor international terrorists, or are incapable of controlling terrorists operating from their territory, have the right to take action to protect their citizens.[95]

According to Haass, the tools for implementation should be diplomatic, economic, military, financial, and legal. The purpose, according to his doctrine, thus clearly extended to nation building in order to address a series of transnational, collective action problems. America, Haass pointed out, could provide leadership but (given their scale and scope) could not address them alone.

Notably, Haass explicitly suggested that coalitions in addressing problems will be fluid in character, as will the issue of using formal institutions as conduits. By implication, the role of the UN would therefore not be embed-

ded in the functioning of this doctrine (one also referred to as constituting a
new norm by Haass). The NATO decision to take military action regarding
Kosovo prior to a Security Council sanction might therefore have initiated
an unanticipated precedent by Russia and (perhaps more significantly) the
People's Republic of China.

Haass's integrationist doctrine was clearly distinct from the doctrine
of preventive intervention. But the linkage was that his doctrine attempted
to specify the legitimate conditions under which preventive intervention
would be appropriate. The doctrine thus justified action that abrogated state
sovereignty. Common to the UN position is its multilateral character, use
of proportional force, willingness to respond in the context of humanitarian crises, and broad moralist component. Its contrast, however, lay in the
centrality of American self-interest, and a willingness to use force to address
issues of liberal trade and democratic governance that emphasized "the liberal peace" argument and extended well beyond any simple humanitarian
mandate. A free-trading liberal democratic world would be a stable one, and
transnational forces should be used to address what Haass characterizes as
transnational problems.[96]

THE DOCTRINE OF "PREEMPTIVE" INTERVENTION

The second doctrine being fermented in the White House by neoconservative proponents at the time was that of "preemptive" intervention (often,
confusingly, referred to interchangeably as "preventive" intervention by
White House staff and military advisers).[97] This alternative doctrine dis-
trusted multilateralism, saw problems with cooperative security (as an at-
tendant attack on American sovereignty), and focused on the use of power for
the purpose of national security defined in narrow terms. While Colin Powell
as secretary of state represented to them the epitome of multilateralism, the
neoconservatives seemed to be gaining the upper hand. That trend, however,
certainly accelerated as a result of the events of 9/11. In effect, Haass lost the
debate, and he resigned to become the president of the Council on Foreign
Relations, where he could continue to advocate his multilateralist agenda. But
although the neoconservatives rejected Haass's argument, some elements of
it nevertheless subsequently resurfaced as a result of political expediency, as
an increasing welter of evidence suggested that the rationale for intervention
in Iraq (unconventional weaponry) was decidedly weak.

As a presidential candidate, George W. Bush clearly signaled an explicit
hostility to multilateralism—to both humanitarian missions and collective
security. He preferred to pursue a narrower definition of self-interest and

state sovereignty in a spirit of unilateralism.[98] The George W. Bush administration's policy responses regarding the Kyoto Accord, the International Court of Criminal Justice, the Biological Weapons Protocol, and the Anti-Ballistic Missile Treaty were reflective of this view.[99]

The Bush administration's posture on preventive intervention was indefatigably stated during the 2000 presidential campaign, summed up with characteristic brevity with the statement that "we should not send our troops to stop ethnic cleansing and genocide in nations outside our strategic interest." Pressed to view American involvement as necessary, conditioned more by American interests in and the structural conditions that others argued necessitated engagement, Bush and his neoconservative advisers seemed immovable on the issue. Their position echoed the sentiment of some commentators that it was not the American role to prevent each tragedy (nor was it capable of doing so) and that American national interest, not moralism, should be the basis of decision-making.[100] Military force was supposedly to be used by the United States quickly and at moderate cost, consistent with supposedly historic (if, in fact, factually inaccurate) accounts of American behavior.[101] Other governments meanwhile—such as the Dutch, Canadian, British, and Swedish—shifted toward fostering far better pragmatic connections between humanitarian assistance and conflict resolution in this period.[102]

Bush, in effect, was echoing and responding to the policies and events of his father's administration. George H. W. Bush had wanted to avoid becoming bogged down in a quagmire when initially engaging in Somalia, driven to act by a humanitarian impulse but keen to avoid the suggestion that Americans were either there to govern or to assist in forming a new government.[103]

Nonetheless, all of George W. Bush's expressed goals were subsequently belied by events in Afghanistan and Iraq. The attacks of 11 September were perhaps emblematic in demonstrating that the United States cannot avoid engagement. Rather than *whether* the United States engages the rest of the world, it is *how* the United States engages it that is key. Bush's version of engagement was signaled early. He emphasized the notion of the "culture of prevention," in speaking of a possible terrorist attack, when he stated, "If we wait for threats to fully materialize, we will have waited too long."[104] Yet the purpose of his "preemptive" intervention has been well documented. The primary goal was to protect US domestic citizens, not foreign civilians. Innocent people were now identified as those on the streets of Boston and not Baghdad, Baltimore, not Basra. The intent in doing so was twofold.

The first was to respond to a perceived imminent threat either by foreign governments or the terrorists that they purportedly harbored in order to thwart attacks against Americans, whether they were located on home or foreign soil. Countries that were considered the launching pad for terrorists were to be held culpable and could not claim immunity from hostile intervention on the grounds of sovereignty.

The second, more extended intention of the doctrine of "preemptive" intervention was to derail the efforts of foreign governments to develop new technologies to create (effectively irresistible) nuclear, biological, or chemical (NBC) weapons that could hold the United States (and its closest allies) strategically at bay—seemingly on an immutable basis. North Korean or Iranian nuclear capacity presented the United States with a nightmare scenario: the possibility that countries could be used as terrorist bases and could develop even more threatening weapons, their safety from American military action guaranteed by their capacity to offer a single, albeit it devastating, military response.

In effect, however, sovereignty was further diluted. Preemptive action on the basis of a clear and present danger has been invoked before. Arab troops massing on the border to attack Israel in 1967 had prompted an Israeli countermeasure, and the notion had gained both legitimacy and currency. But here it was invoked with far less clarity as to the threat, the danger being extended geographically across the globe and (paradoxically perhaps) into the future in order to address a concern that some countries might generate the technological capability of creating an unassailable reprisal capability that might put them beyond the American capacity to intervene. In the doctrine, therefore, clear and present danger in fact came to include the concept of the "potentially materializing danger."

The logic of this position was epitomized by the example of Vice President Richard Cheney's defense of US and allied intervention in Iraq, when he stated:

But we now know that Saddam has resumed his efforts to acquire nuclear weapons. Among other sources, we've gotten this from the firsthand testimony of defectors—including Saddam's own son-in-law, who was subsequently murdered at Saddam's direction. Many of us are convinced that Saddam will acquire nuclear weapons fairly soon. Armed with an arsenal of these weapons of terror, and seated atop ten percent of the world's oil reserves, Saddam Hussein could then be expected to seek domination of the entire Middle East, take control of a great portion of the world's energy supplies, directly threaten America's friends throughout the region, and subject the United States or any other nation to nuclear blackmail.[105]

The counterpart to an emergent foreign threat is the potential injury with which it threatens Americans at home—as articulated by President Bush's subsequent statement that

intelligence gathered by this and other governments leaves no doubt that the Iraq regime continues to possess and conceal some of the most lethal weapons ever devised.
. . . The danger is clear: using chemical, biological, or one day nuclear weapons,
obtained with the help of Iraq, the terrorists could fulfill their stated ambition and
kill thousands or hundreds of thousands of innocent people in our country or any
other.[106]

As Ken Roth summarized it:

[T]he United States–led coalition forces justified the invasion of Iraq on a variety
of grounds, only one of which—a comparatively minor one—was humanitarian.
The Security Council did not approve the invasion, and the Iraqi government, its
existence on the line, violently opposed it. Moreover, while the African interventions were modest affairs, the Iraq war was massive, involving an extensive bombing
campaign and some 150,000 ground troops. . . . To justify the extraordinary remedy
of military force for preventive humanitarian purposes, there must be evidence that
large-scale slaughter is in preparation and about to begin unless militarily stopped.
But no one seriously claimed before the war that the Saddam Hussein government
was planning imminent mass killing, and no evidence has emerged that it was. There
were claims that Saddam Hussein, with a history of gassing Iranian soldiers and
Iraqi Kurds, was planning to deliver weapons of mass destruction through terrorist
networks, but these allegations were entirely speculative; no substantial evidence has
yet emerged. There were also fears that the Iraqi government might respond to an
invasion with the use of chemical or biological weapons, perhaps even against its own
people, but no one seriously suggested such use as an imminent possibility in the
absence of an invasion.[107]

However egregious the administration's claims subsequently proved to
be, the accusations that Iraq was a haven for terrorists, that it was within
striking distance of securing a military capability that would protect it from
US incursion, and that it could soon pose a possible future threat to US security at home found a resonance among the American public—and gave the
neoconservatives within the Bush administration a coherent doctrine upon
which to found their claims.

CONCLUSION

In the last two decades, three doctrines have evolved that challenge the traditional autonomy of states as possessing sovereignty-based rights (summarized
in table 2). Table 2 attempts to classify them according to their characterization of sovereignty, their values, operational attributes, and broader mandate.
They are also listed chronologically in terms of their initial formulations,

Table 2. Four Doctrines of Intervention: The Evolution of a Norm

	Peacekeeping	Preventive Intervention	Imperial Foreign Policy	"Preemptive" Intervention
Nature of Sovereignty	Rights	Responsibilities	Responsibilities	Responsibilities
	Sovereignty sacrosanct	Sovereignty conditional	Sovereignty conditional	Sovereignty highly conditional
Nature of Primary Values	Impartiality	Partiality for victims	Partiality for those denied human rights, democracy, or economic liberalism	Partiality for domestic population
	Consent	Possibly nonconsensual		Nonconsensual
Operational Attributes	Reactive	Proactive	Proactive	Proactive
	Late entry	Early entry	Early entry	Early entry
	Force as last use	Force as appropriate use	Force as appropriate use	Overwhelming use of force
	Self-defense	Citizenry protection	Establishing peace among nations	Domestic citizenry protection
	No political mandate	Possible political mandate		Transformative mandate
	Transparency of operation	Clarity of message	Clarity of message	Clarity of message
Broader Mandate	Humanitarian operation	Commitment to peace building	Construction of world order built on guiding principles	Responding to perceived clear and present danger
	Central but not limited to UN role	Coalitional structure		
	Multilateralist	Multilateralist	Preferably multilateralist	Dominantly unilateralist

although all currently interact with and (in that sense their respective proponents respond to) each other. When George W. Bush contended that "moral truth is the same in every culture, in every time, and in every place," he came close to the assertion that preventive intervention is justifiable because of a universal right of victims to enjoy a "freedom from fear." What they more explicitly share is the belief that sovereignty is conditional upon the upholding of responsibilities. Where they differ is the substance of those responsibilities—and the process by which those responsibilities should be enforced.

The Bush administration soon encountered the limits of the doctrine of "preemptive" intervention. It engaged in limited (and unsuccessful) nation building in Afghanistan and more extensive (although to date by no means any more successful) nation building in Iraq. Moreover, the failure to find any evidence of NBC weapons research or production ultimately drove the Bush administration back to Haass's doctrine to justify its actions in Iraq. And, with no little irony, the subsequent US action in Haiti is perfectly consistent with the doctrine of preventive intervention—the use of forceful action before the number of casualties escalated. These examples demonstrate that while one doctrine may predominate for a while, they all may exist simultaneously—and lack the distinct clarity their proponents suggest they have when actually employed by policy-makers. What makes each distinct, nonetheless, is its purpose, means, and consequences.

Furthermore, the larger picture may portend a trend: In a world in which globalization has already redefined (although not necessarily shrunk) the economic capabilities of states, these prevailing and contesting security doctrines challenge the capacities of states to enhance the safety of civilian populations. The dilution of sovereignty has not been complemented by the blossoming of collective security institutions, nor the support for that concept among those best able to implement such policies. New technologies have created a global capacity for intervention but no accompanying agreement about when or how to intervene. The product is a world devoid of rules, with only contested beliefs about when to abrogate sovereignty. Only one thing is clear; sovereignty, as we routinely enforced it in the second half of the twentieth century, is now largely moribund.

4

By "Any Measures" Necessary

NSC-68 AND COLD WAR ROOTS OF THE 2002 NATIONAL SECURITY STRATEGY

GORDON R. MITCHELL AND
ROBERT P. NEWMAN

ONE PROMINENT VENUE for the public rollout of the George W. Bush administration's 2002 National Security Strategy of the United States of America (NSS 2002) was *U.S. Foreign Policy Agenda*. The preface of that journal's December 2002 issue begins with two quotations from President George W. Bush's letter transmitting NSS 2002 to Congress. It then proceeds to frame the historical significance of the president's words:

With those words President Bush submitted his National Security Strategy (NSS) to the U.S. Congress September 20th. Each administration is required by the Goldwater-Nichols Act of 1986 to submit an annual report to Congress setting out the nation's comprehensive strategic security objectives. The tradition began with President Harry S. Truman in 1950 with NSC-68, a report that focused on the United States and the then–Soviet Union and calling for a doctrine of containment that dominated the ensuing Cold War.[1]

By linking NSS 2002 to NSC-68, the editors of *U.S. Foreign Policy Agenda* present a conundrum that serves as a point of departure for this chapter. The conundrum stems from how NSS 2002 and NSC-68 compare—they share important features in common yet also diverge in ways that make it difficult to fathom how they belong to the same "tradition." Consider that while NSS 2002 is a public document, NSC-68 was classified and hidden from public view for twenty-five years. Further, NSC-68 codified the doctrine of deterrence as the cornerstone of US security strategy, while NSS 2002 declares flatly that against terrorists, "traditional concepts of deterrence will not work."[2] Finally, section 9C of NSC-68 stipulates that "the idea of 'preventive' war—in the sense of a military attack not provoked by a military attack upon us or our allies—is generally unacceptable to Americans,"[3] while NSS 2002 says that today, the United States must be ready and willing to hit enemies first, before threats fully materialize. These vectors of divergence would seem to underscore President Bush's contention that "the basis for our mutual security must move beyond Cold War doctrines."[4]

The conundrum is that while NSS 2002 is clearly billed as a "post–Cold War" security strategy, one that departs significantly from some of NSC-68's key tenets, commentators still draw parallels between the two documents to generate frames of reference for understanding the new Bush security strategy. As Mark Joyce observes, "Just as NSC 68 provided an off-the-shelf strategic rationale for US intervention in Korea and, later, Vietnam, the Bush NSS established an intellectual framework for the subsequent invasion of Iraq and, potentially, for future actions against other perceived sponsors of international terrorism."[5] More generally, in an October 2005 speech addressing the "war on terror," President Bush explained that, "in many ways, this fight resembles the struggle against communism in the last century."[6] Bush's comment suggests that clues for understanding the "current fight" may reside in historical artifacts such as NSC-68, the "blueprint for Cold War defense."[7]

In support of this view, Melvyn Leffler argues that "Bush's rhetoric and actions have deep roots in the history of American foreign policy. Understanding these roots is important because they help to illuminate the different trajectories that inhere in the American diplomatic experience."[8] Specifically, Leffler isolates the "hyperbolic language" of NSC-68 as a precursor to contemporary rhetoric in the "war on terror":

The delicate balance between threat perception, the definition of interests, and the employment of power changed in 1950. The Soviet acquisition of the bomb, the fall of China, the signing of the Sino-Soviet alliance, and the outbreak of hostilities in Korea accentuated the perception of threat, institutionalized the hyperbolic language of NSC 68, and inaugurated a full-scale war on communism everywhere. Eisenhower and Dulles, we now know, were more nuanced than we once thought, but their rhetoric calling on nations to take sides was a precursor of the rhetoric we hear today. The war against communism blurred important distinctions, distorted priorities, and complicated threat perception.[9]

This chapter builds context for the volume's overall assessment of NSS 2002 by studying what Leffler calls NSC-68's "hyperbolic language." We analyze how NSC-68's rhetoric constructs an epistemological framework that blurs important distinctions, distorts priorities, and complicates threat perception, and we chart how NSC-68's approach to security evolves and unfolds across various administrations during the Cold War. Our study traces three threads linking NSC-68 to NSS 2002: the rhetoric in the texts of the strategy documents themselves; the institutional practices deployed to install, legitimate, and implement each strategy; and the identity of the key players involved in the various campaigns undertaken to execute the respective blueprints.

THE MAKING AND MARKETING OF NSC-68

For five years following World War II, there was no definitive statement of American strategic policy. The Joint Chiefs of Staff had developed reasonably effective planning bodies during the war and in 1945 turned to these bodies for advice on how to conduct the expected conflict with the Soviet Union. This was not an apparatus comparable to the notorious German General Staff, but it was a beginning. From 1945 to 1950, ideas came thick and fast from the Joint Intelligence Staff, Joint Intelligence Committee, Joint Strategic Survey Committee, Joint War Plans Committee, and the Joint Chiefs of Staff as a whole.[10] Periodically during these five years, the question of preventive nuclear war surfaced, but never got the support of the Joint Chiefs. As Steven T. Ross suggests,

[T]he final report of the Evaluation Board for Operation Crossroads, the A-bomb tests at Bikini, submitted on June 30, 1947, stated that an atomic blitz could not only nullify a nation's military effort but also demolish its social and economic structures for long periods of time. . . . The United States, therefore, had to amass a large number of weapons of mass destruction, and since a surprise attack with such weapons could be decisive, America had to be prepared to strike first.[11]

Operation Bushwacker, a war plan of 8 March 1948, stated the basic war aim as compelling the Union of Soviet Socialist Republics (USSR) to abandon political and military aggression. Ross observes of Bushwacker that, "given the stated political goal, nothing short of the overthrow of the Soviet regime would have produced the desired results."[12] A later plan, Trojan, of 28 January 1949, carried an annex demonstrating that the "Air Force intended to hit seventy Soviet cities with 133 atomic bombs."[13]

Bushwacker, Trojan, and other nuclear first-strike plans formulated by US war strategists shortly after World War II never received presidential sanction. Truman intended to hold the military budget down; planners knew they had to pull in their horns. But by 1949, the wartime coalition of the Western allies and the Soviet Union had largely broken down, and several traumatic events spurred the president to seek a new look at US defense policy. The collapse of the US's ally in Asia, the Chinese Nationalist regime; the detonation by the Soviet Union of an atomic weapon; and the indictment and ultimate conviction of a high-ranking American diplomat, Alger Hiss, for perjury in denying he had passed state secrets to Soviet agents caused Truman to appoint a committee to review defense policy, chaired by Paul Nitze.

Nitze made sure that only the most dire claims about the hostile intentions of the Soviet Union found their way into NSC-68, the report drafted by his committee. The opinions of those who knew the Kremlin best, George Kennan, Llewellyn Thompson, and Charles Bohlen, were systematically excluded.[14] The Kennan-Thompson-Bohlen group believed that Stalin's primary aim was to maintain his tight control of the USSR and its satellites, but that he had no plan to conquer the world. Their refutation of Nitze's alarmism, when read today, is unassailable. Stalin, they said, was primarily concerned with maintaining his iron grip on the Soviet government, and with developing a cordon sanitaire in depth to prevent another invasion of Russia from the west. Nitze claimed, and wrote into US official policy, that Stalin had the intention of gaining control of the whole of Europe and all strategic points in Asia and Africa, so that the USSR could strangle the United States.

In Nitze's view, the threat from the Soviet system was so powerful that our usual moral superiority to the godless Russians had to yield to the necessity of defeating Communism everywhere: "[T]he assault on free institutions is worldwide now, and in the context of the present polarization of power a defeat of free institutions anywhere is a defeat everywhere."[15] It was to be us or them, there were no alternatives, only complete and total hostility. Those who think NSC-68 was a necessary and legitimate call to arms do not attend to what Leffler calls its "hyperbolic language": the USSR was irrevocably committed to conquering the world. "The issues that face us are momentous, involving the fulfillment or destruction not only of this Republic but of civilization itself. . . . '[W]ith a firm reliance on the protection of Divine Providence, we mutually pledge to each other our lives, our Fortunes, and our sacred Honor.'"[16] As John Lewis Gaddis observes, "the effect was vastly to increase the number and variety of interests deemed relevant to the national security, and to blur distinctions between them."[17] How should the United

States deal with such a totalizing and ominous threat? NSC-68 spelled out the options: "The integrity of our system will not be jeopardized by any measures, overt or covert, violent or nonviolent, which serve the purpose of frustrating the Kremlin design."[18] In short, anything goes, as long as it is not counterproductive. As Gaddis explains NSC-68's logic, "The world crisis . . . rendered all interests vital, all means affordable, all methods justifiable."[19]

Since the United States was not ready to contemplate a war with its one-time ally, the USSR, at the time Nitze wrote NSC-68, the report needed some selling. Truman was one of the last to get behind it. When he got the first draft from Nitze on 7 April 1950, he sat on it for a week, then referred it to James Lay, executive secretary of the NSC, for specification of precise programs that would be required, and what they would cost. Meanwhile, he directed that absolutely no publicity be given to the report or its contents. He also refused to back down from his announced determination to keep the defense budget smaller in 1951 than it was in 1950: $13.1 billion. On 10 June 1950, he told Congress, "We must not become hysterical. Our situation is strong, our strength is growing. We must remain cool, determined, and steady."[20]

Secretary of State Dean Acheson correctly perceived, as he wrote in *Present at the Creation,* that the main purpose of NSC-68 was "to so bludgeon the mind of top government that not only could the President make a decision but that the decision could be carried out."[21] In "Selling NSC 68: The Truman Administration, Public Opinion, and the Politics of Mobilization, 1950–51," Steven Casey explains how difficult this was until the deterioration of the military situation in Korea, the pivotal factor that eventually induced Truman to finally sign off on NSC-68.[22]

THE COMMITTEE ON THE PRESENT DANGER

After embracing NSC-68 as official US strategy, the Truman administration turned next to the challenge of convincing war-weary citizens to implement its tenets. As Casey explains, most historians recount this public relations effort by highlighting State Department official Edward Barrett's statement calling for a "psychological scare campaign"[23] and citing Acheson's memoirs—"throughout 1950 . . . I went about the country preaching" the main points of NSC-68, in language "clearer than truth."[24] However, the rhetorical strategy described by Acheson and Barrett was more nuanced than a straightforward propaganda operation designed to stoke public fear. As Casey points out, after NSC-68, Truman officials were keenly aware that overheating public spheres of deliberation with alarmist rhetoric could backfire, by inducing panicked citizens to call for desperate military measures such as a US preventive nuclear first strike on the Soviet Union. Indeed, these concerns were heightened in 1950 by rumblings in Congress about the viability of war plans such as Bushwacker and Trojan: "[F]or the first time, some members of Congress were beginning to speculate on what had formerly been an almost forbidden subject—preventive war."[25] This delicate situation led the Truman administration to pursue a carefully calibrated approach to management of public opinion, selling NSC-68 in a fashion that would tack between the twin dangers of "atomic apathy and hydrogen hysteria."[26]

Because the popular mood was highly susceptible to such violent mood swings, leaders had tread carefully, tailoring their message to suit current conditions. On occasion, this might well entail overselling, perhaps even exaggerating the importance of an international incident, in order to jolt the populace out of its torpor. But at the same time, clear dangers lurked in going too far in this direction, for such activity might also create an overreaction, perhaps even sparking a widespread popular hysteria. As a result, the goal of any information campaign was to generate interest in times of apathy, but without creating a panic when the mood swiftly began to shift.[27]

As 1950 drew to a close, Truman officials found this rhetorical tightrope increasingly difficult to traverse when a private group named the Committee on Present Danger (CPD) emerged. Led by Harvard president James Conant and atomic scientist Vannevar Bush, the CPD splashed onto the scene with a hard-line manifesto that pressed for full and immediate implementation of the NSC-68 blueprint.

While "the CPD did work hand in hand with the administration to legitimate the policy outlined in NSC-68,"[28] it approached this task like a bull in a china shop, trumpeting hard-line themes with minimal regard for nuance or subtlety. For example, the committee pressed relentlessly for universal military service, pursuit of US nuclear superiority, and permanent stationing of American troops in Europe. It distributed 100,000 copies of a cartoon-captioned pamphlet entitled "The Danger of Hiding Our Heads."[29] A series of CPD Sunday evening radio broadcasts on the Mutual Broadcasting System reached 550 affiliate stations throughout the nation. During one of these broadcasts, CPD member Major General (ret.) William J. Donovan called for "all-out employment of the nation's economic, political and psychological weapons to regain initiative in the Cold War." As an illustration of this NSC-68-style, "any measures" necessary approach, Donovan mentioned the possibility of subversion by means of covert operation, arguing that the United States must "develop countermeasures that would prevent the loss of strategic areas." One area ripe for action was Iran, where Donovan said nationalization of the oil industry was caused by "Soviet maneuvers in the economic and political life of that country."[30]

Donovan's radio broadcast proved prescient—three years later the United States and Britain carried out operation Ajax, a covert Central Intelligence Agency (CIA) mission to oust Iranian leader Mohammed Mossadegh.[31] The second author of this chapter gained insight into this mission from Dick Cottam, professor of political science at the University of Pittsburgh, who had been part of Kim Roosevelt's CIA team that engineered the coup. Cottam was punctilious in observing the oath against revealing sources and methods, but he was abundantly clear about the attitude at the top levels of government: if you lie, don't get caught. An account of how the 1953 regime change in Iran affected US relations with Middle East nations, Stephen Kinzer's *All the Shah's Men*, makes it clear that for American officials, "any measures" necessary to "frustrate the Kremlin design" included deception, as in the case of official US denials that the CIA had played a role in the Iranian coup.[32] A supine mainstream media enabled such falsehoods to persist unchallenged in American public spheres of deliberation—*Newsweek*'s headline echoed the administration's cover story perfectly: "Shah Returns in Triumph as Army Kicks Out Mossadegh."[33]

With NSC-68 fully installed, "frustrating the Kremlin design" frequently meant regime change, eliminating or attempting to eliminate leaders thought to be pro-Soviet, and this happened not only in Iran but also in Guatemala, Cuba, Chile, Indonesia, and Vietnam. Strictly speaking, these were not "preventive wars" in the sense that section 9C of NSC-68 uses the concept to describe a nuclear first strike against the Soviet Union. However, the numerous cases of US conventional (and covert) military intervention against Cold War adversaries—so-called Soviet surrogates—definitely involved preventive use of force. As such, Leffler suggests that it is worthwhile to consider these cases as precursors to the preventive military attacks against Iraq, launched under the aegis of NSS 2002.

After Kennedy's death, intelligence analysts and East Asian experts convinced President Lyndon B. Johnson and McGeorge Bundy that China's acquisition of nuclear capabilities would not endanger vital U.S. interests. Consequently, they did not employ preventative force directly against China or the Soviet Union, but the Kennedy and Johnson administrations did adopt unilateralist, preventative measures in relation to other perceived threats. The most conspicuous case, of course, was the deployment of force to blockade Cuba in October 1962. But Johnson's decisions to send troops to the Dominican Republic and to deploy combat forces to Indochina were preventative in nature, although we often do not think of them in that way. But we should, if we wish to place Bush national security strategy in proper historical perspective.[34]

Some of the Cold War plans to facilitate American preventive war aims with strategic deception strain credulity. Consider Operation Northwoods, a scheme hatched by General Lyman Lemnitzer, chairman of the Joint Chiefs of Staff under Eisenhower and Kennedy. This secret 1962 blueprint for deception came to light after it was declassified under the Freedom of Information Act and highlighted by historian James Bamford in his 2001 book, *Body of Secrets*.[35] Lemnitzer proposed nine covert operations designed to turn public opinion against Fidel Castro and create pretexts for US military intervention in Cuba.[36] His catalog of deception schemes ranged from blunt ("3a. We could blow up a US ship in Guantanamo Bay and blame Cuba"), to terroristic ("4. We could develop a Communist Cuban terror campaign in the Miami area"), to convoluted ("8. It is possible to create an incident which will demonstrate convincingly that a Cuban aircraft has attacked and shot down a chartered civil airliner en route from the United States to Jamaica, Guatemala, Panama or Venezuela").[37]

Lemnitzer's logic shows how deceptive manipulation of US public opinion and preventive warfare went hand in hand in US Cold War strategy. "This plan," Lemnitzer outlined in stark terms, "should be developed to focus all efforts on a specific ultimate objective which would provide adequate justification for US military intervention. Such a plan would enable a logical build-up of incidents to be combined with other seemingly unrelated events to camouflage the ultimate objective and create the necessary impression of Cuban rashness and irresponsibility on a large scale, directed at other countries as well as the United States."[38] Lemnitzer's gambit, which Bamford notes "may be the most corrupt plan ever created by the US government," was approved in writing by each of the Joint Chiefs, and appears to have "originated with President Eisenhower in the last days of his administration."[39] Kennedy and Secretary of Defense Robert McNamara subsequently shelved the extravagant deception proposal when they took power, but that did not stanch the flow of other "pretext" schemes for justifying forcible regime change in Cuba.

In May 1963, Nitze himself proposed to the White House "a possible scenario whereby an attack on a United States reconnaissance aircraft could be exploited toward the end of effecting the removal of the Castro regime." Nitze's ambitions were clear: "[T]he U.S. could undertake various measures designed to stimulate the Cubans to provoke a new incident."[40] While Nitze's and Lemnitzer's unorthodox machinations did little to impress Kennedy, both men continued to leave their mark on US Cold War policy, eventu-

ally winning appointment to the influential "Team B" intelligence group in
1975.

TEAM B

The historical linkage between NSC-68 and NSS 2002 can be clarified by
revisiting the 1975–1976 Team B exercise in "competitive intelligence analysis."[41] In the early 1970s, the appeal of superpower accommodation through
détente gained currency in the wake of Vietnam, and the hard-line NSC-68
consensus began to unravel. With Nitze out of government and much of the
Ford administration's national security team cool to his Cold War fervor,
hard-liners sought new tools to create political pressure for Pentagon re-
armament. As Nitze recalls, "There being no opportunity to be an active
participant in formulating government policy, I devoted my time and energy
to special projects."[42] Enter the Team B exercise in competitive intelligence
analysis, proposed by John Foster and Edward Teller in 1975, cultivated
by Nitze, and approved in 1976 by Director of Central Intelligence (DCI)
George H. W. Bush.

In this exercise, a "Team A" group of "insider" analysts, drawn from the
ranks of the CIA and Defense Intelligence Agency (DIA), was presented with
intelligence data and asked to generate an assessment of the Soviet Union's
strategic military objectives. Another group, comprised of academics, retired
military officers, and other "outsiders," was designated "Team B" and tasked
to generate its own independent assessment by sifting through the same data
set. Advocates of the competitive analysis exercise suggested that by engaging
in dialectical clash, the competing groups could push each other to improve
the National Intelligence Estimate (NIE) process and produce a more reliable
assessment of Soviet strategic objectives.[43] The notion that constructive disagreement and debate among analysts could sharpen intelligence assessments
seems benign, until one sees how the idea was put into practice.

During the exercise, Team A and Team B reached dramatically different conclusions regarding the Soviet military threat. While Team A largely
reproduced the trajectory of analysis featured in previous NIEs, Team B
argued that these assessments "substantially misperceived the motivations
behind Soviet strategic programs, and thereby tended consistently to under-
estimate their intensity, scope and implicit threat."[44] Specifically, in formulating its predictions Team B looked beyond "hard" evidence of Soviet military
capabilities and focused more on "soft" evidence derived from perceptions
regarding Soviet intentions. This methodological difference yielded dramatically more alarmist estimations of Soviet military spending, bomber production, antiballistic missile capability, and technical progress in nonacoustic

antisubmarine engineering. The split on this last issue is telling. While Team A saw little risk of Soviet breakout in antisubmarine warfare capability, Anne Hessing Cahn and Paul Prados point out that "Team B's failure to find a Soviet non-acoustic anti-submarine system was evidence that there could well be one."[45] As the Team B report explained, even though no hard intelligence data existed to establish extant Soviet *capability* in this area, "The implication could be that the Soviets have, in fact, deployed some operational nonacoustic systems and will deploy more in the next few years."[46]

The gulf between the two assessments was not surprising—in addition to Nitze and Paul Wolfowitz, key B-teamers included Richard Pipes, William Van Cleave, Lieutenant General Daniel Graham, Lemnitzer, and several other members of the influential CPD, the group that had succeeded in implementing many of the more extreme planks of NSC-68 during the 1950s. Nitze had honed a framework to "strike a chord of terror" when he had written NSC-68, and now "he brought it back into play."[47] Nitze's group of Cold War veterans proved to be formidable debaters the few times that the two teams met to compare findings. For example, Team A member Jay Kalner recalled that during one encounter, "We were overmatched. People like Nitze ate us for lunch."[48] CIA official Sidney Graybeal reflected, "It was like putting Walt Whitman High versus the Redskins. I watched poor GS-13s and -14s [middle-level analysts] subjected to ridicule by Pipes and Nitze. They were browbeating the poor analysts. Team B was not constructive."[49]

This operation was "strikingly similar" to the earlier NSC-68 campaign,[50] featuring deductive logic rooted in worst-case assumptions, intimidation of dissenters, and strategic use of the classification system to stoke public alarm. In the official CIA history of the episode, Donald Steury writes that "the B-Team abandoned the formula agreed upon for the experiment, in favor of a detailed critique of the assumptions and methodologies that underlay strategic forces NIEs produced over the previous decade or so."[51] Former CIA deputy director Ray Cline labeled the exercise a "subversion" of the official estimative process by a "kangaroo court of outside critics all picked from one point of view."[52] B-teamers such as Graham exerted extraordinary "peer pressure" on mainstream CIA analysts to slant their intelligence findings,[53] while fellow panelists such as George Keegan colored media coverage and primed public fear of the Soviet Union with selective leaks of alarmist data.[54] Richard Lehman, former deputy to the Director of Central Intelligence for National Intelligence, commented that Team B members "were leaking all over the place . . . putting together this inflammatory document."[55] Such leaks had palpable and lasting effects on public opinion and US Cold War policy. According to Senator Gary Hart (D-CO), "The Pro-B Team leak and public attack on the conclusions of the NIE represent but one element in a series of leaks and other statements which have been aimed at fostering a 'worst case' view for the public of the Soviet threat. In turn, this view of the Soviet threat is used to justify new weapons systems."[56]

The leaks roused the CPD from its Vietnam-era doldrums, giving the organization a platform to bully advocates of superpower détente into submission. According to Hart, the Team B exercise "did not promote dissent. To the contrary, it intimidated and stifled the expression of more balanced estimates of the Soviet threat."[57] Ironically, all of this took place while the Soviet empire continued to crumble and Team B's alarmist prognostications about Kremlin backfire bomber production, antimissile research, and military spending were being disproved on the ground.[58]

After the fall of the Berlin Wall, conservative commentators wrote glowingly about the Team B episode and called periodically for follow-on exercises in competitive intelligence analysis. Frank Gaffney opined in 1990 that "now is the time for a new Team B and a clear-eyed assessment of the abiding Soviet (and other) challenges that dictate a continued, robust U.S. defense posture."[59] William Safire followed four years later with the recommendation that "a prestigious Team B" be formed "to suggest an alternative Russia policy to Mr. Clinton."[60] From his academic post at Johns Hopkins in 1996, Wolfowitz restated the rationale for using dialectical argumentation as a tool of intelligence assessment.[61] After the 11 September 2001 suicide airline attacks on the United States, Wolfowitz and other key Bush administration officials seized the opportunity to take B-teaming to a new level.

A TEAM B INTELLIGENCE COUP

Smoke was still billowing out of the Pentagon on the afternoon of 11 September 2001 when Secretary of Defense Donald Rumsfeld began pondering how the suicide airline attacks might enable the United States to oust Iraqi leader Saddam Hussein. According to notes taken by his staff, Rumsfeld wondered whether the 9/11 disaster would allow the United States to "hit S.H. [Saddam Hussein] @ same time—not only UBL [Osama bin Laden]."[62] Cheney, Wolfowitz, and other "Vulcans"—influential White House advisers who had long envisioned war with Iraq as the centerpiece of a bold gambit to reshape the post–Cold War geopolitical landscape—shared Rumsfeld's proclivities.[63]

However, the post-9/11 strategy of folding Iraq into the nascent "war on terrorism" was confounded by official intelligence community (IC) reporting that found a dearth of credible evidence linking Saddam Hussein to terrorist organizations of global reach such as al-Qaida. It was in this context that British intelligence chief Sir Richard Dearlove visited the United States for meetings where the possibility of war against Iraq was discussed. Regarding developments in Washington, Dearlove briefed Prime Minister Tony Blair on 23 July 2002 that "there was a perceptible shift in attitude. Military action was now seen as inevitable. Bush wanted to remove Saddam Hussein, through military action, justified by the conjunction of terrorism and WMD. But the intelligence and facts were being fixed around the policy."[64]

One strategy Rumsfeld, Wolfowitz, and Pentagon deputy Douglas Feith deployed to "fix" the intelligence was to create a Team B–type "Iraqi intelligence cell" within the Pentagon. This cell, the Policy Counterterrorism Evaluation Group (PCTEG), was tasked to study policy implications of connections between terrorist organizations.[65] As George Packer notes, the PCTEG concept "went all the way back to 1976 and Team B, the group of CIA-appointed outside experts, including Wolfowitz, that had come to much more alarmist conclusions about the Soviets than the intelligence agencies."[66] Initially, Wolfowitz and Feith staffed PCTEG with Michael Maloof and David Wurmser, two colleagues Feith knew from working together on the 1996 "Clean Break" report, which called for preventive war against Iraq to bolster Israeli security.[67]

In October 2001, Maloof and Wurmser set up shop in a small room on the third floor of the Pentagon, where they went to work developing a "matrix" that charted connections between terrorist organizations and their support infrastructures. Since both men had security clearance, they were able to draw data from raw and finished intelligence products available through the Pentagon's classified computer system. Sometimes, when they were denied access to the most sensitive material through this channel, Maloof returned to his previous office, where he could download more data. "We scoured what we could get up to the secret level, but we kept getting blocked when we tried to get more sensitive materials," Maloof recounted. "I would go back to my office, do a pull and bring it in."[68]

Early PCTEG work included critical review of a CIA report entitled "Iraq and al-Qaida: Interpreting a Murky Relationship." In its critique, PCTEG lauded the CIA analysis for identifying numerous pieces of evidence linking Iraq to al-Qaida, but noted disappointingly that the force of these citations was blunted by "attempts to discredit, dismiss, or downgrade much of this reporting, resulting in inconsistent conclusions in many instances." PCTEG advised policy-makers to overlook such equivocation and dismiss the CIA's guarded conclusions, recommending that "the CIA report ought to be read for content only—and *CIA's interpretation ought to be ignored*."[69]

It was 1976 redux, with hard-liners deploying competitive intelligence analysis to sweep away policy obstacles presented by inconvenient CIA threat assessments. As Daniel Benjamin and Steven Simon observe, "several members of George W. Bush's inner circle had established themselves as perennial critics of the nation's IC. The roots of this disdain stretched back at least as far as the mid-1970s."[70] Only this time, unlike 1976, they were firmly entrenched in the corridors of power. Control over the levers of White House bureaucracy enabled them to embed a Team B entity within the administration itself. The stage was set for a new kind of Team B intelligence exercise—a stealth coup staged by one arm of the government against the other. Competitive intelligence analysis can be a useful debating tool with potential to shake up settled perspectives and clarify assumptions. However, interlocutors can manipulate the process. One technique of distortion involves feigning commitment to the guiding norms of critical discussion at the outset and later disregarding such norms for strategic gain. This subversion of the dialectical exchange resembles a political coup—the sudden seizure of power through unconventional means such as force or deception.[71]

The coup took shape on 22 July 2002, when a PCTEG staffer sent an e-mail reporting that a senior adviser to Paul Wolfowitz had told an assistant that he wanted him "to prepare an intel briefing on Iraq and links to al-Qaida for the SecDef and that he was not to tell anyone about it."[72] PCTEG secretly went to work, supplementing its earlier critique of the CIA's "Murky Relationship" report by drawing on "both raw and finished IC products."[73] As Bamford describes, "the Wurmser intelligence unit would pluck selective bits and pieces of a thread from a giant ball of yarn and weave them together in a frightening tapestry."[74] However, since the PCTEG officials lacked formal training in the tradecraft of intelligence analysis, their work products were about as sophisticated as "a high school biology student's reading of a CAT scan."[75]

Government entities such as PCTEG are able to access raw intelligence data because of recent efforts to improve "connectivity"—meaning that policy officials can "connect" directly to the data streams that flow through IC channels. As James Steiner notes, "because most senior policymakers and their staffs now have access to raw reporting and finished intelligence on their desktops, they are less reliant on traditional analytic centers at CIA, DIA, and State to tell them what the massive body of intelligence reporting means."[76] The original 1976 Team B exercise needed formal approval from DCI George H. W. Bush to get off the ground. Today, connectivity enables a select few political officials to tap the classified IC data stream by clicking a switch.

Operating largely independently from the IC, PCTEG proceeded to gather its own intelligence and produce a series of briefing slides that were presented to Rumsfeld and Wolfowitz in August 2002. One slide read: "Summary of Known Iraq—al-Qaida Contacts, 1990–2002," and included a controversial item: "2001: Prague IIS Chief al-Ani meets with Mohammed Atta in April." A "findings" slide summed up the Iraq–al-Qaida relationship as "More than a decade of numerous contacts," "Multiple areas of cooperation," "Shared interest and pursuit of WMD," and "One indication of Iraq coordination with al-Qaida specifically related to 9/11."[77]

Another slide entitled "Fundamental Problems with How Intelligence Community is Assessing Information" took direct aim at the IC. Here, PCTEG faulted official intelligence analysts for their use of "juridical evidence" standards and, borrowing a refrain from the 1976 Team B report, criticized the IC for its "consistent underestimation" of efforts by Iraq and al-Qaida to hide their relationship, contending that "absence of evidence is not evidence of absence."[78] The original Team B logic that curiously turned a lack of intelligence data on Soviet acoustic technology into proof of possible USSR antisubmarine warfare breakout capability had returned, this time to bolster the case for preventive war against Iraq.

Following the briefing, Wolfowitz sent an encouraging note to the PCTEG staffers: "That was an excellent briefing. The Secretary was very impressed. He asked us to think about some possible next steps to see if we can illuminate the differences between us and CIA. The goal is not to produce a consensus product, but rather to scrub one another's arguments."[79] So on 15 August 2002 the PCTEG team gave their briefing again, this time for DCI George Tenet and CIA analysts.

Remarkably, this briefing did not include the slide criticizing the IC for "consistent underestimation" by using "juridical evidence" standards. Tenet faced a double whammy—an independent Pentagon cell beyond his control was undermining the integrity of his intelligence analysis in top policy circles, and the cell denied him the chance to respond by concealing the attack. As Senator Carl Levin (D-MI) explains, "unbeknownst to the IC, policymakers were getting information that was inconsistent with, and thus undermined, the professional judgments of the IC experts. The changes included information that was dubious, misrepresented, or of unknown import."[80]

PCTEG's omission of the "Fundamental Problems" slide from the 15 August 2002 briefing raises serious questions about the genuineness of the Department of Defense's commitment to legitimate competitive intelligence analysis in this case, since it is very difficult to have a frank and productive dialectical exchange when one side withholds its most powerful argument— here a frontal assault on the A Team's (CIA) analytical methodology.

With the incendiary slide removed, it is not surprising that Tenet said he "didn't see anything that broke any new ground" in the PCTEG briefing.[81] Although Tenet did agree to postpone release of the CIA's new report, "Iraq and Terrorism," to give time for PCTEG staffers to confer again with official intelligence analysts, the analysts who subsequently met with the Pentagon briefers were unmoved.

This setback did not derail PCTEG's campaign to shore up the administration's evidentiary foundation for war. While Tenet held back release of the new CIA report on Iraq's ties to terrorism, the Pentagon intelligence cell stovepiped its incendiary findings directly to Deputy National Security Advisor Stephen Hadley and the vice president's chief of staff Lewis Libby in a 16 September 2002 briefing that preempted release of the CIA report by two days. According to an internal memorandum, "[t]he briefing went very well and generated further interest from Mr. Hadley and Mr. Libby." Libby requested a number of items, including a "chronology of Atta's travels."[82]

Two aspects of this briefing are especially notable. First, the "Fundamental Problems" slide criticizing CIA interpretive methodology curiously reappeared. Second, DCI Tenet was not aware that the briefing even took place until March 2004, when members of Congress informed him during hearings.[83] Tenet's testy response reflected one of the most daunting challenges facing the DCI in an era when the "red line" separating the policy and intelligence communities is continuously eroded by connectivity. As one group of former intelligence officers observed, "this increased intelligence/ policy proximity, combined with revolutionary growth in information management capacity and data mining tools, has given today's policy-maker the capability to conduct his or her own fairly sophisticated analysis, independent of the traditional intelligence analysis prepared, vetted, and presented by CIA, DIA, and INR."[84] According to Greg Thielmann, these developments "greatly facilitate intelligence cherry-picking, enabling policy officials to generate any kind of report through word searches that look juicy, no matter what the intelligence officials might say about the reliability of the sources on which the report is based."[85]

The PCTEG case shows how connectivity ripens bureaucratic conditions for Team B intelligence coups. Policy-makers and their aides can informally access secure IC databases and use powerful data-mining techniques to cherry-pick intelligence. They can then bolster the persuasive power of such data by packaging them as "talking points" that carry the patina of finished intelligence assessments. The credibility of such B-teamed intelligence can be bolstered further by funneling the data directly to policy-makers, skirting peer review institutionalized by the formal processes of the official IC.[86] Stovepiping turns a competitive intelligence exercise into a Team B coup, something qualitatively different from an exchange of competing

viewpoints designed to simply "sharpen the debate" among contending intelligence entities.[87]

Strong evidence indicates that such informal B-teaming activity was
rife within the Bush administration during the run-up to Operation Iraqi
Freedom.[88] For example, at the State Department, Undersecretary of State
John Bolton pressed hard for his political staff to get electronic access to
INR's Top Secret Secure Compartmented Information.[89] At the Pentagon,
by August 2002 the small PCTEG cell had evolved into a more elaborate
entity, the Office of Special Plans (OSP). The manager of the OSP operation, Abram Shulsky, was familiar with competitive intelligence analysis,
having worked on the staff of the Senate Select Intelligence Committee that
reviewed the original Team B exercise during the Cold War. According to
Kenneth Pollack, Shulsky's cell stovepiped dubious intelligence purchased
from Ahmed Chalabi's Iraqi National Congress (INC) to senior administration officials, fundamentally distorting policy-making on topics ranging
from the threat of Saddam Hussein's alleged nuclear program to the cost of
postwar reconstruction in Iraq.[90] According to Pollack, "The Bush officials
who created the OSP gave its reports directly to those in the highest level of
government, often passing raw, unverified intelligence straight to the Cabinet
level as gospel. Senior Administration officials made public statements based
on these reports—reports that the larger intelligence community knew to be
erroneous."[91] Much of the INC's information came from Iraqi defectors who
were paid to provide testimony about Saddam Hussein's elaborate weapons
programs.[92]

The "intelligence" officials who credited Chalabi exhibited either extreme recklessness or naïveté—there are no kinder words for it. Any lore
whatsoever they had picked up about the many pitfalls of evaluating testimony would have had to make them aware of what Machiavelli said on this
matter. A whole chapter by that sixteenth-century genius is devoted to "how
dangerous it is to put confidence in refugees." According to the L. J. Walker
translation of his *Discourses*, Alexander of Epirus and Themistocles of Athens were both done in by listening to refugees:

[S]o intense is their desire to get back home that they naturally believe much that is
false and artfully add much more: So that between what they believe and what they
say they believe they fill you with a hope which is such that, if you rely on it, either
you incur expense in vain or take up what will ruin you. . . . A ruler, therefore, should
be slow to take up an enterprise because of what some exile has told him, for more
often than not all he will get out of it is shame and the most grievous harm.[93]

Even if the Bush administration planners had not read Machiavelli, a
cursory acquaintance with American history should have given them pause

in believing that they were getting correct evaluations of Iraq.[94] Refugees nourished the long and costly American belief that Chiang Kai-shek was the George Washington of China, and could easily be restored to mainland power. Ngo Dinh Diem's clout with Americans (and not just Catholics) led ostensibly intelligent American statesmen to believe that Ho Chi Minh was nothing but an agitator with little or no following. Take any one of the many American interventions to bring regime change during the Cold War: somewhere in the paper trail you will find that the Iranians were really fed up with Mossadegh and would gladly follow the shah, or that Pinochet was a genuine democrat and Allende a Communist totalitarian.

The latest group of Iraqi refugees had names like "Curveball," and were debriefed "at safe houses outside London, a German castle east of Berlin, a Thai resort south of Bangkok, a Dutch government office in The Hague and elsewhere."[95] Curveball's testimony proved to be the Bush administration's linchpin evidence allegedly confirming the existence of an active Iraqi biological weapons program, even though the official IC harbored severe doubts about his credibility.[96] However, such analytical skepticism was shielded from top policy-makers, who received the defector testimony through a direct stovepipe channel set up to link the INC to the top levels of the Pentagon and White House bureaucracy. While such stovepiping practices are difficult to square with the basic philosophy of competitive intelligence analysis, they reflect Wolfowitz's views on the need for new approaches to mending the intelligence-policy seam in the post-9/11 security milieu. In 2002 congressional testimony, Wolfowitz suggested, "We must also accelerate the speed with which information is passed to policymakers and operators. We cannot wait for critical intelligence to be processed, coordinated, edited and approved—we must accept the risks inherent in posting critical information before it is processed."[97]

In a concrete manifestation of this normative guideline, PCTEG's breakaway from the established IC jettisoned the dialectical checks built into the competitive intelligence assessment process and shut down constructive dialogue within the IC prior to Operation Iraq Freedom. Despite the fact that the State Department's Bureau of Intelligence and Research (INR) is supposed to be an "all source" agency, with access to the full range of intelligence materials circulating throughout the US government, INR's Thielmann says, "I didn't know about its existence. They were cherry-picking intelligence and packaging it for Cheney and Donald Rumsfeld to take to the president. That's the kind of rogue operation that peer review is intended to prevent."[98]

"AT SOME POINT, WE MAY BE THE ONLY ONES LEFT"

This chapter opened by noting how President Bush's October 2005 comparison of "the current fight" with "the struggle against communism in the last century"[99] jibes with Leffler's suggestion that insight regarding NSS 2002's dynamics may be gleaned from study of NSC-68, the "blueprint for Cold War defense."[100] In NSC-68's "hyperbolic language," we find rhetorical precursors to today's absolutist, zero-sum terms that frame official descriptions of the Bush administration's battle against the "evil-doers." The "any measures" necessary logic of NSC-68 that authorized US use of preventive force in Iran, Guatemala, Cuba, Chile, Indonesia, and Vietnam is echoed in the portions of NSS 2002 that underwrote preventive war against Iraq. Parallels also exist in the institutional practices designed to politically legitimate and implement the respective strategies. Just as the 1975–1976 Team B exercise neutralized CIA intelligence assessments that did not accord with the CPD's drive for US nuclear superiority, sixteen years later PCTEG and OSP "fixed the intelligence and facts" on Saddam Hussein's ties to terrorism "around the policy"[101] of regime change in Iraq. Mere coincidence? Not according to analysts such as Daniel Benjamin, George Packer, and Steven Simon, who note that the original Team B subversion of the CIA and the recent PCTEG/OSP end run around the official IC were conducted by several of the same key players.[102] The sense of Cold War déjà vu instilled by these parallels becomes more pronounced after visiting the CPD's new Web site. In 2004, the committee reconstituted yet again, issuing a mission statement that invokes prominently the group's Cold War legacy:

Twice before in American history, The Committee on the Present Danger has risen to this challenge. It emerged in 1950 as a bipartisan education and advocacy organization dedicated to building a national consensus for the Truman Administration's policy aimed at "containment" of Soviet expansionism. In 1976, the Committee on the Present Danger reemerged, with leadership from the labor movement, bipartisan representatives of the foreign policy community and academia, all of them concerned about strategic drift in U.S. security policy and determined to support policies intended to bring the Cold War to a successful conclusion. In both previous periods, the Committee's mission was clear: raise awareness to the threat to American safety; communicate the risk inherent in appeasing totalitarianism; and build support for an assertive policy to promote the security of the United States and its allies and friends. With victory in the Cold War, the mission of the Committee on the Present Danger was considered complete and consequently it was deactivated. Today, radical Islamists threaten the safety of the American people and millions of others who prize liberty. . . . The road to victory begins with clear identification of the shifting threat and vigorous pursuit of policies to contain and defeat it.[103]

The CPD's latest commentary and policy recommendations hearken back to 1953 and the days of Operation Ajax: "Wake Up, America!" exclaims one news release; "Iran is our new Soviet Union."[104] Echoing NSC-68, veteran CPD member William Van Cleave declares: "Islamic terrorism is an unconditional and existential threat not only to America and Israel, but also to Judeo-Christian culture. . . . Only by denying success to this threat—by a combination of anticipatory defensive and offensive measures—can we defeat it."[105]

While these common threads help weave the historical backdrop for subsequent analyses in this volume, points of contrast between NSS 2002 and NSC-68 also frame the study in illuminating ways. In selling NSC-68, Truman administration officials were keenly aware that a "psychological scare campaign" that overhyped the Soviet threat could have a boomerang effect, stimulating a panicked public to call for the one policy that NSC-68 ruled out as too extreme—a preventive nuclear first strike by the United States against the USSR. Steven Casey shows how the Truman White House modulated its rhetoric to avoid this "hydrogen hysteria," employing "clearer than truth" fear appeals to cultivate political support for NSC-68, but easing back when the domestic climate threatened to boil over.[106]

Today, US leaders confront a different variant of this same dilemma. To rally support for the NSS 2002 approach of "acting preemptively" against adversaries, Bush administration officials constructed an exaggerated threat "matrix" that linked Saddam Hussein to al-Qaida and mobilized US public opinion behind a totalizing "war on terror." While this political campaign succeeded in the short-term goal of securing sufficient public support to launch Operation Iraqi Freedom, its boomerang effects undermined US security by "working as a powerful force-multiplier for bin Laden and those he leads and inspires," says CIA terrorism expert Michael Scheuer.[107]

In the case of Truman's advocacy of NSC-68, excessive alarmism threatened to provoke the American public to demand rash actions that would jeopardize US security. For the Bush administration, exaggeration and hyperbole in selling NSS 2002 provokes a different kind of dangerous response, one that plays into Osama bin Laden's script portraying his jihad as a defensive reaction against a US campaign to wage holy war on Islam. When the president says, "at some point, we may be the only ones left. That's okay with me. We are America,"[108] terrorists are invigorated, not dissuaded.[109] As Carol Winkler points out, Osama bin Laden "borrowed heavily from the administration's own narrative frame for the conflict. Specifically, he evoked the settings, characterizations, and themes of the ideologically based Cold War narrative to call Muslims to war against the United States."[110]

For one post–Iraq invasion illustration of this phenomenon, Benjamin and Simon point to comments made by General William G. "Jerry" Boykin. In June 2003, while in military uniform, Boykin told a church group in Sandy, Oregon, that the jihadists "will only be defeated if we come to them in the name of Jesus." He added, "George Bush was not elected by a majority of the voters in the United States. He was appointed by God."[111] According to Benjamin and Simon, these remarks "caused immense damage to American interest by validating an image of the United States military as a Christian army warring with Muslims in the name of Jesus."[112] One senior US official, who was traveling in the Middle East during the Boykin episode, recalled, "It was the worst day of my life. It confirmed their conspiracy theory that the war on terrorism really is a war on Islam."[113] In Benjamin and Simon's view, this episode highlights a choice facing Americans: "We must decide whether we want a strategy for this conflict or a theology."[114]

Ivan Eland is among those who believe that the "new National Security Strategy of primacy and prevention (not preemption, as advertised)" is a "fatal overextension" of our resources. "Flailing around like Don Quixote, the Bush administration . . . is merely making unnecessary enemies and falling into Osama bin Laden's trap. . . . An attack on Iraq (coming after an attack on the Islamic nation of Afghanistan) will merely throw kerosene on the flames of hatred toward the United States in the Islamic world."[115]

History reinforces these observations. Eland writes, "Even stronger than polling results are empirical data showing the links between US interventionist foreign policy and retaliatory terrorism against the United States." He then provides analysis of "more than 60 incidents of terrorism against the United States in retaliation for an activist global U.S. foreign policy." One of his cases is Libya, where Reagan's provocations caused Gaddafi's belligerent response.[116] The nonconfrontational policy of George H. W. Bush reversed this hostility, and Libya eventually ceased attacks and came to terms with the United States. The 1997 report of the Defense Science Board, a panel advising the secretary of defense, verified the link between activism and terrorism.[117]

Partisan commentators frequently decry such analysis as "blame America first" defeatism, invoking what Thomas Goodnight describes in chapter 5 of this volume as an "action/inaction" frame to imply that critics of US military overextension advocate "appeasement" and "giving in to the terrorists."[118] But as William Hartung argues in chapter 11 of this volume, proactive, preventive measures can nip future terrorist attacks in the bud, without resorting to "shock and awe" tactics that stimulate "blowback terrorism."[119]

Of course, American primacy, global interdependence, and catastrophic terrorism present novel security challenges in the present milieu. Yet it is striking how quickly today's leaders look for answers to these challenges by reviving strategic principles and patterns of public argument forged during the Cold War, even when such principles and patterns are so clearly out of step with the current predicament.

PART 2

Public Discourse Justifying Use of Preventive Force

5

Strategic Doctrine, Public Debate, and the Terror War

G. Thomas Goodnight

A DECADE–LONG DEBATE on national security policy had been emerging in fits and starts ever since the end of the Cold War, catching up military, diplomatic, and intelligence institutions as well as fueling controversy between Congress and the executive. The 1990s featured a patchwork of old and new thinking. The Weinberger-Powell doctrine limited intervention to specific military purpose, called for the use of overwhelming force in the interests of victory, and constrained intervention by demanding that clear, militarily attainable goals be set up before any troops are sent in. Alternatively, rationales for expanding the scope of US intervention were created as a response to human rights emergencies and threats of genocide; yet nation building was as much derided as advocated. Indeed, multilateral efforts were supported with great reluctance. Debates over Haiti and Somalia routinely featured congressional histrionics warning that the loss of "even one American life" was not worthy any foreign policy objective. The attack of 9/11 changed this landscape of public debate, totally. The United States now is engaged in an ambiguously defined, global, and open-ended "war on terror," which in the words of the Bush administration is a "new war" that requires "new thinking."

Terrorism was not unknown or forgotten during the 1990s, of course. The largely ignored Hart-Rudman report forecast publicly a major attack on American soil.[1] Yet assaults on ships and embassies, airplanes and troops—and even an effort to topple the World Trade Center itself—played a comparatively minor role within the larger narrative of globalization. The circulation of trade, capital, media, and migration, at ever-increasing rates, in the thinking of the times would create an interconnected world, with rising tides of prosperity that would lift all boats. The spectacle of 9/11 exploded this vision and reset the parameters of public debate. The spreading anxiety loosed by the attack can be phrased as an argument a fortiori: If terrorists could accomplish that much destruction and suffering with but the calculated use of passenger airplanes, how much more damage could be done with a nuclear weapon? The anthrax scare, shortly following 9/11, spread anxieties of insecurity and vulnerability. The attack of 9/11 did not involve "weapons of mass destruction" (WMD), but it could have; that was the point.

There was a single question that had haunted the nuclear age for fifty years: What would happen should deterrence fail? The 9/11 attack on targets in New York and Washington, D.C., the heart of American financial and political power, proved that fear of retaliation was an insufficient deterrent, and that a first strike by a foreign entity could be disastrous.

Deterrence had failed, but in an unexpected way: The attack was made neither by conventional nor nuclear means but by turning a modernist system into a lethal weapon. Moreover, the bolt out of the blue came not from a state but from a network of terrorists, parasitically connected to a "failed state," Afghanistan—itself a region left in ruins after the proxy warfare between the great Cold War powers. That reigning "defenses" had failed, at least in a single case, was clear. The future of defense policy in the United States was up for debate.

This chapter is a study of a novel strategic doctrine, as articulated by different branches of the executive that, after 9/11, radically questioned established doctrines of deterrence and containment, pursued the invasion of Iraq, and ultimately brought into question valid standards of international warfare in a nuclear age. Just as strategic doctrine may powerfully articulate a context for diplomatic and military action, so, too, it may entangle the United States in controversies that impair its prestige and limit American ability to create coherent, persuasive cases directed toward domestic and foreign publics. In the case of Iraq, while preventive force worked as an effective source of invention for prewar justification of policy, it continues to proliferate "postwar" paradoxes that undercut the coherence and effectiveness of justifications for administration actions in relation to the "war on terror."

PRESIDENTIAL PERSUASION AND STRATEGIC DOCTRINE

Foreign policy debate is always a composite language woven from a moving symbolic "nexus of motives."[2] Broad traditions of war and peace—articulated in histories, literature, orations, legal documents, and military strategy—go far back in human cultures. These furnish manifold linguistic resources to communicate the concerns of policy: the strategic requirements of offense and defense, the strengths and limits of realism and idealism, the risks of internationalism and isolationism, and the justifications of war uttered as questions of justice, maintenance of a balance of power, national interest, or collective security. Each strain of thinking, balanced dialectically by an alternative, constitutes a distinctive discourse formation—a site of invention from which arguments can be drawn forward and discourse fashioned to explain, justify, support, and extend policy.[3] Although each formation may be analyzed as a separate philosophy, theory, or tradition, in any live public debate all the resources available are likely to be used in the interest of articulating positions, criticizing opposition, and persuading publics. The strategic deployment of discourse constitutes a rhetoric.

American foreign policy rhetoric traditionally is initiated by the president who, as chief executive, is charged by the Constitution with taking the lead in security matters.[4] In the twentieth century, the president has used public address on significant occasions to announce, articulate, and defend policy.[5] Presidential address is associated with playing a central role in dealing with foreign policy crises.[6] Often such rhetoric finds the president making use of the office as a "bully pulpit," going over the heads of Congress to the people.[7] Speeches meant for short-run success sometimes have long-term impacts. Harry S. Truman's speech on Greece and Turkey, for example, is attributed as defining America's Cold War posture. Whether speaking to crises or overall policy, presidents are expected to make deliberative addresses that satisfy audience expectations and set the terms for subsequent debate.[8] Presidential positions are met with commentary from other branches of government and the press; cabinet members and party affiliates, too, join the fray, and discussions extend across domestic and international elites and audiences—all partisan statements contributing to public argument.[9]

The executive branch annually distributes a national security strategy, which articulates strategic doctrine, a key instrument of foreign policy. The statement informs American publics of the costs and sacrifices that they should be prepared to bear; more broadly, the doctrine sets in place the overall guidelines or thinking of an administration, at least as it wishes to be seen by domestic and foreign publics. Strategic doctrine does not function as a code governing all foreign policy acts, but rather as a set of guidelines that shapes discourse practices of anticipation, interpretation, and justification. Doctrine articulates, and speeches perform, what Thomas Kane has called "commanding ideas" that authorize administration spokespersons and supporters to back policies by drawing upon consistent, persuasive positions across issues and events.[10] When presidential address enacts strategic doctrine, the resulting rhetoric creates "ideographs," (such as "freedom," "security," or "self-defense"), larger symbols that, when couched in public argument, are powerful motivators of opinion that can be difficult to dislodge.[11]

Cold War rhetoric (despite the distinctive doctrinal emphases among presidential administrations) is constituted by a dynamic relationship among commanding ideas and ideographs. On the one hand, Cold War rhetoric is structured within a bipolar style and fueled by a crusading spirit. National symbols are put to strategic use as weapons in a global war between good and evil. On the other hand, room for diplomacy and sensible coexistence is maintained by the language of game theory—with its logic of deterrence and strategic calculation of containment.[12] The end of the Cold War as a historical exigency threw this long-reigning dynamic into question. Nevertheless, President Clinton—who could not rely upon the formulas of anti-Soviet rhetoric and détente to justify policy, of course—formed a loose strategic doctrine that retained presidential flexibility in defining the priorities of "conjunctive diplomacy," while adapting core ideographs of Cold War doctrine, such as deterrence and threat containment, to the present.[13] The aftermath of 9/11 would demand something entirely different.

Presidential rhetoric traditionally situates policy within an ambit of expectations defined more or less by consensus politics. Sometimes events or a special calling intervene. Presidential address then takes on the qualities of a "rhetorical movement" that seeks to overturn standing policy by announcing a new vision. David Zarefsky argues this gambit characterized Lyndon Johnson's wide-ranging "war on poverty."[14] Speeches that articulate change create an alternative policy "imaginary" where old means and ends are questioned and new ones espoused.[15] The new vision meets with debate, and predicaments arise when incompatible claims to honor competing values or accommodate conflicting ends complicate the challenge of securing wide public support.[16] Over time, the new symbolic vision becomes deployed as policy, subjected to review, and advocated in extension. Thus policy follows a "rhetorical trajectory" where discourse and events intertwine and diverge among elites and publics. The trajectory, when read critically, reveals the strengths and limits of an advocacy posture or rhetoric.[17]

Shortly after the 2001 intervention into Afghanistan, in the midst of a yet-to-be-fully-defined "war on terror," the Bush administration began to make public a novel doctrine springing from a distinctive political imaginary. The newly minted doctrine of preventive military intervention in 2002, according to John Lewis Gaddis, had the potential of becoming "the most important reformulation of U.S. grand strategy in over half a century."[18] This chapter examines the unfolding of this doctrine, assessing its strengths and weaknesses in public argument. The legacy of the Bush administration's rhetorical movement will be assessed, as the trajectory of the pivotal term "preemption" paradoxically jettisoned policies of deterrence and containment—the key doctrinal elements underwriting nuclear age foreign policy—while spinning the "war on terror" into a new Cold War.[19]

BUSH AT WEST POINT

In the Bush administration, a different model of presidential persuasion appeared in 2002. A new, presidential foreign policy would be articulated, but not during a dramatic crisis speech—which had become the tradition. Rather, in the summer, a three-pronged campaign was instigated: the president on 1 June delivered a speech at West Point that prepared the grounds for a dramatic shift in American military doctrine; in August, Vice President Richard Cheney filled in the predicate for the general premises laid down by the president—Iraq is a "WMD" threat; and in October of that year the 2002 National Security Strategy of the United States of America (NSS 2002) fully unfolded a new national policy that would turn the United States from a nation that would wait for the first blow to be struck to a shoot-first-and-ask-questions-later power. The pivot for change was pressure put on a single word, "imminent," for depending upon how that term was defined, the traditions distinguishing preemptive versus preventive wars would either be upheld or disappear, and upon this choice hinged the American reputation as a member in a community of nations under the rule of law or, when the chips are down, basically a go-it-alone power.

A graduation speech is expected to be a routine, not-long-remembered oration, perhaps made slightly more noteworthy if delivered by an august figure. Major presidential addresses, by contrast, are broadcast in primetime, with plenty of news coverage and showers of discussion by pundits. George W. Bush's West Point graduation speech of 1 June 2002 was delivered with little fanfare, but it stands with Truman's Greece and Turkey announcement as one of the most significant presidential foreign policy addresses of all time.[20]

"We face a threat with no precedent," because the men who destroyed the World Trade Center were able to cause mass destruction for "much less than the cost of a single tank," the president marvels.[21] Others, like them, are still abroad, hating, waiting, plotting against the United States, he reminds the cadets. Then, a policy vision begins to emerge in language that would have been familiar at the dawn of the nuclear age, a time when many foresaw the arc of mass destruction expanding battlefields of war.

The gravest danger to freedom lies at the perilous crossroads of radicalism and technology. When the spread of chemical and biological and nuclear weapons, along with ballistic missile technology—when that occurs, even weak states and small groups could attain a catastrophic power to strike great nations. Our enemies have declared this very intention, and have been caught seeking these terrible weapons. They want the capability to blackmail us, or to harm us, or to harm our friends—and we will oppose them with all our power.[22]

This situation "without precedent" portends that the "doctrines of deterrence and containment" are no longer operative. "New thinking" is necessary. "Deterrence—the promise of massive retaliation against nations—means nothing against shadowy terrorist networks with no nation or citizen to defend. Containment is not possible when unbalanced dictators with weapons of mass destruction can deliver those weapons on missiles or secretly provide them to terrorist allies."[23] If first strikes cannot be deterred, then they must be prevented, whether the source is a terrorist network, an errant state, or some combination of these actors.

Self-defense is a strong justification for going to war because it draws from moral, legal, and political precedents of long standing. The codes of international law, the customs among nations, the practices of democracy, and common sense all recognize self-defense as a necessity and a right of a victim when attacked. Acts that provoke alarm are imminent within the space of national memory. Public memories of conflict over state frontiers mark sites where the movement of armies signals an impending threat. On a broader scale, spheres of influence are vast stages where the use of force on a small scale in remote regions sends messages to far-distant national powers. The frontiers of nations, like the boundaries of global influence, are contested regions. Smaller incidents that trigger military action, too, are locked in public memory: attacks on foreign nationals, border clashes, exchange of threats, or territorial occupations all may trigger an expanded but genuine justification of self-defense. Incidents prompting war can be manufactured as well. The transparent rationalizations of Nazi rhetoric and the attacks staged by the Japanese in the 1930s, combined with the toothless response to aggression of the old League of Nations, led the United States to champion the United Nations (UN). In the UN Charter, war is legitimate only as a genuine matter of national self-defense.[24]

The West Point speech raised two troubling questions. Is it prudent or right for a nation to wait for an anticipated first, catastrophic blow before "defending" itself? If the answer is no, then what evidence of hostile intentions and unconventional weapons threat capacity should constitute the threshold that triggers a first strike as an act of self-defense? Anticipatory self-defense had long been a controversial doctrine, precisely because it lowers the threshold of war by giving propagandists an opening to manufacture incidents and inflate fears in the interests of promoting conflict. On the other hand, true self-defense was predicated on a rationale that linked making war to an actual or impending attack—and not to a first strike that is imagined as possible, likely, or even inevitable at some future point. The West Point speech did not get into the complex issue of proof standards; rather, its task was to announce that the reigning policies that had won the Cold War—containment—and had kept the peace—deterrence—since the beginning of the nuclear age were now to be considered to be null and void. We should get them, before they get us, the president was saying. Who "they" were, and how this view could be refined into policy, was left for different members of the executive to announce and defend.

CHENEY AT THE VFW

In August 2002, Vice President Richard Cheney delivered a speech that left little doubt how the "new thinking" would be translated into action. The vice president begins with a warning. The shadow world of terrorism has "spread among more than 60 countries"; thus victory in Afghanistan, while welcome, should not lead to complacency.

As we face this prospect, old doctrines of security do not apply. In the days of the Cold War we were able to manage the threat with strategies of deterrence and containment. But it's tougher to deter enemies who have no country to defend. And containment is not possible when dictators obtain weapons of mass destruction, and are prepared to share them with terrorists who intend to inflict catastrophic casualties on the United States.[25]

Oddly, the Cold War is recollected as a successful management exercise, where a risk-averse Soviet state made deterrence work by policing terrorist factions. Cheney has a nomination for the fanatic most likely to share "WMD" with terrorists: Saddam Hussein. Still, Cheney would use the Cold War comparisons, despite little public notice, to define present exigencies.

Cheney's indictment is clear and unequivocal at the outset:

Simply stated, there is no doubt that Saddam Hussein now has weapons of mass destruction. There is no doubt that he is amassing them to use against our friends, against our allies, and against us. And there is no doubt that his aggressive regional ambitions will lead him into future confrontations with his neighbors—confrontations that will involve both the weapons he has today, and the ones he will continue to develop with his oil wealth.[26]

The vice president cannot commit the United States to war; rather, he defers the decision to the president, who will call upon consultation and make time for a full, public debate; but Cheney concludes with a dire warning, drawn forward from the past. "To this day, historians continue to analyze that war [World War II], speculating on how we might have prevented Pearl Harbor." Cheney then adds, "[A] terror network, or a murderous dictator, or the two working together, constitutes as grave a threat as can be imagined."[27] Regret and foreboding coalesce, trigger fear, and motivate, but what would be the threshold at which action should be undertaken? The answer arrives in a pivotal passage.

As former Secretary of State Kissinger recently stated: "*The imminence of proliferation of weapons of mass destruction*, the huge dangers it involves, the rejection of a viable inspection system, and the demonstrated hostility of Saddam Hussein combine to produce an imperative for preemptive action." If the United States could have preempted 9/11, we would have, no question. Should we be able to prevent another, much more devastating attack, we will, no question. This nation will not live at the mercy of terrorists or terror regimes.[28]

The justification reasons: Just as we would have prevented 9/11 with a strike against plotting terrorists, so should we prevent an attack from Saddam Hussein, an outlaw regime. Prudence demands nothing else. That Hussein possesses now, is acquiring, and has used chemical weapons in the past proves the aggressive intentions of his regime; when the evidence becomes definitive, it will likely be too late to prevent loss—just as it is now too late to prevent the 9/11 terrorists from their ghastly deed. The analogy creates an associative rhetoric that foregrounds action against a harm that can still be avoided as compensation for inaction to prevent a loss that cannot be recovered. Such substitutions assuage guilt, sanctify memory, and convert fear to positive motivation. Yet analogical reasoning is incomplete on its own grounds because the comparison of present to past alone cannot articulate a threshold for determining publicly *what* to do and *when* to do it. The past and future surround, yet do not define, the threshold at which a present decision is justified.

International justification for going to war is well established as a response in accord with the needs for self-defense. A nation need not await its adversary to literally strike the first blow, however. Preempting the enemy with a proportionate response is justified when a state "faces an imminent threat that is otherwise unavoidable."[29] The criteria for justifying preemption are clear and of long standing. In the *Caroline* case (concerning cross-border incidents between the United States and Canada), Daniel Webster argued that for self-defense to be legitimate, the British had to demonstrate a "necessity of self-defense, instant, overwhelming, leaving no choice of means, and no moment of deliberation," and acts could not be unreasonable or excessive.[30] Thus three principles became a cornerstone of international law for justifying a preemptive strike: (1) Necessity demands that "all reasonable alternatives to the use of force be exhausted." (2) Proportionality "limits any defensive action to that necessary to defeat an ongoing attack or to deter or to preempt a future attack." (3) Imminence is "a standard [that] combines an exhaustion of remedies component with a requirement for a very high reasonable expectation of future attacks—an expectation that is much more than merely speculative."[31] Scholars conclude that the support for US intervention into Afghanistan was justified as preemptive self-defense and met these criteria.[32] Whereas the standing and conditions of preemption are consensually established, a similar-sounding term and alternative justification for war, "prevention," is much more controversial.

"Prevention is cold blooded," Lawrence Freedman explains; "it intends to deal with a problem before it becomes a crisis, while preemption is a more desperate strategy employed in the heat of crisis. Prevention is the product of calculation, a strategic moment of launching an optimum first strike against a weaker power before it has a chance to grow stronger."[33] From a nineteenth-century perspective, prevention occurs in those situations when there is time for deliberation; then, the costs and benefits of making war can be assessed. Preventive wars have costs that preemptive self-defense does not:

The superior power can expect to be accused of bullying, acting prematurely, perhaps on no more than a hunch. To the extent that A [the state that strikes first] does not care about international opinion, this may not matter, but without a compelling cause, preventive war can soon look like any other sort of aggressive war and thus provoke a reaction elsewhere—from diplomatic isolation to the formation of alliances among potential victims.[34]

The standard of prevention lowers the threshold for conflict by equating the justification for self-defense with the insecurities of any nation wishing war. In short, Jeffrey Record concludes: "[P]reemptive war has legal sanction. Preventive war, on the other hand has none, because the threat is neither certain nor imminent."[35]

The long-standing, important distinction between preemptive and preventive wars put the administration in a predicament. Iraq had not attacked the United States, nor was there evidence of an immediate threat: indeed, the United States had and was continuing to overfly the country without so much as the loss of a single airplane, although thousands of sorties had been conducted. So an invasion fought on the traditional definition of "preemption" would be unjustified. On the other hand, the administration held "no doubt" that Hussein had "WMD" and was "amassing" more. It would be too late to prevent damage, were these weapons to be used; even possession alone would change the balance of power in the Middle East. The key to undoing this tangle and releasing legitimated action is Kissinger's phrase "the imminence of weapons of mass destruction," a phrase that transfers the criteria of imminence from the actions of armies commanded by a state to the possession of certain categories of weapons that themselves constitute a reason for war.

STRATEGIC DOCTRINE

NSS 2002, the 2002 version of a document transmitted by the executive branch to Congress annually, makes the new thinking official.[36] Significantly, NSS 2002 echoes—sometimes directly quoting—the chief executive's West Point speech: "We cannot defend America and our friends by hoping for the best. So we must be prepared to defeat our enemies' plans, using the best intelligence and proceeding with deliberation. History will judge harshly those who saw this danger but failed to act. In the new world we have entered, the only path to peace and security is the path of action."[37] In this view, warfare may be conducted at a place and time of a nation's choosing based on anticipation of an enemy's "plans." This premise would loose the United States from international norms on war making and embrace the strategy of "prevention." Yet NSS 2002 does not embrace this openly controversial justification, but rather attempts to shift the meaning of a single word to put in place a keystone in the arc of thinking for a new age: "imminence."

"We must adapt the concept of imminent threat to the capabilities and objectives of today's adversaries," NSS 2002 reads.[38] Enemies who will not engage in a direct, obvious attack, but who will "use weapons that can be easily concealed, delivered covertly, and used without warning" populate the threat-field of current policy. A nuclear first strike, even if by only a single weapon, however crude, would be catastrophic. So "adapt" the term "imminent" to a new age, the crucial reformulation being:

The United States has long maintained the option of preemptive action to counter a sufficient threat to our national security. The greater the threat, the greater the risk of inaction—and the more compelling the case for taking anticipatory action to defend ourselves, even if uncertainty remains as to the time and place of the enemy's attack. To forestall or prevent such hostile acts by our adversaries, the United States will, if necessary, act preemptively.[39]

NSS 2002 appears to build on Kissinger's idea that the threshold of imminence is the possession of unconventional weaponry by a hostile power and, as such, possession of nuclear, biological, or chemical (NBC) arms falls within the new definition of preemptive war. A national policy grounded in traditional definitions of preemption occupies the moral and political high ground because it makes war a matter of self-defense, when all other alternatives have failed.[40] The high ground works to considerable political advantage in building coalitions, by offsetting political costs. A rationale built for war on grounds of prevention, for instance, reduces the cause for war to the perceptions of an aggressor, thereby imperiling international consensus about the types of war and thresholds at which conflict is justifiable. Since preventive wars lower prestige, even while perhaps increasing threat-credibility, these initiations of conflict may have substantial political costs.

In shifting the definition of "preemption," NSS 2002 tries to capture the rhetorical high ground; yet the argument appears to muddle crucial distinctions in international law and collective security. Since Webster's *Caroline* case, imminence has been connected to an immediate threat-situation. To be true self-defense, there is no time for deliberation and little room for choice because war is in the process of breaking out. The only question is how to respond. In contrast, the Bush doctrine situates the determination of war as a matter of deliberation, a weighing of evidence supporting alternatives for the best time to strike. War is made as a matter of calculation of the likely success of a first strike. In fact, supportive scholars such as Michael Glennon find "no dramatic change" in the Bush doctrine, which, they claim, merely updates policy to take into account international violence with terrorist networks, modern surveillance, threats from NBC weapons, and the necessity of preventing threats on a global scale. It is not Cold War cataclysm but "rogue" state support of terrorism that is the only novel issue.[41] Yet according to Elaine Bunn, preemption accentuates the following policy predicament:

[T]he closer to the "imminent" end of the spectrum a situation falls, the easier preemption is to justify politically, but the harder it may be to be operationally decisive, because the adversary will likely have protected the intended targets of preemption through deception, hardening, burial, dispersal, or predelegation of release. Conversely, the further it is from the imminent use end of the continuum situation is, the less acceptable it is likely to be to world opinion.[42]

Thus the doctrine puts operational success at odds with political efficacy.

The shift of the term "imminence" also imperils an additional con-
straint, "proportionality," with a similar resulting paradox. Preemption is
justified only insofar as an impending attack is thwarted, but unjustified to
the extent that its invocation is a transparent, self-serving pretext for launching an all-out war. Yet in NSS 2002 the idea of proportion is relativized, not
to proper force used to preempt the success of an attack already under way,
but to the costs of waiting and becoming a victim. The harms of sustaining
a first strike, compared to the collateral damage in taking out the shadowy
enemies of a failed state, create a calculus that strongly favors early "preemption." Thus the threshold for evidence of enemy possession and intent requisite for justified "preemption" is substantially lowered by the new doctrine. A
weak evidentiary requirement feeds, rather than unravels, Bunn's dilemma,
however. The weaker the evidence of NBC arms possession, the harder it
may be to build a sense of threat that would spark a coalition; the greater the
evidence of possession of unconventional weaponry, the higher the thresholds
for guaranteeing the success of a first strike become, because a failed effort
would precipitate the very attack and harms that are feared.

The articulation of a new doctrine influences, but does not determine,
the language within which policy is defended by an administration. Condoleezza Rice, the national security advisor, worked rhetorically to tie preemption with traditional approaches justifying war and peace: "The National
Security Strategy does not overturn five decades of doctrine and jettison
either containment or deterrence," she said in defending the redefinition of
"imminence." "As a matter of common sense, the United States must be prepared to take action, when necessary, before threats have fully materialized."
Quoting former secretary of state George Schultz, she concluded: "If there
is a rattlesnake in the yard, you don't wait for it to strike before you take action in self-defense."[43] Lending perspective, familiarity, common sense, and
vividness are reassuring and sophisticated rhetorical strategies. Confusion
sometimes works just as well. What can be made of this statement by Secretary of Defense Rumsfeld? "Prevention is also—has a connotation that's
somewhat more acceptable than preemption. It sounds a little fairer—if there
is such a word; that you're trying to prevent something from happening at the
last minute is the implication—the connotation of that word to me"? This
apparent, guileless confusion is followed with a precise, Orwellian inver-
sion of international law: "Preemption is slightly different in the sense that
it suggest[s] that you have a reason to believe something's going to happen,
could happen, that is notably unpleasant, and you make a conscious decision
to go out and stop that from happening."[44] In the secretary's view, preemption
becomes untethered from what is an imminent event and becomes predicated upon what is "going to" or "could happen" at some undefined future

date, "call it what you wish."[45] Thus the posture of the Bush administration worked to legitimize a war in Iraq by expanding the definition of preemption, and muddling its difference from prevention.

PREWAR LEGITIMATION CONTROVERSY

In a democracy, the decision to take a nation to war requires public support, in the long, if not the short term. The "war on terror" had received unanimous support of the Congress, at least as far as the attack on Afghanistan was concerned. The question of what further engagements would be fought, even in the shadow of 9/11, was more uncertain. The autumn of 2002 saw the US Congress embroiled in a fractious debate whose outcome reached all the way to the UN. The administration had gone to Congress with its newly minted redefinition of preemptive war and proposed an authorizing resolution that would allow the president to take care of problems in the broader Middle East as he saw fit. The proposal was modified substantially and reshaped to answer concerns regarding separation of powers stemming from the War Powers Act; then, in early October, a resolution authorizing the president to determine the necessity for an invasion on his terms was brought to the floor of the US House and Senate. To attain a solid majority, the bipartisan initiative directed the president to first follow the route of gaining a resolution at the UN on arms inspections; only if the inspections failed would the president then be authorized to take stronger measures. Crucially, the president was given nearly unchecked power to determine the success or failure of the arms control process.

Many in Congress, while repudiating the doctrine of preemption, nonetheless supported the resolution because, for them, it was important that the United States "speak with one voice," and this sort of resolution would be the most likely to send a strong message to Hussein and preserve the peace. Nevertheless, the authorization for war had the unmistakable fingerprints of preemptive thinking on it. The resolution reads, in part:

Whereas Iraq's demonstrated capability and willingness to use weapons of mass destruction, the high risk that the current regime will either employ those weapons to launch a surprise attack against the United States or its Armed Forces or provide them to international terrorists who would do so, and the extreme magnitude of harm that would result to the United States and its citizens from such an attack combine to justify action by the United States to defend itself.[46]

The certainty of the administration's public statements and private briefings to Congress that Hussein had "WMD" and was developing more, and would likely share them with terrorists already in Iraq, made opposition to the resolution difficult, especially in the shadow of 9/11. As Miriam Sapiro concludes: "Although the administration has characterized its new approach as 'preemptive,' it is more accurate to describe it as 'preventive' self-defense. Rather than trying to preempt specific, imminent threats, the goal is to prevent more generalized threats from materializing."[47]

The president spoke to the UN to see if a peaceful route to avoiding war could be taken through gaining a resolution that would persuade Hussein to reopen serious weapons inspections. The political leverage the administration was able to muster in persuading the US Congress extended, on a limited basis, to persuading traditional allies of the United States.[48] The UN did vote for renewed inspections, but failure to comply with Resolution 1441 would bring not "war" but the more ambiguous threat of "serious consequences."

In Bush's fall campaign, the new security doctrine had revealed strategic strengths and weaknesses in convincing domestic and international publics. "WMD," which connotes ultimate terror, is a useful symbol that conglomerates three distinct threats—biological, nuclear, and chemical weapons—into an acronym that can be used in an omnibus fashion when describing weapons Iraq had, may have, or could have in the future. Such an omnibus term, however, occludes the size, availability, and specific types of threats faced. Chemical weapons, for example, are not nearly as destructive as nuclear bombs. Still, in the shorthand phrases of political argument, one is associated with the other. So, too, the term "terrorist" was deployed to occlude differences among secular and religious groups that are at war with each other. "Terrorist" filled in the slot for the term "enemy," and it follows that all enemies need to be fought. Finally, Hussein made a tempting target, given his history of warfare in the Middle East, the unfinished status of the 1991 war, and his stature as a dictator. These fears made for sufficient justifications to get the UN to listen to the need to renew weapons inspections. In the shadow of 9/11, fear is as compelling as defending Hussein's regime is politically unpalatable.

The NSS 2002 doctrine is not without critical proof standards, however. If intervention is to be justified on the threat of "WMD," then it would seem to be imperative to show that an adversary has NBC arms, is in the process of developing more in greater variety, will likely cross a qualitative threshold of higher threat, and intends to use new unconventional weaponry either as blackmail or in aggression once developed. What are the kinds and degrees of proof necessary to meet these criteria? Strategic thinking and political consensus-making lead to different answers. The strategy of "preemption" is a desirable strategic posture in a given case to the extent that a proponent is convinced that dealing with an adversary's "WMD" is a now-or-later imperative. Since the costs of enduring a first strike are great, and since political degrees of freedom diminish as the NBC arsenal of an enemy grows, the proof threshold that would necessitate a first strike is low. False positives are risks that preempters are prepared to take. On the other hand, the lower the threshold for war, the greater the risk of provoking violence that could or should have been resolved through other means. Low proof standards increase the risk of fighting an unnecessary and counterproductive war. Thus the reformulated NSS 2002 doctrine invites, even demands, that advocates of force bent on creating consensus wring the greatest degree of proof out of positive evidence supporting the above criteria while minimizing negative evidence on NBC weapons development. First-strike discourse within the strategic establishment requires calculative thinking; public justifications of mounting an invasion—even in the name of liberation—are a matter of broader deliberation. Thus there is an inbuilt impetus within the doctrine to exaggerate evidence of threats to build up a more traditional case for war.

In the end, even with the overstated evidence deployed by President Bush and British prime minister Tony Blair, the public justifications for the American war in Iraq were insufficient to create the kind of consensus that underwrote either the first Gulf War or the invasion of Afghanistan. Despite Secretary of State Colin Powell's best rhetorical efforts, the world remained unconvinced that war with Iraq was necessary.

In the winter of 2003, as the weapons inspections were ongoing, and even as no unconventional weaponry was turning up, President Bush went ahead and "made the tough decision." "He's [Hussein] a master at deception. He has no intention of disarming—otherwise we would have known," the president argued on the eve of invasion. Were Hussein disarming, Bush continued, a few inspectors "could have showed up at a parking lot and he could have brought his weapons and destroyed them." Bush's posited threshold—disarm or war—does not admit to the possibility that there were no unconventional weapons—that inspections, flyovers, and sanctions have done their job already. Bush's test could not be met because—as all commissions studying the prewar situation have concluded—there was nothing to fill up the "parking lot" with.[49]

Thus the NSS 2002 doctrine led Bush to set up proof standards that reversed presumption altogether, thereby drastically lowering the chances of remaining at peace: Hussein had to prove that he did not have "WMD" to avoid war. This is a convincing standard in the climate of post-9/11 anxieties, as insecurity multiplies a network of self-elaborating suspicions among those who support intervention. For instance, US weapons inspector David Kay testified:

The best evidence I would suggest you look at is look at Saddam Hussein. If he had no weapons of mass destruction, why would he not let the inspectors in with full rein? And yet we can describe in chapter and verse the concealment, deception, denial techniques that were used, that ranged from physical intimidation and force, all the way up to much more subtle and technologically sophisticated methods to conceal. If you're not engaged in a prohibited activity, why would you forego $120 billion of oil revenue? I think the best evidence that there is something there is the evidence of the perpetrator of the crime and his behavior.[50]

Still, it is logically impossible to prove a negative, of course. Yet so compelling is this rhetoric to the president that to this day Bush's public narrative justifying his personal decision to end inspections and trigger war continues to hang on a logically invalid argument—that Hussein did not prove that he did not have "WMD."

POSTWAR LEGITIMATION CONTROVERSY

A postwar environment for a democratic victor is expected to be a period where the violence is less, not greater, than the war. Tragically, the postwar environment in the Iraqi conflict has become, if anything, even more uncertain and controversial than the road leading up to invasion. As Thomas Franck put it most starkly: "On September 11, 2001, every nation in the world voiced its support for us, sympathy for our tragedy, and willingness to join in the war on terrorism. Now, almost every nation regards us as the world's gravest threat to peace."[51] While overstated, his point is not without merit. The war is over, but the peace is far from won.

As it became gradually clear that Operation Iraqi Freedom would not be received unambiguously as a moment of liberation by the Iraqis, finding unconventional weaponry became a top priority to sustain justification for the war effort. During the year following the 2003 Iraq War, the world was treated to the spectacle of an army of American specialists searching far and wide to find evidence that would legitimate the president's decision. Scant evidence supporting this prewar rationale emerged, although there could be little doubt—were there any to start with—of Hussein's domestic atrocities. So noticeable was the gap between imagined threat and on-the-ground findings that in the 2004 State of the Union address, President Bush labored to shift the key rationale for the invasion, citing the Kay report, which although it had found no weapons, as the president said, had found "dozens of mass destruction–related program activities and significant amounts of equipment that Iraq concealed from the United Nations."[52] Since a chemical plant or a lab can potentially be converted to weapons production, then any modern industrial state may be said to be a potential NBC weapons threat. The question becomes, crucially, upon what evidence military conflict ought to be initiated.

The threshold for war in a post-9/11 age appears to be "break out," an old, Cold War term used to justify increased defense spending for new technology in light of real or imagined Soviet treaty violations. The key justification for the war, according to Senator John Warner (R-VA), was, from the perspective of 2004, "whether or not Saddam Hussein had some kind of, quote, 'breakout capability' for quickly producing chemical or biological weapons" that would serve as "a basis for constituting a conclusion that there was an imminent threat from Saddam Hussein and his military."[53] Yet the original claims by the administration were that Hussein had weapons, their location was known, the weapons were being amassed, Iraq "WMD" constituted grave and gathering threats to Middle Eastern friends and American interests, and development was going ahead at full speed, with nuclear capabilities within a year possible (or likely). As war opponent Senator Carl Levin (D-MI) put it in questioning Kay: "A different case for war against Iraq can be made, the case which the administration made to the American people was the presence of actual weapons of mass destruction."[54]

If war is predicated on the possibility of weapons acquisition, then the threshold for justifying interstate violence is removed, and the administration appeared to be lowering the standard of self-defense: from "imminence" of an attack on the US territory, allies, or troops; to admitted and known possession of NBC arms; to the existence of suggestive evidence of such possession; to conjectures about the intent of a dictator at some point to develop weapons. This leads to the current central question of American foreign policy: upon what turns the decisions of war and peace for a post-9/11 era? The exchange between Senator Mark Dayton (D-OH) and David Kay probes this question:

Dayton: Just based on your general knowledge, how many countries in the world today would qualify under the category of developing weapons of mass destruction–related program activities or having such activities?

Kay: Oh, I suspect you're talking about probably 50 countries. . . .

Dayton: So if we're going to take out those countries or their governments which are engaged in what we would call weapons of mass destruction–related program activities, we're going to be cutting quite a world swath.

Kay: Well, Senator Dayton, I think you're on to the issue. We no longer are going to be living in a world in which we can control capabilities. Intentions are what are going to be important. And quite frankly, that's what made Saddam so dangerous, in my view. Here was an individual who had invaded his neighbors, used chemical weapons against one of them and used them against the other. So it was hard to have a benign interpretation of that individual's intelligence. And the real challenge for intelligence is going to be getting to our political leadership, not just judgments about capabilities, but judgments about real intentions. And that is tough.[55]

The imputed ambitions of a dictator are unlikely to receive a vigorous public debate because there is zero political incentive to defend leaders of the ilk of the "Butcher of Baghdad." Moreover, to rely on someone who has the international standing of a Saddam Hussein and his pacific intentions is to figuratively sanction the risk of a catastrophic strike on the United States, no matter how remote the actual likelihood. On the other hand, the upside of invasion can be painted in rosy pictures of cheering crowds by naming the conflict as a war of "liberation" within the imaginative horizons of the "rising dominoes" of freedom in the Middle East. As a result of this rhetorical equation, the breaks on policy driven by suspicion and fear—as well as the means to weigh risks and benefits of an invasion impartially—are weakened, if not removed altogether. Kay supplies the motive for lowering the threshold of war: "[A]ny president, when he's presented with intelligence, has got to make a choice about how much risk he's prepared to run for the nation that he leads. It is my belief that regardless of political party, after 9/11, the shadowing effects of that horrible tragedy changed as a nation the level of risk that all of us are prepared to run, that we would like to avoid."[56]

Even as Kay was testifying to the new standards of war making, administration defenders articulated a two-pronged strategy to drain off the controversy. Spokespersons reinforced the idea that Saddam Hussein was a bad actor who eventually would have developed unconventional weapons and shared them with enemies who eventually would have attacked the United States, on the one hand. On the other, some in Congress cast blame on faulty prewar arguments on the broadly defined intelligence community (IC). The Senate Select Intelligence Committee attributed the failure of the IC to "groupthink," a convenient sharing of blame that finds everyone and no one guilty at the same time.[57] Yet an even more important question of leadership remained.

Who was responsible for overestimating and vetting secret, speculative guesswork as hard-won, absolutely certain public fact? The committee demurred on the question of the involvement of administration spokespersons in spreading suspect information. The full, public evaluation of the Bush doctrine was kicked down the road another ten months to March 2005—past a crucial election, when public knowledge of events would matter most, and over three years after the initial debate, a time when old deliberative questions

garner mostly historical interest.[58] The questions of who knew (or should
have known) better in assessing the reports and spreading bad information
to Congress, the public, and the world, and why such systematically distorted
communication filled the public airwaves, largely unchallenged, remain open.
The paradoxes of the NSS 2002 doctrine are not likely to go away, however,
precisely because they reside at the heart of the convoluted questions deterrence, containment, and proliferation pose for the post-9/11 world.

CONCLUSION

In the lengthening shadows of 9/11, the Iraq War, and escalating acts of
global terrorism, the justifications for war and peace are increasingly open
for debate. Jane Stromseth argues, "Doctrinally, the potentially lethal combination of terrorists and weapons of mass destruction requires a rethinking
of the scope of the right of self-defense."[59] As William Taft IV and Todd
Buchwald suggest, "the need to adapt the concept of imminence to the capabilities and objectives of today's adversaries" requires "calculating" the
requirements of self-defense where unconventional weapons "can be easily
concealed, delivered covertly, and used without warning."[60] Yet the problems of threat asymmetry are not new; indeed, they are an integral part of
the nuclear age. Shortly after the invention of the atomic bomb, many were
concerned that technology would eventually make democracies vulnerable
to attacks through sabotage, suitcase bombs, and the like. The strategies of
deterrence and containment provided a secure path through the atomic age,
but the logics of a bipolar Cold War world routed the United States around
basic questions of the age, for a time, and are now in need of review and
repair to face threat configurations that are inherently asymmetrical, chaotic,
and changing. If 9/11 threw the need for fresh thinking into bold relief, and
if the Afghanistan War provided a consensual answer of how to address these
issues, the war in Iraq tore open the uncertainties of the nuclear age with
burning urgency. Indeed, this war is making the connection between the language within which nations fashion collective security and the deeds of war
increasingly problematic, on several levels.

First, the novel NSS 2002 doctrine decreases the security of the United
States. The Iraq War has been so globally divisive and so nationally costly
that it renders unlikely the kind of commitment necessary for preemptive
intervention in cases where intervention is clearly urgent—by Kissinger's
criteria that possession of unconventional weaponry constitutes a threat. US
forces are overextended, while the NSS 2002 doctrine itself threw into controversy the criteria upon which interventions are to be decided. As a result of

Iraq, humanitarian interventions are less likely to receive broad international support, and responsibility is more likely to be shifted over to regional coalitions with unproven effectiveness. Even where NBC arms pose a genuine threat, US persuasion is less effective because overstating evidence "will produce a 'Chicken Little' effect: a crisis of credibility with other countries whose support the United States may need in the future."[61]

Second, the war in Iraq has had equivocal results on the issue of nuclear proliferation. The administration points to the success in Libya, while the cases of North Korea and Iran grow more protracted. The NSS 2002 doctrine narrowly focusing on the threat posed by a particular regime may create a tunnel vision that screens out the wider message sent to potential proliferators. For these regimes, the message may be that if you actually have nuclear weapons, you are in a much stronger bargaining position than if you do not, thereby encouraging nations on the brink of development to completion.[62]

Third, the war in Iraq underscores the imprudence of American neo-isolationist policies of the 1990s. If preventive force is to work, then a substantial commitment to postwar reconstruction has to be made—long before the intervention is executed. If postwar efforts are not successful, then the same problems could reappear, in an even more virulent form. The lack of preparation for assuming responsibilities of "nation building" in Iraq now appears patent, both in the disposition of the understaffed US troops and the failure of the United States to support training of police, emergency relief workers, first responders, and other types of forces necessary to combat "terrorism" through on-the-ground efforts. If preventive war is to be a reigning doctrine, it must have a correlate of postwar reconstruction figured into costs, risks, and outcomes.

Fourth, the on-balance effect of the Iraq invasion on the "war on terror" is still open to question. The NSS 2002 doctrine was useful in framing the justification for invasion as a clear national security issue: terrorism plus nuclear weapons equals a "grave and gathering threat." The United States did eliminate the possibility that Saddam Hussein at some unspecified point might acquire NBC weapons and use them or give them away to some unspecified group; however, the net effect of an intervention based on worst-case thinking may be to drive more people to take up terrorism and to further popularize Islamic movements. The problem with NBC terrorism is not located exclusively in the production programs of states, but on the black market and in potential theft of materials. Radicalizing greater numbers of people multiples worst-case scenarios of a first strike.

Fifth, the doctrine of preventive war exposes paradoxes internal to the logics of policy regarding asymmetrical threats, holes that have yet to be worked out publicly into a coherent, legitimate narrative. At a strategic level, the farther away from actual unconventional weapons deployment an enemy is, the easier it is to accomplish first-strike missions, but the more difficult it is to justify intervention. The closer to full NBC weapons deployment, the easier it is to rouse fears of attack, but the harder it is to complete a successful mission, where goals demand complete success. This dilemma can be undercut by exaggeration of the present enemy threat, but the price of suspect inducement for war is the absence of prewar consensus and spiraling postwar costs.

Sixth, a war that is widely spoken of as preventive (and therefore not defensive), no matter how well linguistically repackaged as preemption, lowers the prestige of an aggressor, especially in a community of democracies. Prestige is necessary for effective public diplomacy. The impact of positive programs that the United States has initiated post-Iraq in areas of AIDS, health care, food, and other foreign aid projects is minimized by a competing frame loosed by the Iraq War and continued with extended, disruptive violence. The extension of power may indeed increase the perception by others that the United States can wield an effective stick, but power without prestige increases the costs and decreases the effectiveness of gestures of goodwill, perceived commitment to the rule of law, and ability to counter adverse propaganda. From a public diplomacy standpoint, the newly defined preemptive wars are disasters from the outset.

Seventh, the NSS 2002 doctrine impairs administration credibility due to its differential weight of technical and public justification. Technically, preventive force may be justified on scant evidence of NBC arms possession, and in the shadow of 9/11 weak evidence apparently was sufficient to convince the administration and the public to support the war. The technical justification, however, does not engage the same proof standards as public discourse, where war is still spoken of as a "last resort," and a "just war" requires more than anecdotal evidence linked to suspicion. Further, even should national trauma motivate action, sustained public support requires a sound rationale for justifying prudent choice, at least over the long term. The result of these rhetorical constraints peculiar to preemption as a doctrine may have led war advocates to exaggerate the certainty of tenuous evidence, overlook counterevidence, and make a case that would eventually be exposed as fraudulent on its face. Preventive force thus creates rhetorical conditions that impair the credibility of an administration, which has important consequences over the long term for the fashioning and support of policy.

The administration rarely speaks of the doctrine of "preemption" anymore, although the consequences of the rhetorical campaign of the summer of 2002 still very much mark its discourse. Indeed, when the administration publicly considered in August 2005 whether it should abandon its signature brand, the "Global War on Terror" (GWOT), in exchange for a new discourse, the "Global Struggle against Violent Extremism (GSAVE), the president put an end to discussion.[63] On 6 October 2005, speaking to the National Endowment for Democracy, Bush returned to Cheney's initial metaphor that America is engaged in a struggle benchmarked by the Cold War. Now, it is "we" who must take it to the enemy, which "[s]ome call this evil Islamic radicalism; others, militant jihadism; still others, Islamo-fascism," he opined. Of course, the GWOT is "war" against a religious/secularist, not a Communist-constructed, movement, involving dispersed nonstate actors, not a Soviet empire, and must be conducted with little help from democratic alliances rather than with a broad, international consensus.[64] In short, absent "preemption" as a doctrine that can be defended on its own, the president must rely upon justification of policy based upon a rather imperfect Cold War simile, an ideograph pushed by the vice president for years without popular success. Such arguments have provided enough political legitimacy to sustain high levels of congressional military funding, but do not draw strong support at home or abroad. The lack of popular appeal appears again to invite overstatement of risk to add policy punch. In a 2005 major speech for the war, Bush supported his call for a crusade at the intensity and clarity of anti-Stalinist zeal and Berlin airlift enthusiasm with what the press found to be, upon interviews with administration officials, publicly unverifiable or equivocal examples of threats and successes.[65]

There is a term for commitments that snarl, bind, twist, reverse, and generate ever more protracted and divisive controversy—"quagmire"—a pivotal term that is as much a metaphor for discourse as a condition of policy. Fresh, clear thinking is needed. To begin, we need to reconsider traditional doctrines that informed American foreign policy and ask probing questions—rather than precipitously propound and extend a radical, new revision. The NSS 2002 doctrine of preventive war requires sustained thinking through recollecting the lessons of deterrence and containment earned through a half century of largely successful American foreign policy. In all candor, the world did not enter a new epoch in 2001; rather, 9/11 constituted but a new, deadly chapter in what we have come to know as the nuclear age.

6

Deliberate before Striking First?

RODGER A. PAYNE

T HE GEORGE W. BUSH administration's "war on terror" has been waged using a diverse array of military and nonmilitary policy instruments. While the armed conflict in Afghanistan initially attracted the most attention, the antiterror effort has also emphasized more vigorous intelligence gathering and worldwide sharing of information, new and contentious law enforcement initiatives, and increased monitoring of financial transactions and banking practices. However, the most controversial "weapon" in the "war on terror" is the "preemptive" war option mentioned almost in passing by the president in a commencement address at West Point in June 2002[1] and without extensive explanation in the September 2002 document issued by the White House, the National Security Strategy of the United States of America (NSS 2002).[2] Former secretary of state Colin Powell, in fact, condemns the Bush administration's domestic and foreign critics for overemphasizing the importance of preemptive use of force in the foreign policy toolkit. Powell boasts that NSS 2002 is a "remarkably candid" public pronouncement of US strategy, but worries that American policy has been misunderstood and distorted by domestic and foreign critics.[3] According to Powell, every US president has retained the option of preemptive war to address certain kinds of threats. The novelty in this case, says Powell, is the explicit public declaration of the strategy.[4]

However, the former secretary greatly understates the unique nature of the Bush administration's preemption strategy. It is true that US presidents, as well as the leaders of other states, have long held the legal option to utilize preemptive force in self-defense. However, as NSS 2002 boldly declares, the United States now asserts that traditional understandings of international law pertaining to the potential defensive use of military force are flawed. Historically, a state could legitimately launch a preemptive attack when facing "visible mobilization of armies, navies and air forces preparing to attack."[5] Such tangible evidence would indicate the existence of an imminent threat. The Bush administration rejects this traditional view because terrorists are prepared to strike without warning against innocent civilians. Administration officials are especially worried about potentially undeterrable threats posed by the proliferation of unconventional weapons to hostile regimes working with terrorists of global reach. Because of the apparently changed circumstances justifying American attack, the military strategy that the Bush administration publicly advocates to meet such contemporary threats is not the same form of preemption that political leaders have previously and privately held in reserve.

Clearly, by making the preemptive attack option publicly explicit, and by openly attempting to alter the standards justifying the use of force in self-defense, the Bush administration has initiated an intense debate about this aspect of its antiterror strategy. Many experts claim that the United States has now embraced a strategy more akin to preventive war, which has long been viewed as illegal under international law.[6] Numerous outspoken critics additionally worry that the new standard sets an extremely risky precedent for international politics. Historian Paul Schroeder offered a sweeping indictment, charging that

a more dangerous, illegitimate norm and example can hardly be imagined. As could easily be shown by history, it completely subverts previous standards for judging the legitimacy of resorts to war, justifying any number of wars hitherto considered unjust and aggressive. . . . It would in fact justify almost any attack by any state on any other for almost any reason. This is not a theoretical or academic point. The American example and standard for preemptive war, if carried out, would invite imitation and emulation, and get it.[7]

Critics fear that states such as India, Israel, and Russia might embrace the new logic of preemption and employ it to justify attacks on various foes. This would likely make the world much more dangerous. Political scientist John

Mearsheimer additionally argues that the Bush administration's confounding of the terms "preemption" and "prevention" has great rhetorical and normative significance and was undoubtedly crafted to influence the public debate in a favorable direction: "The Bush Administration has gone to great lengths to use 'pre-emption' when what it's really talking about is 'preventive' war. Language matters greatly. It lends legitimacy to the administration's case. Saying it's a 'pre-emptive' war gives it a legitimacy that you don't get if you say it's a 'preventive' war."[8]

The Bush administration, of course, stirred up intense domestic and international criticism for its decision to employ the new military strategy against Iraq, a nation with no apparent ties to the 11 September 2001 attacks against the United States.[9] President Bush spent much of 2002 focusing the "war on terror" on Iraq and building support for the plan to topple Saddam Hussein's government by force. In January of that year, Bush controversially claimed that Iraq, Iran, North Korea, and affiliated terrorist groups were part of an "axis of evil" that posed a "grave and growing danger" because of their pursuit of "weapons of mass destruction."[10] In February 2002, Bob Woodward of the *Washington Post* quoted the president as saying on 17 September 2001, "I believe Iraq was involved [in the 9/11 attacks], but I'm not going to strike them now."[11] Then, in a speech before the United Nations (UN) General Assembly in September of that year, Bush specifically called Iraq under Saddam Hussein's rule a "great and gathering danger" because of Hussein's apparent pursuit of "weapons of mass murder."[12] Throughout fall 2002, Bush often linked Iraq and the al-Qaida terrorists that perpetrated the 9/11 attacks. "The danger," he argued, "is that they work in concert. The danger is, is that al Qaeda becomes an extension of Saddam's madness and his hatred and his capacity to extend weapons of mass destruction around the world. Both of them need to be dealt with. . . . [Y]ou can't distinguish between al Qaeda and Saddam when you talk about the war on terror."[13] A few weeks later, referencing fears that Iraq was acquiring nuclear weapons, Bush explicitly invoked the administration's logic justifying early attack: "Facing clear evidence of peril, we cannot wait for the final proof—the smoking gun—that could come in the form of a mushroom cloud. We cannot stand by and do nothing while dangers gather."[14]

Administration critics claim that the failure to find nuclear, biological, or chemical (NBC) weapons in Iraq quite strongly suggests that the administration distorted the prewar debate about Iraq. This is a very serious concern. Government participants in national security debates can undercut the purpose of public deliberation by employing what communications scholar Gordon Mitchell calls "strategic deception."[15] Such governmental trickery is troublesome on matters of war and peace because official participants in public debates about national security policy have substantial advantages over nongovernmental participants. Their job titles grant them authority and credibility, which is further secured by their unique access to classified information.[16] Public debate about national security will be greatly distorted in their favor if authoritative figures exploit their advantages by dubiously overemphasizing evidence that supports their arguments and by ignoring and/or blocking the release of countervailing evidence and caveats. Many political theorists and analysts argue that open and inclusive political debate rewards the ideas that best withstand critical scrutiny in the political marketplace.[17] Indeed, this is a position often taken by classic liberal theorists like John Stuart Mill and Frankfurt-school critical theorists such as Jürgen Habermas. The evidence presented in this chapter substantiates the great danger of distorted debate about the alleged need for preventive war.

In the following pages, I first argue that Bush administration officials clearly recognized the potential risks posed by the new preventive military intervention strategy and thus sought to establish deliberative standards for implementing the policy. Indeed, the standards they put forward would appear to be very difficult to meet in the future and may make Iraq a historically unique case. Next, I demonstrate that the Bush administration's public justifications for attacking Iraq because of its alleged nuclear capabilities were apparently distorted in a number of very important ways. These distortions undercut the deliberative ideals advanced by the Bush administration and provide fertile ground for critics of US policy. Additionally, the virtually inevitable and ongoing revelation of these distortions serves to invite even greater public scrutiny of potential future US applications of preventive strategies against other threatening adversaries. Indeed, these distortions might well make it unlikely that the United States can employ preemption, as it has been historically understood, even when facing serious risk of attack.[18] Thus I conclude by outlining the possible adverse security implications associated with the public declaration of an empty doctrine.

THE LIMITS OF PREVENTIVE WAR

Official public justifications emanating from the Bush White House have attempted to limit significantly the prospective applicability of the new military strategy, despite public boasts that the country's "best defense is a good offense."[19] The administration seems to recognize the potential danger of tampering with international standards justifying preemptive war. This section will summarize the parameters US policy-makers have sought to establish on the future employment of the new strategic doctrine.

To begin, NSS 2002 bluntly warns other states not to "use preemption as pretext for aggression."[20] In that document and elsewhere, US officials have therefore sought to establish fairly clear standards for justifying preventive attack that intentionally serve to narrow its potential applicability. Put simply, the administration promises to use force only as a last resort, after working with US allies to establish the existence of a very grave threat that cannot be addressed in any nonmilitary fashion.[21] The administration's political machinations vis-à-vis Iraq during 2002 and early 2003 also signal the importance the Bush White House places on public justification of its case for preemptive war. As NSS 2002 asserts in regard to potential applications of the preemptive option, "the reasons for our actions will be clear."[22] In September and October 2002, the president himself delivered widely broadcast and discussed speeches to the UN and to the American public. Eventually, in early February 2003, Secretary of State Colin Powell was sent to the UN to present America's best intelligence evidence about Iraq's misdeeds, in the obvious hope of winning broad political support both at home and abroad.

NSS 2002 says, "The United States will not use force in all cases to preempt emerging threats. . . . We will always proceed deliberately, weighing the consequences of our actions." The strategic plan further notes that the United States will "coordinate closely with allies to form a common assessment of the most dangerous threats."[23] According to then national security advisor Condoleezza Rice, the new military strategy requires the United States to pursue diplomatic solutions with the potential targets of attack, until it becomes apparent that those options will fail. In fact, in an address before the Manhattan Institute for Policy Research delivered shortly after NSS 2002 was published, Rice offered an impressive list of caveats to the preventive strategy:

This approach must be treated with great caution. The number of cases in which it might be justified will always be small. It does not give a green light—to the United States or any other nation—to act first without exhausting other means, including diplomacy. Preemptive action does not come at the beginning of a long chain of effort. The threat must be very grave. And the risks of waiting must far outweigh the risks of action.[24]

On a number of occasions, Secretary of State Powell indicated that the case for using force against Iraq was unique precisely because of the prior twelve years of failure to achieve diplomatic success, combined with Iraq's horrible compliance record on a lengthy list of UN Security Council resolutions. The Bush administration's ability to achieve unanimous support for UN Security Council Resolution 1441 convinced many observers that the US view of the Iraq crisis was widely shared. However, the administration and its British allies ultimately failed to win a second UN Security Council resolution backing war against Iraq. France, Germany, and Russia, for example, managed to send repeated and clear signals about their dissent.[25] These states were content to let ongoing weapons inspections take their course.

Even as the Iraq debate raged, however, the United States fairly clearly indicated that it had strong reservations about the application of the preventive military strategy to additional states. Secretary Powell, for instance, reassured the American people and the rest of the world that the United States did not have a "cookie cutter policy for every situation" and would vigorously pursue diplomatic solutions rather than attack North Korea and Iran in regard to their apparent efforts to acquire nuclear weapons.[26] Evidently, US policy-makers did not think that all measures short of using force had been exhausted in these cases. Cynics might point out that it would be materially quite difficult to attack either North Korea or Iran with large number of active forces deployed (or otherwise committed to troop rotations) in Afghanistan and Iraq. Still, the political implications are significant. If the United States does not plan to use military force against two-thirds of the "axis of evil" states, each with relatively advanced nuclear capabilities that gained renewed attention as the United States was pushing toward war in Iraq, it is difficult to imagine another viable target state.

Moreover, even in the case of Iraq, the United States claimed for many months that it would employ force only reluctantly and would prefer a non-military solution. While the United States ultimately used force against Iraq without explicit UN Security Council authorization, President Bush initially claimed not to have made up his mind about the appropriate action necessary to address Iraq's threat. Arguably, in making such a claim and attempting to "sell" the need for war against Iraq, US officials implicitly established the need for public deliberation. More explicitly, starting in September and throughout the fall of 2002, the president and other officials called for public and political debate about US policy toward Iraq. The president, for instance, actively sought input from Congress, even as the overwhelming majority of its members were engaged in reelection efforts. In a letter dated 3 September 2002, the president wrote to members of Congress, "This is an important decision that must be made with great thought and care. Therefore, I welcome and encourage discussion and debate."[27] That same week, the president remarked at a political campaign stop that he wanted to provoke an even broader "debate . . . to encourage the American people to listen to and have a dialog about Iraq. . . . I want there to be an open discussion about the threats that face America."[28] Congress obliged the president's request by conducting nearly a week of floor debate during fall 2002.

The public deliberation, naturally, included citizens talking with each other on coffee breaks and across dinner tables as well as various foreign policy elites attempting to influence the wider public throughout assorted mass media. After former Republican House majority leader Dick Armey (R-TX) publicly questioned the need to attack Iraq without provocation, Defense Secretary Donald H. Rumsfeld declared, "I think it's important for people to say what they think on these things. And that's the wonderful thing about our country. We have a public debate and dialogue and discussion on important issues."[29] Perhaps to signal that the US administration did not merely see the need to engage the domestic electorate, President Bush also sought input from the international community, especially the leadership of other prominent states, such as fellow permanent UN Security Council members China, France, Great Britain, and Russia. "The international community must also be involved," declared the president. "I have asked [British] Prime Minister Blair to visit America this week to discuss Iraq. I will also reach out to President Chirac of France, President Putin of Russia, President Jiang of China, and other world leaders."[30]

The Bush administration proved to be a vigorous participant in the public debates about both the prevention strategy and its apparent application to Iraq. Nonetheless, based upon what numerous public officials said about Iraq, it would be difficult to imagine that other potential cases will easily meet the criteria for the revised version of preventive war. Foreign policy officials, including the president, explicitly and implicitly imposed significant limits on the application of the new strategy. Preventive use of force must be the last resort against an internationally agreed upon grave threat, and it must follow tireless diplomatic efforts. The United States has already announced, as evidence of North Korean and Iranian nuclear proliferation mounts, that it seeks nonmilitary solutions to the threats emanating from the other members of the "axis of evil." Perhaps most important, government officials by their words and deeds instilled a deliberative standard for preventive military attacks.

Some onlookers, euphoric about the immediate military successes, wanted the United States to push ahead and confront Syria in the first weeks of the Iraq War. Cooler heads obviously prevailed, and the growing strength of the insurgency in Iraq tempered even the most vocal war enthusiasts. However, the lack of significant public debate about Syria may also have played a meaningful role in limiting the combat to Iraq. George H. W. Bush's former secretary of state, Lawrence Eagleburger, told the British Broadcasting Corporation at the time that the American political system, which requires public input into such policy choices, precluded this exact possibility: "If George Bush (Jr.) decided he was going to turn the troops loose on Syria and Iran after that he would last in office for about 15 minutes. In fact if President Bush were to try that now even I would think that he ought to be impeached. You

can't get away with that sort of thing in this democracy." Eagleburger added
that the idea was "ridiculous," given the "furor" that preceded the Iraq War,
and that "public opinion and the public, still, on these issues rules [*sic*]."[31]

BACKGROUND TO THE IRAQ WEAPONS DEBATE

The primary rationale for the US attack on Iraq was Saddam Hussein's alleged NBC weapons stockpiles and programs. Iraq's suspected connections
to international terrorism also played a secondary role in justifying US action. The attack was not sold primarily as a humanitarian or democratizing mission, even though Hussein was a horrible tyrant. Former deputy
secretary of defense Paul Wolfowitz, widely viewed as one of the key policy
architects of the war, told an interviewer that "the criminal treatment of the
Iraqi people . . . is a reason to help the Iraqis but it's not a reason to put
American kids' lives at risk, certainly not on the scale we did it." Wolfowitz,
describing the dynamics and arguments advanced in the internal discussion,
further acknowledged that Iraq's alleged links to external terrorism were the
rationale presenting "the most disagreement within the bureaucracy."[32] Iraq,
of course, has not been implicated in the 9/11 terrorist attacks, and very little
evidence tied Saddam Hussein to al-Qaida. Ultimately, the National Commission on Terrorist Attacks upon the United States (commonly known as
the 9/11 Commission) reported in the summer of 2004 that "to date we have
seen no evidence that these or the earlier contacts [between Iraqi officials and
al-Qaida members] ever developed into a collaborative operational relationship. Nor have we seen any evidence indicating that Iraq cooperated with al-
Qaida in developing or carrying out any attack against the United States."[33]
Thus it should not be surprising that the Bush administration, in the words
of Wolfowitz, "settled on the one issue that everyone could agree on which
was weapons of mass destruction as the core reason" for war.[34] Secretary
Powell made an even stronger statement about the centrality of this rationale
in October 2002, in a nationally televised interview: "All we are interested in
is getting rid of those weapons of mass destruction. We think the Iraqi people
would be a lot better off with a different leader, a different regime, but the
principal offense here are weapons of mass destruction . . . the major issue
before us is disarmament."[35] Additionally, in his last prewar press conference
in March 2003, President Bush bluntly declared, "Our mission is clear in
Iraq. Should we have to go in, our mission is very clear: disarmament."[36]

Despite the administration's numerous assertions about great and growing threats from Iraqi arsenals, many more of which will be highlighted below,
it now looks as if the case for attacking Iraq was built upon various distortions

of the public debate. Put simply, the world's most dangerous weapons seem not to have been present in Iraq.

Obviously, a comprehensive review of the quality of the prewar intelligence data about Iraq's unconventional weapons would take much more space than is available here. The US Senate Select Committee on Intelligence, for example, issued a 511-page report on this topic in July 2004, and the final report of the US weapons search team in the fall of 2004 includes more than 1,000 pages. The next section of this chapter focuses on the major public distortions of the intelligence about alleged Iraqi nuclear weapons, which were arguably the most egregious points raised in the debate. The emphasis is on the way the Bush administration publicly employed the information available to it, rather than on the accuracy of the intelligence itself. However, it should certainly be noted that an array of governmental and nongovernmental agencies, as well as various academics and journalists, have reviewed the prewar intelligence data and have concluded that it was rife with substantial errors that inflated the threat. For example, the systematic evaluation of the prewar intelligence about Iraq's alleged unconventional weapons and terrorist connections by the Senate Select Committee on Intelligence found that the information was quite flawed. Put simply, Iraq did not have threatening stockpiles, and there was very little reason to believe that it would have worrisome programs in the foreseeable future. The committee devoted substantial attention to the National Intelligence Estimate (NIE) dated 1 October 2002, which was the most important summary of prewar data prepared by the intelligence community (IC) and made available to American policy-makers:

The major key judgments in the NIE, particularly that Iraq "is reconstituting its nuclear program," "has chemical and biological weapons," was developing an unmanned aerial vehicle (UAV) "probably intended to deliver biological warfare agents," and that "all key aspects—research & development (R&D), production, and weaponization—of Iraq's offensive biological weapons (BW) program are active and that most elements are larger and more advanced than they were before the Gulf War," either overstated, or were not supported by, the underlying intelligence reporting provided to the Committee.[37]

The Senate committee additionally concluded that the IC's conclusions reflected pessimistic biases and serious mistakes of tradecraft. Moreover, the NIE did not adequately explain the uncertainties surrounding the quality of the evidence. Analysts from the Carnegie Endowment for International Peace and other nongovernmental organizations (NGOs) that have reviewed the publicly available data also concluded that the case for war against Iraq was built on very weak evidence.[38]

After more than eighteen months of ongoing US government inspections by hundreds of highly trained personnel, the Iraq Survey Group (ISG)
turned up evidence only of "dozens of weapons of mass destruction–related
program activities" rather than actual Iraqi weapons or weapons-production
infrastructure.[39] The original chief weapons inspector, David Kay, left Iraq
in December 2003 and resigned his position a month later. Kay apparently
considered the search to be a pointless waste of time. He subsequently gave
numerous interviews and speeches stating that Iraq had no weapons to find
and that an enormous prewar intelligence failure occurred. In July 2004, Kay
declared that the Bush administration should abandon its "delusional hope"
of finding such weapons in Iraq.[40] Finally, on 30 September 2004, Kay's
replacement, Charles Duelfer, presented the *Comprehensive Report of the
Special Advisor to the DCI on Iraq's WMD.*[41] While Duelfer emphasizes that
Saddam Hussein very badly wanted various unconventional weapons, and
that corruption in the oil-for-food program may have provided an economic
resource base to develop such arms in the future, the regime destroyed its
chemical stockpile and ended its nuclear program in 1991. It then abandoned
its biological program in 1996 after the destruction of the key research facility. Duelfer's report also concluded that Hussein wanted such weapons to
assure Iraq's position in the region and to threaten Iran, not to attack the
United States.

Given that the intelligence undergirding the central argument for war
was fatally flawed, the public debate about the need for war was bound to
be greatly distorted. Under ordinary circumstances, third-party observers
should perhaps absolve errors made by any administration that relies upon
faulty information, so long as it uses the best available data in a manner that
reflects good faith. How can policy-makers, after all, be blamed as consumers
for the errors of those that produce the poor intelligence? In the pages to
follow, on the other hand, I argue that the Bush administration knowingly
overstated some of the IC's most important assessments of the Iraqi threat
and also employed dubious rhetorical strategies that ultimately served to
overemphasize alleged weapons developments in the public debate. This had
a serious negative effect on the public deliberations.

THE INFLATION OF THE NUCLEAR THREAT

As former intelligence analyst and National Security Council staffer Kenneth
M. Pollack has argued, Iraq's alleged nuclear program "was the real linchpin
of the Bush Administration's case for an invasion."[42] Indeed, a recent scholarly
study found that many members of Congress "gave the nuclear threat as the
main or one of the main reasons for their votes" supporting the war resolution

in October 2002.[43] Yet it now seems virtually certain that the administration publicly exaggerated the status of the Iraqi nuclear program. Officials also strategically manipulated their prewar rhetoric about the Iraqi threat so as to mislead the general public and mass media. This often meant, for instance, blurring certain kinds of policy distinctions that would otherwise have suggested greater caution in the pathway to war. In many cases, moreover, it meant emphasizing the strong certainty rather than the real ambiguity about key evidence and thus implying the worst about the Iraqi threat.

Though the Bush administration apparently started planning for war against Iraq soon after the 9/11 attacks, and frequently claimed that the ongoing "war on terror" would have to include states like Iraq that allegedly sponsored terrorism, it began the serious public discussion about Iraq threats in late summer 2002. On 26 August 2002, for example, Vice President Richard Cheney delivered a widely noted speech to the Veterans of Foreign Wars (VFW). In that address, Cheney declared with great certainty that "we now know that Saddam has resumed his efforts to acquire nuclear weapons. . . . Many of us are convinced that Saddam will acquire nuclear weapons fairly soon."[44] This comment preceded by about five weeks the production of the NIE that was later carefully scrutinized by the Senate Select Committee on Intelligence. Soon, the image of a potential "mushroom cloud" caused by an Iraqi bomb was invoked prominently by both the president and by National Security Advisor Condoleezza Rice. While President Bush used the phrase in his 7 October 2002 speech in Cincinnati, Rice had made worldwide headlines when she uttered these words earlier in an interview with CNN on 8 September 2002: "The problem here is that there will always be some uncertainty about how quickly he [Saddam Hussein] can acquire nuclear weapons. But we don't want the smoking gun to be a mushroom cloud."[45] Again, Rice's comments preceded the production of the NIE by many weeks.

The administration strongly implied that the worst fears were related to very real threats. The president himself declared in mid-September: "Should his [Saddam Hussein's] regime acquire fissile material, it would be able to build a nuclear weapon within a year."[46] Just days before the war was launched, on the Sunday morning NBC television program *Meet the Press,* Vice President Cheney told journalist Tim Russert that Saddam Hussein "has been absolutely devoted to trying to acquire nuclear weapons. And we believe he has, in fact, reconstituted nuclear weapons."[47] Altogether, these various statements surely helped create the very strong and false impression that Iraq had an active and dangerous nuclear weapons program that was precariously close to success. According to USA Today/CNN/Gallup national poll conducted 31 January to 2 February 2003, just after the president's State of the Union address, 28 percent of the respondents were "certain" that

"Iraq has nuclear weapons," while another 49 percent said that it was "likely, but not certain."[48]

The nuclear threat was not nearly as grave as the administration suggested, however, and this was fairly well known to foreign policy elites prior to the war. Indeed, before the terror attacks of 9/11, and thus before the fall 2002 buildup to war, some prominent Bush administration officials had publicly asserted that Iraq had not developed threatening programs. Secretary of State Powell, for example, noted in early 2001 that "the sanctions exist—not for the purpose of hurting the Iraqi people, but for the purpose of keeping in check Saddam Hussein's ambitions toward developing weapons of mass destruction. . . . And frankly they have worked. He has not developed any significant capability with respect to weapons of mass destruction."[49] Condoleezza Rice, while serving in 2000 as George Bush's primary foreign policy adviser, had written in *Foreign Affairs* that "rogue regimes" like Iraq were "living on borrowed time, so there need be no sense of panic about them. Rather, the first line of defense should be a clear and classical statement of deterrence—if they do acquire WMD, their weapons will be unusable because any attempt to use them will bring national obliteration."[50] These were bold statements not only about Iraqi incapability but also about the unimportance of Iraqi threats, even if the regime had developed nuclear capabilities.

How could these Bush administration advisers and officials have made such definitively dismissive statements about Iraqi weapons? Put simply, they apparently relied upon the latest information produced by the IC, which did not believe Iraq was a serious threat. As recently as December 2001, the pertinent NIE declared that "Iraq did not appear to have reconstituted its nuclear weapons program."[51] According to the Senate Select Intelligence Committee, this same finding appeared in various yearly reports from 1997 until drafts of the 2002 NIE were circulated around the IC in late September of that year. It seems quite clear, in retrospect, that intelligence sources depended greatly upon the international weapons inspectors who were in Iraq through the end of 1998, when they were asked to withdraw by the Clinton administration so the United States could commence bombing.[52] Working with the United Nations Special Commission (UNSCOM), which was established in 1991 after the Persian Gulf War, the International Atomic Energy Agency (IAEA) had essentially completed its nuclear disarmament mission in Iraq by December 1998: "By the time the inspectors were withdrawn, the IAEA had been able to draw a comprehensive and coherent picture of Iraq's past nuclear weapons programme, and to dismantle the programme. The IAEA had destroyed, removed or rendered harmless all of the physical capabilities of Iraq to produce amounts of nuclear-weapons-usable nuclear material of any practical significance."[53]

In short, the IAEA found by the time of its withdrawal on 16 December 1998 that Iraq had "significant hurdles" to clear before it could build a nuclear device. The various conclusions were quite authoritative. In addition to overseeing the destruction of Iraq's gas centrifuge program that had been designed for enriching uranium, the IAEA concluded that "all nuclear material of significance to Iraq's nuclear weapons programme was verified and fully accounted for, and all nuclear-weapons-usable nuclear material (plutonium and high enriched uranium) was removed from Iraq." Furthermore, "There were no indications that there remained in Iraq any physical capability for the production of amounts of nuclear-weapons-usable nuclear material of any practical significance." Perhaps most startling, at least politically, Iraq's official disclosures about its nuclear program matched the IAEA findings. Iraq was a disarmed nuclear state almost completely in compliance with its international obligations by 1999. Moreover, even after IAEA inspectors withdrew from Iraq in 1998, they were able over the next four years to confirm the continued sealed status of Iraq's known nuclear materials (such as its stores of nonenriched uranium).

The intelligence thus supported the statements by Rice and Powell in 2000 and 2001, which dismissed the threats from Iraqi NBC weapons. How then did members of the Bush administration come to make the very frightening claims documented above about Iraq's nuclear program? Did any new information about Iraq's arms support new interpretations of the threat? Arguably, this is precisely what happened. The US IC's assessments did not dispute the IAEA's successes in Iraq or state that the country was making progress on its nuclear program until the 2002 NIE.[54] That assessment, however, published 1 October 2002, completely reversed course and found that "Baghdad began reconstituting its nuclear program shortly after the departure of UNSCOM inspectors in December 1998." Since the NIE reports over the previous five years had suggested that Iraq might be able to build a nuclear bomb within five to seven years once its program was reconstituted, this was a potentially earth-shattering declaration. In addition, the NIE had with "high confidence" concluded that Iraq was "continuing, and in some areas expanding," its various arms programs and that the IC was not fully able to detect "portions of these weapons programs."[55]

Iraq's disarmament was not clearly apparent to US officials until well after the war's early goals had been achieved and the United States and its coalition partners occupied Baghdad. American weapons inspectors returned to Iraq in March and April 2003, in the form of the Seventy-fifth Exploitation Task Force and as covert Task Force 20. These groups were succeeded and supplemented, respectively, by the larger ISG in June 2003. Only after months of inspections did it become evident to these agencies and inspectors that Saddam Hussein had not, in fact, made meaningful progress toward a nuclear program—nor really to any significant unconventional weapons program. David Kay testified about the nuclear dimension for the ISG in October 2003: "[W]e have not uncovered evidence that Iraq undertook significant post-1998 steps to actually build nuclear weapons or produce fissile material."[56] Kay added in January 2004 that Iraq's "program-related" activity in this area merely involved the construction of new buildings that could eventually host a nuclear program. "It was not a reconstituted, full-blown nuclear program."[57] Charles Duelfer's fall 2004 report goes much further, finding that Iraq's ability even to reconstitute a nuclear weapons program "progressively decayed" after 1991, when Saddam Hussein ended Iraq's program.[58]

This timeline, of course, is missing some critical information that undermines the credibility of the Bush administration's prewar statements. Most important, many of the most politically charged and definitive statements occurred before the IC produced a new report. Thus the administration's public assessments of the Iraq nuclear program were substantially different from the secret December 2001 NIE, and may have served to shape the later NIE. Democratic senators John D. Rockefeller, Carl Levin, and Richard Durbin noted the importance of the timing in their addendum to the 2004 Senate Select Intelligence Committee report: "In the months before the production of the Intelligence Community's October 2002 Estimate, Administration officials undertook a relentless public campaign which repeatedly characterized the Iraq weapons of mass destruction program in more ominous and threatening terms than the Intelligence Community analysis substantiated." The senators added, "These high-profile statements . . . were made in advance of any meaningful intelligence analysis and created pressure on the Intelligence Community to conform to the certainty contained in the pronouncements."[59]

Even in October 2002, the IC did not think that Iraq had a nuclear weapon or that it was likely to acquire one any time soon. The threat was not imminent. The national intelligence officer for strategic and nuclear programs told the Senate Select Intelligence Committee that Iraq had not fully reconstituted its nuclear program immediately after the inspections ended in 1998 and that the "five to seven year clock" on Iraq's nuclear capability did not start running until 2002. As a result, the same NIE noted with "moderate confidence" that "Iraq does not have a nuclear weapon or sufficient material to make one but is likely to have a weapon by 2007 to 2009."[60] The NIE also included "alternative views" of some of the agencies that helped put together the intelligence assessment. The State Department's Bureau of Intelligence and Research (INR) was "unable to predict when Iraq could acquire a nuclear device or weapon," but argued that it was not persuaded by the key pieces of evidence thought to be critical to the changed assessment.[61] Below, this internal dissent will be discussed in more detail. Note, however, that Senators Rockefeller, Levin, and Durbin allege that "the qualifications the Intelligence Community placed on what it assessed about Iraq's links to terrorism and alleged weapons of mass destruction were spurned by top Bush Administration officials."[62]

Also missing from the narrative is the return of IAEA inspectors to Iraq in late 2002 and through March 2003. These international nuclear weapons inspectors operated freely in prewar Iraq and visited over 140 Iraqi sites looking for signs of nuclear activity. IAEA inspectors also conducted interviews with Iraqi scientists and other personnel of interest, and reviewed a significant amount of written documentation related to Iraq's nuclear program that was provided by the regime. Thus it is very significant that before the war began, the IAEA concluded that Iraq had no nuclear program. In January 2003, agency director Mohamed ElBaradei told the UN Security Council, "We have to date found no evidence that Iraq has revived its nuclear weapon programme since the elimination of the program in the 1990's."[63] By 7 March 2003, ElBaradei was able to further cement this finding: "After three months of intrusive inspections, we have to date found no evidence or plausible indication of the revival of a nuclear weapon program in Iraq."[64] While Vice President Cheney sometimes publicly disparaged the work of the IAEA, the administration offered no detailed public critique of these prewar inspections and continued to rely upon the work of the IAEA to assure nonproliferation goals in North Korea and Iran.[65] As noted above, US intelligence agencies were quite dependent upon on-site inspections from Iraq throughout the 1990s. Moreover, these inspections should have been highly credible. As Kenneth Pollack succinctly noted, "nuclear-weapons production is extremely difficult to conceal."[66]

DISTORTING THE DETAILS

The Bush administration overstated the intelligence about a number of specific elements of the Iraqi nuclear program. For example, in his September speech to the UN, President Bush referenced Iraq's apparent pursuit of aluminum tubes in the global marketplace, which Bush alleged would be "used to enrich uranium for a nuclear weapon." In the following sentence, the president implied that this was a particularly urgent problem: "Should Iraq acquire fissile material, it would be able to build a nuclear weapon within a year."[67] That same month, Condoleezza Rice declared that these tubes were "only really suited for nuclear weapons programs, centrifuge programs."[68]

In an apparent reference to these tubes, Vice President Cheney, just days before the first anniversary of the 11 September attacks, declared on *Meet the Press*: "[W]e do know, *with absolute certainty,* that he [Saddam Hussein] is using his procurement system to acquire the equipment he needs in order to enrich uranium to build a nuclear weapon."[69] While Iraq apparently sought thousands of aluminum tubes that might withstand great heat and stress, the American IC was not uniformly convinced that these tubes were sought to build nuclear weapons. Their eighty-one millimeter diameter and one meter length arguably made them a poor fit for enriching uranium, but they did seem appropriate for a 1950s-era centrifuge design. Eventually, Department of Energy (DOE) analysts discovered that the tubes were a perfect fit for their well-known eighty-one millimeter conventional rocket program and that Iraq had literally tens of thousands of these tubes in its arsenal during the previous decade. In January 2003, former IAEA weapons inspector David Albright, who in the words of the *Washington Post*, "has investigated Iraq's past nuclear programs extensively," told that paper that the information about the tubes appeared to serve only the administration's political goals: "In this case, I fear that the information was put out there for a short-term political goal: to convince people that Saddam Hussein is close to acquiring nuclear weapons."[70]

Within the United States, both the DOE's Office of Intelligence and the State Department's INR concluded before the war that the tubes were "probably not intended for a nuclear program."[71] The IAEA physically inspected the aluminum tubes and concluded in March 2003 that "extensive field investigation and document analysis have failed to uncover any evidence that Iraq intended to use these 81 mm tubes for any project other than the reverse engineering of rockets."[72] Moreover, the IAEA found that even if Iraq had tried to make these poorly sized tubes work in some kind of uranium enrichment process, "it was highly unlikely that Iraq could have achieved the considerable redesign needed to use them in a revived centrifuge programme." US intelligence services learned in February 2003 that the aluminum tubes were, as Iraq had declared, exactly like the tubes it had used earlier for its rocket program.[73] In January 2004, David Kay testified that it was "more than probable" that the aluminum tubes were intended for a conventional missile program rather than a centrifuge.[74]

Following Vice President Cheney's lead, Secretary of State Powell offered similarly weak intelligence about Iraq's nuclear program in his widely acclaimed presentation to the UN Security Council. The speech was designed to present the administration's best evidence about Iraqi threats and was thoroughly vetted by the CIA and the State Department's INR, which was perhaps the internal agency most skeptical about Iraq's weapons capabilities. Indeed, the INR sought the removal of dozens of "incorrect or dubious claims" from the speech draft and later reported that twenty-eight were either deleted or changed to eliminate its concerns.[75] This attentiveness almost certainly added to the credibility of the February 2003 presentation, as Powell's dramatic appearance was widely viewed as convincing and compelling, even by domestic political opponents of the administration.[76] A survey by *Editor and Publisher* magazine found that literally the day after Powell's speech, "daily newspapers in their editorials dramatically shifted their views to support the Bush administration's hard-line stance on Iraq."[77]

Despite these public relations successes, however, a substantial portion of the secretary's claims have not held up to critical scrutiny. Consider first the acquisition of magnets thought to be useful for Iraq's centrifuge program for enriching uranium. According to the Senate Select Intelligence Committee, this was the only new evidence the secretary presented relating to Iraq's nuclear program:

We also have intelligence from multiple sources that Iraq is attempting to acquire magnets and high-speed balancing machines. Both items can be used in a gas centrifuge program to enrich uranium. In 1999 and 2000, Iraqi officials negotiated with firms in Romania, India, Russia and Slovenia for the purchase of a magnet production plant. Iraq wanted the plant to produce magnets weighing 20 to 30 grams. That's the same weight as the magnets used in Iraq's gas centrifuge program before the Gulf War. This incident, linked with the tubes, is another indicator of Iraq's attempt to reconstitute its nuclear weapons program.[78]

Based on the DOE's prewar analysis, however, the magnets were significantly smaller than those Iraq would have needed to use with the eighty-one millimeter aluminum tubes and were no more than half the weight of magnets Iraq had previously used in its centrifuge damper designs.[79] Similar sorts of technical and production constraints were reported by the IAEA's ElBaradei in his 2003 public presentations before the start of the war. Based on physical examination, the IAEA was able to observe strict limits on the utility of the magnets that Iraq was supposedly attempting to import and/or manufacture. Six months after Powell's UN presentation, an Associated Press analysis of the major evidence found that the secretary's entire briefing file "looks thin" in retrospect.[80] Powell himself acknowledged in September 2005 that he feels "terrible" about the presentation, which he considers a painful "blot" on his record.[81]

Perhaps the best-known distortion of the intelligence related to the alleged Iraqi importation of tons of uranium from Niger. Someone, as yet unnamed, forged documents purporting to support this claim. In his January 2003 State of the Union address, President Bush uttered these words, "The British government has learned that Saddam Hussein recently sought significant quantities of uranium from Africa."[82] The truth about this dubious assertion become a major political issue in the United States in 2003. The *Washington Post* reported on 12 June 2003 that the CIA had dispatched a retired ambassador, who was not named in the article, to Africa in 2002 in order to investigate the claim that Iraq had attempted to purchase uranium. Upon return, the official reportedly dismissed the alleged transaction.[83] In July, not long after Ambassador Joseph Wilson went public with his findings, CIA director George Tenet took personal responsibility for the faulty intelligence and acknowledged that the inclusion of this allegation "was a mistake."[84] News reports revealed that the CIA previously convinced the White House to remove a similar statement from the president's October 2002 speech in Cincinnati. As a result of these developments, administration officials publicly acknowledged the allegation was a mistake and retracted the president's claim: "Knowing all that we know now, the reference to Iraq's attempt to acquire uranium from Africa should not have been included in the State of the Union speech."[85]

Once again, however, those closely following the public debate before the war already knew the claims were dubious. The IAEA reported in early March—before the war began—that documents it received from the United States only one month earlier related to this alleged transaction were forgeries: "Based on thorough analysis, the IAEA has concluded, with the concurrence of outside experts, that these documents—which formed the basis for the reports of recent uranium transactions between Iraq and Niger—are in fact not authentic. We have therefore concluded that these specific allegations are unfounded."[86] Had the US IC been offered the chance to incorporate evidence based on the IAEA's latest on-site inspections, it too might have concluded before the war that Iraq had not, in fact, reconstituted its nuclear weaponry. Likewise, if the public debate had centered upon the significant doubts about the nature of the threat, domestic support for the war might have collapsed, and the administration might have aborted or delayed the attack.

CONCLUSION

The Bush administration's case for war against Iraq was significantly distorted by the public manipulation of dubious intelligence and other communicative misdeeds. Specifically, prior to launching a war in mid-March 2003, the Bush administration greatly inflated the threat from Iraq's nuclear program. A large number of general and specific claims turned out not to be well supported by the available intelligence. While it also appears that the intelligence itself was flawed, as the Senate Select Committee on Intelligence concluded in 2004, White House officials blatantly oversold the status of the overall Iraqi nuclear program. Its hyperbole failed to include important caveats that were included in the intelligence data and gave the false impression that Iraq was very close to making nuclear weapons.

Moreover, the administration apparently failed to live up to its own standards for employing the preventive military strategy. From fall 2002, officials claimed that the United States would employ the new "preemptive" strike doctrine only as a last resort, after working with allies to establish the existence of a grave threat amenable only to military action. The president himself called for public and global debate about the nature of the threat and the need for a response. Yet by distorting the evidence that framed the debate, the administration almost completely undercut the role of public deliberation. The certainty in their public statements served to drown out informed critics and skeptics like former weapons inspector Scott Ritter, Cambridge academic Glen Rangwala, and even the IAEA, whose assessments turned out to be far more accurate than the administration's about Iraq's unconventional weapons threats.

The next time a US administration contemplates preventive attack, it will almost surely find itself engaged in a more spirited debate. Fooled once, the mass media, the Congress, and the general public will have strong incentives to seek out information that at least challenges the claims presented by the executive branch. Moreover, even if few skeptics doubt the veracity of the publicly available intelligence, analysts will point out some of the difficulties in building international support for using force, financing and staffing war and nation-building missions, and dealing with the potentially violent aftermath of even successful attacks against particular worrisome threats. Ideally, an open and inclusive debate about the prospect of using preventive military force will create public consensus for the most appropriate policy course.

Essentially, the public sphere failed to stop the US attack of Iraq because most domestic audiences did not have access to accurate information. The administration behaved in a manner that was strategically deceptive. Most of the evidence about Iraq's nuclear program was classified, and the administration monopolized control of those secrets. To understand how this might have worked differently, consider one of the few occasions when the administration's monopoly on information was successfully contested. In September 2002, standing next to British prime minister Tony Blair, President Bush erroneously claimed that the IAEA had previously produced a report that Iraq was "six months away from developing a [nuclear] weapon. I don't know what more evidence we need."[87] However, no such report existed, and an agency spokesperson quickly denied this specific claim. The *Washington Times* interviewed Mark Gwozdecky of the IAEA and reported on 27 September 2002, "There's never been a report like that issued from this agency. We've never put a time frame on how long it might take Iraq to construct a nuclear weapon in 1998."[88] The administration did not repeat this claim again, though it did sometimes point more generically to IAEA findings from the early 1990s.

This chapter has focused on the Bush administration's use of evidence about Iraqi nuclear weapons, but it could just as easily have applied to its public claims about Iraq's chemical or biological weapons, missile program, or ties to al-Qaida. The Senate Select Intelligence Committee found similar shortcomings in most of the key evidence undergirding the administration's various assertions. Furthermore, many of the independent organizations that have produced reports criticizing the content of US intelligence assessments have additionally provided quite negative evaluations of the administration's prewar employment of that intelligence. Their findings often suggest, as one prominent report found, that the administration "systematically misrepresented the threat from Iraq's WMD and ballistic missile program."[89] Democratic senators Rockefeller, Levin, and Durbin, who served on the Senate Select Committee on Intelligence, wrote an "additional view" to the lengthy document that publicly accuses the administration of distorting the intelligence: "By selectively releasing and mischaracterizing intelligence information that supported an Iraq–al-Qaeda collaboration while continuing to keep information classified and out of the public realm that did not, the Administration distorted intelligence to persuade Americans into believing the actions of al-Qaeda and Iraq were indistinguishable, 'part of the same threat,' as Deputy Secretary Wolfowitz asserted."[90] Former State Department INR official Greg Thielmann, who served Colin Powell until September 2002, likewise charges that "the administration was grossly distorting the intelligence."[91] Thielmann reflects at greater length on various intelligence questions in a later chapter in this volume.

Some members of the administration apparently attempted to bypass bureaucratic checks within the government so as to emphasize the intelligence that favored its anti-Iraq position. In practice, this apparently meant that officials cherry-picked pieces of the most worrisome available intelligence and then "stovepiped" that information to top-level government leaders, in order to bypass skeptical intelligence analysts. This allegedly occurred even if the evidence was of questionable accuracy or obtained from dubious and self-interested sources provided by representatives of the exiled Iraqi National Congress.[92] According to former National Security Council member Kenneth Pollack, "The Bush officials who created the OSP [Pentagon's Office of Special Plans] gave its reports directly to those in the highest levels of government, often passing raw, unverified intelligence straight to the Cabinet level as gospel. Senior Administration officials made public statements based on these reports—reports that the larger IC knew to be erroneous."[93]

American intervention in Iraq based on faulty and distorted intelligence has almost certainly created new international security dangers. Most important, the credibility of US intelligence gathering (and analysis) might be seriously undermined. This is critically important to the future of the preventive war doctrine. As David Kay points out, "If you cannot rely on good, accurate intelligence that is credible to the American people and to others abroad, you certainly cannot have a policy of preemption. . . . Pristine intelligence—good, accurate intelligence—is a fundamental benchstone of any sort of policy of preemption to even be thought about."[94] Bush administration officials, of course, continue to argue that a firm and clear public declaration about preemption may be genuinely important to an effective antiterror strategy. They promote the strategy as a means to deter undesirable behavior by foes—and perhaps even to compel more desirable behavior. Their argument for prevention goes well beyond deterrence, however. Confronted by a genuine threat, it might at some future date be necessary for the United States to strike before such threats are fully apparent. Since 11 September 2001, in fact, US leaders have often expressed concern that deterrence will fail to mitigate threats from terrorists and the outlaw states that provide them safe harbor.

Officials now argue that the mere prospect of preventive action has already served as an effective warning to some potentially hostile states. As former secretary of state Powell has written, an important "reason for including the notion of preemption in the NSS was to convey to our adversaries that they were in big trouble."[95] In his 2004 State of the Union address, President Bush specifically credited the attack on Iraq for the success in convincing Libya to abandon its unconventional weapons programs: "Nine months of intense negotiations involving the United States and Great Britain succeeded with Libya, while 12 years of diplomacy with Iraq did not. And one reason is clear: For diplomacy to be effective, words must be credible, and no one can now doubt the word of America."[96]

Except, of course, other states do doubt America's words, or at least the words about threats related to proliferation and terrorism. As Nikolas Gvosdev noted in 2003, diplomats around the world now quite publicly doubt the veracity of US claims in regard to North Korea.[97] Though Powell charges that critics distort the significance of the administration's preemption policy, it is even clearer that Bush officials have sent very mixed messages. Too often the administration's own words and deeds since the beginning of 2002 have served to limit US options by undermining American credibility. Because of the all-too-apparent distortions in the Iraq debate, it may well be impossible to convince even close American allies to address threats the United States identifies.

Given the complete demonization of Saddam Hussein's regime, and the twelve years of sanctions against Iraq, it is difficult to imagine the United States now making a convincing case for attacking any other state absent an imminent threat. Hussein was unfavorably compared to Adolf Hitler and Joseph Stalin, he attacked multiple neighbors, gassed his own people, allegedly attempted to assassinate a former American president, and at one time had very advanced unconventional weapons programs, including a very worrisome nuclear program. If the United States could not rally the world behind a preventive attack against Iraq, and could not after the fact produce evidence of the grave dangers it had cited, it will not likely be able to convince many other states to help attack Iran, North Korea, Syria, or some other potential adversary.

7

On Justifying the
First Blow

TOM ROCKMORE

THE 2002 NATIONAL Security Strategy of the United States of America
(NSS 2002) authorizes first-strike, or preventive, military action under
the guise of providing a new and (substantially) different meaning to
the term "preemptive" warfare. In examining the distinction between preemptive and preventive military strikes, this chapter focuses on the justification of war of any kind. In the framework of the so-called war on terror, in
an unusual use of the term "preemption," what would ordinarily be called
preventive military action is currently being applied in the war against and
continuing occupation of Iraq. In standard usage in policy and scholarly
circles, as distinguished from the term "prevention," the term "preemption"
refers to a military strike that prevents an adversary from inflicting an attack that is imminent. A good analogy comes from martial arts. An attacker
begins an attack, say through launching a punch to the jaw; the person about
to be struck preempts the blow with a kick to the stomach of the attacker. A
preventive attack is one in which the attack is not expected in the immediate
future. For example, if the United States launched a "surgical strike" against
North Korea targeting all of its nuclear facilities and weapons (on the grounds
that it expected a nuclear attack from North Korea in six months), the US

attack would be considered preventive, not preemptive. Since in both cases
the adversary possesses the capacity and presumably desires to launch an
attack, one important difference between military preemption and military
prevention concerns whether the attack is imminent or only extremely likely
in the near future.

In the final analysis, war of any kind can only be justified on moral
grounds, which, on an average, ordinary interpretation restricts military action to defensive responses, or preemptive attacks.[1] By "moral" I have in mind
the well-known distinction between what one does (or conceivably could do)
and what one ought to do. Since all actions of any kind are not necessarily
moral, what one does or conceivably ought to can only be regarded as moral
if the principle that motivates one's acts is moral. This conception of morality
presupposes Scottish philosopher David Hume's notorious is-ought distinction, which has generated so much discussion. In simplest terms, suffice it
say that actions can be chosen for (and justified in terms of) prudential, utili-
tarian, religious, military, medical, political, legal, or other reasons. Actions
are said to be moral if and only if the principle on which they are chosen
concerns what ought to be the case. I will assume that in time of war, when
two or more countries are opposed in armed conflict, it is justified to take a
person's life if and only if to do so is the only realistic way to protect citizens
against the consequences of foreign aggression. I further argue that, from
this angle of vision, what is being called preemptive war in Iraq, and which
corresponds to a version of what until now has usually be called preventive
war, is simply unjustified.

WHAT IS "PREEMPTIVE" MILITARY ACTION?

Since the new national security doctrine radically revises standard terminology for a specific purpose, much of the work of this essay will consist in
analyzing the differences and consequences with respect to standard usage.
"Prevention" is an ordinary word that is usually employed with the sense of
stopping or arresting someone or something. "Preemption" is a less frequent
term that is usually often utilized with respect to property. Thus the right of
eminent domain can be exercised by a governmental entity in certain specifiable conditions. An example might be when a city or local government, in
order to build a road, expropriates property a citizen owns but does not desire
to sell.

In normal usage, the terms "prevention" and "preemption" function
asymmetrically. Ordinarily, "prevention" includes "preemption," but "preemption" does not, or normally does not, include "prevention." If I prevent
you from doing something, I am not usually preempting you in any way. Yet

if I preempt you, I am also preventing you. If this is correct, then it follows that "preemption" is a subclass within the wider concept of "prevention."

This link, which occurs in normal English usage, is apparently absent in normal scholarly discussion. In standard scholarly usage, the link between "prevention" and "preemption" is severed, since these terms refer to different types of military threats in different, discontinuous time frames. In NSS 2002, the link is reestablished since there, "preemption" is made to refer to the normal objects of both "preemption" and "prevention."

In a passage devoted to "weapons of mass destruction" (WMD), NSS 2002 says in part that "the US has long maintained the option of preemptive actions to counter a sufficient threat to our national security," and then adds, "even if uncertainty remains as to the time and place of the enemy's attack . . . to forestall or prevent such attacks, the United States will, if necessary, act preemptively."[2] What this amounts to is unclear and controversial. The unclarity and controversy concern both the precise nature of the new doctrine and its desirability as a relevant part of NSS 2002. In part, the difficulty is purely linguistic and is due to the fact that ordinary words are arguably being used in unusual and possibly inconsistent ways.

A rough way to put the point is that it is usually accepted that preemptive military action, that is, military action directed against a clear and present danger, is acceptable, but preventive military action, that is, military action directed against a future but not imminent danger, one that may or may not someday occur, is not legitimate. The same point can be restated in terms of the intuitive test of a clear and present danger. Preemptive military action is justified in cases of a clear and present danger that currently exists. But preventive military action, which reacts by anticipation to a potential danger that may never materialize, that is, may never become a clear and present danger, is not justified.

The difficulty in understanding preemptive military action is that NSS 2002 uses this term in an unusual, nonstandard sense. This revision specifically authorizes so-called preemptive military action by calling preemptive that which, in normal usage, falls under the heading of prevention. As a result of this revision, there are two purely linguistic changes, which, taken together, result in a doctrine that specifically authorizes what used to be called preventive military action. On the one hand, the old distinction between the terms "preemption" and "prevention" is simply obliterated, since "preemption" now covers what earlier was known as preemption as well as prevention—that is, both a clear and present danger and a possible future danger. On the other hand, as a consequence of the new usage of "preemption," preemption replaces what used to be called prevention.

Scholars are clearly confused about what is being said as well as its lessons and consequences. A number of observers, including Chomsky, Kröning, Freedman, Schlesinger, Knight, and Crawford, detect a deliberate effort to conflate doctrines of preventive and preemptive war.[3] According to Noam Chomsky, who employs the terms "prevention" and "preemption" in their ordinary scholarly senses, the new strategy authorizes preventive but not preemptive war.[4] Chomsky restates a more developed version of this claim in a recent book by utilizing the term "preemption" in the new, nonstandard way outlined in NSS 2002. In referring to the difference between preemptive war ("whatever that might be")—he imagines a case in which Russian bombers are approaching the United States with clearly aggressive intent—and preventive war ("which falls within the category of war crimes"), where the latter justifies "the use of military force to eliminate an imagined or invented threat."[5] Volker Kröning, a member of the German Bundestag, refers to the US Department of Defense's own *Official Dictionary of Military Terms* to suggest, plausibly, that the new US doctrine really favors preventive war.[6] Lawrence Freedman thinks that the new US use of "preemption" means "prevention," as when steps are taken to prevent disease before it starts, such as through vaccination.[7]

The scholarly confusion is warranted since the term "preemptive" is being used, perhaps deliberately, in a nonstandard way that extends and broadens the justification for the United States to wage war against real or imagined adversaries. The consequence is to turn on its head the very idea that military action should be defensive only—hence, initiated in response to an attack already under way or at the very least one already looming or about to occur—substituting in its place a principle that authorizes attacks on adversaries in response to no attack at all. The result, which is arguably deliberately sought in the revised doctrine, is to extend the legitimacy that would normally be accorded to a preemptive strike, understood as a response to a clear and present danger, which no one other than a pacifist normally questions, to what would normally be regarded as a preventive strike, whose justification is not automatic, and which requires a highly unusual case by case defense as well as a general justification. On the contrary, as a result of the new language, in simply conflating what would normally be regarded as preemptive military strikes with what would normally be regarded as preventive military strikes, the doctrine now in force obliterates any difference in authorizing the extension of what would normally be a reaction to a clear and present danger, hence to an actual situation, to be extended to any potential situation whatsoever.

The new doctrine deserves careful scrutiny. The statement that "the US has long maintained the option of preemptive action to counter a sufficient threat to our national security" both conflates the normal use of the terms "preemption" and "prevention" as well as suggesting that a threat of any kind invites a military response when it crosses an unspecified sufficient threshold. As the doctrine is worded, crossing a sufficient threshold might include a specific threat, such as the verified use or even simply the discovery of nuclear, biological, or chemical (NBC) weapons in Iraq, which in turn justifies military action to eliminate threats posing a clear and present danger. Or it might include reference to the bare possibility that though Iraq does not now possess NBC weapons, it might conceivably have such weapons at an unspecified future time. In the latter case, there is no clear and present danger, though such a danger might exist at some point in the future. The NSS 2002 seems to leave what is being said completely indefinite in adding, "even if uncertainty remains as to the time and place of the enemy's attack."[8] It is reasonable to infer that the change in terminology, and hence military doctrine, is not accidental, but intentional, a strategic move designed to gain further space for military action that would not otherwise be permissible. The claim being made shifts attention from a clear and present danger— from the response to an immediate threat—to a threat that is situated in an indeterminate future, without distinction between these two possibilities.

My view presupposes that there is a relevant difference between an immediate threat, which in fact presents a clear and present danger, and an undefined future threat, which at some later time will, or at least possibly might, become a clear and present danger, but which does not now present that characteristic. In other words, the revised version of NSS 2002 can reasonably be construed as referring not only to presently existing threats, which have already "materialized" as it were, and which call for immediate action, but also to future threats that might never "materialize," but against which military action is justified. It seems reasonable to suppose that though many things are indeed possible, and the security of the United States might later be threatened in many different ways, some of these possible threats will never become actual. It seems obvious that if Iraq did not possess unconventional weaponry at the time it was attacked by the United States, as a result of the attack and the subsequent occupation it is highly unlikely to possess them in the near or even in the distant future.

The distinction on which my claim rests is controversial. Some observers might not want to admit my assumption that there is a difference between military action in regard to a clear and present danger and military action in regard to a danger located only in an indeterminate future. This distinction, which many find crucial, can be denied in various ways. One is to say that the mere capacity to develop such weapons is, or at least should be regarded as, tantamount to actually possessing them. A further, more extreme claim is that there is no difference between having such weapons at a time in the past and having them again in the future. In an interview with Diane Sawyer on ABC television, President Bush, who was obviously interested in justifying the invasion of Iraq, took both approaches simultaneously. In answer to the "hard fact that there were WMD, as opposed to the possibility that [Saddam] might move to acquire these weapons," the president's considered response was, "What's the difference?"[9] He then added: "I'm telling you I made the right decision for America because Saddam Hussein used weapons of mass destruction and invaded Kuwait."[10] The first passage in effect says that there is no difference between possessing NBC weapons and conceivably acquiring them later, or between a mere potential to possess weapons and actually possessing them, since in both cases military action is equally justified. The second, more extreme passage suggests there is no difference between once having had such weapons in the past and possibly later possessing them in the future for precisely the same reason.

In the heat of the moment, Bush, who is not a scholar, could be using words imprecisely or even simply for political effect. Yet the perhaps intended result is to deny the well-established practice of distinguishing between a reaction based on a clear and present danger and a threat that might never materialize. To return once more to the Iraq example, from Bush's perspective, there seems to be no significant difference between the fact that Iraq once possessed NBC weapons, now possesses them, or may possess them in the future.

The NSS 2002 doctrine of "preemptive" military action can be construed in different ways, all of which are troubling. The radical view that henceforth the only acceptable defensive policy is a "preemptive" military stance, understood as military prevention extending to threats that have not and might never become actual, simply threatens the permanent possibility of naked aggression. This view, which features the argument that a defensive, or preventive, posture is inadequate in practice, abandons any connection between the specific case and the specific response, as in the adage that the punishment must fit the crime. In its place, the new doctrine offers a general response to any and all cases in relying on the revised conception of preemptive warfare through an enlarged conception of legitimate defense as charged with anticipating and countering any possible threat in advance. In effect, this is a form of the Old West so-called cowboy approach of shooting first and asking questions later.

The new "preemptive" view of national defense as attacking first and asking questions afterward is held at the highest levels of the Bush administration. For instance, President Bush has said: "Terrorists and terror states do not reveal these threats with fair notice, in formal declarations—and responding to such enemies only after they have struck first is not self-defense, it is suicide."[11] This statement, which reflects a short-term political intention, retrospectively justifies the preemptive attack on Iraq on the grounds that this was and remains, even now when the fraud concerning unconventional weaponry has been thoroughly exposed, the only adequate response. I take Bush to be suggesting that, in his opinion, the United States was in effect faced with a clear and present danger of such magnitude that the only reasonable course of action was to strike first before being struck, since an Iraqi strike on the United States was likely to be so devastating as to impede, or even to prevent, an adequate response. If granted, this point would effectively destroy any distinction between preemption and prevention as these terms are usually understood in suggesting that when the dust settles, prevention rather than preemption is the just course of action, or in the terms of the NSS 2002, "preemption," since, in a time of NBC weapons, the permanent possibility of an anticipatory form of "preemptive" war against real or simply imagined threats is the only responsible military stance.

This suggestion, which has the undoubted political merit of playing well in the hustings, and perhaps betrays the irrational fears of certain neoconservatives who claim to detect real and imagined enemies everywhere, is difficult to take seriously. In the case of Iraq, such capable observers as Hans Blix, David Kay, and Lord Butler say there never have been reliable reasons to believe such weapons existed at the time the United States decided to invade. All indications now point to the idea that a number of important figures in the Bush administration, including Bush himself, but also Paul Wolfowitz, Donald Rumsfeld, Condoleezza Rice, Richard Cheney, and others, were committed to the idea of invading Iraq even before they came to power.[12] Even had there been such weapons, it does not follow that military aggression is the only or even the best course of action. Negotiation rather than war, where negotiation is still possible, is always the better alternative, as the United States, which attributes the possession of "WMD" to North Korea, is now sporadically negotiating with that country. Other responses can be imagined that might be more useful than a military conflict in which human beings will be certainly killed. In the case of North Korea, where there is large-scale hunger, shipments of food and technical aid directed toward helping the North Koreans to feed themselves, which would ameliorate the situation and perhaps reduce the military threat to others, is arguably preferable to launching a war.

The idea that a preemptive military response is the preferred course in all, or even the majority of cases, hence the only responsible way to react to a possible future threat, simply fails since it cannot be shown that other responses are not better. "Preemption" as it figures in the new doctrine, or what is usually called prevention, can also be interpreted more moderately as selective preemption. According to this interpretation, a posture of military "preemption," understood in the sense of a preventive attack against a foe that is not yet poised to strike, is justifiable, if not as a rule in all situations, at least under some specifiable circumstances. When all else fails, the preemptive option, that is, the possibility of a military strike against a really existing threat, must still be on the table.

Even a selective use of "preemptive" military action as the new NSS 2002 doctrine redefines it appears problematic. As a recent Brookings Institution Policy Brief points out, it is difficult to distinguish "justifiable preemption [that is, as this term is now redefined in NSS 2002] from unlawful aggression in ways that will gain widespread adherence abroad."[13] The authors of this Policy Brief are worried about whether, if this distinction cannot be defended, this particular policy might not result in justifying the opposite intention, that is, unjustified military strikes when a real threat is not already present or looming. They seem to believe that if the United States can win the hearts and minds of its allies and critics around the world, then what the NSS 2002 deems preemptive military action is acceptable. Implicit in this reasoning is the idea that there are at least some identifiable situations in which preemptive military action, that is, not as the term is usually employed but as it is redefined in the NSS 2002 doctrine, is not only justified but even a good thing. If this were true, then a policy of preemptive unilateralism would be justified as long as others agreed to it.

This view is absurd and very dangerous. Though reputable thinkers continue to conflate consensus with truth, this is a deep mistake.[14] The idea of basing politics on what people seem to desire has led to the widespread practice of incessant public opinion polling, a practice that is as widespread in Europe as in the United States. But agreement or consensus, however obtained, has absolutely nothing whatever to do with truth, which does not depend on the fact of actually being believed. In the 1930s a large number of Germans agreed to a series of policies that Germans and others now find reprehensible, and no one, except the odd unrepentant Nazi, still regards as true.

ON JUSTIFYING WAR

There is an important distinction between the morality of going to war and the morality of how it is conducted. A war can be morally justified, but carried out in a morally unjust manner; or it can be morally unjust, but fought in a morally just manner. Whether the Vietnamese War was morally just—and I believe it was not—has no bearing on the moral injustice of the massacre perpetrated at My Lai.[15] The scandal at Abu Ghraib prison near Baghdad focuses attention on persistent disregard of human rights by the United States in Afghanistan, Guantanamo Bay, Iraq, and perhaps elsewhere, but says nothing at all about the legitimacy of the war in and occupation of Iraq.

Wars can and have been "justified" in a large variety of ways. An incomplete list of reasons, all of which have at one time or another been invoked for the war in Iraq, might include the mere whim of the maximum leader, electoral imperatives, the political ability to obtain authorization, a religious belief that this is God's will, to gain access to fossil fuel, to deflect attention from interior political and economic difficulties, to respond to a real or imagined threat of some kind in the name of national defense or in terms of national interest broadly defined, and so on. Certainly, it is not enough to say that a given war is conducted according to rules—for instance, military or legal rules, or the rules of the Geneva Convention—since the rules themselves require justification.

Since any justification of war of whatever kind ultimately comes down to claiming that a particular war in a particular time and place is legitimate as necessary to protect human beings, all efforts of whatever kind to legitimate a particular war, not war itself, presuppose a moral justification. Yet even when a moral justification can be given, there are important moral limits to what one can do in ordinary and even in extraordinary times if our actions must respect other people not merely as means to an end but as ends in themselves. More generally, war must protect the citizens of one country while respecting as much as humanly possible the lives of others. This is obviously one of the things that was not being done at Abu Ghraib, hence one of the reasons why moral justification is so important in focusing our views about this war.

The general idea that some individuals, or groups, have privileged access to mind-independent reality is the basis of all just war theories. Just war theories, which are rooted in theology and therefore are grounded in faith rather than reason, invoke the support of sacred texts to justify military action. Just war theories are interpreted to suggest that a particular course of military action is sanctioned by, or at least generally agrees with, divine authority as understood by one group of believers, though not necessarily by other groups of believers. For a religious believer, it makes sense to claim one ought to carry out divine will, if necessary, through military intervention. In a just war theory, the grasp of reality as mediated through the authorized interpretation of the sacred texts of a particular religion justifies military action.

There are at least three insuperable difficulties in any just war theory. First, a theological justification of war is only convincing to someone who accepts the specific religious framework on which it rests. An atheist, agnostic, or even a religious believer who doubts claims to know God's (or Allah's) mind will probably not be convinced by reference to sacred texts. Second, there is no rational, nonarbitrary way to distinguish between a correct ("true") and an incorrect ("false") identification of what a given religion requires of its faithful. The strife of textual interpretation, including interpretation of sacred texts, is literally endless. There is no way to know one is getting it right, hence no way, other than through arbitrary decision, to be sure one is carrying out the dictates of a particular religion, let alone to justify military action based on religious insight. Third, there is also no rational way to distinguish between actions that religion in general, as opposed to a specific religion, approves or disapproves. For instance, a distinction cannot be rationally drawn between the Bush administration's wars in Afghanistan and Iraq and the jihad (or "just war") launched by Osama bin Laden and his Muslim associates. Both cases involve appeals to a primitive, intuitive concept of just war to justify action.

War is a form of social action in which some individuals try to inflict grievous bodily harm on others in the course of furthering their ends. A moral approach to the justification of military action differs from Platonism, which insists on knowing the real, in abandoning any claim to know the mind-independent world as it really is, and from just war theories in relying on reason as opposed to religious faith as a guide. A moral approach to war relies on the mere force of argument to legitimate military action. It seeks to determine what it is right to do in a given situation in formulating arguments an impartial observer might find convincing.

If morality requires us to treat each individual as an end and not as a means, then it is moral, hence justified, to defend those who are attacked; but it is immoral, hence unjustified, to attack others, to attempt to take lives through military action, when one has not been attacked in a way that puts one's life in danger. It follows that defensive, or preemptive, war, which is intended to respond to a clear and present danger, including an ongoing or clearly looming attack, is moral, hence licit or justified. But what the Bush administration calls "preemptive" war, which is widely regarded as preventive, or offensive, war, designed for a situation when an attack is not clearly in the offing, when it may not ever take place, is immoral, hence illicit or unjustified.

If war must be moral, then it cannot be offensive and can only be defensive. This rules out the very idea of justifying war in general. It seems obvious that in the case of the wars in Afghanistan and Iraq, this test was not met. No one pretends that Afghanistan attacked the United States. At most, it is claimed that one or more terrorist organizations operating from within Afghanistan carried out an attack on the United States, which does not morally justify attacking and destroying Afghanistan in response.

If the punishment must fit the crime, then the military response in a case of aggression must be proportional to, hence cannot exceed, the nature of the harm inflicted. A proposed war of self-defense of legitimate interests becomes illegitimate if the means employed do not take into account and respect the limits of the particular situation.

A religious approach, which regards life as intrinsically sacred, as an ultimate value, cannot permit the taking of life ("Thou shalt not kill") even for the supposed purpose of realizing God's will.[16] To be consistent, religious thinkers should forbid war of any kind and adopt pacifism as the only justified stance in response to aggression. Yet from the moral point of view, it is legitimate to take the lives of human beings understood as ends in themselves and never as means to an end in the course of defending the lives of other human beings.

MILITARY ACTION WITHOUT JUSTIFICATION

Thus far I have assumed that war requires an adequate justification, and, as concerns the NSS 2002, which authorizes preventive warfare under the heading of "preemptive" warfare, none can be given. This is unlikely to trouble the Bush administration and its foreign policy friends since the idea that scholarly or even informal justification is required before engaging in military action is not an important concern. But suppose we take the line that none needs to be given since international relations is a field that has nothing to do with morality, which has no role to play in the international arena?

The central foreign policy theme of the Bush administration can be summed up as the claim that a powerful nation like the United States does not need to pay attention to what others want since it can do as it pleases. This suggests that the might of the United States, the world's only remaining superpower, is itself a sufficient justification for whatever it wants to do. The only limit on US action lies in its power as a nation, which entitles it to do as it pleases. The idea that "might makes right" suggests that we can somehow get beyond the need to justify what we do.

Garry Wills refers to Bill Clinton's summary of his approach to foreign policy as cooperating whenever possible and going alone only when we must, and to George W. Bush's view as going it alone whenever possible and cooperating only when we must.[17] This insight sums up the Bush administration's position that there are no limits on its foreign policy, hence none as concerns military actions. Since 11 September 2001, under the transparent guise of responding to terrorism, which is legitimate, the United States has illegitimately waged war against, as well as substantially destroyed and occupied, Afghanistan and Iraq. It has further restricted civil liberties in an important way within the United States and undertaken to intern so-called enemy combatants in a kind of legal limbo in defiance of international conventions and even US law at Guantanamo Bay for an indefinite period.[18]

The idea that military actions do not require moral justification since "might makes right," which apparently inspires the Bush administration in its conduct of foreign policy, is almost as old as Western philosophy. In the first book of the *Republic*, written some two and a half millennia ago, Socrates draws attention to a distinction between what is consistent with the prevailing set of laws, hence is legal, and what, though not necessarily legal, is advantageous, or useful, to at least some individuals. He has in mind the idea that the rulers of the state may be wrong about where their advantage lies. In countering Socrates, Thrasymachus, who has often been seen as presenting a cynical form of realism, argues that "right" has no natural meaning, and merely means whatever the strongest elements of the state decree it to mean, pointing to the idea often abbreviated as the claim that "might makes right." This view has been influential in later political theory as well as in political practice. Thucydides attributes this view to the Athenians in their unsuccessful negotiations with the Melians, and Machiavelli later restates this view in his argument that the true statesman must not acknowledge any moral limits on his effort to garner power.

The main difference in the present situation is that because of intervening technological advances, the situation is now unlike anything Plato or even Machiavelli ever contemplated, for the world's only remaining superpower and a number of other countries (for example, Russia, probably France and the United Kingdom, possibly Israel and China, and potentially India, Pakistan, and perhaps Iran), and indeed any other nation in possession of a sufficient number of nuclear weapons with reliable delivery vehicles and the willingness to use them, are in a position to destroy the world. Yet in other respects, Socrates' rejoinder remains appropriate. While it is true that a strong country, such as the United States, the strongest country the world has ever seen, can, within constantly changing limits, do virtually as it wishes, in the Bush administration's version of foreign policy, which is mainly unconcerned to justify its actions either publicly or privately, the United States often acts in ways that, to an independent observer, might seem to run contrary to its deeper interests. Thus the invasion of Iraq, which is contrary to international law, including the United Nations (UN) Charter, weakens rather than strengthens the legal ties binding the various nations together, and encourages other violations of international law in what is deemed national interest. This invasion can only be counterproductive in failing to reach its objective of the establishment of democracy as the end in view, since meaningful forms of democracy cannot be imposed by force from above but must rather emerge from below. Further, the failure to respect even the most elementary form of human rights in dealing with enemy combatants, as symbolized by the scandal at Abu Ghraib, which, like My Lai for Vietnam War, will forever be the symbol of the invasion and occupation of Iraq, simply destroys whatever goodwill might have accrued to the United States as a result of the idea of liberating Iraq from Saddam Hussein.

PREEMPTIVE WAR, PREVENTIVE WAR, AND MORALITY

NSS 2002 authorizes offensive, first-strike, preventive, or, in its revised use of terminology, "preemptive" military action, as opposed to a defensive reaction to a prior or ongoing attack. The intentions of the Bush administration seem clear: in pursuit of its purposes, it has announced its intention to wage war against literally any country without restraint of any kind, undeterred by international law, multilateral or bilateral treaties, or international organizations, in what looks very much like an effort to attain and maintain global hegemony.[19]

In ordinary scholarly usage, preemption relates to defense as prevention relates to aggression. Preemptive military action suggests by definition that the country contemplating it has already been or shortly will be attacked. Preventive military action, what the NSS 2002 calls "preemptive" military action, suggests the country contemplating it has not so far and perhaps might never be attacked, but is justified in going to war. Advocates of the new view of justified "preemptive" military action, who presumably invoke a widened concept of defense (for example, the best defense is a good offense), see the very possibility of a future attack as warranting such a response in advance.

The practice of preventive warfare is not new. There have always been countries that, on the grounds of legitimate self-defense, have attacked other countries without being attacked. Prevention is sometimes conflated with "anticipatory self-defense," which is recognized by Article 51 of the UN Charter. Anticipatory self-defense is not aggressive, thus not preventive, but defensive, hence preemptive. It is often suggested that when Israel launched a military strike on Egypt in 1967 in opening the Six Days' War at a time when Egypt's forces were massively deployed in the Sinai, this was an instance of anticipatory self-defense. Since in this case a clear and present danger was identifiable as imminent by all observers, one can say that anticipatory self-defense, as illustrated at the outset of that war, constituted a variation on the theme of legitimate self-defense against aggression.

Partisans of the Bush doctrine of "preemptive" military strikes, like former national security advisor Condoleezza Rice, present it as merely old wine in new bottles.[20] In part this is correct, since US history is littered with preventive strikes, often on weak, virtually defenseless targets—for instance, the unprovoked attack on Grenada. Yet in another sense, this doctrine is genuinely new, a clear break with past US practice, which has long been based on a defensive posture. As a veteran Sovietologist, Rice should know that the US policy throughout the Cold War period was based on mutual détente for defensive purposes, not preemptive aggression.

But one can ask: if we knew that a particular country harbored aggressive intentions toward another country, intentions that were likely to or even possibly might later lead to aggression, would that be sufficient to justify preemptive military action? For instance, it might be argued that rather the sign a treaty with Nazi Germany in 1938, the Allies would have been well advised to launch a preemptive war against Nazi Germany.

This question raises a problem that is not easily answered in an imperfect world, where the future cannot simply be deduced from even the most thorough knowledge of the past. In a perfect world, we would be able to forecast with certainty what will necessarily later occur. Yet no one suggests this is currently the case, and the information at our disposal in the field of foreign affairs appears woefully inadequate as a moral basis to justify killing other people.

If one knew with certainty that a situation posing a clear and present danger would surely later develop, it would be difficult not to have recourse to military action as a legitimate response when the lives of one's citizens would clearly later be in danger. But since no one knows the future, it is self-serving to claim that the possession of unconventional weapons and the putative intention to acquire them are really one and the same. At most we know that at this time, there is no reason to think that Iraq possessed NBC weapons, hence there was in fact no clear and present danger justifying a preventive war and occupation of a sovereign country. And since we do not know that Iraq was certain to have unconventional weaponry at a future time, it was also unjustified to wage a preemptive war against Iraq.

The Hobbesian mindset of the Bush administration reflects a kind of bunker mentality in which the United States, understood to be under attack from all quarters, is mightily defending itself against real or imagined enemies everywhere. According to this model, a responsible form of national defense must on occasion be preventive, or what in the new lingo is now called "preemptive" war, in order to defend American democracy. Yet "preemptive" war, as NSS 2002 understands it, and which is in fact a form of preventive war, is not the most adequate way to defend US democracy, is never morally justified, and, for this reason, should never be allowed to occur.

PART 3

From Boardroom to Battlefield

8

Intelligence in Preventive Military Strategy

Greg Thielmann

> *I would never advise Your Majesty to declare war forthwith, simply because it appeared that our opponent would begin hostilities in the near future. One can never anticipate the ways of divine providence securely enough for that.*
>
> —Chancellor Otto von Bismarck to Kaiser Wilhelm I, 1875

ACCURATE INTELLIGENCE is important. In-depth understanding of current realities and prescience about the future have always been major assets in the execution of foreign and military affairs. In the modern era, the detailed demands of government on intelligence services have mushroomed along with the technical capacity of the intelligence collectors. Particularly in the United States, the intelligence community's (IC) sixteen agencies devour a significant (and still classified) share of the national budget.

This American commitment to the intelligence function is partly the result of national traumas induced by instances of failed warnings. The Japanese attack on Pearl Harbor helped to create a national obsession with receiving advance warning of foreign aggression. The Cuban Missile Crisis engraved on our collective consciousness the importance of hypervigilance in matters involving nuclear weapons; it may also have bequeathed the public an excessive confidence in the ability of the IC to monitor events. The 9/11 attacks on New York City and Washington, D.C., dramatically demonstrated the dangers posed by nonstate actors. In light of the destructive potential of organized foreign terrorists willing to commit suicide, it became obvious that major intelligence assets would need to be focused on the murky world of international terrorism.

Just as the threat of terrorism has redirected the intelligence enterprise in the twenty-first century, the development and deployment of intercontinental ballistic missiles (ICBMs) with nuclear warheads had a powerful effect on establishing the primacy of intelligence as a component of national defense during the Cold War. Strategists worried that the power, range, size, and speed of modern weapons might foreclose the option of waiting for a putative threat to be actualized. However improbable the notion that any state would contemplate a nuclear attack on the United States, there was (and remains to this day) no reliable means of thwarting an attack by ICBMs once they are launched.[1] This was a particularly uncomfortable realization for the United States, which matured on the notion that it was protected by two broad oceans.

Preventive war is not new to the cogitations of national security managers and other strategic thinkers. It was in response to the new dynamic of the nuclear threat that some Americans called for preventive war against the Soviet Union in the 1950s—and some Soviets used a similar rationale in calling for preventive war against China during the 1960s.[2] In his seminal 1959 book, *Strategy in the Missile Age*, Bernard Brodie described preventive war as "a live issue [in the early 1950s] among a small but important minority of American citizens."[3] Even then, it never received sufficient backing to become part of US national security doctrine. Henry Kissinger referred to preventive war as "contrary to the sense of country and the constitutional limits within which American foreign policy must be conducted."[4] By the end of that decade, Brodie observed that "the ranks of the preventive war advocates appear now to be practically deserted."[5] And yet as a deterrent to Soviet nuclear attack, the United States retained the preemptive options of launching on warning—before any enemy weapons were fired—or launching under attack—before any weapons reached their targets on US territory.

It is a relatively new feature of American political dialogue to hear preventive war justified as a formula for defeating nonstate actors. The application of this doctrine should not be confused with the US attack on Afghanistan, which was undertaken *after* al-Qaida's 11 September 2001 attacks on American citizens (and bears some resemblance to the US Army's pursuit into Mexico of Pancho Villa's forces in 1916 after Villa's attack on a US town in New Mexico). This most recent rationale for making war before being attacked was spawned by the past successes of al-Qaida terrorists and nourished by the particular fear of terrorists acquiring and using "weapons of mass destruction" (WMD) in the future against urban civilian targets. Harkening back to the 9/11 attacks, President George W. Bush offered the following dark vision in his State of the Union address on 28 January 2003: "imagine those 19 hijackers with other weapons and other plans, this time armed by Saddam Hussein."[6] Americans feel particularly vulnerable to nuclear terrorism from nonstate groups, which achieve global reach operating out of sanctuaries in hostile or chaotic states. This anxiety is likely to grow—at least until the international community gets much better control over nuclear warheads and fissile material. Advocates of the preventive war doctrine argue that civilized nations cannot allow legal niceties to block them from taking prompt military action against terrorist cells, wherever those cells can be found.

Intelligence gathering and analysis are at the heart of implementing any doctrine of preemptive/preventive war, since such a doctrine presumes the ability to know both the intentions and capabilities of potential enemies. It is therefore necessary to take a close look at the nature of strategic intelligence—particularly as it has evolved in the post–World War II era—so that its contributions and limitations can be fully understood. In the following analysis, the first section places the capabilities and limitations of strategic intelligence in historical context, elucidating key episodes and salient trends that shape the backdrop for contemporary discussions of preventive war. The second section looks at how interactions between the realms of intelligence and policy complicate efforts to institutionalize preventive war as military doctrine. The final section contributes to the ongoing dialogue on intelligence reform by proposing several policy recommendations that follow from the chapter's findings.

WHY INTELLIGENCE FALLS SHORT

Even a cursory review of the way intelligence has been formulated and used during the last half century shows that it has not been a consistently accurate indicator of the capabilities and intentions of foreign governments. Notable blunders range from overestimating the size of the Soviet bomber force in the late 1950s and underestimating the staying power of the North Vietnamese in the face of American intervention in Vietnam in the 1960s, to overestimating the range of the Soviet Backfire medium-range bomber in the 1970s and exaggerating the motives for and significance of the Soviets' illegal construction of a large-phased array radar at Krasnoyarsk, Siberia, in the 1980s.

As the United States enters a period conducive to intelligence reform, it is tempting to believe that, whatever its past failings, the IC can adjust to the more demanding requirements of the preventive war doctrine. I contend that such an expectation cannot be fully met because, while the doctrine demands clairvoyance, intelligence assessments will always be subject to incomplete information and flawed interpretations.

To acknowledge the weaknesses of many past intelligence assessments is not to belittle the role of intelligence or to deny the contributions it has made to US security, for it has been an indispensable tool of government. Intelligence does not need to be infallible to be valuable, but neither should it be pushed beyond its natural limits. For intelligence analysts to overstate their confidence level is to set up the policy-maker for disaster, and for the political leadership to exaggerate the precision of estimates is to break trust with the public. Further examination of the historical record elucidates this delicate dynamic.

INTELLIGENCE EXAGGERATES THREATS

Intelligence serves several functions: warning of what could happen; predicting what is likely to happen; and analyzing why things happen the way they do. Ever since the surprise attack on Pearl Harbor in 1941, US intelligence at the strategic level has put a premium on the warning function. The loss of a major portion of the US Pacific Fleet in a single attack was so dire, dramatic, and avoidable that being able to warn in advance of a similar catastrophic event quickly became enshrined as the holy grail of US intelligence efforts. The vast Cold War intelligence bureaucracy was principally focused on providing warning of Soviet strategic attack and gauging the capability of Soviet offensive forces to carry out such an attack.

The detection of Soviet efforts to deploy nuclear-tipped missiles to Cuba in 1962 was the most conspicuous post–World War II triumph of the intelligence warning function. But even in its most triumphant manifestation, the limits of intelligence can be perceived. The reading of intentions in Moscow and Washington was done through a glass darkly. US intelligence agencies did not receive timely information when the Soviet and Cuban governments decided on the deployments; it only detected the deployments once they were under way. Moreover, intense US scrutiny of the island during the crisis missed entirely the nuclear capability of Soviet tactical missiles deployed there.

One of the most serious limitations on confidently predicting hostile action by another state is that governmental leaders themselves may not know their own minds or may not be in complete control of events. We are now well aware of how much trouble Washington was having discerning Soviet intentions during the height of the Cuban Missile Crisis. That Moscow was having similar difficulty assessing whether the Kennedy administration intended to invade Cuba was at least partly a consequence of mixed signals being sent by a government that itself had not yet decided what its course of action would be. Both Kennedy and Nikita Khrushchev had concerns about provocative military actions being taken without their specific authorization.[7] The world is indeed fortunate that the United States chose a naval quarantine and diplomacy rather than a preventive attack. The Cuban Missile Crisis should stand as "Exhibit A" in making the case that intelligence will be insufficient to justify attacking first.

Recent episodes reveal other limitations of the intelligence function. Failures to provide warning—for example, of Indian nuclear testing in May 1998 or of the 9/11 attacks in 2001—were occasions for severe criticism of the Central Intelligence Agency (CIA) and the other intelligence agencies. Partly as a consequence of such reactions, the IC has preferred to warn of improbable events or sensationalize relatively insignificant developments rather than to risk a failure to warn against the unexpected. Following pointed criticism of US assessments of foreign ballistic missile threats as too sanguine by the Commission to Assess the Ballistic Missile Threat to the United States (Rumsfeld Commission) and the Republican leadership in Congress during 1998, the IC essentially adopted the hyped rhetoric and inflated criteria of the Rumsfeld Commission report in subsequent yearly estimates. The US IC thereby presented the nation with a series of implausible timelines and unrealistic threat scenarios that proved very wide off the mark in predicting actual missile deployments. The prognostication record was particularly lacking concerning those countries that had been the document's principal focus—North Korea, Iran, and Iraq.[8]

Another factor predisposing US intelligence to exaggerate threats is susceptibility to deception by hostile states. It is bad enough that the United States has a habit of embellishing threats to the nation, but the states that the United States is monitoring also have an incentive to exaggerate their own capabilities, particularly those states that fear intervention from stronger powers. Such self-aggrandizement can be motivated by a leader's desire to claim credit domestically for defense efforts and/or to increase the deterrent effect of military forces against potential aggressors. While China was quietly pursuing its own nuclear weapons program in the 1950s, it publicly disparaged the effectiveness of nuclear weapons and declared itself immune to intimidation and threats by the nuclear powers because of its large population and revolutionary zeal. Self-aggrandizement can also simply be a manifestation of national pride. North Korea has exaggerated its scientific and military capabilities to bolster pride and to intimidate the United States, claiming, for example, that it succeeded in launching a satellite on 31 August 1998, even though US intelligence declared the Taepo Dong 1 space launch attempt a failure.[9] Even the United States, in announcing that its inadequately tested strategic ballistic missile interceptors in Alaska would be "operational" in 2004, seems willing to play the exaggeration game.

The incentive states have for exaggerating their capabilities are matched by the incentives intelligence agencies have for believing such claims. While intelligence analysts are trained to recognize both "denial" and "deception," they are professionally inclined toward concentrating on the former—uncovering the secrets that could save the nation from a disastrous surprise (and burnish the reputation of the sleuthing analysts in the process). To argue that a hostile state is less threatening than it appears is to risk being labeled as naive. Few intelligence analysts have gained glory and institutional reward from finding that foreign capabilities are less alarming than previously believed.

Political and military leaders prefer that the IC err on the side of warnings that are too many or too strident rather than too few or too ambiguous. For example, they judge it far better for the United States to deploy a military force trained and equipped to operate in a chemical weapons environment that does not materialize than to deploy a less encumbered military force more quickly, which is then surprised by the use of chemical weapons.

Even though it is understandable and relatively common for states to exaggerate their capabilities, foreign intelligence organizations often fall for it anyway. Ironically, tactical success at exploiting the "worst-case" bent of most intelligence services can lead to counterproductive and catastrophic results over the longer term. Moscow's bravado over Soviet military capabilities and the secrecy shrouding its military and scientific activities in the late 1950s helped spur the United States to launch the largest nuclear modernization program in history—excessive when measured retrospectively against the actual threat. It is likely that the more convincing the Pentagon is in convincing the world of its missile defense capabilities, the more countries like Russia and China will improve their offensive strategic deterrents—doing so at much less cost than what the United States spends on deploying its defensive systems.

By stretching intelligence, politicians can also contribute to exaggerated threat assessments. The problem with intelligence goes beyond the inability of the intelligence services to get everything right every time. Whatever the good faith findings of the intelligence services, the political leadership choosing to pursue war will be tempted to misrepresent the actual evidence to the public. There is ample evidence of such misrepresentation in past US military interventions. One can go back to the erroneous claim that the USS *Maine* had been attacked in Havana harbor in 1898—or turn to the much more recent example of the 1964 Tonkin Gulf affair, when the Johnson administration requested a congressional resolution authorizing a military response to the second of two "unprovoked" attacks on US warships "on routine patrol" in international waters. In the latter case, neither the US Congress nor the public at large had any idea that the US government had been supporting clandestine raids on North Vietnam by South Vietnamese commandos (Operation Plan 34A).[10] They were also unaware of the emerging doubts within the US military at the time that a second attack had actually occurred, because President Johnson had described the evidence as "unequivocal."[11] Yet the resulting Tonkin Gulf Resolution served for years as the constitutional equivalent of a congressional declaration of war.

Dire warnings based on exaggerated depictions of the threat have become standard fare in political campaigns. Alarming descriptions of Soviet strength during the Cold War fueled the political success of John Kennedy in the 1960 election and Ronald Reagan in the 1980 and 1984 elections. Inflated estimates of the foreign ballistic missile threat contributed to the election of George W. Bush and the demise of the Antiballistic Missile (ABM) and Strategic Arms Reduction Treaty (START) treaties. Indeed, before the aftermath of the 2003 Iraq War, there appeared to be little penalty attached either to the IC or the political leadership for excessive warning.

IRAQ AS HARBINGER?

If the Cuban Missile Crisis is "Exhibit A" in the intelligence case against preventive war, "Exhibit B" is provided by a more recent case. The implications of intelligence geared only to warning are just beginning to be understood as the facts of the Iraqi "WMD" fiasco begin to sink in. In many ways, the Iraqi example stands as a harbinger of a grim alternative future when inherently imperfect intelligence combines poisonously with an aggressive approach to war. In examining the Iraqi threat, the IC again assigned warning top priority, arriving at a classical "worst-case" assessment. The Key Judgments of the classified October 2002 National Intelligence Estimate (NIE) on Iraqi "WMD" were full of frightening scenarios that, even at the time, many analysts regarded as either unlikely or possibly only relevant to some more distant future.

Later, the 2004 report of the Senate Select Committee on Intelligence[12] and the findings of the Iraq Survey Group (ISG)[13] both provided conclusions significantly at odds with the official estimates of the US IC and the statements of senior Bush administration officials immediately prior to the Iraq War. The October 2002 NIE claimed high confidence in asserting that Iraq "had chemical and biological weapons" and moderate confidence that Iraq was "likely to have a [nuclear] weapon" by 2007 to 2009.[14] The NIE also warned that Iraq "*could* make a nuclear weapon within several months to a year."[15] The Senate Select Intelligence Committee bipartisan report delivered a blunt verdict on the quality of these assessments: "the major Key Judgments in the

[October 2002 NIE] . . . were either overstated, or were not supported by, the underlying intelligence reporting."[16]

The conventional wisdom about the dearth of reliable intelligence on Iraq prior to the 2003 invasion refers mostly to the poor quality and quantity of human intelligence. However, the US IC actually knew a great deal about the history of Iraqi programs for unconventional weapons as a result of the 1991 Gulf War, the subsequent activities of United Nations (UN) inspectors, and intense ongoing scrutiny of Iraq through national technical means. Considerably more was known at that time about Iraq than about North Korea and Iran, the other two charter members of President Bush's "axis of evil." Indeed, the United States probably knew much more about the specific capabilities of the Iraqi military prior to the 2003 war than it knew about the Japanese and German militaries prior to entering World War II in 1941. The discovery that the US government had significantly misassessed the unconventional weapons capabilities of Iraq prior to the US invasion therefore raises an especially troubling issue for those who expect the IC to provide the kind of information requisite to waging preventive war. The case of Iraq should constitute a sobering wake-up call on the dangers of expecting too much from intelligence. Specifics of this cautionary tale can be gleaned by reviewing key dimensions of the intelligence failure that took place prior to the US invasion of Iraq in 2003.

Nuclear weapons are so much more destructive than the other categories of "WMD" that intelligence analysts, members of the press, and politicians should resist the temptation to use "WMD" as a collective in referring to chemical and biological weapons. In the case of Iraq, what was for government officials and the press mostly a stylistic convenience was for some politicians a mechanism for spreading and harnessing fear. The president and his advisers reported that intelligence showed Iraq possessed "WMD," conjuring up images of mushroom clouds, but the already thin evidence pointed to nonnuclear stockpiles or "WMD-related program activities." For example, when Deputy Secretary of Defense Paul Wolfowitz claimed in a May 2003 interview that "there's been very little dispute about the WMD, except for some of the borderline issues,"[17] he was referring to chemical and biological weapons. Yet the public had been conditioned to think of nuclear weapons, the most destructive unconventional weapons category by far, whenever it heard "WMD."

When senior intelligence figures summarized the detailed and comprehensive analyses of intelligence on the Iraqi nuclear program, they consistently featured worst-case scenarios, and did so prominently—giving greater credibility to supporting evidence and dismissing contrary evidence. As a result, the timetables of concern were advanced.[18]

In forecasting how soon Iraq could acquire its first nuclear weapon, the NIE concluded: "probably . . . during this decade."[19] Little noticed was the qualifier for this projection: "if left unchecked." "Unchecked" could mean either "not blocked" or "not examined." The former meaning would constitute a very pessimistic assessment of the effectiveness of the stringent arms embargo then in force, along with the US-British enforcement of no-fly zones. The latter meaning may have been intended to reflect the absence of UN inspectors at that time, but it would seem to be an inaccurate reflection of the intense international scrutiny to which Iraq was being subjected. If the important qualifier was the absence of inspectors, then it is remarkable that the return of inspectors in November 2002 had no discernable impact on the administration in judging the urgency of military action.

Later in the NIE's Key Judgments, an even more alarming timeline for development of the first Iraqi nuclear weapon appeared: *"several months to a year."*[20] Curiously, when Director of Central Intelligence (DCI) George Tenet tried to justify the CIA's prewar estimates on the nuclear issue in July 2003, he referred to sensitive foreign intelligence reports indicating that Hussein had specifically instructed his nuclear scientists to reconstitute the nuclear program.[21] In the same account, which Tenet cited for its credibility, he mentioned that one scientist told Hussein it would be possible to have a bomb within eighteen to twenty-four months of getting sufficient fissile material.[22] This boast was more than twice as long as the NIE said would be required. Yet the shorter, more alarming time frame was retained in the published estimate.

Moreover, the context for the "several months to a year" scenario was Iraq's acquisition from abroad of sufficient fissile material. There was no indication of any evidence that Iraq was seeking a foreign source of enriched uranium or plutonium. Without it, the NIE predicted that at least five to seven years would be required—and only based on the assumption that Iraq was already reconstituting its own uranium enrichment effort.[23] This latter judgment was vigorously challenged by the State Department's Intelligence Bureau (INR), citing the Department of Energy's (DOE) analysis of the unsuitability of the intercepted aluminum tubes as the most critical flaw in the reconstitution theory. In a separate section of the document, the careful reader could discover that the IC had only "moderate confidence" in even the five-to-seven-year projection. When used by key policy-makers and members of Congress, however, the shorter timelines were headlined, and the careful qualifications of the analysts were ignored. After its exhaustive review of the evidence, the Senate Select Intelligence Committee report later agreed with the State Department's dissenting view in the October 2002 NIE that the available evidence did not "add up to a compelling case for reconstitution."[24]

The front-loading of alarming timelines and subtle obfuscations of the uncertainty and fragility on which the projections were made misled even some who were conscientiously seeking answers. However, for an administration that already had its answers long before the questions were posed to the IC, there was no interest in ensuring that Congress and the public got a faithful rendition of expert opinion.

The NIE's treatment of vehicles capable of delivering unconventional weapons followed a similar pattern. The classified Key Judgments of the NIE included the statement, "Gaps in Iraqi accounting to UNSCOM [United Nations Special Commission] suggest that Saddam retains a covert force of up to a few dozen Scud-variant SRBMs with ranges of 650 to 900 km."[25] This was one of the most important assessments relating to any determination of an imminent threat posed by Iraq, because these missiles would have been the only means Iraq might have had available in 2003 for effectively threatening population centers in Israel, Saudi Arabia, and Iran. According to the Senate Select Intelligence Committee report, the UN inspectors had been able to account for the destruction of all but two of the Scud missiles previously acquired from the Soviet Union and all but seven of the indigenously produced al Husayn, Scud-type missiles.[26] The committee reported that it was "unclear" how the IC established the higher ("up to a few dozen") figure, since "the IC had no estimate of the number of components that may have been withheld from inspectors."[27] DCI Tenet implied a slightly less imposing and more justifiable quantity—"a small number of SCUD missiles"—in testimony to the Senate on 11 February 2003.[28] However, by stating flatly that "Iraq *retains* a small number of" these missiles, and dropping the explanation of how the estimate was derived—that is, "[g]aps in Iraqi accounting . . . *suggest* . . . that Saddam retains"[29]—he misled Congress and the public about the confidence intelligence experts had in the accuracy of this assessment. He implied that an educated guess was a statement of fact, neglecting to acknowledge that there was no hard evidence that even a single Scud missile remained in the Iraqi inventory. And he did so almost three months after the UN inspectors had regained the opportunity to search for covert inventories.

Both the classified NIE of October 2002 and the unclassified summary of the NIE referred to another category of delivery vehicles for "WMD"—unmanned aerial vehicles (UAVs). The Key Judgments cited one type of UAV as "probably intended to deliver [a] biological warfare agent," but identified it as a "developmental" program rather than an operational system.[30] The unclassified version did not reveal that the intelligence entity most qualified to comment on its intended use, Air Force Intelligence, believed that this UAV was intended primarily for reconnaissance rather than for weapons delivery.

Nor was the public informed when the Defense Intelligence Agency (DIA) and the army joined the air force in dissenting from the majority view on the issue during the coordination of another NIE on "nontraditional threats to the US homeland through 2007" in January 2003.[31] That majority view in the October 2002 NIE was: "Baghdad's UAVs could threaten Iraq's neighbors, U.S. forces in the Persian Gulf, and if brought close to, or into, the United States, the U.S. Homeland."[32] Since the UAVs were not yet operational, the "could" referred to a future contingency rather than a present capability. Moreover, the judgment of Air Force Intelligence about the primary purpose of the UAVs appears to have been vindicated by the ISG after Iraq was occupied. The contingent clause about threatening the US homeland had turned sober weapons intelligence analysis into farce. The casual reader was thereby led to the conclusion that a platform, which was probably not even designed to deliver chemical or biological agents as tactical battlefield weapons, might be an active threat to the American homeland 5,000 miles away. The Senate Select Intelligence Committee report took the IC to task for "overstating" what was known and what was judged about the mission of the UAVs,[33] "failing to discuss" the conventional missions most analysts believed were primary,[34] and describing a mission, attacking the US homeland, that was not supported by intelligence.[35] It also criticized the CIA for failing to share with other agencies details of the dubious intelligence on alleged attempts to acquire US mapping software.[36]

These were consequential failings. The Senate report itself judges that the lack of information sharing by the CIA on alleged Iraqi plans to use UAVs against the United States "may have led some analysts to agree to a position they otherwise would not have supported."[37] A more faithful rendering to the public on the dearth of hard evidence concerning the existence of delivery vehicles for the "WMD" agents of concern would almost certainly have affected public willingness to wage war. At least one member of Congress, Florida senator Bill Nelson (D–FL), has said that the statements about the alleged evidence of Iraqi attempts to acquire mapping of the US homeland for targeting was instrumental in convincing him that Iraq posed an imminent threat.[38]

Iraqi deception further reduced the likelihood of accurate intelligence analysis. At the same time Saddam Hussein was pleading to the world that Iraq had no illicit weapons and that sanctions should therefore be removed to spare the Iraqi people from further suffering, he was publicly awarding medals to his "nuclear mujahideen" and refusing to cooperate fully with UN inspectors. Hussein appears to have been trying to convince US intelligence agencies and the Iraqi people that Iraq did have some chemical and biological weapons capability—to avoid a sense of national humiliation and to dissuade foreign intervention. The former head of the UN inspection mission, Hans

Blix, explained the latter possibility in the following way: "Yet like someone who puts up a sign warning BEWARE OF DOG without having a dog, perhaps the Iraqi regime did not mind inspiring in others the thought that it had weapons of mass destruction and was still dangerous."[39] This was a delicate double game, which succeeded as deception but failed to have its intended policy effect. Hussein underestimated international support for the return of inspectors and overestimated the ability of presumed possession of chemical and biological weapons to deter US and British military action.

In the period leading up to the 2003 Iraq War, Bush administration officials helped exaggerate the Iraqi threat by stretching already thin data. A close reading of pre–Iraq War statements by President Bush, Vice President Richard Cheney, National Security Advisor Condoleezza Rice, Secretary of Defense Donald Rumsfeld, and Deputy Secretary of Defense Paul Wolfowitz shows a consistent pattern of exaggerating what the IC was reporting about operational ties between Iraq and al-Qaida and about the prospects for an early nuclear weapons capability by Iraq. After the invasion, Wolfowitz acknowledged that the links to terrorism was one of "three fundamental concerns," the one "about which there's the most disagreement in the bureaucracy."[40] Yet the rhetorical drumbeat in the speeches and interviews of senior officials asserting a close association between Hussein and al-Qaida carried no hint of this disagreement in the months leading up to the invasion.

The Bush administration's 2002 National Security Strategy of the United States of America (NSS 2002) promised: "The reasons for our actions [using military force] will be clear."[41] Indeed, the preinvasion statements of senior administration officials did make clear that the reason for war with Iraq was to counter the urgent threat posed by Hussein's "WMD." Yet the postinvasion statements of Bush, Cheney, and Rice constitute reluctant witness that the danger from Iraqi "WMD" was either a spurious or incomplete rationale for war. Each of these officials has denied that foreknowledge of the absence of unconventional weapons in Iraq would have changed the substance or timing of the administration's decision to invade the country. In other words, they have inadvertently conceded that there were compelling reasons for going to war in March 2003 other than the officially stated casus belli. The rhetorical approach of the Bush administration before the war (exaggerating Iraq's "WMD" capabilities and conflating Iraq with al-Qaida) was carefully constructed and consistently followed.

IS IRAQ THE EXCEPTION OR THE RULE?

Most of the intelligence dynamics described so far will not change. The intelligence process will continue to manifest a bias toward warning. Thus the most salient political criticism of the IC will continue to be "Why did you not warn us of an attack before it was too late?" rather than "Why did you imply that an attack was coming that never materialized?" Homeland Security's color-coded public alert system, of little use to the common citizen, is a recent example of how eager political authorities are to protect themselves against charges of culpability in not warning of any future terrorist attack. History will judge that the IC provides far more instances of false alarms than missed alarms. The larger US intelligence entities, like the CIA, DIA, and National Security Agency (NSA), will continue to prioritize the goal of warning against military surprise and will make every effort to avoid under-estimation. The efforts of the INR to emphasize predictions of the probable over warnings of the improbable will often be drowned out.

Some continued exaggeration of foreign threats by the US IC is nearly inevitable, and the larger the intelligence gaps are, the greater will be the tendency to assume the worst. For those states labeled as "rogues" by our political leadership, sinister motives will be assumed, and it will be judged prudent not to regard the lack of solid evidence as exculpatory. Such states may be just as likely to encourage US exaggerations of their capability as to correct such inaccuracies. As the post–World War II era repeatedly dem-onstrated in the cases of the Soviet Union and China, and as the Iraq case has recently demonstrated once again, the perceived need of foreign states to deter US attack or intimidation can tempt them into claiming capabilities they do not have.

One does not have to assume a capacity for malfeasance on the part of future presidents, however, to recognize an inherent problem with the use of intelligence. Democratic societies do not go to war easily—even with the wolf at the door. In making the case for war, it is natural to simplify the evidence and remove qualifiers. The issues are complicated; many of the details are classified; and the qualifications attached by professional analysts are tedious. Yet gaining sufficient popular support is critical. So it is not surprising that American political leaders from the eighteenth century to the modern era have engaged in striking rhetoric to call the nation to war—sometimes em-bellishing the facts in the process.

If democratic governments have a tendency to exaggerate present facts, the temptation to exaggerate future dangers is even greater. The rationale for preemptive war extends only from the present to the immediate future; pre-ventive war can be justified by engaging the most imaginative speculations about an eventual future. Moreover, since the future has infinite possibilities, it is difficult to persuasively refute the claim that something could happen.

HOW INTELLIGENCE AND PREVENTIVE WAR DOCTRINE WILL INTERACT

Pursuit of a preventive war doctrine will increase the need for highly accurate, definitive intelligence, even though the IC will often fail to deliver it.
The influence of those organizations that possess military or paramilitary
capabilities—the Department of Defense (DOD) and the CIA, for example—will be expanded; the influence of those that specialize in nonviolent
methods—the State Department, among others—will be reduced. The gap
between what intelligence is needed and what is provided will make matters
worse, since pressure will increase on intelligence agencies to make actionable assessments, whether or not they have sufficient information. There will
be a tendency to ignore or suppress efforts by intelligence professionals to
hedge their estimates or accurately label the low confidence levels of their
judgments. Bottom-line judgments of the IC will be conveyed to the public
and tailored for policy advocacy. This will increase the chance that public
manifestations of classified intelligence judgments bear low fidelity to the actual evidence. For those cases where the evidence is ambiguous or otherwise
unsuitable for making a convincing public case, the national security leadership will more seriously consider clandestine operations, which do not arouse
public opposition and which do not require congressional sanction.

In an atmosphere tolerant of preventive war, even more energy would be
devoted by the IC to detecting foreign military capabilities than uncovering
political intentions, since the former are more subject to discovery by technical means and the latter are very difficult to discern with high confidence.
There would be a greater incentive to focus on short-term intelligence rather
than underlying dynamics and long-term trends. Preventive war implies a
resort to immediate, unilateral, and violent solutions rather than multifac-
eted efforts through multilateral forums to achieve more gradual change in
fundamental economic and political trends. The ongoing trade-off between
defense intelligence most relevant to the "war fighter" and strategic intelligence most relevant to the political leadership would be further tipped in
the direction of the former.

THE NATURE OF THE DILEMMA

The virtual impossibility of achieving near-certain confidence in the accuracy of intelligence confronts us with a paradox and a dilemma. The paradox
is found in the logic of NSS 2002: the United States must be ready to wage
war in order to prevent the more dangerous war that is bound to come. "We
cannot let our enemies strike first."[42] The dilemma in such a doctrine is that
the self-evident value of preventing damage from a possible future attack may

not outweigh the certain negative consequences of declaring and implementing a preventive war doctrine. These consequences will include, at the very least, de-legitimization of the US military action in the eyes of many countries, and probably an increase in the number of wars initiated by the United States on the basis of erroneous information or unnecessarily provoked by the posture of US military forces.

Choosing to strike first in the face of a "gathering danger" means adopting the traditional logic of the aggressor—that is, if eventual war is considered necessary or inevitable, it is better to attack than be attacked. In this way, the anticipated victim of aggression becomes the actual aggressor. If the United States proclaims and exercises a right of preventive war, the international community is likely to identify it as the aggressor, even if the circumstances prompting US military action would otherwise generate sympathy and support. Even accurate intelligence on preparations for war by a US enemy could fall short of the demonstrable proof necessary to maintain the high moral ground in the court of public opinion. The legal and moral responsibility for the brutal business of war will still be assigned to the party that launches it. And if the most powerful country in the world deems it unacceptable to wait until there is unimpeachable evidence of an attack before striking back, the constraints on much smaller and more vulnerable states will be considerably weakened.

The first negative consequence of the preventive war doctrine is definitional and straightforward—being blamed for the breach of the peace. A second negative consequence derives directly from the first. Countries that disagree with the preventive war doctrine or fear its application may become less likely to cooperate with US intelligence services. A third negative consequence is ironically and integrally connected with the intelligence function. The preventive war doctrine will orient intelligence toward providing early and definitive judgments of malevolent intent. Because the NSS 2002 doctrine itself implies a lower tolerance for risk, the intelligence agencies will also accept less risk in their identification of danger. It is likely, therefore, that there will be more occasions when warning-focused intelligence finds threatening situations. Just as history provides spectacular examples of strategic surprise, it is also replete with instances of intelligence organizations exaggerating threats and assessing erroneously that neighboring states harbored aggressive intent when they were, in fact, only preparing to defend themselves from aggression. Thus the NSS 2002 doctrine will stimulate more occasions for putting troops on alert, forward-deploying ships and aircraft, and interdicting suspicious movements of ships and aircraft from hostile states. The preparations consistent with such a doctrine will then result in a more provocative posture, which will be interpreted in turn by other parties as evidence of malevolent US intent, engendering political opposition and in-hibiting the flow of intelligence. A vicious cycle will thus be created.

PREVENTIVE WAR DOCTRINE FURTHER INCREASES COSTS OF ACTING ON EXAGGERATED THREATS

Some Americans argued for preventive war against the Soviet Union dur-ing the 1950s when the United States enjoyed overwhelming superiority, just as preventive war against China was advocated by members of the Soviet military during the 1960s. However, the sobering realities of the nuclear age eventually prevailed over the hard-liners in both countries. While America's long and painful involvement in Vietnam could be considered a kind of pre-ventive war against the spread of Communist insurgency in Southeast Asia, the introduction of a preventive war doctrine is a relatively new phenomenon for the United States.

Until the Bush administration incorporated preventive war into US military doctrine, the primary consequence of precipitous and exaggerated warnings from intelligence was unnecessary defense spending and missed opportunities for negotiated security arrangements. The cost was in the form of money and aggravated risk of war. We are now entering an era in which the existing emphasis on warning may lead not only to undertaking unnecessary and expensive defense measures but to waging unnecessary and expensive wars against other countries. As a result, friends and allies may be alienated, and the proliferation of unconventional weapons to hostile states may be ex-acerbated.

WHAT WARS MIGHT WE HAVE MISSED?

It is instructive to contemplate alternative histories that could have resulted if a muscular policy of preventive war had been practiced in years past. A review should be prefaced with a reminder about imperial Japan's attack on Pearl Harbor. The decision to launch preventive war was a logical one from Tokyo's perspective. It followed two decades of hostile acts by the United States: the 1924 Exclusion Act; the US Navy's war planning to contest con-trol of the western Pacific; the US oil embargo imposed after the Japanese invasion of Manchuria; and finally the 1941 freezing of Japanese assets in the United States. The Japanese government had no trouble "connecting the dots" to convince itself about America's hostility and the inevitability of war. The Japanese military's tactical intelligence was also impressive, even con-sidering the lack of information about the location of the Pearl Harbor–based US aircraft carriers on 7 December. The fatal flaw was in the strategic analy-sis of American intentions and the underestimation of the effect of a surprise attack on America's will and determination.

Our world would have certainly been altered if American advocates of preventive war against the Soviet Union had been more persuasive. Provocations like the Berlin Blockade in 1948–1949, the crushing of the 1956 Hungarian revolt by Soviet tanks, and the construction of the Berlin Wall in 1961 would have provided ample opportunities to rally the American people behind an attack.

During the 1962 Cuban Missile Crisis, active consideration was given to a preventive attack on the island. With the accumulation of personal interviews by participants and the opening of important archives, it has become increasingly obvious that the preventive war option against Cuba was actively considered. The provocation was clear, and the "window of opportunity" was fleeting. The brevity of medium-range ballistic missile flight times and the days-and-hours estimates of the time before the missiles would become operational made a strong argument for a US attack under a preventive war rationale—even though strategic intelligence on Soviet intentions was almost completely lacking. Fortunately for the world, President Kennedy rejected preventive war and chose a quarantine instead.

HOW NONSTATE ACTORS CHANGE THE EQUATION

The Bush administration contends that in a post-9/11 world, the potential interaction between "rogue" states developing unconventional weapons and nonstate actors with global reach has fundamentally altered the strategy and tactics required to protect the United States. However, contrary to the insinuations of the president and his vice president, the comprehensive research of the bipartisan 9/11 Commission found no evidence of a collaborative operational relationship between Iraq and al-Qaida.[43] To date, the IC has offered little empirical backing for the plausibility of asserting a close connection developing between organizations like al-Qaida and the governments of states possessing or seeking to possess nuclear, chemical, or biological weapons. Such states are usually loath to transfer sensitive technologies to nonstate actors outside their direct control. Not only might such transfers strengthen domestic opponents of the regime, but they could also lead to US retaliation for any use against US territory or US forces.

It is reasonable to assume that there are limits to the risk states are willing to run. Even North Korea's desperation to raise revenue through the sale of missiles and missile technology did not induce Pyongyang to respond favorably to Iraqi expressions of interest in purchasing missiles. A greater concern regarding the supply of sensitive technologies to terrorists arises from the operations of nonstate entities like the enterprises of A. Q. Kahn. The US-led attack on Afghanistan to remove the Taliban and pursue al-Qaida provided ample evidence that sponsorship of an organization responsible for attack-

ing the United States was hazardous to the survival of any regime supporting such a group. In the event that the government of a country possessing
unconventional weapons fell to radical fundamentalists—a fundamentalist
Pakistan is one of the worst such eventualities—that country would still have
to consider the reaction of the United States to any aid offered to terrorist
groups. Intelligence thus plays an increasingly important role in maintaining
the credibility of the US deterrent, for it is important to convince foreign
governments that the United States would detect significant covert assistance
flowing to terrorist groups. While there is no assurance US intelligence would
be able to prove such a connection, successful investigation of past terrorist
incidents like the sabotage by Libyan agents of Pan Am 103 over Lockerbie,
Scotland, deprive conspirator states of confidence that they could keep such
involvement hidden.

In spite of increasingly imaginative terrorist attack scenarios under discussion involving chemical, biological, or radiological weapons, the threat
posed by nuclear weapons use dwarfs all others. Fortunately, identifying the
sources of existing nuclear weapons or nuclear weapons–related technology
is not a new challenge for the IC. And in many respects, it is less demanding than penetrating the terrorist cells that might be interested in obtaining
nuclear technology or material. Because nuclear weapons require an extensive
national infrastructure to develop and produce, and because technical means
of detection are growing ever more sophisticated, intelligence services have
multiple opportunities for tracking progress among proliferators. Multilateral
organizations like the International Atomic Energy Agency (IAEA) have won
new arrangements to safeguard the use of nuclear energy and prevent nuclear
proliferation. The ability of the IAEA to monitor nuclear activities increased
dramatically between the first and second Iraq wars. Negotiated agreements
like the Comprehensive Nuclear Test Ban Treaty and the proposed Fissile
Material Cutoff Treaty hold the potential for further increases in the international community's ability to contain the threat of nuclear terrorism. Following the sources of fissile material, nuclear weapons–related technology,
and the activities of key experts will continue to be a high-priority task for
intelligence agencies. US intelligence can make an enormous contribution as
well to effective enforcement of international nonproliferation regimes.

While it may be hotly contested which lessons for national doctrine
should be drawn from contemporary circumstances, there is little doubt
about the implications for intelligence of the quantum leaps in weapons lethality, speed of employment, and capabilities of nonstate terrorist groups.
More than ever, intelligence must be fast and reliable if it is to be actionable.

These increasing demands on intelligence providers have exacerbated
the long-standing challenge of trying to understand the intentions and ca-

pabilities of potential enemies—whether foreign governments or nonstate entities. Requiring the IC to provide the kind of high confidence and rapid assessments needed to launch preemptive/preventive war goes a large step beyond the previous challenges of warning, prediction, and evaluation—from difficult to virtually impossible.

WHERE DOES THIS LEAVE US?

With the end of the Cold War, the consequences of an enemy attack are no longer a matter of national survival. The need to act with haste militarily in advance of an attack is much less critical than earlier. While a well-honed warning capability retains value for the nation, it no longer assumes an existential role in national defense. A surprise biological attack by terrorists or chemical weapons use against US troops is more likely to result in a localized catastrophe or temporary setback to American forces in the field than to the destruction of the nation or the end of life on Earth as we know it. In the long run, the United States is better off using its resources cooperatively to detect and prevent an attack in the first place, or to mitigate the lethality of any attack that does occur, than lashing out unilaterally at all enemies real and imagined. The breathing space provided by the end of the Cold War calls for exploiting the opportunity to retool intelligence and reinvigorate cooperation with the international community, which overwhelmingly opposes the activities of international terrorists.

REFORMING OUR INTELLIGENCE STRUCTURE

Although I have argued that the quality of intelligence required for preventive war cannot be reliably attained, this realization should not preclude efforts to improve the intelligence on which the nation continues to rely. Indeed, the better the intelligence, the more likely the United States will be able to avoid attack and to minimize damage from any attacks that do occur. More successful intelligence along with more intelligent foreign policy would make the radical and counterproductive doctrine of preventive war even less attractive.

A number of serious recommendations for reforming the US post–World War II intelligence structure have been made in recent years by high-level commissions and study groups. The unusual circumstances leading to the 9/11 Commission report and the unanimous, bipartisan nature of the report's recommendations led Congress to make significant statutory changes in December 2004. It would be wise also to incorporate lessons from misassessing Iraq—the other significant US intelligence failure of the new century—in any reform effort. The Senate Select Committee on Intelligence provided in

July 2004 an unusually comprehensive, insiders' perspective on the prewar performance of the IC in assessing Iraq's unconventional weapons programs and Hussein's connections to al-Qaida. The Commission on the Intelligence Capabilities of the United States Regarding Weapons of Mass Destruction (Silberman-Robb Commission) released its report on overall proliferation intelligence in March 2005. The promised phase two report of the Senate Select Committee on Intelligence will address the way prewar intelligence on Iraq was used. It is hoped that these reports will also be able to influence the current round of intelligence reform.

FORMULAS FOR CHANGE

While recommendations here for specific changes in intelligence structure risk being overtaken by swiftly moving events, several broad principles of reform to enhance the quality of intelligence assessment can be safely asserted.

The roles of the CIA chief and the leader of the IC must be kept structurally and functionally separate. For many years, the same individual performed these two jobs. In practice, this meant that the challenge of coordinating all of the intelligence agencies and representing their collective judgment to the president was subordinated to the institutional or personal interests of the head of the CIA. By the time of the Iraq War, not only was the President's Daily Brief (PBD) being drafted by the CIA with no coordination by other intelligence agencies, the final product was not being shown to the heads of those other agencies. When the PDB carried the headline "Bin Ladin Determined to Strike in US" on 6 August 2001, that PDB was not shared with the Federal Bureau of Investigation's (FBI) director of intelligence, the head of the DIA, or the State Department's assistant secretary for intelligence and research. When the CIA informed the White House that Iraqi purchases of high-strength aluminum tubes were going into Baghdad's nuclear weapons program, no one represented the two dissenting agencies (the DOE and the INR) to make the case for the contrary explanation, which ultimately proved correct. Moreover, DCI and CIA chief Tenet, along with the National Intelligence Council (NIC) reporting to Tenet, minimized this interpretation in statements to the public and the Congress. The Intelligence Reform and Terrorism Prevention Act of 2004 was designed to remedy these problems by creating a new and more powerful supervisory authority over the entire IC, the Director of National Intelligence (DNI). This statutory reform will eliminate the inherent conflict of interest in the CIA director wearing both hats.

The organization responsible for producing IC assessments, currently the NIC, should be truly independent. It should be headed by someone who is not responsible for running individual intelligence agencies or defending any particular policies, but is instead free of pressure from political, operational, and resource concerns. This goal would suggest that the head of the IC's assessment function should be appointed by the president and subject to congressional confirmation, but not be part of the White House.

The sources of human intelligence must be more rigorously evaluated. More information on the sources should be made available to those with the proper clearances. If trustworthy reliability labeling cannot be achieved under the existing structure, as appears to have been the case with so much of the human intelligence relating to Iraqi biological and chemical weapons, then an evaluative mechanism needs to be established outside of the CIA's Directorate of Operations.

The analytical integrity of individual IC agencies must be maintained. Each of the sixteen separate agencies and entities of the US IC have a unique institutional mission and perspective. Some are oriented around the means of collecting information—for example, NSA specializes in signals intelligence. Others perform all-source analysis, but are oriented around the specialized needs of a particular customer—for example, the DIA serves the DOD. Interagency discussions of complicated issues serve as a form of peer review when hypotheses are suggested to explain evidence. While consensus is sought when the IC produces an estimate, conclusions dissenting from the majority view are permitted, if not always encouraged. The failure to take published dissents seriously on Iraqi "WMD" led to serious consequences. The most conspicuous examples of such dissents were the contentions of DOE and INR that the aluminum tubes were not intended for a nuclear weapons program, and of Air Force Intelligence that the UAVs were not intended for weapons delivery. In these cases, the appropriate level of attention was never extended to the agencies that commanded the greatest technical expertise on the matter under investigation. That said, a more centralized and tightly controlled intelligence directorate might never have allowed the dissenting views to surface in the first place.

Congressional oversight needs to be strengthened. In recent years, there appears to have been little congressional scrutiny of how the IC "sanitizes" classified information for public consumption or how it reaches its conclusions on complicated issues. In the case of Iraq, this situation allowed the CIA's leadership to present information to the public (and to members of Congress not on the intelligence committees) in a manner that was not faithful to the detailed analyses in highly classified documents. In many cases, this seems to have been done not to protect sensitive sources and methods, but to make a more persuasive political case for the policies being pursued. The magnitude of the IC's failure and the misuse by senior administration officials of the IC's findings also bespeaks a failure in congressional oversight. Yet only the Senate has so far taken modest steps to reform its procedures and structure in parallel with the statutory measures of the Intelligence Reform and Terrorism Prevention Act of 2004.

RENOUNCING PREVENTIVE WAR

In 2002, President George W. Bush introduced the preventive war doctrine into the national security strategy of the United States for the first time. In order to be morally justifiable, preventive war must be based on the firm knowledge of a hostile opponent's capabilities and intentions. Yet the Bush administration has twice demonstrated convincingly within a short period of time that the elaborate intelligence services of the United States could not be relied upon to deliver definitive and timely knowledge of opponents' capabilities—first al-Qaida and then Iraq. Discerning the exact intentions of Saddam Hussein proved even more elusive than smoking out his unconventional weapons capabilities.

Preventive war is not a feasible formula for addressing the urgent security challenges facing the nation, because it unleashes problems even worse than those it is intended to remedy. Preventive war doctrine should, therefore, be explicitly rejected. Doing so would not preclude all military action against terrorists, although police action would be the principal tool. Military actions would carry the presumption that they had been authorized either by the governments of the territories on which they occurred or by the UN.

While improving US intelligence collection and analysis is desirable and possible, the intelligence services cannot be expected to deliver the quality of information needed to merit preventive war. To initiate war without such certain knowledge of intentions and capabilities is a prescription for ignominy—and an invitation to join the multitudinous ranks of aggressors throughout history. If even Bismarck, as chancellor of the German Empire in the nineteenth century, could foreswear preventive war because of the inherent limits of strategic intelligence, it is not asking too much for the president of the world's most powerful democracy in the twenty-first century to do the same.

Military Capabilities in Preventive Military Strategy

PETER DOMBROWSKI

THE FOREIGN POLICY of the United States has long been informed by the implicit assumption that military force can be used to counter imminent threats to national security,[1] but seldom if ever has the United States publicly declared a preference for limited preventive strikes and/or preventive war. The doctrine of preventive military intervention, announced formally with the publication of the 2002 National Security Strategy of the United States of America (NSS 2002), changed this reticence by indicating that the United States would no longer wait to be attacked before responding; instead the George W. Bush administration pledged to strike potential attackers before they acted. Years later, senior Bush administration officials continue to support the preventive use of force despite a firestorm of domestic and international criticism and charges that it contributed to the Iraq disaster.

Sustaining an explicit commitment to preventive military strategy raises an important question: Does the United States have the military capabilities necessary to implement a doctrine of preventive military intervention over time?[2] On initial consideration, this question might seem irrelevant. Recent

US military actions in Afghanistan and Iraq, not to mention Kosovo and the first Gulf War, have been successful, in an operational sense, if not in strategic terms.[3] Further, as has been widely reported, US military spending exceeds that of the rest of the world combined, so there appears little chance that any single country or even group of countries could challenge US military supremacy any time soon. The Bush administration, the Office of the Secretary of Defense, and the military services have also committed to maintaining American predominance by actively encouraging a process of transformation designed to increase substantially the nation's military capabilities in the coming decades. In short, how could the United States have difficulty implementing preventive military strategy?

Answering this question will help determine how credible the doctrine will be as future presidents grapple with terrorist groups, state sponsors of terrorism, "rogue" states, and proliferators of nuclear, biological, and chemical (NBC) weapons.[4] It is likely that the preventive force option will remain available, in one form or another, for the foreseeable future.[5] If so, the US military must have the wherewithal to implement the policy successfully. Otherwise, the United States might face operational failures, the loss of credibility, and, perhaps, an erosion of national security.[6]

This chapter is divided into five sections. First, it explores the general military capabilities required to implement the doctrine of preventive military intervention. Second, it considers whether the United States has these capabilities in sufficient quantity and quality. The next section considers US capabilities vis-à-vis two countries—Iran and Syria—that are potential targets of US preventive military action. Section five discusses how US military limitations, within the wider context of the doctrine of preventive military intervention, might affect international perceptions of US credibility, legitimacy, and security. The chapter concludes by examining options for increasing the US capacity for preventive military intervention.

PREVENTIVE INTERVENTION AND THE USE OF FORCE

Most analyses bemoan the fact that the Bush administration has used the term "preemption" promiscuously, thus muddying the distinction between preemption and prevention. Debates over the Iraq War and whether it was undertaken under the auspices of the new strategic doctrine or for other reasons, such as upholding the credibility of the United Nations (UN) Security Council, have not helped matters. Nor have the recent findings that Iraq neither possessed nuclear weapons capable of imminently threatening the United States nor had close ties with terrorist groups such as al-Qaida bolstered international confidence in the ability of the United States to execute a first-strike strategy in good faith. Earlier chapters in this volume consider these arguments in detail and clarify the theoretical distinction between preemptive and preventive military action. My analysis focuses on the military challenges involved in implementing a strategic doctrine based on preventive use of force.

To help understand what military capabilities are required to implement the doctrine of preventive military intervention, it is first necessary to clarify what it means in terms of military requirements. Conceptually, there are two general types of preventive military actions: strike operations involving limited attacks against a discrete set of targets, and full-scale military interventions intended, for example, to topple a regime pursuing NBC weapons or harboring terrorists.

The US military must be prepared, out of necessity, to undertake preventive military action alone; hence, in this chapter I do not focus on how the United States might undertake preventive action alongside allied or coalition forces, although, as will be discussed in the chapter's final section, this may be an option in the future. In the near term, unless the Bush administration or its successors radically shift their relations with the UN, regional security organizations, or even members of ad hoc "coalitions of the willing," the military actions associated with either limited preventive strikes or preventive wars will largely fall upon the American armed forces. One reason is practical; few countries have types of military forces necessary to conduct either strike or full combat operations far from home. Another reason is political; few states agree with the US assertion that it has the unilateral right to undertake preventive military intervention. The apparent lack of trained troops and appropriate equipment among potential partners is a relatively minor obstacle compared to the divergence between American understanding about when and how force might be used, legally and ethically, and the positions held by many members of the international community, including long-standing US allies like France and Great Britain.[7] The net result of international opposition to the American position on the use of force is that many countries are reluctant to participate in American-led actions.

The problems associated with how the Bush administration made its case against Iraq have also affected the willingness of other states to join the United States in undertaking preventive military actions. Having been misled on the presence of nuclear weapons capabilities, the imminence of the threat, the extent of Iraq relations with al-Qaida, and the prospects for peace in postwar Iraq, many countries are reluctant to believe in the legitimacy of NSS 2002 itself or have full confidence in the ability of US intelligence and military services to support the preventive military actions. Additionally, many countries have expressed skepticism about recent American claims against Iran, Syria, and even North Korea.

US MILITARY CAPABILITIES

NSS 2002 is a guide for using force, but it tells the world little about whether the US military can do what is expected of it.[8] Does the United States have the military forces to strike weapons production facilities and/or terrorist facilities? The preceding conceptual distinction between limited preventive strikes and preventive wars helps answer this question. Limited preventive strikes are focused attacks against discrete targets, while preventive wars involve more sustained campaigns designed to end, by regime change if necessary, a "rogue" state's ability to threaten the United States.[9] Preventive war also implies that regime change will be accompanied by reconstruction, both political and material; the United States must be prepared to help create and support the establishment of a successor to the regime it just displaced. At a minimum, this requires that the United States help supply security—including constabulary functions—while the new regime becomes viable. The Afghanistan and Iraq wars and postconflict period have taught the world that skimping on security undermines the orderly transfer of power.

MILITARY BALANCE AND EFFECTIVENESS

The American military has downsized substantially since the height of the 1980s buildup, but this does not necessarily mean that the individual services are less capable or that they are not able to accomplish assigned roles and missions. The US Navy, for example, has fewer ships than the nearly 600 it could deploy in the late 1980s, but by other measures, such as firepower, the navy is stronger today. The nature of threats have also changed, although how and why are often in dispute, so few expect the US military to maintain the size and composition it held when it faced the forces of the Soviet Union and the Warsaw Pact.

Historically, the most common benchmark for assessing the appropriate size of American forces was the two-war standard. In short, the standard maintains that the United States should maintain sufficient military forces to fight and win two conflicts nearly simultaneously. In the post–Cold War period, the two-war standard has been debated and revised continuously. More recent variants discuss preparing for two simultaneous major regional contingencies and other "lesser included cases" such as noncombatant evacuation operations.

The relationship of US military force structure to the planning standards, such as the ability to fight two wars, has often been more theoretical than real. It is unclear whether the country met its own planning objectives at any point since World War II. A true test of fundamental US planning objectives has never really occurred, however, because for the most part the military has not been called upon to fight two major conflicts at once. Efforts to sustain multiple smaller operations simultaneously suggest that shortfalls are myriad, especially with regard to "high value, low density assets" such as air refueling tankers, surveillance and communications satellites, and language specialists, to name a few prominent examples. The US military's readiness to fulfill its planning objectives in the past, today, and in the future is in dispute. Witness, for example, the debate between the Bush and John Kerry campaigns (not to mention congressional partisans) during the 2002 presidential race over whether the army needs more troops to sustain operations in Iraq, Afghanistan, and other hotspots in the global war on terror simultaneously.

What is not in dispute is that the US military today is smaller than it was prior to the collapse of the Soviet Union and the Warsaw Pact. Currently, US forces consist of approximately 1.37 million active duty forces and 1.28 million ready and stand-by reserves. Table 3 provides a rough outline of America's military strength by military service and major fighting components. While this is not necessarily the best measure of the strength of the US armed forces, it does enable a first order assessment.

Regardless of abstract planning metrics, as a global power the United States prepares for multiple conflicts simultaneously, including both the so-called wars of choice that fall under the rubric of the preventive military intervention and conflicts that are thrust upon it due to prior commitments or new adversaries.[10] This is especially true if the country remains locked in counterinsurgency, policy, and occupation roles in Iraq. Many reputable analysts inside and outside the government argue that a long-term military commitment to Iraq, including combat forces, is straining, and will continue to strain, US forces, especially the army, marine corps combat units, and specialized military capabilities. For this chapter, let us assume that in the

Table 3. US Military Active Duty Personnel and Current Force Structure, 30 September 2004

Army	Navy	Marine Corps	Air Force	total
499,543	373,197	177,480	376, 616	1,426,836
10/8 Active/National Guard Divisions	301 Ships	3/1 Active/National Guard Divisions	10 Air and Space Expeditionary Units	

Source: Adapted from United States, Office of the Secretary of Defense, *Annual Report to the President and the Congress,* 2004 (Washington, D.C.: Government Printing Office, 2004), http://www.defenselink.mil/execsec/adr2004/index.html.

short to intermediate term the United States will maintain between 120,000 and 130,000, if not more, troops in Iraq with an appropriate level of support by air force and naval airpower as well as intelligence assets of various types. Obviously, the demand for combat troops would diminish rapidly if the United States chooses to withdraw its forces from Iraq or was asked to leave by an elected Iraqi government.

PREVENTIVE STRIKE CAPABILITIES

The ability to launch strikes, preventive or otherwise, remains perhaps the greatest single strength of the US military; in fact, it is perhaps the only capacity not diminished by the Iraq commitment. Unlike other countries, the United States is able to strike targets anywhere in the world within a relatively short period of time. Repeatedly during the long shadow war against al-Qaida prior to 9/11, the Clinton administration attacked and prepared to attack al-Qaida facilities and leaders, including Osama bin Laden; missions were often aborted not because the military was not ready to launch air strikes, cruise missiles, or special operations, but because intelligence was not always actionable.[11] Within months of determining that al-Qaida, under the protection of the Taliban regime of Afghanistan, had planned and carried out the 9/11 attacks, the United States attacked and destroyed virtually all terrorist and military targets in the country. What makes this feat impressive is the geographic distance of Afghanistan both from the United States and from its forces stationed abroad on land and at sea. The United States was able to strike at will using a wide array of precision weapons and "dumb" bombs launched from US-based strategic bombers, carrier-based attack aircraft, both air- and sea-launched cruise missiles, and, in a few cases, combat-equipped unmanned aerial vehicles (UAVs) such as the Global Hawk. It was also able to deploy special forces and other covert troops on Afghani territory by December 2001, once President Bush made the decision to remove the Taliban from power.

Admittedly, some elements of the American attacks were improvised. Military analysts called it a "pick-up game." A *Nimitz*-class nuclear aircraft carrier that normally carries a complement of eighty-four strike and reconnaissance aircraft was reconfigured to host special operations forces and associated air power. Covert forces operating outside the control of the US military provided much of the early on-the-ground firepower in Afghanistan. Much of the actual ground fighting was done by an Afghan rebel group, the Northern Alliance, with US financial, logistical, and intelligence assistance. Improvisation, though, serves only to highlight the ingenuity and training of the American military when faced with an especially difficult military objective.

Operations Northern and Southern Watch over Iraq following the Persian Gulf War are also instructive—because of the demonstrated capacity of the United States to sustain strike operations over time when necessary. For nearly six and a half years the United States, with the support of British (and French for a while) forces, as well as with the use of the facilities and airspace of Iraq's neighbors, was able to both surveil Iraq's territory—including both the land under no-fly zone restrictions imposed by the UN and areas where Iraqi sovereignty remained technically intact. More to the point, US planes repeatedly struck Iraqi air defense systems, intelligence facilities, and other targets to enforce the UN arms and oil embargoes, prevent Saddam Hussein's forces from punishing Kurds and other rebellious groups within Iraq, and ensure that Hussein was unable to launch a full-scale NBC production program.[12]

These two examples, while extreme, illustrate the range of US strike capabilities. Even the most heavily defended airspace is eventually accessible to US tactical and strategic aircraft. American air defense suppression systems, stealth technologies, radar-jamming capabilities, satellite surveillance technologies, battle space management techniques, and virtually unfettered access to the global commons of space and the high seas ensure access. There are, of course, gaps and weaknesses in US strike operations—poor flying weather, heavy jungle canopies, mobile targets, and so forth present formidable technical and operational challenges that have not yet been resolved.

The logic underlying preventive military intervention requires more than retaliatory, one-shot, limited preventive strikes or even sustained operations, however. The ambitious objectives of regime change, democratization, and nation building are not attainable with limited preventive strikes. Launching preventive strikes is analogous to treating the symptoms rather than the disease or its underlying causes; the best-case outcome is that a regime is deterred or discouraged from harboring terrorists or proliferating unconventional weapons. In the worst case, a recalcitrant regime continues covert efforts to attain NBC weapons and/or assist anti-American terrorists groups. Preventive wars address the root of problems posed by adversaries by removing the regime in power and installing a new one that, if the Bush administration has its way, will have similar institutions and aspirations to the United States and its democratic allies. Drive-by shootings will not, indeed, lead bad guys to stop acquiring NBC weapons or from harboring terrorists. These goals require larger, more sustained commitments to the use of force.

PREVENTIVE WARS

The most controversial and militarily challenging option is to launch a preventive war against a "rogue" state to effect regime change. Preventive wars, at least as discussed by members of the Bush administration and its supporters, is for the opponent akin to total war. The regime that is attacked is literally fighting for its life and, depending on the circumstance, the lives and freedom of its political leaders. As a consequence, there is possibility that it will use whatever military means are at its disposal to ward off the attack or increase the costs on the attacking nation even to the point where preventive war is no longer an attractive option. This logic underlies the assumption of many analysts prior to both wars with Iraq that, if pushed to the extreme, Saddam Hussein would deploy and use chemical and biological weapons.

The type of military force required to effect regime change is determined by the particular characteristics of the regime in question—its military capabilities; its possession, or not, of NBC weapons; the support that could be expected from the populace; the terrain; access from the sea and air; in addition to many other factors. Even for a military as experienced as the United States' the types and qualities of forces required are often subject to dispute. For example, relatively small operations such as preparations for the potential invasion of Kosovo generated disputes between General Wesley Clark, North Atlantic Treaty Organization (NATO) allies, the Pentagon leadership, and civilian leaders.[13] While preparing for the 2003 Iraq invasion, the Bush administration was, at least temporarily, beset by internal strife, as those who advocated for a large force capable of winning through a *coup d'main* and handling all possible contingencies vied with Secretary of Defense Donald Rumsfeld and others, who insisted that a much smaller military force, if used properly, could win through rapid decisive operations and "shock and awe" tactics.[14]

As both Iraq wars demonstrated, however, defeating the enemy's forces on the battlefield is insufficient to win a victory, especially in the case of preventive war where regime change is expected. For a viable political settlement to be arranged, the military must secure the territory of the government it has defeated. The reasons are both military—it is not in the interest of the invader to allow a resistance movement, insurgency, or even civil war to develop—and political—for a new regime to replace its predecessor, the invader needs political legitimacy and must demonstrate that it can protect civilians and infrastructure until a new government is ready and able to assume its responsibilities.

As a consequence, military operations do not necessarily stop once major battles are completed. Rather, the nature of the military's tasks and assignments changes. This often requires troops and equipment different from those required for major combat operations, thus creating a different type of strain on the nation's military forces.

POSTCONFLICT OPERATIONS/NATION BUILDING

Iraq has retaught the United States that it is not enough to simply destroy an adversary's army, air force, navy, and other military capabilities to ensure a lasting peace and reduce the possibility that the nation will have to go to war against the same adversary in the future. Unfortunately, the US military has not focused on occupation and reconstruction for some time. Even as the administration was preparing for the Iraq invasion, it was simultaneously closing down the Peacekeeping Institute at the US Army War College—one of the few assets designed to prepare troops for succeeding in the postconflict environment it would face in Iraq as soon as the main battles were decided.[15] The US military suffered from what has been called "the problem of forgetting."[16]

The mantra of US military forces in recent years is the equivalent of "we don't do windows."[17] Time and time again, general officers have argued that the military services should focus on war fighting as opposed to all the various operations categorized as "military operations other than war." Yet in the Balkans, Afghanistan, and now Iraq, the US Army has increasingly found itself employed as the main implementer of a grand strategy of nation building and democratization. Contrary to popular belief, these are tasks that the US Army and Marine Corps have historically carried out—from the army's decades-long efforts to pacify the western frontier in the nineteenth century to US long-term commitments to Nicaragua, the Philippines, and a host of larger countries such as Germany, Japan, and South Korea. Nowhere is this trend more evident than in Iraq. The Bush administration made public and extravagant commitments to rebuilding the nation's economy and introducing democratic political institutions, objectives whose fulfillment is contingent on the ability of the United States to provide internal and external security for the new government.

Despite history and rhetoric, neither the US civilian nor military leadership appears to have prepared especially well for what the military calls Phase IV, or posthostility, operations.[18] As David Reiff argued, "[t]he real lesson of the postwar mess is that while occupying and reconstructing Iraq was bound to be difficult, the fact that it may be turning into a quagmire is not a result of fate, but rather (as quagmires usually are) a result of poor planning and wishful thinking."[19] Reiff's interpretation has been confirmed by General (ret.) Tommy Franks's insider account of the preparations for the Iraq War.[20] Yet no amount of planning and no amount of can-do spirit among US military personnel could entirely overcome the fact that American soldiers are no longer trained and equipped to serve in the postconflict environments presented in Iraq and, perhaps, in the future if other preventive wars are launched.

At some future date, the United States will, in all likelihood, find itself once again in a position of nation building, democratic or otherwise. But if the past is a guide, the United States can no longer walk away once the last full-scale battle has been fought. It must help create the conditions for self-governance, preferably democratic. If this means keeping significant forces in-country to perform policing or even counterinsurgency operations, so be it. To do otherwise is to risk having to intervene militarily again and again, as the United States has done in Haiti, Nicaragua, and a host of other small countries circling the globe. Further, given that military spending, expertise, capital, and human resources are likely to exceed by an order of magnitude the other components of American foreign operations budgets, the military will be the primary instrument used to exercise American power.[21]

AGAINST WHOM?

In his 2002 State of the Union address, President Bush specifically identified three members of the so-called axis of evil—Iraq, Iran, and North Korea. Months later, then undersecretary for arms control and international security John R. Bolton took the president's proclamation one step further by identifying Cuba, Libya, and Syria as states that might be subject to preventive action.[22] Events appear to have taken Libya off the list of candidates for preventive war;[23] although as experts from the International Atomic Energy Agency (IAEA) still seek to verify whether Libya has fulfilled its pledges to the international community, longer-term worries remain.[24] Cuba, however, remains a remote candidate but still a real possibility as a target for preventive war, as neither the Democratic nor Republican Party can resist pandering to the Cuban exile community for votes; the Bush administration has even claimed, despite a paucity of evidence, that Cuba may be sharing biological weapons or the technologies to make them.[25]

Other possible targets for preventive war may also warrant consideration. Several states not mentioned by President Bush have nuclear weapons, have NBC development programs, and have at least been rumored to be shopping these weapons to outlaw states and perhaps even terrorist groups. Chief among these is Pakistan. Prior to 9/11, one of President Bush's special assistants on the National Security Council, Kori Schake, developed a list of "rogue" states and potential proliferators (see table 4).[26] In short, there is no shortage of potential targets for preventive military intervention in the future.

The next section considers most closely two cases: Iran and Syria. Both countries have been explicitly warned and even threatened by senior officials in the Bush administration. Both also represent hard cases in that they have relatively large militaries and the type of popular support that would make

Table 4. Potential "Rogue" States

State	NBC Programs	Terrorism Sponsor	State	NBC Programs	Terrorism Sponsor
Algeria	Yes	Yes	North Korea	Yes	Yes
China	Yes	No	Russia	Yes	No
Cuba	No	No	Serbia	Yes	No
Iran	Yes	Yes	Sudan	Yes	Yes
Libya	Yes	Yes	Syria	Yes	Yes

Source: Adapted from Kori N. Schake and Justin P. Bernier, "Dealing with Rogue States," in *The Global Century: Globalization and National Security,* vol. 1, ed. Richard L. Kugler and Ellen L. Frost (Washington, D.C.: National Defense University Press, 2001).

them unlikely candidates for the sort of regime change "lite" represented by schemes to undermine the regime using exiles or disgruntled tribal groups. Other potential rogues have been set aside, for this analysis anyway, in large part because of the reverse insight offered by an Indian officer. When asked about the lesson of the 1991 Persian Gulf War, the officer said: "Never fight the US without nuclear weapons."[27] The United States is not eager to initiate a preventive attack against a nuclear-armed adversary.

CAPABLE FOES?

A traditional defense planner seeking specific answers to the specific question motivating this chapter might begin by generating scenarios for fighting potential target states and then war game these scenarios using existing or projected capabilities, strategies, and tactics for the United States and its possible allies and for the target state and its possible allies. More recently, defense planners have used capability-based techniques that address iteratively questions of strategy, budgets, and uncertain threats. Given the staffing requirements, expertise, and extensive resources required for these processes, they are obviously far beyond the scope of this chapter. As a very rough substitute, this chapter will assess the relative difficulty of launching a preventive war against the two countries based on three parameters: geography; military balance and military effectiveness; and intensity of resistance before and after military intervention by the United States to impose regime change.

Geography will be discussed because a prerequisite for launching a preventive war is access to the target country. Although the United States could plausibly threaten most parts of most countries with military strikes (and even with a significant number of troops using airborne landings, austere bases, and so forth), a full-scale preventive war would much more viable if the military could introduce its forces in significant numbers through land routes, major ports, and/or access to functional air bases.

Military balance, for these purposes, refers simply to the numbers and nature of the military forces controlled by a particular country. According to Ken Pollack, military effectiveness "refers to the ability of soldiers and officers to perform on the battlefield, to accomplish military missions, and to execute strategies devised by their political-military leaders. If strategy is the military means by which political ends are pursued, military effectiveness refers to the skills that are employed."[28] In brief, a country can have an imposing military force structure but remain militarily ineffective when confronted with actual combat. Assessment of Iraq's military before and after the 1991 Persian Gulf War represents an extreme example of this phenomenon.

Intensity of resistance refers to how likely or unlikely the United States is to win the support and/or acquiescence of significant segments of the target country's population, political elites, and regular or irregular military forces. It also considers the likelihood that remnants of the previous regime will continue to fight as "dead enders" and/or whether there are major tribal or ethnic groups that can and will serve as alternative sources of political, economic, ideological, and thus military power. The presence or absence of neighboring countries also opposed to regime change and/or an American-led invasion and reconstruction will also be considered.

IRAN

Iran remains the favorite candidate of neoconservative activists for the next preventive war to be launched by the United States. As Charles Krauthammer argues, there were once five countries supporting terrorism and pursuing unconventional weapons—two junior-leaguers, Libya and Syria, and the axis of evil varsity: Iraq, Iran, and North Korea.[29] The Bush administration has eliminated two: Iraq, by direct military means, and Libya, at least according to Bush administration partisans, by example and intimidation. As Krauthammer views the situation:

Syria is weak and deterred by Israel. North Korea, having gone nuclear, is untouchable. That leaves Iran. What to do? There are only two things that will stop the Iranian nuclear program: revolution from below or an attack on its nuclear facilities. The country should be ripe for revolution. The regime is detested. But the mullahs are very good at police-state tactics. The long-awaited revolution is not happening which makes the question of preemptive attack all the more urgent.[30]

American relations with the government of Iran have been largely conflictual since the Iranian revolution in 1979. But unlike Iraq,[31] Iran has not received a great deal of attention until recent years, in large part because both Presidents Clinton and George W. Bush were preoccupied with Iraq.

Iran, however, has played a checkered role in supporting and/or hindering American objectives in Iraq both before, during, and after the 2003 Iraq War. The heart of recent American antagonism toward Iran lies with evidence that Iran has pursued and may still be pursuing nuclear weapons capabilities. In combination with alleged Iranian interference in Iraqi affairs during the post-Hussein period, Iran's nuclear ambitions have moved Iran to the forefront of potential threats to US interests.

Geography

Iran is both a long way from the United States and, at least until the recent occupation of Iraq, relatively difficult to access for American armed forces. Moreover, it is a very large country with an incredibly diverse terrain. The climate ranges from arid to semitropical. Of its five neighboring states, some are friendly and sympathetic to the regime, while others have long histories of conflict and even outright warfare. The coastline on the Persian Gulf might allow for logistical operations in addition to those based in Iraq, but all shipping must pass through the Straits of Hormuz and other bottlenecks, thus leaving a potential invading and resupply force vulnerable to sea-based attacks and access denial through mining operations. In short, Iran is an in-hospitable country with access limited to a relatively small coastline and such landlines of communication as exist between Iran and its longtime enemy Iraq.

Military Balance and Effectiveness

Iran's conventional military is large but low-tech, especially given arms embargoes in place since the fall of the shah and the tremendous losses of the Iraq-Iran War. Iranian conventional power projection, aside from terrorism, is limited to its immediate neighbors. In defending in its own country, Iran remains a formidable military force, however. One expert notes that "a ground force of a substantial number of divisions" would be required to "completely defeat it."[32]

The state of Iranian NBC programs remains in dispute. Most experts acknowledge a measure of biological and chemical capability, but the biggest worry is the country's nuclear capabilities. Few think that an invading foe can rule out being attacked by dirty bombs and other nonatomic or thermonuclear explosions. In the Iran-Iraq War, Iranians demonstrated a will to fight that should not be ignored. Despite the Western weapons and intelligence channeled to Iraq, Iran was able to hold its own largely through the fanaticism of its troops and the ruthlessness of its leaders.

Intensity of Resistance

As the Iran–Iraq War demonstrated, the nationalism of the Iranian people and their willingness to sacrifice lives and social well-being are quite serious. Iraq's political landscape is divided and contentious. Iran is relatively homogeneous in terms of religion and ethnicity. Homogeneity can work for and against a potential invader. On one hand, the invader cannot hope to support one ethnic group against the others, thereby perhaps securing a territorial base and a base of support among at least some of the local populace. On the other hand, the possibility of finding a postconflict political settlement is not complicated by intricacies of confessional and ethnic politics such as institutional power sharing, the disenfranchisement of minorities, and the aftershocks of long-standing historical grievances.

In sum, if the doctrine of preventive military intervention and the fundamental precepts of the Bush administration's approach to foreign and security policies are to be taken seriously, Iran is a potential target for preventive war or limited preventive strikes. Some analysts believe Iran might be willing to transfer its nuclear knowledge and capabilities to one or more of the terrorist groups it has supported for the past several decades, develop its own nuclear weapons and delivery systems, and perhaps even choose to use them in service of its wider regional ambitions in the Persian Gulf and the greater Middle East. Iran will remain a serious threat to American security interests.

Yet limited preventive strikes against Iran, much less a preventive war, will be much more difficult than in the Afghanistan and Iraq cases. Limited preventive strikes are not very likely given that, like most states with nuclear ambitions, Iran has spread its facilities widely and buried many deep underground.[33] Preventive war would be equally difficult because of the geography of Iran. Even more than Iraq, Iran possesses great strategic depth, with layers of military assets that complicate enemy attacks. It also has a large and relatively homogeneous population with long history of independence, nationalism, and antagonism toward the United States. Finally, although some might calculate that Iraq would provide a convenient launching pad for a war against Iran, large numbers of American troops will be tied up supplying basic security services in Iraq for the foreseeable future.

SYRIA

In some respects, Syria is an unlikely target of the preventive war doctrine. It was a US ally in the first Gulf War. Following the death of President Hafez Assad, Syria has been led by his son, Bashar, who is Western educated and, by some accounts, more interested in accommodation with the United States

Table 5. Basic Comparison of Potential Target States: Geography, Military and People

	Iraq	Syria	Iran
Geography			
Land area	438,317 sq km	185,180 sq km	1.648 million sq km
Borders	6	5	8
Coastline	58 km	193 km	2,440 km
Military			
Armed forces personnel (in thousands)	429	316	513
Weapon holdings (aggregate number of heavy weapons)	7,580	11,932	5,113
Defense budget (in US dollars)	$1,300,000,000	$858,000,000	$4,300,000,000
People			
Population	23,331,985	16,728,808	66,128,965
Ethnic Makeup	Arab (75–80%) Kurdish (15–20%)	Arab (90.3%) Kurds, Armenians, and other (9.7%)	Persian (51%) Azeri (24%)
Religions	Shi'a (60–65%) Sunni (32–37%)	Sunni (74%) Alawite, Druze, and other Muslim sects (16%) Christian sects (10%)	Shi'a Muslim (89%) Sunni Muslim (10%)

Sources: Bonn International Center for Conversion (BICC); *CIA World Fact Book,* and *Middle East Directory,* http://www.cia.gov/cia/publications /factbook/index.html; and http://www.middleeastdirectory.com.

than conflict. Yet major points of contention remain. Syria remains a frontline state against Israel and continues to support terrorist groups operating in Lebanon and the Occupied Territories. Most important are reports that Syria was secretly aiding Hussein's regime until its final collapse and in recent months has served as a base of operations for insurgents and terrorists attacking American troops in Iraq. Although the sources of these reports are not definitive, the US government has warned Syria not to interfere in Iraq and not to sponsor terrorists.[34] Several of the Bush administration's staunchest domestic allies, including Richard Perle, have repeatedly called for action against Syria.[35]

Geography

Syria presents a similar case to that of Iraq and Iran in terms of distance from the United States and its major bases. Unlike Iraq and Iran, however, it can be accessed from the Mediterranean Sea rather than the more treacherous Persian Gulf. With the American occupation of Iraq, Syria is surrounded by countries (such as Israel and Turkey) that, if not openly supportive of a potential preventive military intervention, would be unlikely to act against the United States. Two other border countries—Jordan and Lebanon—are too weak and strategically compromised to offer much support to the Syrian regime in the event of an invasion, although Lebanon may remain home to terrorists supported by Syria. In terms of terrain and climate, Syria is mostly arid desert plains and plateaus broken by some mountains in the west (see table 5). In short, the country's geography offers little by way of an obstacle should the United States seriously consider preventive military action.

Military Balance and Effectiveness

The historical record of Syria's armed forces is not very strong, unless various internal military operations are counted as successes.[36] In its wars with Israel, Syria has been badly overmatched on land and in the air. As part of the grand anti-Hussein coalition for the 1991 Persian Gulf War, Syria was assigned few tasks of substance. Hence it is difficult to assess Syrian capabilities beyond the simple measures such as numbers of troops and quantity and quality of weapons. Syrian armed forces, while numerically large, are plagued by short-falls in modern weapons systems, technologies, and the technical expertise to operate those advanced systems it manages to acquire. Moreover, some analysts maintain existing forces are weakened by continued reliance on habits inherited from Soviet-era military advisers—a lack of tactical initiative and an unwillingness to modify predetermined plans.[37] Experts suggest that the Syrian military is largely a "hollow" force that has adopted "asymmetric warfare" as the strategy of necessity to combat its primary enemy, Israel. Thus it maintains a large tank force to slow potential Israeli thrusts into its territory, while seeking NBC weapons and delivery systems, building up its special operations capabilities, and continuing to fund terrorist proxies like Hezbollah and Amal.[38] In view of its conventional weaknesses, however, Syria may have acquired unconventional deterrents "on the cheap with chemical and biological capabilities that, coming from close distances, are quite threatening."[39]

DAUNTING TARGETS

In these brief descriptions of the challenges posed by Iran and Syria, it is clear that while both countries would present military resistance, the force-on-force stage of a preventive war would result, relatively quickly, in an American victory. Iran would probably present the most serious challenge because of the nation's large size, the number of military personnel, and the fact that relatively soon the status of Iran's nuclear programs, especially nuclear weapons production, would force the US military to proceed cautiously. Planners for either deep strikes against facilities or an all-out invasion would need to take the same care as was involved with both Iraq invasions.

Yet both Iran and Syria would conceivably require long and strenuous commitments of military force to maintain security and stability during postconflict operations. In Iran and Syria, forces opposing the United States, whether "dead enders" from the previous regime or others, could find refuge in territories unoccupied by US forces or even perhaps in neighboring countries. Moreover, other countries in the region could readily supply weapons and materials to surviving government forces or insurgents if massive commitments of US personnel to close the borders were not made. Worse, even if collaborators and members of the exile communities could be found (à la Ahmed Chalabi and Iyad Alawi), ethnic, religious, and tribal leaders could lead military and political opposition to American occupying forces that would tie down large numbers of troops for years if not decades.

In brief, even if the strength and military capabilities of the US armed forces were increased (through ongoing transformation efforts or increases in the numbers of US servicemen and women), the prospect of pursuing another preventive war against likely targets is daunting. The difficulties would be less if the United States could disengage most of its combat troops from Iraq; but short of an unexpected political settlement or serious rethinking by Bush administration officials, this seems unlikely. Limited preventive strikes, on the other hand, are always possible if the United States is willing to assume the political risks associated with missed targets, collateral damage, and, in the case of NBC facilities, the consequence of materials spread into the atmosphere or surrounding territory. This, of course, assumes that US goals, such as punishing or warning adversaries, could be achieved by strikes.

WHAT DOES IT MATTER?

Does it matter whether the United States has the capacity to undertake preventive military intervention in the near-to-intermediate term? With preventive military intervention as US declaratory policy, implementation difficulties, real or perceived, will affect American credibility, legitimacy, and, ultimately, security.

CREDIBILITY

Ever since former presidents Johnson and Nixon tried to present their unwillingness to pull back from the Vietnam War on the basis of maintaining

American "credibility," many international relations experts have been reluctant to invoke the concept. Credibility is a nebulous concept ripe for posthoc analysis and political manipulation.

Yet in the contemporary unipolar world, the stakes may be higher even than during the Vietnam era. Underlying the doctrine of preventive military intervention is the assumption that "rogue" states and terrorists may actually use NBC weapons against the United States proper, US government facilities overseas, or even large concentrations of American civilians living abroad. By threatening to invade or strike adversaries before they have the opportunity to attack, the United States has sought to change the dynamic of its relationship with enemies and potential enemies. Rather than assuming a reactive and defensive posture, the United States has served notice that it will act quickly and decisively when it is threatened. To achieve the desired effect of unsettling potential enemies and deterring them from attacking, the United States must have an unambiguous capacity to carry out its threats. Otherwise, the United States risks being seen as a paper tiger.

LEGITIMACY

Apologists for American hegemonic aspirations, unilateralism, and even imperialism sometimes argue that the world is yearning for a strong leader.[40] Even a benign hegemon, willing and able to play the role of a global police force and even enforcer, may provide a stable security environment that benefits all members of the international community.[41] America's ability to make and fulfill threats against terrorist groups and "rogue" states, then, is part and parcel of American global legitimacy.

One thesis that supports this notion, albeit indirectly, is the argument that the international outcry over Iraq was less about anger over American actions than about the process by which the United States pursued military intervention. At its simplest, the claim is that opponents to the war objected to the truncated inspection process, the badly handled politics at the UN, and the lack of consultation on war and postwar operations, even with members of the so-called coalition of the willing. Some European countries made this argument during the run-up to the Iraq War and have subsequently reiterated their position.

The overwhelming dominance of the US military power exacerbates this problem. At least for conflict operations, the United States does not need military support to "win" military victories against most nonstate and "rogue" state opponents. Some US military analysts even argue that including coalition forces actually impedes American military effectiveness.

The same cannot be said for postconflict operations, including policing, counterinsurgency operations, and general constabulary functions. These functions are labor intensive, whereas even the US Army and Marine Corps are by training, doctrine, and sheer numbers of troops reliant on capital intensive firepower, mobility, and intelligence. Hence, as it became increasingly clear that many Iraqis would not greet their American "liberators" with open arms, the Bush administration turned, with very limited success, to coalition members, other interested parties (such as the Saudis and Pakistanis), and the UN to provide the military and constabulary capabilities needed in postconflict operations.

How long American military predominance will continue and how military transformation might exacerbate the existing shortfall of labor-intensive, low-technology, "boots on the ground" capabilities remain to be seen. What is clear is that America's legitimacy as the sole superpower with responsibility, explicit and desired or implicit and unwanted, will be damaged if it does not demonstrate the ability to meet its own or the international community's security needs. Should Iran, for example, finally acquire serious nuclear weapon capabilities and begin to play a more a threatening role in the Middle East, most other states in the region, much less the regions of the world dependent on Persian Gulf energy supplies, will be looking for ways to blunt Iranian aggression. The multilateral diplomacy currently being used to dissuade and contain Iranian nuclear ambitions may eventually give way to a desire for more coercive measures. For the foreseeable future, only the United States possesses even the remotest potential to offer a credible military option. The legitimacy of the US position within the international system depends on maintaining that capacity.

SECURITY

It is possible that the United States might indeed find it necessary to launch limited preventive strikes or engage in preventive war. Some reports suggest that the "war on terror" has not made a significant dent in al-Qaida, although undoubtedly a large number of pre-9/11 leaders have been killed or imprisoned. Yet recruitment has risen, and an even more networked structure has developed, to give al-Qaida a resilience few expected. Even as President Bush claims the United States has killed approximately 75 percent of the al-Qaida leadership since 9/11, both public and private analyses suggest that al-Qaida's membership has actually grown in the same period. Clearly, the Madrid bombings and other actions credited to al-Qaida suggest that whatever the status of the pre-9/11 leadership, the organization continues to have serious terrorist capabilities.

With the United States committed to preventive military intervention, the US military must be capable of carrying out limited preventive attacks and, in extremis, even preventive wars. Given existing and projected strike capabilities, there seems little doubt of the American capacity to do "drive-by shootings" both now and in the future. Many new weapons programs—from UAVs to the Joint Strike Fighter—will only serve to increase American deep-strike capabilities. Whether the US intelligence community can supply the necessary actionable intelligence remains an open question that is addressed by at least two other authors in this volume.[42]

The ability to launch a preventive war against a "rogue" state or perhaps a failed state providing safe haven to terrorist groups is much less certain. This uncertainty is especially acute if it is necessary, as seems likely, to provide for nation building (including security) during the postconflict operations. US Army and Marine Corps units are, at least as presently trained and equipped, not especially well suited to such operations. Moreover, the technological restructuring in progress, such as the Future Combat Systems (FCS) of the army, focuses on constabulary, policy, and civil affairs activities only as a sideline. The main thrust of the FCS is to fight and win wars against the main battle forces of nation-state adversaries. Counterinsurgency and counterterrorist operations are dealt with largely as lesser-included cases.

WHAT SHOULD BE DONE?

Despite the overwhelming military superiority of the United States and intense efforts to transform the US military, implementing a strong variant of the NSS 2002 doctrine would present a serious challenge. At a minimum, it would require strengthening links with civilian intelligence agencies and improving their own indigenous intelligence capabilities so that vast improvements in strike assets (including both platforms like UAVs and the most recent generations of precision-guided munitions) can be used more effectively. In effect, it would require rebalancing American military forces in ways that are largely antithetical to the thrust of American military modernization, at least since the Vietnam era and quite possibly longer. The long-term trend toward replacing humans with technology and increasing the intensity and accuracy of military firepower may continue, but it would have to be supplemented by providing more attention to the less glamorous aspects of the US military: civil affairs, combat engineering, policing functions, and on-the-ground peacekeeping and peace enforcement.

MILITARY TRANSFORMATION

It would be intellectually dishonest simply to project current military capabilities forward into the future. Both the Clinton and Bush administrations have emphasized the need to transform the US military to take advantage of the ongoing "revolution in military affairs." But will military transformation and the prospects for fulfilling these plans leave the United States better equipped to conduct either limited preventive strikes or preventive wars in the long term?

Although it is too early to make a definitive assessment of transformation, early returns are positive. Some of the most thoughtful scholars have argued that the precision-guided weaponry, stealth technologies, and integrated battlefield management characteristic of the new American way of war have roots dating back thirty years. Yet transformation advocates may have oversold the concept. Transformation is touted as the means to "lock in" American operational advantages for the foreseeable future. Although transformation may provide a lasting competitive edge in mid-to-high-intensity conflicts, it is not clear the currently planned transformation force is suited to operations other than war, much less low-intensity conflicts, including counterinsurgency and counterterror operations.

It is not too late for transformation to shift course. Already the army and the marine corps have begun adapting to the security challenges posed by al-Qaida, Afghanistan, and Iraq. For example, infantry and armored officers are waging largely internal debates over the nature of armored vehicles. In preparing for the Iraq War, based largely on experiences in the Balkans and Somalia, some experts advocated that the army and the marines be equipped with smaller, faster, lighter vehicles. The thinking then, as now, was that such vehicles would be better suited to the low-intensity conflicts of the future, where speed and deployability would triumph over armor and firepower. Events in Fallujah and elsewhere in Iraq, for example, now may suggest otherwise.

The US military is the most powerful instrument of military force ever, both in absolute terms and in a relative sense. The United States spends more money overall, buys more high-technology systems, invests more in research and development, and trains its soldiers better than virtually any country or combination of countries in the world. The US military is optimized largely for high-intensity conflicts against conventional forces and, secondarily, to provide a safe and effective strategic deterrence with its nuclear forces. It can strike virtually anywhere on Earth at any time. Yet the United States has not yet recognized that if it is going to fight Mary Kaldor's "new wars,"[43] and if it is going to provide stability and security to conquered territories, it must have sufficient numbers of troops trained and equipped for peacekeeping, constabulary actions, and civic affairs. As it is currently pursued, military transformation will not solve the problems best addressed by low-technology "boots on the ground."

REBALANCE AMERICAN MILITARY FORCES?

Much of the transformation rhetoric focuses on providing more strike capabilities, even though this element of military power is already among the most developed and successful components of the American armed forces. Less attention is devoted to mundane tasks like the requirements of managing the postconflict environment. Indeed, if many military and civilian leaders had their way, there would be no need for such follow-on forces. Once the military forces of an opponent were defeated, other US government agencies, foreign militaries, or local forces could then assume the role of military operations other than war. Unfortunately, both Iraq and Afghanistan, not to mention the Balkans, have demonstrated that a serious security presence is essential.[44]

The US military has taken steps toward reforms. Both the army and air force vision statements tout the need to become more expeditionary. Even the navy, which has prided itself for generations as providing the long arm of American power, is working with the other services to provide even greater capabilities. The sea-basing initiative found in Chief of Naval Operations Vernon Clark's Seapower 21 plan will help free American forces from relying on land bases donated or rented from allies and states that are willing to tolerate an American presence. Yet these efforts largely avoid the problem of numbers. Effective postconflict operations, whether in Iraq or in the future in Iran or elsewhere, require large numbers of well-trained, prepared, and equipped troops on the ground. If the Bush administration and subsequent political leaders do not recognize this, and indeed resist the efforts of Congress and outside experts to increase the number of American combat troops available, the United States may win every force-on-force encounter but lose wars because it will be unable to provide the security necessary for political and economic stabilization in defeated countries.

STRENGTHEN CIVILIAN CAPABILITIES?

If one of the greatest difficulties facing the United States is training, preparing, and equipping the military for postconflict operations, perhaps other US government agencies or departments could be created or persuaded to fill these roles. Niall Ferguson's analysis of the British Empire lauds the imperial or colonial service and, at least by implication, advocates the creation of an American variant.[45] However, it should be noted that Ferguson doubts Americans have the "right stuff" for such a venture.[46] Presumably, postconflict operations in Iraq and other future preventive wars could be handled by an American imperial service in conjunction with military elements. For another related alternative, Tom Barnett proposes a "progressive bifurcation of the US military into a Leviathan force focused on waging wars and a System Administrator force focused on winning the peace." The Systems Administrator force would be "supportive, nonlethal, and willing to submit to recognized authorities such as the International Criminal Court and the UN."[47] Presumably, the Systems Administrator military force will support and be supported by other US government agencies, such as the Agency for International Development and the Department of State. Another option already in widespread use in Iraq, not to mention by other countries across the globe, is relying more on private military firms (PMFs).[48] In Iraq, PMFs provide food, housing, training, and maintenance functions for the US military and its coalition counterparts. Reports suggest that the ratio of personnel from PMFs to official US military personnel is roughly one to ten, approximately ten times the ratio during the first Persian Gulf War.[49] The trend toward using PMFs is not, of course, limited to the United States, nor is it an entirely new phenomenon, but it does appear the United States is taking the trend to the extreme.[50] There is no reason why such outsourcing cannot be used to overcome shortfalls in personnel, expertise, and even equipment in the future if national policies and strategies demand it. The effectiveness of mercenary forces relative to regular military remains a serious question, however.

WORK MORE CLOSELY WITH ALLIES?

Just because preventive action is taken does not mean it has to be the sole responsibility of US forces. In the first presidential debate of the 2004 campaign, Democratic candidate Senator John Kerry made much of his proposal to work more closely with allies in providing security in postwar Iraq. Kerry's campaign theme simply gives voice to the actual efforts of the Bush administration since the early days of the war and much of the scholarly literature on the relationship between the US military and those of friends, allies, and temporary coalition members.

The most likely allies to turn to would be in Europe, by revitalizing the transatlantic relationship, along with tightening ties with allies such as Japan and perhaps even strengthening the military capabilities of the UN. Given the events of the recent past, this diplomatic turn may be very difficult to sell—the controversy over the intelligence findings the Bush administration used to justify the war, the eventual decision to act without a renewed mandate from the UN, and the various contretemps over the post–Iraq War period have, by some accounts, undermined the willingness of other countries to support US initiatives.

Of course, even if the diplomatic and political difficulties can be overcome using a combination of deft diplomacy and generous incentives, the reality is that few countries have or will have significant military forces capable of being deployed far from home. After several decades of trying to close the gap between US and European military capabilities, the distance has, if anything, widened.[51] Shortfalls in strategic intelligence and long-range airlift, to name two examples, will remain for the foreseeable future. One oft-raised option is to divide labor with the less capable European militaries so that they supply troops while the United States contributes technologies. Yet many European countries have resisted the de facto division because it puts more of their troops at risk, cedes important political-military decisions to the United States, and fails to provide domestic benefits (such as large defense contracts or the potential for technology spillovers from investment in cutting-edge military technologies).

Discussions about burden sharing with like-minded allies or more temporary coalition members will lead nowhere if the United States continues to alienate much of the world through both its policies and its apparent disdain for diplomacy and international political processes. The apparent lack of planning for a post-Hussein Iraq and the obvious difficulties that the US Army have had in providing an appropriate occupation force have exacerbated tensions between the United States and several key allies over the decision to go to war.[52] If Iraq had turned out as Vice President Cheney and Secretary of Defense Rumsfeld, among others, had optimistically predicted—with a cakewalk military victory and a smooth transition to a post-Hussein Iraqi regime—critics would have had less resonance. Instead, postwar complications have reinforced international doubts about America's Iraq policies. The same reasoning often holds with punitive and limited preventive strikes—when missions succeed, the criticism is muted; when there are failures, such as allegedly misidentified targets (in Sudan) or large numbers of civilian casualties, the United States is vilified. Military capabilities then are part and parcel of the overall position on the world stage, not just in a basic sense of raw military power, but also in a perceptual sense involving legitimacy and credibility.

10

A Sheep in Wolf's Clothing?

FRANCE'S STRUGGLE WITH PREVENTIVE FORCE

Jacques E. C. Hymans

THE GEORGE W. BUSH administration has shown a marked preference for bypassing multilateral security institutions in favor of "coalitions of the willing"—variable line-ups of states that choose to fall in line behind one or another American initiative. The administration argues that traditional multilateralism is incompatible with a new world of emerging threats from "rogue" states and "terrorists," where credible signaling of military options and, on occasion, quick recourse to military action are essential.[1] A considerable number of eminent practitioners of American diplomacy have, however, strongly criticized the administration's eagerness to bypass established decision-making processes in the United Nations (UN) Security Council and even in the North Atlantic Treaty Organization (NATO).[2] These critics argue that by rejecting traditional multilateralism so openly, the administration has offended its traditional alliance and Great Power partners, thus complicating its ability to tackle emerging threats.

The administration and its domestic critics have different foreign policy prescriptions, but they share at least one perception: France, the so-called oldest ally of the United States, is incorrigible. Indeed, the idea that France is still chasing after a Gaullist fantasy of leading Europe and the world against the American "hyperpower" is a key pillar of each side's assessment of the merits of multilateralism. Those who support forming "coalitions of the willing" argue that since France is incorrigible, its current importance in both Western and world diplomatic forums dooms any effort to build a muscular multilateralism.[3] Meanwhile, those who support continuing to work within traditional structures suggest that France's incorrigibility is the very reason why a serious American effort at multilateralism is so important—to push France into a diplomatic corner and thus keep its global ambitions in check.[4]

This chapter argues that the general American impression that the United States' "oldest ally" is a wolf in sheep's clothing is basically wrong. Indeed, it is more accurate to say that France today is a sheep in wolf's clothing. Behind the rhetorical flourishes, French elites understand that the country they lead is, at best, merely a "residual great power."[5] They know that it simply does not have the resources to lead Europe, let alone the world, as a durable counterpoise to the world's only superpower. That France briefly found itself in that very position during the Iraq crisis of 2003 was, paradoxically, a testament to its basic weakness. Therefore, a more supple American diplomacy, one that reflected a truer understanding of the sources of French foreign policy, might well have been able to avoid the intense Franco-American tussle of that period, even without abandoning the ultimate objective of cashiering Saddam Hussein. This suggests in turn that a renewed commitment to multilateralism—at least, to the mini-multilateralism of NATO—would not necessarily greatly constrain US freedom to maneuver on the international stage.

The chapter first explains France's pre-9/11 position for lifting the Iraq sanctions as deducible from its traditional Gaullist foreign policy outlook. It then charts France's steady post-9/11 abandonment of much of its principled stance on Iraq, and it explains this movement as a consequence of the US policy shift and of France's desire to maintain good relations with the world's only superpower. The next section focuses on the crucial turning point, mid-January 2003, when France refused to join the American war effort. It explains France's refusal as a downstream consequence of the categorical antiwar stance of Germany. The crucial German dimension of France's choice to stand up to the United States at this juncture is something that has not been fully recognized by previous analyses. The chapter then looks at the period of intense diplomatic conflict, from mid-January to the formal beginning of the war on March 20. It shows that even at this late date, French diplomacy was still endeavoring to minimize direct confrontation with the United States. That Paris in the end could not avoid the confrontation is explained again by the country's weakness, this time relative to the United Kingdom. The final section draws lessons from this case for US foreign policy.

FRANCE'S STANCE AGAINST THE IRAQ SANCTIONS

From today's vantage point, it takes no small effort to recall that the international debate in the mid-1990s was over whether and when to *lift* the sanctions on Saddam Hussein's Iraq. The UN Security Council, including France, had approved heavy sanctions on the Hussein regime in the wake of the Gulf War. In 1994, recognizing that the international oil embargo was strangling the country, Hussein finally agreed to submit to those Security Council resolutions that related to arms control. But instead of welcoming this development, the United States and United Kingdom began arguing that Iraqi conformity with the arms control resolutions was not enough; Iraq had to comply fully with all of the Security Council resolutions before the oil sanctions could be lifted. France—and many others—took issue with this stance, which the *New York Times* editorial page stated amounted to "changing the rules" on Iraq. As the *Times* put it, "The resolution's direct linkage between arms control and oil sanctions is not simply a technicality. . . . Indefinite, symbolic sanctions—punishing a regime simply for being loathsome—tend to lose their meaning and effectiveness over time."[6] This was the French position, too, and over the years the French (joined by Russia and China, among others) became increasingly insistent that the sanctions had to be curtailed.

Why did France refuse to go along with the US-UK determination to continue containing Hussein? It has become all too common for journalistic accounts to stress the French economic interest in ending the sanctions. French oil companies did stand to benefit, but it is just as simplistic to say that they dominated French Iraq policy as it is to say that US oil interests dominated US Iraq policy.[7] In fact, the French position on the sanctions was easily deducible from France's basic tradition in international affairs. This tradition can be labeled Gaullist, as it was codified by Charles de Gaulle after his return to power in 1958—though Gaullism has deeper lineages going back all the way to Cardinal Richelieu.[8] "Gaullism" is not just a synonym for French nationalist ambition. It also offers a particularly French "political" vision of international order, at the heart of which sits the rational state, unpenetrated by private interests and unmoved by religious fervor.[9] The Gaullist vision of international affairs naturally produces relative sympathy for secularist and nationalist states such as Saddam Hussein's Iraq, though of course the French did not endorse Hussein's bloody excesses. In particular, as Jacques Beltran has explained, successive French governments of different political parties promoted an end to the sanctions regime in order to promote the following core French foreign policy objectives: stability in the Arab world and between the Arabs and the West, to which the French thought a chastened

Hussein could contribute; avoidance of an even greater humanitarian disaster in Iraq—an important goal not only in itself but also for the fulfillment of the first goal of stability; and respect for the letter of UN Security Council resolutions by all states, be they great or small.[10]

Until September 2001, France held fast to its principled Iraq policy, even though this produced a certain level of Franco-American tension.[11] France notably withheld its assent from Operation Desert Fox, the four-day bombing of sensitive Iraqi facilities that the United States and United Kingdom carried out in December 1998, as well as from UN Security Council Resolution 1284 of December 1999, which created a new UN inspection commission for Iraqi illicit weapons. Indeed, throughout the 1990s France's consistent and coherent defense of its position gradually gained more adherents internationally, so that by the early days of the George W. Bush administration, there was widespread international support for ending the sanctions regime entirely. In order to counter this trend, the Americans and British found it necessary to propose a new, "smart sanctions" formula that would significantly lighten the burden on Iraqi civilians, while reinvigorating the export controls hampering Iraq's military reconstruction. France, not surprisingly, supported the new UK-US initiative, since the shift to "smart sanctions" represented a major victory for French diplomacy.[12] Indeed, the Iraqi propaganda machine even singled France out for violent criticism as the true originator of the UK-US "smart sanctions" idea.[13]

THE CONSEQUENCES OF 9/11

The Bush administration regained the diplomatic offensive after 11 September 2001, however, and it used its new political capital to push for a major shift in the set of internationally legitimate Iraq policy options. Before 9/11, the limits of mainstream international debate were, on the dovish extreme, reintegrating Saddam Hussein's Iraq into the international community, and, on the hawkish extreme, maintaining the "dumb sanctions" regime. The even more hawkish official US policy of "regime change" was widely seen outside the United States as mere rhetoric. But as early as November 2001, Bush and his team began to assert a new spectrum of legitimate policy options: continuing the sanctions as the dovish extreme, and preventive war with the objective of regime change as the hawkish extreme.[14]

The long-standing, coherent, and consistently defended French stance for a rapid end to sanctions clearly stood outside the new discursive limits defined by the Bush administration. In the face of Bush's discursive maneuver, the French wilted.[15] The French policy reversal would eventually be consolidated in the "yes" vote on the famous UN Security Council Resolution

1441 of November 2002. What explains this change? The answer, in short, is that the French believed they were too weak to do anything else. It is often claimed that French foreign policy is driven by an exaggerated sense of national power, with its leaders fancying themselves as the heirs of Charles de Gaulle—or even of Napoleon Bonaparte.[16] French leaders undoubtedly overindulge in what the French call "*cocorico*," or crowing over their domestic and external successes. But in fact, the broad trajectory of French foreign and especially defense policy over the 1990s was toward an acknowledgment of France's diminished position in the international system.[17] France's post-9/11 cave-in on Iraq was just one more indication of this growing modesty.

During the 1990s, France still held on to its self-image as a "residual great power," in Ulrich Krotz's formulation,[18] but the accent was increasingly on the word "residual." For many in France, especially those close to the military, the first Gulf War had already demonstrated the superiority of American power and the need for greater French "interoperability" with that superior force. A decade later, the United States was spending more on its national defense than the entire national budget of France. French decision-makers were not ignorant of these facts, and they responded to them with a sometimes rocky, but nevertheless ever-closer reintegration with the NATO alliance: rejoining the Military Committee in 1993; attending the Defense and Foreign Ministers' meetings beginning in 1995; signing a joint declaration with the United Kingdom for a European Union (EU) defense capacity "in conformity with our respective obligations in NATO" at Saint-Mâlo in 1998; and sending significant French forces to serve under NATO command in the 1999 Kosovo war—a war that, like the Iraq War of 2003, was not sanctioned by the UN Security Council.[19]

The attack on 11 September accelerated this preexisting French tendency to come back into the American fold. France's participation in the American "war on terror" went far beyond the atmospherics of *Le Monde*'s front-page editorial, "Nous sommes tous Américains,"[20] or President Jacques Chirac's 18 September visit to the White House. France made a strong contribution to the enhancement of international counterterrorism policing cooperation, and indeed it would eventually make a major biological terror bust in the midst of the diplomatic fight over Iraq. It also contributed significant troop strength, including crack special forces teams, to Operation Enduring Freedom in Afghanistan—essentially accepting the principle of participation in an ad hoc, US-led "coalition of the willing." Though the Afghanistan War was not without some of the usual Franco-American friction, the fact that the French were there at all testified to their recognition that hyperpower has its privileges.[21] This recognition was more broadly reflected in the French defense budget plan that was (not coincidentally) released on 11 September

2002. The clear objective of the plan was to make France's military more "British"—that is to say, more useful to the United States.[22]

The very day after the release of the French defense budget plan, President Bush gave a speech to the UN General Assembly explicitly challenging the UN to stand up to Saddam Hussein. In so doing, he forced the French to choose between their traditional, principled stance on Iraq and their desired partnership with the United States. France chose partnership. To be sure, the negotiations over UN Security Council Resolution 1441—the resolution on returning weapons inspectors to Iraq—were long and arduous.[23] For the French and many other Security Council members, the main sticking point was the US desire that the resolution threaten the use of "all necessary means"—meaning military force—to secure its enforcement. The French, Russians, Chinese, and several nonpermanent members wanted to require a second resolution to authorize force. Though the issue was serious and the debates were proportionately intense, at no time did the French threaten a veto. This was a sign of their willingness to play by America's rules, though not to rubber-stamp America's desires.[24] In the end, on 8 November 2002 the Security Council unanimously approved a compromise resolution declaring that Iraq was being given "a final opportunity to comply with its disarmament obligations." The resolution warned of "serious consequences" in the case of Iraqi noncompliance, but it did not automatically condone the use of military force. In retrospect, some have viewed this compromise as a mere papering over of fundamental differences on Iraq, a simple postponement of the inevitable Franco-American clash. But President Bush, for one, told Bob Woodward after the fact, "In the end, we got a great resolution."[25] Bush's satisfaction with Resolution 1441 reflected the great distance that the French (as well as the others on the Security Council) had moved to get even within shouting distance of his hard-line position on Iraq.

GERMANY STIFFENS FRANCE'S SPINE

The fact that the French moved so far in the direction of the American position on Iraq was particularly remarkable because, in so doing, they were leaning away from the position of their major European partner, Germany. German chancellor Gerhard Schröder issued a categorical "no" to an eventual Iraq war—even, he said, if it were to receive the Security Council's blessing—with increasing insistence over the course of his electoral campaign in the summer and fall of 2002. Fearing that France would be tarred with the same brush that Washington had begun vigorously applying to Schröder, Chirac, and Dominique de Villepin hastened to put some daylight between them and their German partners on the Iraq issue. In late August, de Villepin told the

French ambassadorial corps, "We Europeans know all too well the price of weakness in dealing with dictators. . . . We must thus maintain as firmly as possible our demand of an unconditional return of UN inspectors."[26] In a long interview with the *New York Times* published on 9 September, Chirac backed up his foreign minister, stating that, for France, the military option was indeed on the table, and that Schröder had gone overboard because he was "very close to the election."[27] These statements may have encouraged Bush to take the UN route, which he announced in his General Assembly speech of 12 September.[28]

Some have suggested that the hints of flexibility sent out by the French at this juncture were simply meant to ensnare the US war machine forever in the cobwebs of international diplomacy. That the French wanted a bona fide diplomatic process is beyond doubt; but it is also beyond doubt that they were seriously considering participation in an eventual war. On 20 December, France announced that the aircraft carrier *Charles de Gaulle* would be ready for a voyage by late January—a significant date because the inspectors were to make their first report to the UN Security Council on 27 January.[29] The next day, a French general visited the Pentagon to discuss a potential French contribution of 15,000 troops, 100 aircraft, and naval support. This proposal amounted to about the same level of commitment as the French had made in the first Gulf War.[30] Then, on 7 January, Chirac stated portentously in his annual address to the French military that they should get ready; he was seconded on the podium by the army chief of staff, General Henri Bentegeat, who said that the stars were aligning for a military mobilization in the year 2003.[31]

Even so, in early January the French were still not ready politically or militarily for war, and indeed they were shocked to learn that the Americans were. When Chirac's diplomatic adviser, Maurice Gourdault-Montagne, visited Washington to sound out the administration on 13 and 14 January about its intentions, the administration put its cards on the table. National Security Advisor Condoleezza Rice, Deputy Secretary of Defense Paul Wolfowitz, and Deputy Secretary of State Richard Armitage, in separate meetings with the envoy, ridiculed the French desire to give more time to the inspectors. Wolfowitz flatly labeled the French position as "irresponsible."[32] Incredibly, such beating about the head appears to have been necessary for the French finally to understand that the administration was dead set on war.[33] With weapons inspector Hans Blix's first report to the Security Council due on 27 January, the time for the French decision had arrived.

The decision Chirac made was to stand up against the Americans. On 20 January, de Villepin "ambushed" Powell by inducing him to come to a meeting on "terrorism" that, contrary to what had been promised, quickly devolved into a debate on Iraq. After the session, an energized de Villepin told the press that "Nothing! Nothing!" justified this war. The break between the diplomats was now open—and personal.[34] A few days later, during the celebration of the fortieth anniversary of the Elysée Treaty that links France and Germany, Chirac informed Schröder that France was joining Germany in its antiwar posture on Iraq.[35] Then, in front of the media, with Schröder at his side, the French president indulged in the near-pacifist statement that "war is always the worst solution."[36] This turn of events was a surprise to many observers. Even American conservatives with a deep mistrust of France were surprised that it had replaced its typical diplomatic smoothness with antiwar tirades.[37] Why, after giving so much ground to the American position, did Chirac and de Villepin finally decide to stand and fight?

A number of factors were clearly at work in this decision, including a genuine distaste for what they saw as an unjustified rush to war; shock and disappointment over France's treatment at the hands of the Americans; and perhaps a natural political impulse to run to the front of the increasingly vocal antiwar parade in European mass opinion. But the elephant in the room, which other accounts of this story strangely have tended to obscure, is the incredibly close Franco-German relationship. It was not by chance that Chirac took up the antiwar cause with Schröder standing at his side. To choose to be "with" Bush in mid-January 2003 was to choose to be "against" Schröder, and, in fact, no French president could have made such a choice.

Even when American postmortems of the diplomatic crisis over Iraq do not ignore the Franco-German "couple" (as it is called in France), they tend to warp its impact on events. For instance, the Brookings Institution's resident France experts have written that "Bush's isolation of Schröder may have actually pushed him into the arms of Chirac at a time when his preference might have been to mend fences with the United States."[38] This statement misfires on two levels: it reflects an outdated, Cold War understanding of the relative commitments of Germany and France to Atlanticism; and, more fundamentally, it reflects an outdated assumption that the foreign policy choices of Germany and France are truly independent of each other—that they reflect traditional "hard-shell" state sovereignty over foreign policy.

The Cold War pattern of Atlanticist devotion of Germany and truculence of France no longer holds. In the case studied here, clearly it was Chirac who seconded Schröder's categorical anti–Iraq War position, not the other way around. As one British official recalled, "We weren't looking closely enough at the Elysée anniversary. We misunderstood the Germans. It suited them to have Chirac as political cover. We have had a consistent problem misreading Franco-German intentions going back through the 1980s."[39] The problem stems from a failure to update Cold War understandings of

France's and Germany's relative commitments to the Atlantic alliance. During the Cold War, Germany indeed straddled between starkly contrasting French and US positions on the nature and function of the West. But the Cold War ended a long time ago. We have already seen how far France moved toward American stances during the 1990s.[40] Germany moved, too—but in a different direction. During the Cold War, the Federal Republic had kept a relatively low international profile because of its security dependence on America, as well as its desire to avoid inflaming still-vivid memories of Nazi atrocities. But Germany and the world changed in 1989, and the new, reunified Germany subsequently displayed much greater self-confidence on the international stage. This independent streak was particularly evident in the leftist coalition government that came to power in 1998 promising to build a Germany that can "say no."[41] Heavily influenced by the German peace movements of the 1970s and 1980s, contemporary left-of-center German elites evince no small degree of skepticism about the true motivations behind US foreign policy. Moreover, they have a positive agenda of ending the dominance of violence in international affairs (though they also increasingly send German troops abroad, in peacekeeping or peacemaking capacities).[42] Given this background, it is not surprising that in the immediate aftermath of 9/11, Chancellor Schröder privately stated that he thought the Bush team was going to try to use this as a pretext for invading Iraq, and that he was going to try to stop them from doing so.[43] This crucial piece of evidence demonstrates, contrary to the opinion of many American observers, that Schröder's campaign against the Iraq War was not mere election-year opportunism. Rather, it reflected strong convictions, which he was gratified to learn on the campaign trail that most Germans shared.

That Chirac signed up with Schröder's policy on Iraq, rather than vice versa, is clear. But why did he do so? Why did he not let the Schröder government bear the full consequences of its self-righteousness? Many American and British observers had expected him to do just that.[44] Such expectations were based on the second major misconception noted above: that France and Germany are independent foreign policy actors. They are not.

The Franco-German "couple" is not just a cute journalistic turn of phrase; it is an institutionalized fact of life.[45] Ironically, it was Charles de Gaulle, the champion of French foreign policy "independence," who fathered the 1963 Elysée Treaty that has ended up binding France irrevocably to Germany. De Gaulle had thought the treaty signaled Germany's willingness to show unstinting support for French foreign policy initiatives; when this belief turned out almost immediately to have been erroneous, he essentially acted as if the treaty had never happened.[46] But the treaty had indeed happened, and slowly but surely the twice-yearly leadership summits it envisioned have become no less than "joint Franco-German cabinet meetings,"[47] where all government ministers and hundreds of civil servants hold detailed discussions of all major aspects of the two countries' foreign and domestic policies. Of particular relevance to the concerns of this chapter are the discussions of the Franco-German Defense and Security Council, which is a top-level decision-making body whose "formal legal authority is so wideranging that it could decide to create a joint Franco-German army without special parliamentary procedures."[48] Moreover, the formal cooperation of the summit meetings has spilled over into a large number of other collaborative activities, including permanent secretariats for the Franco-German councils, joint ministerial trips and ambassadorial conferences, exchange programs for diplomats and other civil servants, and many informal contacts. To manage all of this activity, each side appoints a full-time, very senior "coordinator" of cooperation, whose tasks include managing the multitude of cooperative endeavors, reporting regularly on the state of cooperation, and proposing further areas for cooperation.

In short, given the realities of the Franco-German "couple," once Germany had turned left, France had to follow. The Bush administration in January 2003 was essentially asking for the immediate surgical separation of two Siamese twins connected at the head. It is no wonder that the twins in question, France and Germany, did not agree to the operation. But this raises another question: if France had known all along that it could not break with Germany, and if it knew that Germany had placed itself in a position of categorical refusal of any future Iraq war, how could Chirac have waited until January 2003 to come out against such a war? The answer to this question lies in the delicate power balance inside the Franco-German "couple." Although France today is clearly becoming the junior partner by most measures of power, it still has a claim to leadership in matters of international high politics, a claim largely based on France's permanent seat at the Security Council.[49] But even here, with each passing year the bases for French leadership are slipping away, as Germany develops its diplomatic and military muscle and as the French permanent seat appears increasingly anachronistic. Thus when, as in the case of Iraq, Germany decides to take a strong stand, France is in a bind. In such cases, to reassert its leadership France generally must do two things: first, it must appeal over Germany's head, to the authority of the UN; and second, it must assert ownership of the issue through a much greater investment of thought and energy than the Germans have done. Often this means becoming "more German than the Germans," at least for a while, until the French lead on the issue is secure. For their part, the Germans are generally willing to play along with the French desire for leadership because it produces a force multiplier effect for their preferred position in the short term, while handing off most of the diplomatic and military risk.

The Franco-German dance over Balkan diplomacy in the 1990s was an early iteration of this basic pattern. Over France's objections, Germany unilaterally recognized Slovenia and Croatia in December 1991; France, still cherishing its historic alliance with Serbia, grumbled but followed suit in early 1992. By mid-1992, France had retaken leadership on the issue—but with a markedly "German" twist, as President François Mitterrand declared Serbia responsible for the war and made a dramatic visit to besieged Sarajevo. Thereafter, Paris was clearly in the foreground.[50]

The French were following the same script in the recent Iraq crisis, but the Bush administration—in spite of France's desperate pleading, right up to the last minute, for even a mere few extra weeks—did not give Paris the time it needed to reclaim ownership of the issue from Berlin.[51] Therefore France in the spring of 2003 ended up with the sucker's payoff: it was pursuing Germany's, not its own, preferred policy; and for this the Bush administration was punishing it severely, indeed more severely than the administration was punishing Germany.[52] Such are the wages of weakness.

THE WEAK SUFFER WHAT THEY MUST

Bush had forced France to choose sides, and France had chosen Germany and its antiwar position. But even so, the French well understood that they could not stop the war from happening, and they also understood Donald Rumsfeld's dictum that when you are in a hole, stop digging. The best they could hope for at this late stage was a replay of December 1998, when the United States and United Kingdom failed to get France, Russia, and China to agree to a Security Council resolution for Operation Desert Fox but went ahead with it anyway. That episode had been difficult, but the Franco-American relationship had recovered soon thereafter. The French thus suddenly became converted to the American thesis that Resolution 1441 provided the United States and United Kingdom with sufficient grounds for war against Iraq. According to Charles Grant, beginning in January "the thrust of the French message was: 'If you must go to war, do it on the basis of 1441; we would criticize you, although moderately. However, if you seek another resolution to authorize war, we shall fight against it.'"[53] This was an ironic twist, considering France's strong push for a two-resolution requirement during the negotiations over 1441. But it made perfect sense in the context of French damage limitation.

France expected that its proposal would find receptive ears in a Bush

administration aching to get out of the UN and into Iraq. But British prime
minister Tony Blair, fighting a rebellion within his own Labour Party,
thought he needed the second resolution, so on 31 January Bush gave it to
him.[54] In yet another demonstration of French weakness, Washington again
was inclining toward London, even though this time Paris was telling it what
it wanted to hear.

The stage was thus set for a fight to the finish. Still, the French were
backing into it. In particular, they were very worried about having to use their
precious Security Council veto, which they know is an anachronism. And—
despite all the bad blood that had accumulated by this point—they especially
wanted to avoid using the veto against their Western allies, something France
has not done since 1956.[55] France's desire to avoid a veto—which, again, was
born of its profound sense of weakness—led it to undertake a lobbying effort
among other Security Council members, a step that probably angered the
Americans even more than a veto would have. By early March, the lobbying effort had escalated to the point where de Villepin was running around
Africa in an attempt to round up a blocking majority against the second
resolution (Colin Powell, saving himself the trip—and the indignity—limited himself to telephoning those same leaders in advance of de Villepin's
arrival).[56] The race was very tight until 10 March, when Chirac declared in
a television interview that "whatever the circumstances," France would vote
no. After Chirac's seemingly categorical statement, Security Council support
for a second resolution evaporated, and the resolution was withdrawn.[57] In
the end, then, France had succeeded in avoiding a veto only by threatening to
use it—a Pyrrhic victory, at best.

Pyrrhic though the French victory may have been, clearly the Americans
and British also did not emerge from this fight unscathed. This raises the
question of why they picked it. It is often said that Blair "needed" the second
resolution for domestic reasons. But despite his fabled optimism,[58] in calling
for a second resolution Blair had to consider the possibility that the Security
Council would not give it to him. Whereas going to war without trying to get
a second resolution would have raised questions in Britain, going to war after
failing to get a second resolution would have been viewed in many quarters
as wholly illegitimate. Was Blair courting even further domestic problems by
taking his second-resolution gamble? Not necessarily.

Blair appears to have calculated that a knockdown, drag-out fight with
the French at the Security Council—even one that Britain ultimately lost
—would in fact leave him strengthened at home, at least temporarily, for in a
pinch, he could always count on Britain's deeply ingrained anti-French sentiment.[59] In an interview with Bob Woodward, Bush gave a revealing explanation for his decision to back Blair's second-referendum request: "Blair's got

to deal with his own Parliament, his own people, but he has to deal with the French-British relationship as well, and its context within Europe. And so he's got a very difficult assignment. Much more difficult, by the way, than the American president in some ways. *This was the period where slowly but surely the French became the issue inside Britain.*[60] Indeed, Blair knew that his second-resolution bet was a winner because the more "the French became the issue," the stronger his domestic position would become. Even so, he did not leave to chance the scapegoating of France for the failure at the Security Council. In the weeks leading up to the war, British cabinet ministers were given "the highest authority" to say whatever they wanted to about the French. Meanwhile, Blair's spinmeister, Alastair Campbell, let loose the hounds of Fleet Street. The tabloid the *Sun* notably featured "separated-at-birth" photo spreads of the French and Iraqi presidents.[61] Pillorying the French for the disaster at the UN was all too easy, and it smoothed the way for British participation on the side of the Americans.

But as Bush also indicated to Woodward, Blair's anti-France play was not merely domestically oriented. It also was part of his bid for a leadership role in Europe. On 29 January, Blair held a rare private meeting with French ambassador Gérard Errera in his Downing Street office. The two men exchanged ideas in a cordial and apparently unguarded way. Then, a few hours later, the media were handed an open letter challenging French and German leadership and signed by eight EU states, including ringleader Great Britain. "France's ambassador," John Kampfner writes, "had been spectacularly double-crossed."[62] The publication of this letter—and a second one signed by ten eastern European NATO partners—revealed how dramatically the tables had turned between Britain and France since the mid-1990s even on France's supposed home turf of Europe, and even when France and Germany were working together. Chirac may have been hailed by the masses that packed European streets on 15 February,[63] but Chirac, like his mentor, de Gaulle, understood that appealing to the street was an act of political desperation, the consequence of having lost the elites.[64] In the only opinion poll that mattered in the short run—that of European chancelleries—Britain and America finished far ahead. As one of Blair's aides put it, "You must admit that as insults go, this one was well-judged."[65] Indeed, during February and March only Belgium and Luxembourg proved reliable friends of the self-proclaimed Franco-German "motor" of European integration.[66] Chirac's frustration boiled over in his comment that the eastern Europeans had "missed a good opportunity to keep quiet . . . . Remember that all it takes is for one country not to ratify by referendum, for [EU enlargement] not to happen."[67] This unfortunate statement rendered France's difficult situation even more so.

It is necessary to plumb beneath Blair's and Chirac's tactical maneuvering to understand why France lost this fight. The waning of French (and waxing of "Anglo-Saxon") influence in Europe is another phenomenon with deep structural roots, in this case the "reuniting" of Europe east and west after the end of the Cold War. On the one hand, the eastern Europeans are anxious to ensure their security against Russia and overwhelmingly view NATO, not the EU, as the means of achieving that goal. Given France's still-tentative reintegration into NATO, it has little to offer eastern Europeans on this issue of central importance, while as America's best friend in Europe, Britain, can offer a great deal. On the other hand, the eastern Europeans also want economic development, and they overwhelmingly view the EU as the means of achieving that. This desire for EU membership gives France some political capital; but, bowing to domestic political imperatives, France consistently spends most of that capital on one issue: the protection of its farmers. Because of the tenacious French defense of its agricultural entitle-ments in EU accession negotiations, in enlargement after enlargement new member-states have arrived in Brussels eager to settle scores with Paris (and indeed, more than a little Euro-skeptical).[68] Thus, over time, Britain, the first applicant to be mistreated by France—its candidacy was twice suddenly halted by French vetoes—has a natural opportunity to gain adherents to its camp. Britain has long enjoyed this structural advantage, but the inability of its Tory governments even so much as to feign commitment to the European idea had prevented it from cashing in. Having been told by Bill Clinton that his usefulness to America stood in direct proportion to his ability to carry Europe, Tony Blair did not make the Tories' mistake.[69] As a result, by 1999 he and Gerhard Schröder, not Jacques Chirac, were the clear leaders of Eu-rope.[70] The Iraq crisis demonstrated that in the new, wider Europe, when Britain joins forces with America, its stock in Europe can stand higher even than the combination of France and Germany.[71] And France knows it.

LOOKING FORWARD

This chapter has focused primarily on the diplomatic maneuvering in the pre-lude to the Iraq War. But the Iraq War is simply the most dramatic instance to date of the general American doctrine of preventive war. Given that the preventive war doctrine is likely to stick, are we therefore fated to more years of international, and in particular Franco-American, tension? Not necessar-ily. This chapter has argued that although France was opposed on principle to the Iraq War and to the wider preventive war doctrine, its behavior was not fundamentally driven by principle. Rather, the zigzagging policy the French pursued reflected their deep sense of weakness on the international stage, no-tably vis-à-vis the United States, Germany, and the United Kingdom. This conclusion is more in line with the available evidence than the "incorrigible France" picture that most commentators have painted. As a result of this study, therefore, we can derive some novel lessons for US diplomacy.

First, the preventive war doctrine in and of itself does not mandate a Franco-American clash. The fact that France was not primarily guided by principle in the Iraq crisis suggests that even if the United States decides to go to the mat with Iran, North Korea, or some other "rogue" state, a repeat of the Franco-American train wreck of 2003 is not inevitable. France recognizes its weakened international power position and determines its policy accordingly. On the other hand, the present diplomatic context is not the same as the context of late 2002. Then, the French position was muted and ambiguous; now, it has been broadcast to the four corners of the earth. It will not be easy for the French to extricate themselves from the principles they have so loudly proclaimed, even if they want to do so. Moreover, Franco-American relations today are in an execrable state. The misunderstandings and doubts of the 1990s gave way to open contempt and accusations of bad faith in 2003; even now, many of the emotions that were stirred by the crisis of 2003 have yet to dissipate. Nevertheless, there is some cause for optimism in the conciliatory noises that started coming from France almost as soon as the war began.

Second, the road to Paris leads through Berlin. Many have criticized the vindictiveness toward France that is suggested by Condoleezza Rice's tripod formulation for US diplomacy after the Iraq crisis: "Punish France, ignore Germany, and forgive Russia."[72] But in fact, the worst miscalculation in that phrase is Rice's injunction to "ignore Germany." If it had not been for Germany's categorical refusal to countenance an Iraq war, France probably would have bowed to its inevitability. More research is needed on the precise sources of the German "no," but in any event a deep and intensive German-American dialogue is clearly essential for Western unity.

Third, US diplomacy needs to adjust to the reality of the new Europe. The point here is not that France can be ignored. If the United States wants NATO at its side in the future, it has to open the lines of communication with both sides of the Franco-German "couple," for, like most couples, each side has influence over the other. For instance, in the case of Iraq, if the United States had given the French more time—perhaps even just the few more weeks they were asking for—it is not inconceivable that France could have reclaimed leadership over the issue from Germany and then gradually reshaped the "couple's" policy in a less confrontational direction.

There is a deeper lesson for US diplomacy here as well. Not just the Bush administration, but also most US foreign policy elites appear to view the EU still today as they did de Gaulle's squabbling "Europe of States."[73] But in reality, that Europe is a distant memory, even in the areas of foreign policy and defense. Therefore, a diplomacy of divide and rule—seemingly endorsed by Secretary of Defense Donald Rumsfeld's infamous comment about "old" and "new" Europe—is destined to fail. But at the same time, it is evident that the EU is far from becoming a truly supranational state, so there is no need to treat it as a potential peer competitor. Rather, the EU is best described as a set of national capitals bound together by strong, heavily trafficked transgovernmental networks.[74] As we have seen, this networked relationship is especially close between Paris and Berlin. The key to US influence in Europe is to take an active part in those networks. Because of the continuing centrality of NATO, this is still possible in the security issue area. The United States has tremendous resources at its disposal. If it uses them wisely, it can have both the international freedom of maneuver it desires and the international legitimacy that the mini-multilateralism of NATO can provide.

PART 4

Outlook

11

Promoting Practical Alternatives to Preventive Force in the Wake of Operation Iraqi Freedom

William Hartung

WHEN THE GEORGE W. BUSH administration unveiled its new national security strategy in September 2002, foreign policy analysts and media pundits alike wondered whether it marked a new departure comparable to NSC-68, the directive that ushered in the policy of containment at the beginning of the Cold War. In the preface to the new strategy, President Bush suggested a quicker trigger for US military action based on the new danger posed by catastrophic terrorism, a threat that exists at "the crossroads of radicalism and technology." He asserted that it is simply "common sense" to "act against such emerging threats before they are fully formed." He further suggested that "we must be prepared to act against our enemies' plans, using the best intelligence and acting with deliberation. History will judge harshly those who saw this danger coming but failed to act. In the new world we have entered, the only path to peace is the path of action."[1] The body of the strategy document amplifies this point, suggesting a need to take "anticipatory action to defend ourselves, even if uncertainty remains as to the time and place of the enemy's attack."[2]

On first glance, Bush's more aggressive stance seemed to fit the tenor of the times in the wake of the 11 September terror attacks. No US president would want to be perceived as sitting passively by while adversaries prepared to strike. But as always in matters of strategy, the devil would be in the details. How early would the US strike under the new doctrine, against what kinds of plans and activities, and against what sorts of potential adversaries?

Based on its application in Iraq, it appears that the 2002 National Security Strategy of the United States of America (NSS 2002) is in fact a strategy of preventive war dressed up in the language of preemption. Nevertheless, the new strategy has been widely mislabeled a "doctrine of preemption," which would have implied an intention to strike at nations or groups poised to strike the United States in short order. Preventive war, on the other hand, implies a willingness to strike whether or not one's adversary is imminently prepared to attack. This crucial difference has major ramifications, both for domestic discourse on the wisdom of particular cases of intervention and on the implications of the doctrine for US and global security. Iraq is an object lesson in how high the costs of a preventive intervention can be, in lives, treasure, strained alliances, international institutions undermined, and negative impacts on the reputation of the United States in the Islamic world and beyond.

My aim in this chapter is twofold: to outline a policy of preventive diplomacy that can serve as an alternative to the NSS 2002 doctrine of preventive war; and to analyze how best to promote such an approach in the midst of emerging public policy debates over prevention and preemption opened up by the implosion of the Bush administration's case for war in Iraq. The alternative policy suggested here would make force an option of last resort, utilized as part of a layered defense in which a web of preventive measures based on diplomacy, treaties, rigorous inspections, intelligence, law enforcement, and economic leverage would take precedence, backed up by the threat of force in particularly tough cases.

Articulating an alternative approach requires some understanding of the Bush administration's stated and actual reasons for going to war in Iraq, how these arguments were received by the public, and what the practical consequences of this particular case of preventive intervention have been for US and global security. Along the way, I will discuss the extent to which the Iraq example was unique, and the extent to which it holds lessons that can be applied to future potential cases of intervention. In short, was Iraq the preventive intervention to end all preventive interventions, or are the difficulties there just a small detour in the longer arc of history in which policy is tending toward the acceptance of a new paradigm for military intervention?

THE LOGIC OF INTERVENTION IN IRAQ

The most consistent theme running throughout the Bush administration's case for intervening in Iraq was the claim that Saddam Hussein was rapidly rebuilding his nuclear weapons capability and would be willing to share nuclear, chemical, or biological (NBC) weapons with a terrorist organization that might in turn use them against the United States. For example, in his 7 October 2002 speech in Cincinnati, Bush asserted that if Saddam Hussein could buy, steal, or otherwise acquire a quantity of enriched uranium the size of a softball, he could build a nuclear weapon in less than a year. He then resorted to the inflammatory phrase that had been used by his national security advisor Condoleezza Rice in a television interview a month earlier: "we cannot wait for the final proof—the smoking gun—that could come in the form of a mushroom cloud." Later on in the speech Bush made the "sharing with terrorists" argument: "Iraq could decide on any given day to provide a biological or chemical weapon to a terrorist group or individual terrorists. Alliance with terrorists could allow the Iraqi regime to attack America without leaving any fingerprints."[3] Bush reiterated the theme in his January 2003 State of the Union address, asserting that "with nuclear arms or a full arsenal of chemical or biological weapons, Saddam Hussein could resume his ambitions of conquest in the Middle East and create deadly havoc in that region. . . . Secretly, and without fingerprints, he could provide one of his hidden weapons to terrorists, or help them develop their own."[4] In his address to the nation on the eve of the war, in March 2003, Bush returned to this theme yet again: "The danger is clear: using chemical, biological, or, one day, nuclear weapons, obtained with the help of Iraq, the terrorists could fulfill their stated ambitions and kill thousands or hundreds of thousands of innocent people in our country, or any other."[5] Stockpiles of chemical and biological agents that had not been accounted for going back ten or fifteen years or more were treated as if they were still active and ready to go. Severe worst-case scenarios were presented about the possible impact of these imagined chemical and biological arms stockpiles, making it sound to the untrained ear as if they were every bit as dangerous as nuclear weapons, a transparent falsehood. Thus those who listened to the president's January 2003 State of the Union speech were treated to references to "enough doses" of anthrax in Iraq "to kill several million people," and "materials sufficient" to produce enough botulinum toxin "to subject millions to death by respiratory failure."[6]

Absent these graphic images implying a serious and direct threat to the United States, it is highly unlikely that the Bush administration would have been able to muster the requisite public and congressional support needed to launch the war to overthrow Saddam Hussein's regime that commenced in mid-March 2003. Arguments about improving the human rights situation in Iraq, or spreading democracy, or punishing an "evildoer" probably would not have been enough to get most Americans to support major combat operations halfway around the world. But by the spring of 2004, within a year of the decision to intervene in Iraq, the main pillars of the administration's case for war were in tatters, contradicted by evidence collected once Hussein's regime was gone. There were no massive stockpiles of chemical and biological weapons. There was no active nuclear weapons program. There were no mobile biological weapons laboratories of the kind described by Secretary of State Colin Powell in his February 2003 presentation to the United Nations (UN) Security Council. There were no major underground weapons facilities. Basically, the regime of UN sanctions and inspections that the Bush administration had ridiculed in the run-up to the war had been far more effective in disarming Hussein's regime than anyone had realized. For example, an analysis by the historian Thomas Powers indicated that the preliminary report of the US-funded and staffed Iraq Survey Group (ISG) was unable to find evidence for any of the twenty-nine major factual assertions in Powell's Security Council presentation on Iraq's weapons programs: "The conclusion seems inescapable: on the eve of war, Iraq had no weapons of mass destruction [WMD], and it had no active program to build them."[7] Or, as chief UN inspector Hans Blix put it in his book-length treatment of the subject, "We now know that Iraq under Saddam almost certainly did not have any weapons of mass destruction, and that the regime was, in fact, deterred from maintaining or reviving prohibited weapons programs by the presence of UN inspection and the US/UK threat supporting it. The much maligned, relatively low-cost policy of containment had worked, and the high-cost policy of counter-proliferation had not been needed."[8]

The administration's own handpicked group of inspectors, the ISG, also concluded that Iraq had no active NBC programs, and that any weapons that did exist had been destroyed in the early to mid-1990s. On the nuclear question, the group's final report—popularly known as the Duelfer report for its director, Charles Duelfer—said the following: "Saddam Hussein ended the nuclear program in 1991 following the Gulf War. ISG found no evidence to suggest concerted efforts to restart the program." As for chemical weapons, the report had a similar assessment: "While a small number of old, abandoned chemical munitions have been discovered, ISG judges that Iraq unilaterally destroyed its undeclared weapons stockpile in 1991. There are no credible indications that Iraq resumed production thereafter." And so it was for Hussein's biological weapons program: "ISG found no direct evidence that Iraq, after 1996, had plans for a new BW [biological weapons] program or was conducting BW-specific work for military purposes."[9]

In the face of the Duelfer report's seemingly incontrovertible evidence that Iraq had no NBC weapons—and no imminent plans or programs to develop them—the Bush administration shifted gears and cited Saddam Hussein's "intent" to start up such programs once UN sanctions were lifted. Bush asserted that Hussein was "systematically gaming the system, using the UN oil-for-food program to try to influence countries and companies in an effort to undermine sanctions." Bush continued: "He was intent on doing so with the intent of restarting his weapons program once the world looked away." Vice President Richard Cheney struck a similar note, arguing that "as soon as sanctions were lifted, he had every intention of going back to business as usual. So delay, defer, wait was not an option."[10] This suggests an extreme version of the preventive war theory—taking military action against a country because of its perceived intentions, even if they cannot be implemented until many years later. The consistent application of such a doctrine would put a hair trigger on potential conflicts worldwide.

Greg Thielmann, a proliferation expert who worked at the State Department's Bureau of Intelligence and Research (INR), has noted that even if a state like Iraq had developed a nuclear weapon along with ballistic missiles to deliver one or another type of these deadly weapons, the concept of nuclear deterrence would still operate:

For emerging missile powers to anticipate effectively intimidating the United States with threats of a direct missile attack on the American homeland is a dubious proposition. There is no empirical evidence that even the most erratic foreign leader would believe himself immune from . . . [a US] counterattack. . . . There are no plausible scenarios for disguising the source of an ICBM [intercontinental ballistic missile] attack on the United States. . . . Devastating retaliation and the end of the attacker's regime would have to be assumed.[11]

Bush administration claims about Iraq–al-Qaida ties have also been largely disproved by several bipartisan investigations undertaken since the start of the Iraq War. The administration's claims on this score ranged from on-again, off-again intimations of an April 2001 meeting in Prague between 9/11 hijacker Mohammed Atta and an Iraqi intelligence officer to assertions by President Bush that Iraq was "an ally of al Qaeda" that "provided al Qaeda with chemical and biological weapons training."[12] The report of the bipartisan commission that investigated the 9/11 attacks determined from a variety of sources, ranging from security camera photographs to cell phone records to travel records, that "the available evidence does not support" the original claim of an Atta meeting with an Iraqi official in Prague on the stated date.[13] More important than any single detail, both the 9/11 Commission and a Senate Select Committee on Intelligence investigation of US intelligence in the run-up to the Iraq War concluded that there were no operational ties between Iraq and al-Qaida. The key findings in the Senate report with reference to al-Qaida were: (1) "The Central Intelligence Agency's assessment that Saddam Hussein was most likely to use his own intelligence operatives to carry out attacks was reasonable, and turned out to be accurate"; (2) "The Central Intelligence Agency reasonably assessed that there were likely several instances of contacts between Iraq and al-Qaeda throughout the 1990s, but these contacts did not add up to a formal relationship"; and (3) "The Central Intelligence Agency's assessment that to date there was no evidence proving Iraqi complicity or assistance in an al-Qaeda attack was reasonable and objective. No information has emerged to suggest otherwise."[14] Secretary of Defense Donald Rumsfeld also acknowledged—once the war with Iraq was under way—that he had seen no evidence of Iraq–Al-Qaida ties.[15]

Not only have Iraq–al-Qaida links not been found, but experts on the region question the premise that there is a basis for a relationship in the first place. As former National Security Council (NSC) analyst Daniel Benjamin has put it, "Iraq and al-Qaida are not obvious allies. . . . They are natural enemies." He further argued that before being deposed from power, "Mr. Hussein ha[d] remained true to the unwritten rule of state sponsorship of terror: never get involved with a group that cannot be controlled and never give a weapon of mass destruction to a group that might use it against you."[16]

GROUPTHINK AND IDEOLOGY

The huge disparity between the administration's main arguments for the war and the reality of Iraq's military capabilities suggest one of two possibilities: groupthink and worst-case scenario building run amok, or a policy of outright deception. Since so many prominent policy-makers in the Bush administration—including Vice President Cheney, Secretary of Defense Rumsfeld, Deputy Secretary of Defense Paul Wolfowitz, and many of their key aides—were "true believers" in the cause of "regime change" in Iraq long before joining the administration, it can be difficult to distinguish ideological distortion from conscious efforts to deceive the public. Rumsfeld and Wolfowitz were both signatories, for example, of a 26 January 1998 letter organized by the conservative Project for the New American Century (PNAC) urging President Clinton to undertake a strategy aimed "at the removal of Saddam Hussein from power."[17]

George W. Bush's first treasury secretary, Paul O'Neill, notes that targeting Iraq was on the administration's agenda within its first ten days in office, and that the rationale seemed to be a sort of reverse domino effect: "A weak but increasingly obstreperous Saddam might be useful as a demonstration of America's new, unilateral resolve. If it could be effectively shown that he possessed, or was trying to build, weapons of mass destruction—creating an 'asymmetric threat' in the neoconservative parlance, to US power in the region—his overthrow would help 'dissuade' other countries from doing the same."[18]

O'Neill was skeptical, to put it mildly, noting, "There was never any talk about this sweeping idea that seemed to be driving all the specific actions. From the start, we were building the case against Hussein and looking at how we could take him out and change Iraq into a new country. And, if we did that, it would solve everything. It was all about *finding a way to do it.* That was the tone of it. The President saying, 'Fine. Go find me a way to do this.'"[19] It was perhaps this attitude, more than anything else, that corrupted the collection and, more important, the use of intelligence in the run-up to the war with Iraq. O'Neill experienced the effect of this at the very first meeting of the NSC, when Central Intelligence Agency (CIA) director George Tenet showed a satellite photo of a building that he said "might be a plant that produces either chemical or biological materials for weapons manufacture." When O'Neill pointed out that he had seen "a lot of factories around the world that look like this one. What makes us suspect that this one is producing chemical or biological weapons?" Tenet was finally forced to acknowledge that there was no "confirming intelligence" as to what was being produced at the plant.[20] But it was clear that Vice President Cheney and other enthusiasts for going to war were going to take it as hard evidence of illicit weapons activity. Multiply this bias systematically, scores of times over, and you get the kind of exaggerated intelligence estimates that were used to convince Congress and the American people to go to war in Iraq.

In its very measured assessment of whether the intelligence in the run-up to the Iraq War was politicized, the Carnegie Endowment for International Peace cited five factors that suggested that analysts may have felt undue pressure to hype the threat in the preparation of the 2002 National Intelligence Estimate (NIE) on Iraq that was released shortly before Congress voted to authorize military action in the fall of that year: Vice President Cheney's multiple visits to CIA headquarters to inquire about the Iraq estimates; demands by top administration officials for access to raw intelligence; the haste with which the estimate was written (roughly three weeks time); the high number of dissenting opinions (most of which were not made public until after the congressional vote); and the fact that political appointees at the Pentagon set up a separate intelligence analysis unit that gave its own spin to the data.[21] Add to this the fact that a number of important pieces of data in the administration's case were uncorroborated assertions from Iraqi defectors who were later proven to have little credibility, and the picture emerges of information being shaped to fit a preexisting case rather than an effort being made to objectively evaluate the threat posed by Iraq.

Selective use of intelligence is nothing new. Recent examples include the Commission to Assess the Ballistic Missile Threat to the United States, a 1998 panel chaired by Donald Rumsfeld that claimed that any nation with Scud-based missile infrastructure could develop a long-range ballistic missile capable of reaching US territory within five years of a decision to do so. The Rumsfeld commission's estimate was far shorter than existing estimates in the intelligence community, and it was utilized to full effect in promoting missile defense spending and encouraging the United States to abandon the Anti-Ballistic Missile Treaty. According to *Washington Post* defense correspondent Bradley Graham, the main source of information for the commission's assertion that a nation like North Korea could build a crude long-range ballistic missile in relatively short order came from an interview with two engineers from Lockheed Martin, a major missile defense contractor that had a vested interest in exaggerating the threat.[22] The Rumsfeld report's prediction has proved to be far off the mark, because it underestimated the difficulties of developing long-range ballistic missiles at every turn while vastly overstating the ease with which a developing nation could go through all of the necessary steps to develop such a complex system.[23] Further back, there is of course the infamous "Team B" exercise of the 1970s, when the neoconservative Committee on the Present Danger pressed for an outside panel to take a second look at the CIA's assessment of the Soviet threat. Paul Wolfowitz served on one of the Team B panels, and Ford administration Secretary of Defense Donald Rumsfeld sided with their harsher (and ultimately incorrect) view of Soviet capabilities and intentions.[24] Among the "lessons" of these experiences is that there is often little political price to be paid for exaggerating the threat to the United States; that is to say, the individuals involved in "crying wolf" or systematically overstating the threats rarely have difficulties finding positions of power and authority in future administrations. "Better safe than sorry" seems to be the motto. That is, better to have erred on the side of exaggerating the threat than underestimating it. The Bush administration's equivalent of this argument in the run-up to the war in Iraq was to say that the costs of not acting would be far greater than the costs of acting. As we will see below, this truism proved disastrously wrong in the Iraqi case. Advocates of more balanced approaches to security strategy need to do a better job of demonstrating and publicizing the costs of unilateralist action and threat inflation—in dollars, in lives, and in diversion of resources from more urgent priorities.

Evidence that emerged in mid-2005 gives credence to the argument that the Bush administration may have gone beyond exaggerating the Iraqi threat to actively distorting it in support of an intervention it had already decided upon. British foreign policy aide Matthew Rycroft distributed a secret memo, dated 23 July 2002, to the British defense secretary, foreign secretary, and other key officials that included the following passage: "C reported on recent talks in Washington. There was a perceptible shift in attitude. Military action now seemed inevitable. Bush wanted to remove Saddam, through military action, justified by the conjunction of terrorism and WMD. But the intelligence and facts were being fixed around the policy."[25] The "C" referred to in the memo was Richard Dearlove, the head of MI6, the British overseas intelligence service. The memo further indicated that the issue involved the timing of the war and the means of selling it to the US and British publics, not whether to intervene in Iraq. Analyst Mark Danner has noted that "the idea of the UN inspectors was introduced not as a means to avoid war, as President Bush had repeatedly assured Americans, but as a means to make war possible."[26] The relevant passage of the Rycroft memo reads:

The Foreign Secretary said he would discuss this with Colin Powell this week. It seemed clear the Bush had made up his mind to go to war, even if the timing was not yet decided. But the case was thin. Saddam was not threatening his neighbors, and his WMD capability was less than that of Libya, North Korea, or Iran. We should work up a plan for an ultimatum to Saddam to allow back the U.N. weapons inspectors. This would also help with the legal justification for the use of force.[27]

Other sources such as Paul O'Neill, *Washington Post* reporter Bob Woodward, and former Bush adviser Richard Clarke have traced the administration's preparations to go to war in Iraq from as early as January 2001 to September–November 2001.[28] But the Rycroft memo sheds further light on the political strategy pursued by US and UK officials to sell the war to the public.

Reaction within the United States to the huge gulf between the arguments for war and the reality on the ground in Iraq has been mixed, as has the opinion among elites. Historian Arthur Schlesinger Jr. has bluntly excoriated the preventive war in Iraq as "illegitimate and immoral," arguing that no government will ever have the kind of perfect foresight required to make the momentous decision to commit troops to combat based on an imagined threat that might come into being at some future date.[29] Moderate to neoconservative columnists like Jim Hoagland and Charles Krauthammer have defended the application of the preventive war doctrine in Iraq on grounds ranging from the notion that it represents a potential first step in the democratization and stabilization of the Middle East to continued adherence to the idea that Saddam Hussein's history of bad actions and future intent to reconstitute his arsenal of NBC weapons were reason enough to act. These two sets of arguments mirror the shifting rationales put forward by the Bush administration: Saddam Hussein was a "madman" with evil intent, and the United States could not risk letting him rebuild his arsenal of mass terror; and removing Hussein's regime opens the way to building a free and democratic Iraq, which will be a model for the development and spread of democracy throughout the Arab world, with the added bonus of depriving Palestinian extremists and other terror groups in the region of a key source of support, thereby opening the way to a viable peace between Israel and the Palestinians.

Both of the Bush administration's "fallback rationales" for the war have roots in neoconservative thinking that preceded the 2000 presidential election. In the infamous 1996 "Clean Break" memorandum prepared by a team led by Richard Perle in conjunction with Douglas Feith and David Wurmser—all of whom went on to be key officials or advisers in the Bush administration—"removing Saddam Hussein from power in Iraq" is seen as the linchpin of an aggressive new strategy in which Israel will "contain, destabilize, and roll back some of its most dangerous threats."[30] Although these are put forward as policy prescriptions for a new Israeli government, the implication is that they will be supported by the United States. Similarly, in their January 1998 letter to President Clinton, Donald Rumsfeld, Paul Wolfowitz, Richard Perle, John Bolton, and their colleagues, writing on behalf of the PNAC, stressed regional concerns rather than direct threats to the United States. They argued that if Hussein's regime were allowed to develop "WMD," "the safety of American troops in the region, of our friends and allies like Israel and the moderate Arab states, and a significant portion of the world's supply of oil will all be put at hazard."[31] Several prominent neoconservatives who either have ties to the Bush administration or took positions in the administration have advocated a sort of "democratic domino effect" for the Middle East in which the United States by force, pressure, or other means topples a whole series of undemocratic Arab regimes, with Iraq just serving as a starting point.

A more modest version of the domino theory is President Bush's claim in his 2004 State of the Union address that America's intervention in Iraq has changed the behavior of other states by showing them that "America's words now have meaning." He was referencing, in particular, Libya's decision to renounce its nuclear weapons program and open it to international inspections.

So the terrain of justification for the war in Iraq shifted from the idea that Saddam Hussein was an imminent threat who possessed weapons that could kill millions of people, and was on the verge of getting more, to more abstract notions. The first, "better safe than sorry" rationale held that it was better to strike early before he got too far along in his intentions to get such weapons. The second, "democratic domino" argument suggested that overthrowing one tyrant by force would radically transform the political and security landscape of the Middle East, giving the United States and its allies tremendous leverage to reshape the region in ways that suit their long-term interests.

How did domestic constituencies accept this bait and switch? Support for the war eroded over the first year or so, but a solid core of Americans continued to "rally around the troops" and back the war effort, even if they did have questions about the precipitating cause of the conflict. To the extent that questions about the war arose, they seemed to have more to do with costs and casualties, not the original rationales put forward by the administration. In fact, a remarkable survey published by the Program on International Policy Attitudes at the University of Maryland in April 2004 found most Americans still believed the administration's principal arguments for the war, despite numerous high-profile testimonies of key experts asserting strong evidence to the contrary. A majority of Americans continued to believe that Iraq had given substantial support to al-Qaida, and a majority believed that Iraq either had "WMD" prior to the war or a major program for building them.[32] Furthermore, Americans who believed that Iraq had "WMD" or supported al-Qaida were much more likely to continue to support the war in Iraq and to say that they would support the reelection of George W. Bush.[33] The persistence of these inaccurate views even after a number of high-profile experts had discredited them indicates the heavy burden that opponents of preventive war may face. It is extremely difficult to sway public opinion against the powerful "bully pulpit" of the presidency, which can often set the tone for major electronic and print media coverage of an issue at critical decision points. Even so, by the summer of 2004 a *New York Times*/CBS poll demonstrated what one *Times* reporter described as "a deep post-Iraq skepticism about war, with 59 percent of voters . . . saying the United States should not attack another country unless attacked first."[34] By the summer of 2005, another *New York Times*/CBS poll found that a slight majority of Americans (51 to 45 percent) believed that the United States should have stayed out of Iraq, and 60 percent believed that US efforts to bring stability to Iraq were going badly.[35] Even if this plunge in support is based on costs and casualties and not opposition to the justification used for going to war, it still suggests an opening for discussion of alternatives to the doctrine of preventive war.

TOWARD PREVENTION, NOT INTERVENTION

Perhaps the most important contribution of the Iraqi case to the discussion of preventive war is as a cautionary tale. It is a reminder that there are cases when, contrary to the Bush administration's mantra, the costs of military action can be considerably higher than the costs of pursuing the same objective using other tools (or what Bush officials refer to as "inaction").

Because preventive wars are by their nature controversial, the likelihood of persuading allies to share the financial and military burdens of the conflict is greatly reduced. That has certainly proved true in Iraq, where the United States expended roughly $200 billion on the war and occupation in the first two years of the conflict, with ongoing expenses running at $6 billion or more per month.[36] More than 2,350 US troops have been killed, as have tens of thousands of Iraqis. US military personnel injured were well over 17,000 as of the spring of 2006, with many injuries requiring expensive medical procedures.[37] Many states and scores of cities, towns, and villages have suffered indirect impacts as members of the National Guard and Reserve who work as police, firefighters, public health personnel, and government officials in their hometowns have been absent on extended duty in Iraq. Because the war is being financed in the midst of a policy of continuing tax cuts, it has added directly to budget deficits in the range of $300 billion to $400 billion per year. If the war in Iraq were truly in response to an imminent security threat to the United States that could be met in no other way, these economic burdens would be acceptable. But in a situation where the war appears to have been a "war of choice," not necessary to deal with an imminent threat, the issue of cost is relevant.

The costs of the war in Iraq loom even larger in the wake of Hurricane Katrina, which devastated large parts of Louisiana (especially New Orleans), Mississippi, and Alabama in the summer of 2005, incurring a pledge from the Bush administration to spend at least $62 billion rebuilding the region. The full bill could be much higher, perhaps as much as $100 billion to $200 billion. Not only did the war in Iraq soak up funds that might have been available for disaster relief in the Gulf Coast region of the United States, but the stationing of large numbers of National Guard personnel from each of the affected states in Iraq hobbled relief efforts.

The economic costs of preventive war in Iraq pale in comparison with the potential security costs. As former White House counterterrorism adviser Richard Clarke has noted, the diversion of money and specialized troops (especially special forces personnel) from Afghanistan to Iraq served to slow the hunt for public enemy number one in the global campaign against terrorism,

Osama bin Laden. Even worse, *New York Times* reporter Douglas Jehl has summarized a classified CIA analysis of the situation in Iraq as of mid-2005: "The Central Intelligence Agency says Iraq may prove to be an even more effective training ground for Islamic extremists than Afghanistan was in Al-Qaida's early days, because it is serving as a real-world laboratory for urban combat."[38]

While preventive war in Iraq has backfired disastrously, a wide array of homeland security priorities could benefit from money spent in the United States instead on the conflict there, from protecting ports, bridges, and tunnels, to safeguarding nuclear and chemical facilities, to creating appropriate means for key antiterror agencies to share information on suspects in a timely manner. And, as is discussed below, there are smarter ways to reduce the odds that terror groups will get their hands on the makings of an NBC weapon that are much cheaper and more effective than overthrowing governments. Last but not least, if $100 billion or more per year was not being drained from the US Treasury for the occupation of Iraq, there would be funds available to promote positive programs in education, economic assistance, and other areas that would help improve the image of the United States around the world and build lasting relationships that will be crucial to fighting a multifaceted campaign against terrorism.

It is worth reflecting on the fact that there are other, even worse cases of preventive war that are possible. During the 1962 Cuban Missile Crisis, US officials did not learn until years later that although Havana did not yet have nuclear-armed ICBMs from Moscow, Cuba did have ships armed with medium-range nuclear missiles. Thus if President Kennedy's cooler head had not prevailed and he had taken up preemptive/preventive military options suggested by his military aides, a nuclear confrontation could have been sparked. One could imagine a scenario in which a US military strike against North Korea, if viewed as the prelude to the death knell for the regime and its leader, might lead to a last-gasp use of any nuclear weapons Pyongyang might have developed against South Korean targets and US troops. And even a conventional conflict could involve tens or hundreds of thousands of casualties, given the proximity of the North Korean border to the South Korean capital of Seoul.

Finally, of course, there is the question of what kind of instability would be sparked if a new international norm of preventive war were to begin to be established as a result of a US doctrine that implicitly or explicitly endorses the concept as an acceptable, routine foreign policy option. Russian leader Vladimir Putin has threatened to use "all of" Moscow's military might against supporters of Chechen terror groups; India and Pakistan have had numerous bloody cross-border incidents over the status of Kashmir; and large parts of Africa, the Middle East, and South Asia have unresolved border disputes, resource conflicts, and refugee crises that could easily escalate when managed by a demagogic leader armed with a doctrine of preventive war. US actions alone will not spark wars in any of these areas, each of which have their own local and regional dynamics. But giving legitimacy to a doctrine of preventive war could give aggressor groups and nations yet another rationale for starting wars rather than negotiating peaceful accommodations.

CONSIDERING THE ALTERNATIVES

There wasn't exactly a raging debate on the issue of preventive war during the 2004 election season, but the major candidates did take distinct positions on the issue, and it rose to the level of discussion in major news and opinion pieces from time to time. While he was still a candidate for the presidency, John Edwards released a position paper arguing that the threat of "WMD"—especially nuclear weapons— should be addressed by a strategy of preventive diplomacy, not "preemptive war."[39] In his acceptance speech at the July 2004 Democratic convention, John Kerry made a point of saying that "as President, I will bring back America's time-honored tradition: the United States of America never goes to war because we want to, only because we have to." He elaborated briefly by saying he would not send troops into battle unless he could tell their parents "we had no choice. We had to protect the American people, fundamental American values from a threat that was real and imminent." He went on to say that "this is the only justification for going to war."[40] The impact and meaning of this apparent departure from the Bush doctrine of preventive war were called into question a few weeks later when Kerry announced that even if he knew then what was known postinvasion about Iraq's capabilities, he still would have voted to authorize military action against Saddam Hussein's regime. This would seem to contradict his statement that under his administration the United States would only go to war "because we have to," which implies an imminent threat.

Leaving aside the political posturing of the campaign trail, what would a practical alternative to the Bush doctrine look like? The first principle of a policy of preventive diplomacy backed by force would involve setting priorities. The two greatest threats facing the United States and its allies in the coming period are mass-casualty terrorism and the spread of nuclear weapons. The combination of the two—nuclear weapons in the hands of a terrorist organization—although not as high probability an event as some analysts suggest, could have such devastating consequences that preventing it from occurring deserves serious attention. This was one of the original rationales used by the Bush administration for going to war in Iraq—that Saddam Hussein was reconstituting his nuclear weapons program and might one day share those weapons (or his chemical or biological weaponry) with a terrorist group that would then use them against the United States. This was a highly unlikely scenario for a variety of reasons. Not only did Saddam Hussein not possess the weaponry in question, but if he had he would have been loath to hand it over to a terrorist group like al-Qaida, whose activities he could not control. Nor would he want to risk a connection being made between the terror group employing the weapons and their origins in Iraq, risking massive retaliation by the United States that could destroy Iraq as a functioning society.

That being said, there is a far more likely route for a terrorist group to get access to a nuclear weapon. When the bank robber Willie Sutton was asked why he robbed banks, he said, "because that's where the money is." If a terrorist group wanted to acquire a nuclear weapon or materials to make a crude nuclear device, it would go where the weapons are. The largest stockpiles of poorly secured nuclear weapons in the world are in Russia. In January 2001, shortly before President Bush's inauguration, a bipartisan task force chaired by former Senate majority leader Howard Baker and former White House counsel Lloyd Cutler reported that "the most urgent national security threat facing the United States today is the danger that WMD or weapons-usable material in Russia could be stolen and sold to terrorists or hostile nation-states and used against American troops abroad or American citizens at home."[41] The task force recommended the development of a long-term project to safeguard, destroy, or neutralize Russia's vast stockpile, estimated to include up to 40,000 strategic and tactical nuclear weapons, plus enough enriched uranium and plutonium to build tens of thousands more. If implemented, the Baker-Cutler plan would cost $3 billion per year, a tripling of current US spending for those purposes.

The Baker-Cutler proposals are not untested or theoretical. They suggest an acceleration of programs that have already been working. Since the end of the Cold War, over 6,000 strategic warheads, 700 long-range ballistic missiles, and tons of bomb-grade nuclear materials have been destroyed or secured under the US-funded Nunn-Lugar Cooperative Threat Reduction program. With additional investments and stepped-up cooperation, the pace could be picked up substantially. A recent study by the Belfer Center at Harvard estimated that at current rates, it would take thirteen years to destroy or secure Russia's remaining warheads and nuclear materials. The study suggests a program of stepped up investment and cooperation that could accomplish that same goal in four years time.

The authors of the Belfer Center report identify the key element of a successful strategy as sustained presidential attention to the issue, including appointment of a national coordinator to focus on a plan and create concrete goals for the reduction of vulnerable nuclear weapons and bomb-grade materials worldwide.[42] Graham Allison of the Kennedy School of Government has also devised an extensive plan for thwarting terrorist efforts to acquire nuclear weapons in his book *Nuclear Terrorism: The Ultimate Preventable Catastrophe.*[43]

Russia is not the only potential source of nuclear weapons or nuclear materials that could fall into the hands of a terrorist organization. A change of government in Pakistan, where pro-Taliban and Islamic fundamentalist factions have a foothold in the military, intelligence, and political elites, could also pose a significant risk of leakage of nuclear weapons or nuclear materials to terrorist organizations. And there are scores of nuclear plants and research reactors that have generated bomb-grade materials in countries that may not themselves have developed their own nuclear weapons yet. For example, in August 2002 the United States purchased enough material to make at least two nuclear weapons from a research laboratory in Yugoslavia. To do so, it was necessary to seek $5 million in private financing from the Turner Foundation, because the US government could not come up with adequate funding on short notice to remove this obvious proliferation threat. In order to prevent this sort of ad hoc approach from governing future nonproliferation efforts, Senator Richard Lugar (R-IN) has proposed globalizing the Nunn-Lugar Cooperative Threat Reduction program that has been applied to nuclear weapons and nuclear materials in Russia, so that there would be adequate, flexible funding available to purchase and destroy loose nuclear weapons or nuclear materials from any source on short notice.[44] As of this writing, his idea has yet to be implemented due to lack of sufficient support from the executive branch or Congress.

While securing and destroying so-called loose nukes and bomb-grade materials is a crucial first step toward keeping nuclear weapons out of the wrong hands, the highest margin of security depends on reducing global nuclear arsenals to the lowest possible levels while stopping production of new nuclear weapons and new bomb-grade materials. An excellent first step in that direction would be to strengthen the Strategic Offensive Reductions Treaty between the United States and Russia. As it currently stands, the agreement calls for reductions in deployed strategic warheads on both sides to roughly one-third of current levels, but there is no timeline for reductions, and no requirement that warheads taken off of active status be destroyed. Also, either side can pull out of the agreement on thirty days notice. Adding a timeline for reductions and requiring that warheads taken out of service under the agreement be destroyed rather than stockpiled would make the treaty far more meaningful, both as a stepping stone toward further US and Russian reductions and as leverage for bringing other nuclear weapons states into discussions about reducing their arsenals as well.

As for "problem states" like Iran or North Korea that pursue nuclear weapons despite current international agreements like the Non-Proliferation Treaty, there are ample options short of war for dealing with these difficult cases. In retrospect, the Iraq case shows that the regime of sanctions and monitoring set up in the wake of the 1991 Persian Gulf war was actually quite effective in dismantling Baghdad's NBC weapons programs, and that to a significant degree Saddam Hussein's efforts at subterfuge prior to the 2003 US intervention were, if anything, more of an effort to hide his military weakness than to hide his strength.[45] The Iraq case is somewhat unique in that the sanctions regime that was set up the early 1990s was as strict as it was because Iraq was defeated after waging a war of aggression against Kuwait. In cases like North Korea and Iran, where these circumstances do not obtain, it will be necessary to engage in hard bargaining to create a mix of carrots and sticks designed to get the country in question to give up its nuclear ambitions. Despite its on-again, off-again character, the 1994 framework agreement between the United States and North Korea is a good model for this kind of negotiation. In broad outline, it offered North Korea economic benefits, including an end to US sanctions and resumption of energy assistance, plus security benefits in the form of an end to US enmity leading to an eventual normalization of relations, in exchange for Pyongyang giving up nuclear bomb making. Despite press accounts the contrary, during periods when the United States was able to hold up its end of the bargain, North Korea generally did the same. When the United States delayed or backed out on either the economic or security front, North Korea shifted gears and resumed or threatened to resume nuclear activities.[46]

An important addition to the nonproliferation tool kit would be a substantial increase in funding for the International Atomic Energy Agency (IAEA), which has a regular budget of just $270 million per year to carry out inspections and impose safeguards for the entire world. By contrast, the UN inspectors and the US-backed ISG spent over $1 billion to learn that there were no active NBC weapons in Iraq.[47]

The only true "undeterrables" in the new nuclear equation are the practitioners of catastrophic terrorism, like the 9/11 suicide hijackers. Tyrants with state power are first and foremost survivors. Their desire to survive can be exploited to create enforceable mechanisms short of war for eliminating their ability to develop or use "WMD." Dealing with tough cases like Iran or North Korea through concerted diplomacy—backed up by the threat of force only as a true last resort—would free up time, energy, and resources for the urgent task of building a global coalition to eliminate, secure, and protect the world's stockpiles of unconventional weapons so that terrorists seeking these awful weapons will have the odds firmly stacked against them.

The most recent case of a so-called rogue regime abandoning its nuclear weapons program—Libya—owes far more to diplomacy than to threats of force, but one would never have known it from listening to the rhetoric of the Bush administration. The president tried to claim Libya's shift in policy as a victory for its doctrine of preventive war as evidenced by the following passage from the 2004 State of the Union address: "Nine months of negotiations involving the United States and Great Britain succeeded with Libya, while twelve years of diplomacy with Iraq did not. For diplomacy to be effective, words must be credible, and no one can now doubt the word of the United States of America."[48] The clear implication is that the US intervention in Iraq put such fear in the heart of the Gaddafi regime that it felt compelled to cough up its "weapons of mass murder." Under this theory, preventive war has a sort of deterrent or leveraging effect on terrorists and tyrants, who will change their behavior once they know that "America means business." An alternative interpretation has been offered by, among others, Flynt Leverett, who served as senior director for Middle Eastern Affairs at the NSC in 2002 and 2003. Leverett points out that Libya's interest in striking a deal to renounce its NBC weapons programs predated the US intervention in Iraq, and is grounded in a longstanding desire to get out from under US sanctions. With a growing population of unemployed youth and a need for US technology to expand oil production, the Gaddafi regime was anxious to have the sanctions lifted as quickly as possible to avoid having to deal with a fundamentalist challenge to its legitimacy. The deal was also made possible by a new, pragmatic attitude on the part of Bush policy-makers—a willingness to offer a quid pro quo to a difficult regime in exchange for verifiable changes in behavior. Furthermore, the Libya deal was made possible by explicitly keeping the neoconservative, interventionist camp in the Pentagon and State Department (John Bolton's office) out of the policy loop. Leverett suggests that it is this more nuanced, diplomatic approach that is likely to bear fruit in tough cases like North Korea and Iran, not the guns-blazing Iraq model that President Bush alluded to in his 2004 State of the Union address.[49]

As for dealing with the threats posed by chemical and biological weapons, a good start would be for the United States to support efforts to strengthen the enforcement provisions of the Chemical Weapons Convention (CWC) and the Biological Weapons Convention (BWC). Instead, the Bush administration walked out of an international conference on strengthening the BWC, and has resisted more robust inspections of potential chemical weapons sites because it refuses to be subjected to the same level of inspection as other adherents to the accord.[50]

A preventive approach to fighting terrorism and ensuring US national security interests also requires renewed engagement in helping to resolve deep-seated regional conflicts, from the Israeli-Palestinian dispute, to India and Pakistan's conflict over Kashmir, to the divide between North and South Korea. Rather than letting these important regional issues fade into the background as blood, treasure, and executive attention are lavished primarily on the occupation of Iraq or other potential preventive wars, they should be brought back to the forefront as the United States seeks to reposition itself as an honest broker in helping to resolve conflicts rather than being an outside interventionary force trying to impose its will on key nations. This is important in reality, and also in how the United States is perceived by key allies in Europe and Asia and in the Arab and Muslim worlds. First and foremost, this will mean taking a more independent line vis-à-vis Israel's decision to put up a security wall that impinges on land formerly offered to the Palestinians as part of a land-for-peace deal, pressing for a cutback in settlements in the West Bank, and otherwise indicating that US support for Israel's right to exist within secure borders does not translate into unquestioning support for every policy shift of the Israeli government of the moment. On the Korean peninsula, it will mean being more supportive of Seoul's sunshine policy of gradual rapprochement with Pyongyang, which could over time lead to reunification and an elimination of the North Korean threat, even if it takes a decade or a generation to accomplish. And in India and Pakistan, it will mean building a more consistent nexus of economic and political ties that can be put to work in helping to broker an understanding over contentious regional issues such as the status of Kashmir and the future of the two nations' nuclear programs.

More broadly, a preventive approach to dealing with terrorism and other key threats to US security will require a diversification of the foreign policy tool kit beyond the current overemphasis on military solutions. Dealing with a distributed network like al-Qaida, which operates via cells in sixty or more countries and can sustain itself with or without state sponsorship, with a doctrine that emphasizes preventive military strikes against nation-states is misguided at best, if not actively counterproductive. It is the equivalent of trying to kill a swarm of disease-bearing mosquitoes with a sledge hammer, rather than taking comprehensive public health measures such as drying up pools of stagnant water that serve as breeding grounds, educating the public to seek early treatment if symptoms of disease arise, and similar measures. The parallel approach for dealing with terrorism would entail a diversified plan that involves cooperating with allies on military, diplomatic, intelligence, economic, public relations, and law enforcement efforts to root out and delegitimize terrorist organizations. To the extent that unilateral or near-unilateral military efforts like the US intervention in Iraq undermine the prospects for this kind of broad cooperation, that is another strike against them in the calculus of setting strategic priorities.

In the FY 2006 federal budget, military tools for addressing threats to US security are funded at $449 billion, or seven times as much as non-military tools such as homeland security and international affairs accounts ($64.7 billion), without taking into account the costs of the wars in Iraq and Afghanistan.[51] A task force of retired military officers, former Pentagon officials, and civilian experts organized by the Center for Defense Information and Foreign Policy in Focus has suggested a rebalancing of the overall national security budget—civilian and military—that would cut $53 billion from military accounts and shift $40 billion into nonproliferation, diplomacy, economic development, peacekeeping, and homeland security. The result would be an overall national security budget that spends four times as much on the military as it does on international affairs and homeland security, a considerable improvement on the current seven to one ratio. Reductions would come from cutting back or eliminating Cold War systems like the F-22 fighter, the DDX destroyer, the missile defense program, and new and excess nuclear weapons, as well as military base restructuring and adjustments in the National Guard and Reserve. Major new investments would include $1.2 billion in Nunn–Lugar–style nonproliferation programs, a $10 billion annual increase in foreign economic aid, $14 billion to increase preparation for emergency responders (police, fire, and public health) across the United States, $2 billion for port container inspections, and $6 billion for public transit security.[52]

The details of this "security shift" are open to debate, but the need for a shift is clear. Continuing to build advanced combat aircraft like the F-22 for roughly $200 million a copy when US adversaries in every conflict of the past two decades have barely had air forces worthy of the name makes little sense, particularly if upgraded versions of current-generation aircraft can be had for one-quarter of the price. Increasing spending on cooperative threat reduction is a far more effective way to prevent nuclear weapons and nuclear materials from getting into terrorist hands than launching costly wars of counterproliferation and occupation, or air strikes based on imperfect intelligence. Increasing economic assistance not only helps improve the image of the United States in key countries and regions but, properly managed, can help build stability and stave off the creation of "failed states" that all too often become operating grounds for terror organizations.

Finally, a preventive strategy will require a thorough rethinking of US arms sales policy. Too often arms transfers are considered as merely instruments of policy, as means to an end that can be swapped for access to military facilities, or as ways to build military-to-military relations, or as symbols of closer relations with a given regime. The potential negative consequences of these dangerous exports—in fueling regional arms races, empowering repressive regimes, and, in too many cases, arming groups and regimes that later become US adversaries—are rarely given adequate consideration. The destabilizing impact of current US arms sales policies is considerable. Since 9/11, thirteen of the twenty-five major US arms customers in the developing world have been undemocratic regimes, undermining President Bush's claim that fostering democracy is a top priority of US foreign policy. For the most recent year for which statistics are available, eighteen of twenty-five active conflicts worldwide involved US-supplied weaponry.[53] In addition, the growing role of US government subsidies for arms exports, which have grown to $6 billion to $8 billion per year, has become a drain on foreign aid resources available for nonmilitary purposes.[54] The role of US covert aid to Afghanistan in helping to launch Islamic fundamentalist groups like al-Qaida, not to mention the role of US credits and dual-use technologies in aiding the development of Saddam Hussein's arsenal in the run-up to Iraq's invasion of Kuwait in August 1990, are just two of the more extreme examples of how relatively unfettered arms transfers can backfire disastrously years after the original decision to transfer weapons or technology is made.[55] A policy that puts strict limits on arms transfers to regimes with poor human rights records or undemocratic practices would offer a measure of protection against this "boomerang effect," while opening the way to substituting other, nonmilitary tools of influence such as diplomacy, aid, and trade as America's calling card to key players in the international system. To have the required effect, US restraint would eventually need to be duplicated on a multilateral basis, but as the world's leading arms exporting nation, US leadership would go a long way toward getting the process started.

None of the above-mentioned steps rule out the use of force to deal with truly imminent threats to US security, such as intelligence that a terrorist organization has acquired an NBC agent, or that a regional power is poised to strike a major US ally. But even in these instances, an assessment would need to be made as to the most effective form of action (for example, special forces versus air strikes, reliance on allies versus direct US intervention), and intelligence would ideally need to be a good deal more accurate and de-politicized than it was in the run-up to the war in Iraq. Obviously, in the absence of perfect information, a decision to initiate hostilities would have to be made on a case-by-case basis. That is all the more reason to pursue a preventive strategy dedicated to diminishing the most serious risks to US security so that the need to use force is reduced accordingly.

12

Preventive Force

UNTANGLING THE DISCOURSE

WILLIAM W. KELLER AND
GORDON R. MITCHELL

SPEAKING TRIUMPHANTLY from the deck of an aircraft carrier in May 2003, President George W. Bush declared, "[M]ajor combat operations in Iraq have ended. In the battle of Iraq, the United States and our allies have prevailed."[1] While this optimism drew a predictable response from the live military audience, the credibility of President Bush's proclamation gradually faded as US forces were drawn into a bloody and costly counterinsurgency campaign that eventually alienated many war supporters. As 2005 drew to a close, rising casualties and spiraling war expenses fueled skepticism of President Bush's "mission accomplished" message and raised serious doubts about the wisdom of "staying the course in Iraq."[2] One prominent Republican lawmaker commented, "the White House is completely disconnected from reality,"[3] while other Republicans called on the Bush administration to produce an exit plan.[4] However, as Karl-Heinz Kamp points out, such arguments were drawn narrowly and did not include calls for an overall exit from the US doctrine of first-strike force spelled out in the 2002 National Security Strategy of the United States of America (NSS 2002):[5] "It is noteworthy that despite the disaster in Iraq, the Bush doctrine of preemptive strike has not been discredited with the American public. Domestic criticism is directed against the developments in Iraq, but not against the idea of anticipatory self-defense. There is essentially no political pressure on the administration to disavow the Bush doctrine."[6]

Perhaps the willingness of war skeptics to spare NSS 2002 from the stinging criticisms levied at Operation Iraqi Freedom is the product of a successful White House effort to establish a rhetorical firebreak between its preventive use of force doctrine and the specific example of the 2003 Iraq War. As part of this effort, then national security advisor Condoleezza Rice stated in 2003 that the United States "would never want to do another Iraq."[7] In one sense, Rice's comment stands today as a truism, since ongoing military commitments in Iraq are likely to tie down US forces for the foreseeable future and complicate new missions requiring substantial troop deployments. Assessing how these constraints limit options for further pursuit of the Bush administration's strategic vision, Donald Daniel, Peter Dombrowski, and Rodger Payne argue that "from an operational perspective, the doctrine is presently a dead letter."[8] Consistent with this analysis is a shift in the tenor of the White House's approach to foreign policy in President Bush's second term. Marking this turn, Rice raised the status of diplomacy as a tool of US statecraft after her appointment as secretary of state. According to Guillaume Parmentier, head of the French Center on the United States in Paris, "We Europeans see that Condi Rice has convinced the president that diplomacy should be tried before other means, and as Secretary of State she is pursuing that conviction on a wide variety of issues."[9]

For example, Rice jump-started stalled multilateral negotiations on Iran's controversial nuclear program during her first visit to Europe as secretary of state, explaining that "we're going to continue to work however we can diplomatically."[10] The Bush administration faced strong pressure to follow Rice's lead and stay on the diplomatic track, given the paucity of satisfactory options for dealing with Iran militarily. In chapter 9 of this volume, Peter Dombrowski illuminates how the US military is unprepared to support the massive postconflict reconstruction effort that a preventive intervention to oust the Iranian mullahs would entail. Military options on the lower end of the force spectrum appear similarly unpromising. As Dan Reiter shows in chapter 2, Iran has learned the lesson of Osiraq, dispersing and burying its nuclear assets, thus rendering them much less vulnerable to limited preventive strikes.[11]

Shortly after release of NSS 2002, commentators asked whether the strategy document was a blueprint to "run the table" and "go all around the Middle East taking over governments."[12] The fact that this has not come to pass can be interpreted as validation for Colin Powell's argument that critics have "exaggerated both the scope of preemption in foreign policy and the centrality of preemption in U.S. strategy as a whole."[13] While Powell's comment may reassure those skeptical about the wisdom of preventive military action against Iran, the Bush administration's frequent warning that "all options including the military one are on the table" signals that fresh first-strike attacks are under serious consideration.[14] Richard Clarke and Steven Simon punctuated this point, observing in April 2006 that "the current level of activity in the Pentagon suggests more than just standard contingency planning or tactical saber-rattling."[15] More generally, in an October 2005 update on the "war on terror," President Bush reasserted that "we're determined to prevent the attacks of terrorist networks before they occur."[16] While rolling out the 2006 National Security Strategy, National Security Advisor Stephen Hadley renewed the White House's commitment to first-strike force: "The President's strategy affirms that the doctrine of preemption remains sound and must remain an integral part of our National Security Strategy."[17] In President Bush's address at the 2005 Naval Academy commencement, he recounted his administration's investment of $16 billion in "transformational military capabilities" that "will help us keep the peace by redefining war on our terms."[18] What are these investments, and how might they "redefine war"? While a comprehensive answer to this question lies beyond the scope of this chapter, a brief discussion of "global strike capability" suggests why technological developments may move the topic of preventive war up on the agenda of political discussion sooner rather than later, sustaining public controversy about the value of hitting first as a central tool of US foreign policy.

THE ARRIVAL OF GLOBAL STRIKE CAPABILITY

Section three of this volume shows how the utility of preventive military force is constrained by factors including soldier scarcity, the dispersal and hardening of military assets by adversaries, and the need to secure consent from other governments before projecting force. In summer 2004, Secretary of Defense Donald Rumsfeld approved a top secret "Interim Global Strike Alert Order," laying the groundwork for *nuclear* first-strike attacks that would be largely unencumbered by these constraints.[19]

In an apparent follow-up to Rumsfeld's order, a draft document from the Department of Defense (DOD) Joint Chiefs of Staff entitled "Doctrine for Joint Nuclear Operations" was posted on a military Web site in spring 2005. This document proposes that US regional military commanders may seek approval for nuclear first strikes against adversaries "intending" to use "weapons of mass destruction" (WMD).[20] According to Hans Kristensen, "The result is nuclear pre-emption, which the new doctrine enshrines into official U.S. joint nuclear doctrine for the first time, where the objective no longer is deterrence through threatened retaliation but battlefield destruction of targets."[21] After the existence of this planning document was amplified by Jeffrey Lewis,[22] it vanished from the DOD Web site.[23] Yet sixteen members of the US Congress still followed up, arguing that the "Doctrine for Joint Nuclear Operations" "removes the ambiguity of the previous [1995 version of the] doctrine, and now suggests that your [the Bush] administration will use nuclear weapons to respond to non-nuclear WMD threats and suggests that this use could include pre-emptive nuclear strikes thereby increasing reliance on nuclear weapons."[24]

William Arkin explains that "global strike" has become one of the "core missions" for US Strategic Command (STRATCOM), a Pentagon agency that traditionally served as the steward of the US nuclear arsenal during the Cold War.[25] One result is CONPLAN 8022-02, a STRATCOM contingency plan for neutralizing "WMD" threats from North Korea or Iran by combining pinpoint bombing, cyber warfare, and specially configured earth-penetrating nuclear bombs to destroy deeply buried targets.[26] As Arkin notes, "STRATCOM established an interim global strike division to turn the new preemption policy into an operational reality."[27] According to Seymour Hersh, "one of the military's initial option plans, as presented to the White House by the Pentagon this winter [2005], calls for the use of a bunker-buster tactical nuclear weapon, such as the B61-11, against underground nuclear sites," including Iran's main uranium centrifuge facility at Natanz.[28] Under the guidance of Admiral James O. Ellis Jr., STRATCOM also moved to integrate space assets into its global strike package. As Ellis explained in 2003 congressional testimony:

Space capabilities will dramatically enhance US Strategic Command's newly assigned global strike mission, which extends our long-standing and globally focused deterrent capabilities to the broader spectrum of conflict. The incorporation of advanced conventional, nonkinetic, and special operations capabilities into a full-spectrum contingency arsenal will enable the command to deliberately and adaptively plan for and deliver rapid, limited-duration, extended-range combat power anywhere in the world.[29]

General Richard B. Myers, then chairman of the Joint Chiefs of Staff, used the occasion of Admiral Ellis's July 2004 retirement ceremony to announce that global-strike capability had made major strides:

Jim, the President charged you to "be ready to strike at any moment's notice in any dark corner of the world." That's exactly what you've done, and in superb fashion. Within months, you compressed the conventional planning process, and accelerated execution timelines from weeks to days, and in some cases down to only hours. To-day we can recognize a threat, develop a plan of action, and execute a mission faster than ever before.[30]

In the words of a STRATCOM concept paper, the "defining charac-teristic" of a global strike is its ability to target the enemy "without resort to large numbers of general purpose forces traditionally associated with major combat operations."[31] This implicates debates on the wisdom of preventive first strikes, since, as Jeffrey Lewis observes, "Objectors have long derided a strategic posture based on preventive warfare as needlessly provocative in light of the technological futility of the task. Warfighting proponents view space systems as a solution to these objections."[32]

RECONSIDERING NSS 2002 AFTER IRAQ

According to the Pentagon, the "global-strike" capability afforded by "bun-ker-buster" nuclear bombs and space assets will improve preventive warfare's prospects for operational success. High technology, on this logic, enables planners to surmount many of the traditional obstacles that constrain at-tempts to project military force, some of which are discussed by Dombrowski (chapter 9) and Hymans (chapter 10). However, one drawback of technical wizardry is what Seyom Brown calls "the illusion of control," a tendency of military planners to believe that the "polyarchic" nature of international rela-tions can be tamed magically by advanced technology.[33] Such hubris, Brown reasons, is bound to produce unwise decision-making and dubious military misadventures. Similarly, Jeffrey Record warns further that one result of the technology-driven transformation of the US military may be to "increase the incidence of politically sterile military victories," where ostensibly successful missions contribute little to long-term security.[34] As a counterweight, Brown proposes a set of eight normative guidelines governing the use of military force (see table 6).

Brown's guidelines dovetail with many findings presented by the authors of this volume. For example, guideline one is the logical extension of William Hartung's call (chapter 11) for a "web of preventive measures" that includes treaties, rigorous inspections, and other diplomatic tools, along with military force. Hartung advises that the nonmilitary measures of prevention take pre-cedence in his system of "layered defense." But to ensure this prioritization, it is necessary to keep the boundaries separating the elements "thick and clear," as Brown's overarching guideline stipulates.

In the context of Iran policy, such boundaries are steadily eroded by the Bush administration's calculated ambiguity regarding the delineation

244   WILLIAM W. KELLER AND GORDON R. MITCHELL

Table 6. Guidelines for Judicious Use of Military Force

Category	Individual Guidelines
Overarching Guideline	1. Keep the threshold between nonviolent diplomacy and war thick and clear.
Guidelines Based on Substantive Principles	2. Be assured that the interests and values at stake are of sufficient weight—and have sufficient support from the country—to warrant going to war. 3. Be convinced in each case that the resort to military force will better serve the interests at stake than will nonmilitary actions. 4. Be convinced that the harm likely to result from the contemplated war will not exceed the good expected. 5. Be willing to commit the United States to whatever postwar responsibilities and resources will be required to restore at least minimal civic life where it has been severely disrupted by the war. 6. Scrupulously adhere to rules of engagement that prohibit attacks on unarmed civilians, and expand the prohibition to include indirect attacks. 7. Explicitly define and reinforce "firebreaks" between different kinds and levels of warfare, making sure that they are clearly reflected in deployments, strategies, military training manuals, and war games.
Deliberative Guideline	8. Integrate guidelines 1–7 into both the domestic and international deliberations and decision-making processes that play a crucial role in determining whether and how to use force.

Source: Table compiled from Seyom Brown, *The Illusion of Control: Force and Foreign Policy in the 21st Century* (Washington, D.C.: Brookings Institution Press, 2003), 154–75.

between diplomatic and military policy tracks. The rhetoric of coercive diplomacy, backed by "all options are on the table" military threats, blurs the boundary between nonviolent diplomacy and war. As Arkin notes, this blurring heightens the risks of miscalculation and frustrates prospects for peaceful resolution of the nuclear dispute.[35]

Guideline three can be read as a natural counterpart to Thomas Goodnight's analysis (chapter 5) of how the White House's "action/inaction" frame for preventive war decision-making generates presumptive momentum toward the use of force. Brown's military/nonmilitary frame acts as a countervailing brake, pushing back the tendency to evaluate the military force option in a strategic vacuum. It also lays a foundation for the type of intelligence analysis that Thielmann (chapter 8) says is necessary to remedy the predilection of error-prone analysts to derive alarmist, worst-case projections from the assumption that "doing nothing" becomes the default mode of US policy toward adversaries if force is not used. On another level, guideline five reflects the findings of Dan Reiter's survey (chapter 2) of preventive attacks, which shows that extensive postconflict reconstruction is the key factor accounting for the success of previous attempts to neutralize nuclear, biological, and chemical weapons programs through preventive invasions that result in regime change.

Guideline eight integrates Brown's entire set of guidelines into a process of political legitimation conducted through deliberative exchange of viewpoints. Since this normative move resonates deeply with the overall focus of *Hitting First*, further examination of this synergy is in order. One general insight emerging from the analyses in this volume is that the Bush administration's first-strike force doctrine suffers from intrinsic defects that are likely to become manifest in preventive wars of the future, even if technological innovation succeeds in resolving some of the outstanding operational dilemmas. For example, although Bush administration officials promise that the United States will not "do another Iraq,"[36] the framework for public discussion set up by the White House to redefine Saddam Hussein as an imminent threat prior to the 2003 Iraq War remains intact. Many of the same patterns of argument isolated by Goodnight (chapter 5) and Payne (chapter 6) have been applied in the public debate surrounding Iran's nuclear program in 2005–2006.[37] As Joseph Cirincione notes, "the parallels are striking. . . . [T]he unfolding administration strategy appears to be an effort to repeat its successful campaign for the Iraq war."[38] Additionally, it has proved difficult to correct the record on Iraq prewar intelligence that Bush administration officials manipulated through what Mitchell and Newman (chapter 4) call "Team B intelligence coups"—political gambits to slant intelligence analysis under the guise of "competitive intelligence exercises."[39]

Several official investigations have examined the IC's role in producing flawed prewar intelligence on Iraq, but a Senate probe looking into White House use of intelligence bogged down when, in former intelligence officer Paul R. Pillar's words, it "got stuck in the partisan mud."[40] One major sticking point involved access to documents and witnesses related to the intelligence activity of Pentagon deputy Douglas Feith and others associated with the Policy Counterterrorism Evaluation Group (PCTEG) and the Office of Special Plans (OSP). Democrats pushed for information on these subjects, but were denied by committee chair Senator Pat Roberts (R-KS).[41] Roberts justified limiting the scope of his committee's "phase two" inquiry by arguing that Senate investigation of White House Team B activities should be deferred until an internal review of the matter by the Pentagon inspector general was completed.[42] This bureaucratic impasse once again denied the public an opportunity to learn more about the extent to which PCTEG and OSP affected public argument prior to Operation Iraqi Freedom.

Disconcertingly, evidence suggests the Bush administration's antipathy toward public deliberation, documented by Payne in chapter 6, is less a single-case aberration and more an endemic manifestation of systematic attempts to control public opinion. Consider the appearance of official documents in 2003 that lay out American deception plans: "In a document last autumn, the joint chiefs of staff stressed the need for 'strategic' deception and 'influence operations' as tools of war. The army, navy and air force have been directed to devise plans for information warfare."[43] According to Arkin, the Bush approach includes goals for information warfare that pursue "D5E": "destruction, degradation, denial, disruption, deceit, and exploitation." While deception has long been recognized as a legitimate tool of psychological warfare to confuse enemies,[44] Arkin notes that the wide array of sites and practices of information control brought under the purview of the Bush policy "blurs or even erases the boundaries between factual information and news, on the one hand, and public relations, propaganda and psychological warfare on the other."[45]

The political implications of blurring the boundary that demarcates military strategic deception and public sphere propaganda are significant, given Arkin's concerns that "while the policy ostensibly targets foreign enemies, its [deception's] most likely victim will be the American electorate."[46] This fusion of military deception with media propaganda is what led the Office of Strategic Influence to commission officers from the US Army's Psychological Operations Command to work as interns in the news division of CNN, and, as noted in chapter 1, also helped turn the US 305th Psychological Operations Company's mission at Firdos Square on 9 April 2003 into a worldwide propaganda event.[47] When the Office of Strategic Influence's existence was leaked to reporters in 2002, Secretary Rumsfeld was forced to close the propaganda unit. Yet less than a year later, he stipulated that his action had only been symbolic, and that the same information warfare missions had been shifted to other Pentagon offices: "And then there was the Office of Strategic Influence. You may recall that. And 'oh my goodness gracious isn't that terrible, Henny Penny the sky is going to fall.' I went down that next day and said fine, if you want to savage this thing, fine, I'll give you the corpse. There's the name. You can have the name, but I'm gonna keep doing every single thing that needs to be done and I have."[48] Rumsfeld kept his word.[49] In November 2005, it was disclosed that US Army officials secretly paid Iraqi journalists to publish upbeat stories about American military operations, based on press releases written by US Army psychological warfare experts.[50]

Another Pentagon psychological operations campaign, "Villainize Zarqawi/leverage xenophobia response," came to light in April 2006. As Colonel Derek Harvey, a military intelligence officer in Iraq, describes the effort: "Our own focus on Zarqawi has enlarged his caricature, if you will—made him more important than he really is, in some ways." Internal military documents belie official Pentagon assurances that the Zarqawi villainization initiative was purely a foreign propaganda operation. One briefing slide explicitly lists the "U.S. home audience" as a propaganda target, while another slide in the same briefing notes that a "selective leak" about Zarqawi was made to *New York Times* reporter Dexter Filkins. According to the *Washington Post*, Filkins's resulting article, about a letter supposedly written by Zarqawi and boasting of suicide attacks in Iraq, ran on the *Times* front page on 9 February 2004.[51]

One name is sufficient to dramatize the ominous security implications of this commitment to strategic deception: Operation Northwoods. As Mitchell and Newman show in chapter 4, General Lyman Lemnitzer's secret 1962 plan to deceive the American public into supporting a US first strike on Cuba illustrates that top US officials have been willing to conceive of strategic deception as a legitimate tool to justify preventive wars that might be difficult to sell publicly. With deception schemes ranging from a fake civilian airline hijacking to a plot designed to "make it appear that Communist Cuban MiGs have destroyed a USAF aircraft over international waters in an unprovoked attack," Lemnitzer's plan was as imaginative as it was audacious.[52] Notably, President Bush picked up General Lemnitzer's line of thinking almost exactly prior to the 2003 Iraq War. An official British memorandum reveals that during a 31 January 2003 White House meeting between Bush and British prime minister Tony Blair, Bush "was thinking of flying U2 reconnaissance aircraft with fighter cover over Iraq, painted in U.N. colours." The memorandum quotes Bush telling Blair: "If Saddam fired on them, he would be in breach [of UN resolutions]."[53]

While it may be tempting to dismiss the Lemnitzer and Bush cases as eccentric aberrations, the historical record reflects other instances where apparently saner deception schemes interacted precipitously with the quick trigger of first-strike force. In 1967, the Soviet Union attempted to inflate the threat of Israeli military mobilizations against Syria. "The evidence pointing to deliberate deception about the supposed Israeli threat to Syria is overwhelming," explains historian Michael Handel.[54] While this Soviet strategy worked for a time as a pressure tactic against the United States, eventually the campaign to flood Arab newspapers with exaggerated estimates of Israeli troop deployments inadvertently triggered the Six Days' War, by sparking Israeli preemption: "Above all, this example illustrates the difficulty of controlling a deception operation involving volatile and unstable allies and of knowing where it will lead. The threat to Syria operation is the quintessential runaway deception campaign. It also backfired on the instigator, creating results that were exactly opposite of those desired."[55]

Payne's reconstruction (chapter 6) of the "deliberative caveats" embedded in the logic of NSS 2002 illustrates still another way that strategic deception turns the Bush administration's military doctrine against itself. The concern of NSS 2002's drafters that the strategy document would be emulated by other states has materialized—Russia, Australia, France, Japan, and Indonesia have each followed the US lead and asserted a first-strike prerogative.[56] Whether these states exercise such military options judiciously or use them as "pretexts for aggression" may depend largely on whether they also copy NSS 2002's "deliberative caveats" requiring political leaders to justify and explain decisions to use preventive force before applying it. But the embrace of deception policies by the White House and Pentagon may seriously undercut the credibility of US diplomats urging restraint by other nations.

TOPICAL REMEDIES FOR DISCOURSE FAILURE

Decision-making prior to the 2003 Iraq War was not integrated carefully into the kind of deliberative process Brown recommends. As Arthur Schlesinger Jr. observes, for many months "President Bush's extraordinary reversal of the direction of American foreign policy had little effective opposition, or even debate."[57] According to Chaim Kaufmann, a "failure of the marketplace of ideas" resulted in breakdown of the US political system's ability to "weed out exaggerated threat claims and policy proposals based on them."[58] Peter Neumann and M.L.R. Smith call this phenomenon a "discourse failure," where "constriction of the language and vocabulary" produces a "failure of comprehension."[59] How can discourse failure be averted in future situations when decisions on war and peace hang in the balance? Ironically, Brown sees a role here for some of the advanced technologies that facilitate projection of preventive military force:

The technological revolution in communications—paradoxically a source of both greater control and potential loss of control over conflict escalation—is making it possible to slow down the decisionmaking process to ensure that use-of-force issues are given the serious consideration they deserve. It makes it technically feasible for everyone who should be "in the room" to be there when actions of profound consequence for the nation and the world are being considered. It should no longer be acceptable that, because of a presumed lack of time, the crucial technical, political, legal, and ethical implications are not given due attention.[60]

Brown hopes that communication technology can animate his deliberative guideline (see table 6) by getting everyone "in the room" for prospective discussions on proposed usage of military force. However, as students of deliberative democracy are keenly aware, there is no guarantee that once assembled, interlocutors will deliberate in a manner that pushes leaders to govern responsibly.[61] Indeed, as Kaufmann observes about the 2003 Iraq War case, "careful phrasing of official rhetoric can allow even claims with especially weak evidentiary bases to be persuasive to the public, because often only experts are in a position to parse what certain official statements did and did not say."[62] In the parlance of rhetorical theory, this dynamic reflects a lack of rhetorical invention on the part of citizens, journalists, and lawmakers—failure to come up with apt lines of argument fitting for the situation.

Since the time of ancient Greece, scholars have worked to understand and explain this challenge of "rhetorical invention."[63] In his treatise *On Rhetoric,* Aristotle argued that effective speakers should hold in reserve "selected statements about what is possible and most suited to the subject, and when unexpected problems occur, to try to follow the same method, looking not to the undefined but to what inherently belongs to the subject of the discourse."[64] His system for helping speakers create arguments "most suited to the subject" centered on the topoi (commonplace topics). Aristotle created twenty-eight topoi, which Eugene Garver describes as "argumentative means of organizing practical domains."[65] Aristotelian topoi are designed to help speakers "identify common lines of argument"[66] that can enrich discussion on "the important subjects on which people deliberate," including "finances, war and peace, national defense, imports and exports, and the framing of laws."[67]

As we observed in chapter 1, a key factor differentiating preemptive from preventive warfare situations is that the latter afford time for deliberation before decisions to use force become faits accomplis. Brown's guidelines lay out a salient set of issues that warrant careful attention in these deliberations (see table 6). However, as he clarifies, "the guidelines are not specific policy prescriptions or strategies. Rather they are a statement of considerations that are essential to take into account in formulating and executing national security policy."[68] Left untheorized by Brown is precisely how citizens can best press their leaders to "take into account" these substantive considerations.

In highlighting how government officials leveraged their information monopoly to control public deliberation prior to the 2003 Iraq War, Kaufmann paints a bleak picture of the prospects that US citizens will be able to overcome similar dynamics in future public debates. However, the availability of dialogue strategies, modeled after Aristotle's commonplace topics, may help equalize the playing field. Given the myriad military, political, economic, and moral issues implicated in preventive war decision-making, a comprehensive catalog of salient dialogue strategies could easily fill the pages of another book. Yet it may still be useful to generate a narrowly focused list, one that is tailored to stimulate argumentative creativity in a specific area of public dialogue. A key area of discourse failure during the run-up to Operation Iraqi Freedom that this volume isolates as especially prone to breakdown is deliberation unfolding at the interface where intelligence analyses are converted into evidence and offered as support for public arguments on policy positions. The following sections spell out three dialogue strategies designed to facilitate productive deliberation in future contexts where these dynamics may be in play.

DIALOGUE STRATEGY 1: SHAKE THE TREE FOR UNPICKED CHERRIES

The quality of public deliberation may improve if interlocutors pursue a dialogue strategy that locates and evaluates the origins of intelligence analysis supporting public justifications for proposed uses of preventive force. Almost by definition, deliberation regarding proposed use of preventive military force is an exercise fraught with uncertainty, since the purpose of attacking preventively is to forestall threats that have not yet fully materialized, and may possibly never reach fruition. Goodnight (chapter 5) points out how this dynamic creates a thorny dilemma for political leaders seeking political support for preventive war missions: It is difficult to back up arguments for war with definitive evidence when only uncertain or ambiguous intelligence data are at hand. Hartung (chapter 11) and Thielmann (chapter 8) detail how White House officials dealt with this dilemma prior to the 2003 Iraq War, cherry-picking select data points from various intelligence sources to support claims that Iraq posed a "great and gathering" danger to the United States. Similarly, Mitchell and Newman (chapter 4) chronicle ways that the White House circumvented official intelligence channels to convey intelligence directly from Iraqi defectors into administration speeches and statements. As Payne (chapter 6) shows, subsequent investigations have revealed many of these cherry-picked data points to be highly suspect. The magnets thought to be useful for Iraq's centrifuge program turned out not to have threatening uranium enrichment applications. The key documents alleging that Iraq sought uranium from Niger turned out to be forgeries. Alleged Iraq–al-Qaida ties were based on vanishingly thin reeds of evidence. In fact, later scrutiny exposed the dubious quality of almost every single piece of intelligence data referenced in Colin Powell's pivotal February 2003 address to the United Nations (UN).[69]

As UN secretary general Kofi Annan indicates, the fallout from these revelations has dealt a significant blow to US credibility: "The bar has been raised. People are going to be very suspicious when one talks to them [US officials] about intelligence. And they are going to be very suspicious when we try to use intelligence to justify certain actions."[70] Yet there is a danger here. Taken to the extreme, the suspicious impulse could result in a blind form of hyperskepticism on the part of audiences evaluating US claims in preventive war deliberations. Goodnight (chapter 5) and Payne (chapter 6) both point out how this "Chicken Little effect" could jeopardize US security, making it difficult for Washington to act when truly imminent and grave threats materialize.

A more constructive response by those evaluating the merits of US arguments for the preventive military missions of tomorrow would entail locating the specific intelligence analyses employed by government officials to justify use of force, and then folding discussion of these analyses back into ensuing deliberations. While classification laws designed to protect confidential "sources and methods" of intelligence gathering often make it difficult for citizens to participate in public debates on the credibility of specific intelligence sources, it may be easier to enter public dialogue at the level of intelligence analysis. As Pillar observes, "Any time policymakers, rather than intelligence agencies, take the lead in selecting which bits of raw intelligence to present, there is—regardless of the issue—a bias. The resulting public statements ostensibly reflect intelligence, but they do not reflect intelligence analysis, which is an essential part of determining what the pieces of raw reporting mean."[71] Consider the example of Vice President Richard Cheney's claim on 16 March 2003 that upon invading Iraq, US forces would be "greeted as liberators."[72] Hindsight suggests that this important claim was not based on any coordinated intelligence analysis conducted by authorized experts in the US intelligence community (IC), but rather on unofficial defector testimony "stovepiped" to Cheney by Iraqi National Congress chief Ahmed Chalabi.[73] One could imagine the following series of questions being posed to Cheney during the *Meet the Press* appearance where he made that statement.

— *Is your claim that US forces will be "greeted as liberators" personal opinion, or is it based on coordinated intelligence analysis?* Since arguments for war based on personal conjecture have marginal appeal, this question establishes a burden of proof on the interlocutor to specify a specific intelligence analysis underwriting the substantive claim in question.

— *On what basis do you judge the credibility of intelligence analysis supporting your claim that US forces will be "greeted as liberators"?* This question isolates the credibility of the relevant intelligence analyses as a topic of deliberation.

— *Have agencies of the US IC conducted any official analyses that assess the strength of intelligence data backing your claim that US forces will be "greeted as liberators"?* This question opens discussion of the "stovepiping" possibility, couched in a way that can proceed without the interlocutor necessarily being forced to reveal "sources and methods."

In future settings, deliberators might adapt variants of the above questions as creative tools to focus public discussion on the origins and strength of intelligence analyses backing claims for war (or the fact that supporting intelligence analysis is absent). These lines of argument eschew ad hominem attacks designed to neutralize the credibility of government officials, and focus instead on bringing the substance of specific details regarding the nature of intelligence analysis (not necessarily specific sources) to the surface of public debate.

A vivid example of this dialogue strategy in action involves media follow-up to President Bush's claim on 13 March 2006 that "Tehran has been responsible for at least some of the increasing lethality of anti-coalition attacks by providing Shia militia with the capability to build improvised explosive devices in Iraq."[74] The next day, journalist Charlie Aldinger pressed Pentagon officials for evidence supporting Bush's claim: "You said that Revolutionary Guards and IEDs [improvised explosive devices] and weapons are moving across the border from Iran. What you have not said conclusively is whether the government of Iran and the mullahs are sponsoring that activity. Do you have proof that they are, indeed, behind this, the government of Iran?" After Secretary Rumsfeld handed off Aldinger's probing question to General Peter Pace, Pace admitted: "I do not, sir."[75]

DIALOGUE STRATEGY 2: CAST A PEBBLE INTO THE POND

By probing pat characterizations of IC judgments, questioners can deepen understanding of public arguments advanced in support of proposed preventive war missions. The official US IC is composed of sixteen separate agencies and entities that each serves different customers, and each has a distinct approach to intelligence analysis. On a flow chart, this looks like a disjointed hodgepodge of bureaucracy. But as Thielmann argues in chapter 8, the analytical heterogeneity produced by this structure is actually an important strength of the IC, since it enables consensus judgments to be enriched by the cross-pollination of diverse perspectives. The Silberman-Robb Commission, charged by President Bush to investigate the 2003 Iraq War intelligence failure, concurs with Thielmann's point: "Analysts must readily bring disagreement within the Community to policymakers' attention, and must be ready to explain the basis for the disagreement. Such disagreement is often a sign of robust independent analysis and should be encouraged."[76]

The texture of these internal IC debates tends to be flattened when intelligence analysis is converted into evidence for specific policy positions in public argument. In the Iraq case, Thielmann shows that while interagency IC debates raged on key points of intelligence analysis undergirding the White House's case for war, the existence of these debates was hidden in public statements that portrayed consensus IC findings as settled judgments. For example, while the CIA viewed Iraq's importation of aluminum tubes as convincing proof that Saddam Hussein was attempting to reconstitute his nuclear weapons program, Department of Energy (DOE) and Bureau of Intelligence and Research (INR) analysts strongly disagreed. Such doubts were communicated directly to President Bush in the October 2002 President's Summary of the National Intelligence Estimate (NIE), which indicated that although "most agencies judge" that the use of the aluminum tubes was "related to a uranium enrichment effort . . . INR and DOE believe that the tubes more likely are intended for conventional weapons uses." Murray Waas reports that the one-page summary was written specifically for Bush, was handed to the president by then CIA director George Tenet, and was read in Tenet's presence.[77] Nevertheless, these intelligence dissents were hidden from public inspection by a selective declassification policy that the Bush administration used to present a one-sided picture of the NIE's contents.[78] White House statements on aluminum tubes projected an air of certainty that belied the vigorous technical debate simmering within the IC.[79]

In a December 2002 press conference, Secretary of State Powell stated: *"We also know* that Iraq has tried to obtain high-strength aluminum tubes, which can be used to enrich uranium in centrifuges for a nuclear weapons program."[80] Here, Powell's definitive characterization of the intelligence silenced the vigorous dissenting views advanced by INR and DOE, the latter agency being the most technically qualified authority to weigh in on the issue. With few exceptions, most journalists, citizens, and members of Congress uncritically accepted Powell's characterization of the intelligence and would not come to grips with the INR and DOE dissents until after the war, when multiple investigations concluded that the aluminum tubes in question were not intended for uranium enrichment.[81] Perhaps events would have unfolded differently if journalists had challenged Powell with probing questions like the following that would have punctured the smooth veneer of certainty shrouding his statement.

— *Your statement that "we now know" about Iraq's aluminum tube imports implies that any uncertainty about this technical issue within the official IC has been resolved. Do any official intelligence agencies disagree with your conclusion that the aluminum tubes are suitable for production of nuclear weapons?* This question pushes for an explicit characterization of the state of debate within the IC. A candid reply would acknowledge the existence of official dissents and open additional lines of argument spelled out in dialogue strategy 3. Conversely, a deceptive answer denying existence of any dissent would provide an opening for relevant IC officials to correct the record.[82]

— *Which intelligence agency has the most technical expertise to analyze whether the aluminum tubes are suitable for uranium enrichment, and what is its position on the issue?* This question highlights the importance of comparing the relative credibility of analyses produced by competing official intelligence entities.

A similar line of questioning might have flushed out hidden intelligence dissents on the topic of Iraq's alleged ties to terrorism. During the rollout of NSS 2002, Bush, Cheney, and Powell frequently cited statements from Libyan detainee Ibn al-Shaykh al-Libi as "credible evidence" that Iraq was training al-Qaida members.[83] Yet their certainty sharply contradicted intelligence reporting by the Defense Intelligence Agency (DIA), which warned in a February 2002 document that it was possible that al-Libi "was intentionally misleading the debriefers."[84] (DIA's analysis proved correct—al-Libi later recanted.)[85] "Just imagine," Senator Carl Levin (D-MI) said, "the public impact of that DIA conclusion if it had been disclosed at the time. It surely could have made a difference in the congressional vote authorizing the war."[86]

Consider another example of the cherry-picking argument pattern, this one unfolding after the war had already begun. On 29 May 2003, fifty days following Hussein's ouster, President Bush asserted that two small trailers confiscated by US troops were mobile "biological laboratories." He declared, "We have found the weapons of mass destruction."[87] For months, others in the Bush cabinet echoed this unequivocal line of argument. Speaking in Italy in June 2003, Powell said, "[W]e have already discovered mobile biological factories of the kind that I described to the Security Council on the 5th of February. We have now found them. There is no question in our mind that that's what their purpose was."[88] Such unqualified proclamations are difficult to explain in light of an official intelligence report by a DIA fact-finding team sent to Iraq to investigate the trailers. "There was no connection to anything biological," said one expert who studied the trailers and transmitted a skeptical report to Washington on 27 May 2003, two days before the president's flat declaration on Polish television. Another expert on the nine-person team of scientists and engineers with extensive experience in the technical fields involved in making bioweapons recalled an epithet that came to be associated with the trailers: "The biggest sand toilets in the world."[89] Had journalists used dialogue strategy 2 to probe beneath the surface certainty of the Powell and Bush statements on alleged Iraqi weapons laboratories, it is possible that the classified (and ultimately correct) DIA finding would have been brought to light before its existence was finally revealed by the *Washington Post* almost three years after the critical DIA report was filed. Even if Bush and Powell had failed to acknowledge existence of the report, their denials might at least have created an opening for intelligence officials (such as then CIA director Tenet) to step forward and correct the record.

A timely and carefully worded question can be the pebble in a pond destabilizing the placid surface projected by political leaders' pat characterizations of intelligence data. Such questions may have salutary effects, since as William Odom notes, "What initially appears to be an intelligence failure often turns out to have been a failure of interaction between political and military leaders on the one hand and intelligence officials on the other."[90] Pressure from lawmakers, journalists, and citizens could prompt those on both sides of Odom's divide to pay more attention to the details of these interactions, particularly when it comes to the treatment of uncertainty in intelligence analysis. The need for more careful approaches to these interactions seems apparent in light of postwar revelations that President Bush and then national security advisor Condoleezza Rice were not even aware of the INR/DOE dissents appended to the 2002 NIE on Iraq. "They did not read footnotes in a 90-page document," a senior White House official told the *Washington Post*.[91] The Silberman-Robb Commission recently argued that intelligence analysts also have room for improvement on this count, since accurate and consistent depictions of uncertainty must first be crafted carefully in official IC reporting before they can be injected into the public debate.[92]

In addition to conveying disagreements, analysts must also find ways to explain to policymakers degrees of certainty in their work. Some publications we have reviewed use numerical estimates of certainty, while others rely on phrases such as "probably" or "almost certainly." We strongly urge that such assessments of certainty be used routinely and consistently throughout the Community. Whatever device is used to signal the degree of certainty—mathematical percentages, graphic representations, or key phrases—all analysts in the Community should have a common understanding of what the indicators mean and how to use them.[93]

While the Silberman-Robb Commission stops short of suggesting a specific template to standardize characterizations of uncertainty in IC analysis, its findings highlight the need for one in the wake of the Iraq prewar intelligence failure.[94] A possible exemplar comes from Richards Heuer Jr., who builds on the earlier work of Sherman Kent to fashion a table designed to work as a common reference tool for intelligence analysts and political leaders. This table facilitates translation of "words of estimative probability" into approximate confidence levels, and vice versa (see table 7).

Table 7. Words of Estimative Probability in Intelligence Analysis

Words of Estimative Probability: Synonym Groups	Confidence Level: Approximate Percentage Range	Confidence Level: Rough Probability
"Virtually certain" "All but certain" "Overwhelming odds"	95–99%	Almost certain
"Highly likely" "Highly probable"	80–94%	Very probable
"Likely" "Good chance"	61–79%	Probable
"Could go either way" "Chances a little better (or less) than even"	40–60%	Chances about even
"Probably not" "Improbable" "We doubt"	21–39%	Unlikely
"Small chance" "Possibility can't be excluded" "We doubt"	6–20%	Very unlikely
"Very slight chance"	1–5%	Almost certainly not

Source: Adapted from Richards J. Heuer Jr., personal communication with Gordon Mitchell, 9 July 2005; see also Sherman Kent, "Words of Estimative Probability," in *Sherman Kent and the Board of National Estimates,* ed. Donald P. Steury (Washington, D.C.: Central Intelligence Agency, 1994).

DIALOGUE STRATEGY 3: ONLY FOOLS RUSH IN

In the third dialogue strategy, interlocutors use official acknowledgments of uncertainty to extend time for deliberation and leverage arguments for non-military forms of prevention. There is a good reason why White House officials couched their arguments for war against Iraq in definitive terms such as "there is no doubt in our minds," "absolutely," and "there is overwhelming evidence."[95] The patina of certainty surrounding these phrases helped soften preventive warfare's political paradox—use of first-strike force only seems like self-defense if there is unequivocal evidence of an imminent threat. When used to counter threats that are vague or uncertain, preventive warfare looks very much like conquest or even naked aggression. Anatol Lieven notes that the American people "are willing—even overwilling—to fight if America is attacked or even insulted, but are not committed to the permanent celebration and projection of military power and values."[96] This conservative sentiment has potential to work as a natural brake against reckless use of the preventive war option. Hitting first with preventive force is not the same as striking back in retaliation or scrambling to forestall an imminent enemy attack. The time available for reflection in preventive war deliberation affords citizens the opportunity to carefully consider threat assessment, efficacy of possible military response, and utility of nonmilitary forms of prevention.

To understand how, consider Director of Central Intelligence George Tenet's admission of uncertainty in his 7 October 2002 letter to Congress: "Our understanding of the relationship between Iraq and al-Qa'ida is evolving and is based on *sources of varying reliability.*"[97] As veteran intelligence analyst Ray McGovern explains, "this is intelligence code for 'Whoa!'"[98] Translating this code effectively into productive outcomes presents a rhetorical challenge, one that can be explored further by considering another example—intelligence analysis of Iraq's alleged unmanned aerial vehicle (UAV) program.

During preparation of the 2002 NIE, there was vigorous intra-IC debate not only about the technical specifications of aluminum tubes but also about the question of whether Iraq's UAV program had threatening weapons applications. Specifically, Air Force Intelligence disagreed with the consensus NIE Key Judgment that Iraq's UAVs were intended to be used as tools of biological warfare. This was a significant dissent, since, as Thielmann notes in chapter 8, Air Force Intelligence was the agency most technically qualified to comment on the issue. While the specific terms of the agency's dissent were omitted from the CIA white paper declassifying portions of the NIE, this public document did obliquely acknowledge the presence of disagreement within the IC regarding the UAV judgment: "Iraq maintains a small missile force and several development programs, including for a UAV that *most analysts believe probably* is intended to deliver biological warfare agents."[99]

Here is another example of what McGovern calls "intelligence code for 'Whoa'"—the sort of caveat that can be coaxed to the surface by pointed questions that flow from dialogue strategies 1 and 2. However, in the absence of follow-on efforts to interpret the meaning of such caveats and explore their implications, the drumbeat of war may simply drown out such expressions of uncertainty. The following lines of argument illustrate how deliberators might have used the official acknowledgment of uncertainty regarding Iraq's UAV program to extend time for deliberation and leverage arguments for nonmilitary prevention as preferred strategies for dealing with Iraq.

— *Before committing to preventive war, we should be sure that Iraqi UAVs pose a grave threat to US security. The greater our uncertainty about this judgment, the more likely our use of force will constitute unprovoked aggression.* This line of argument frames the confidence levels on threat assessments as indicators of whether a proposed preventive attack is more accurately characterized as a legitimate act of self-defense or an opportunistic use of military power.

— *Uncertainty about the Iraqi UAV threat is a sign that more time is needed to gather information and deliberate about whether the danger posed to US security justifies preventive use of force. A rush to war based on uncertain*

*evidence turns the United States into an aggressor nation that treats violence
as a preferred option rather than a last resort.* This line of argument uses
the uncertainty of threat assessments to slow down the decision-making
process and win more time for intelligence gathering and nonmilitary
forms of prevention.

— *Nonmilitary measures of prevention can minimize the possible Iraqi UAV
threat, while also indemnifying the United States against risks that preventive attacks launched on the basis of uncertain intelligence will mistakenly
cause unnecessary bloodshed.* This line of argument challenges the assumption that a decision to defer use of force in the face of uncertainty
requires the United States to passively accept security risks. It emphasizes that nonmilitary strategies of prevention are active security strategies that also provide insurance against downside risks of intelligence
failure.[100]

Expressions of uncertainty in official characterizations of intelligence
analysis are like yellow traffic lights—they signal a need to proceed with caution. For the most part, the Bush administration's case for war against Iraq
was a series of bright green lights—overconfident summaries of intelligence
findings that were largely bereft of caveats or qualifications. However, there
were a few instances where Bush administration officials acknowledged the
existence of uncertainty in the intelligence assessments upholding their case
for war. Unfortunately, the implications of these qualifiers were not explored
robustly in public deliberation, another factor contributing to "discourse failure" prior to Operation Iraqi Freedom. Perhaps deliberators can adapt the
preceding dialogue strategies to future use of force discussions and thereby
guard against repetition of this error.

A near-term opportunity to test these dialogue strategies involves public deliberation on the proper policy response to Iran's nuclear program. In
2005, the IC completed an NIE on Iranian nuclear capability. That estimate, reflecting the consensus view of all official US intelligence agencies,
forecasts that even with a full-scale effort that avoids significant technical
obstacles, "Iran will be unlikely to produce a sufficient quantity of highly
enriched uranium, the key ingredient for an atomic weapon, before 'early to
mid-next decade.'"[101] This finding is in tension with statements that Iran's
atomic bomb program is "very advanced and near completion, so that they
might soon perform a nuclear test."[102] This latter statement, from Representative Curt Weldon (R–PA), is based on unofficial, uncoordinated intelligence
passed to Weldon by an anonymous Iranian informant identified only as
"Ali." The wide discrepancy between the worst-case NIE timeline of five to
ten years and the Weldon/Ali near-completion forecast should provide rhe-

torical leverage for interlocutors to argue that advocates of quick-trigger force must acknowledge that their assertions regarding imminence of the Iranian nuclear threat are rife with uncertainty. Such yellow-light acknowledgments may slow down the momentum of a drive for preventive war and win more time for the type of preventive nonproliferation diplomacy that Alexander Montgomery suggests is the best bet to produce long-term security in the region.[103] As David Albright and Corey Hinderstein argue, "estimates of Iran's nuclear capabilities, accomplishments, and timelines need far greater public and Congressional scrutiny than they are currently receiving. This scrutiny becomes even more important as those in the Bush Administration who favor confronting Iran and pressing for regime change may be hyping up Iran's nuclear threat and trying to undermine intelligence assessments that Iran is several years from having nuclear weapons."[104]

An additional yellow light factor confounding any rush to use force is uncertainty regarding the effects of limited preventive strikes against Iran. A Bush administration adviser told Seymour Hersh that White House military planning was premised on a belief that "a sustained bombing campaign in Iran will humiliate the religious leadership and lead the public to rise up and overthrow the government."[105] Such optimism, reminiscent of 2002 predictions that "liberating Iraq would be a cakewalk,"[106] is contradicted by analysis that "outright U.S. hostility, instead of weakening the regime, is more likely to strengthen the die-hard conservatives."[107] Limited bombing, in this view, would enable Iran's ruling clerics to consolidate political power and crush dissent by invoking popular memory of Operation Ajax in 1953, when US and British secret agents conspired to overthrow Iranian prime minister Mohammed Mossadegh.[108] Corroboration for this theory comes from unexpected quarters. Reza Pahlavi, whose father was installed as the Shah of Iran following the 1953 US-UK coup, said in March 2006 that a military strike against Iran "will rally nationalistic sentiments which will work to the regime's advantage, and consequently, give the theocracy a much longer lease on life."[109] Will such concerns check repetition of the 2002-2003 "discourse failure" that resulted in the ill-fated war of choice against Iraq? The answer may hinge in part on whether interlocutors can use the preceding dialogue strategies to leverage arguments for a US policy approach toward Iran that privileges nonmilitary forms of prevention.

CONCLUSION

Lieven notes that episodes of reckless militancy in US history tend to be followed by a return to more tolerant and moderate phases. There is a "self-correcting mechanism" that works like a pendulum, swinging American society back to equilibrium after bouts of extremism.[110] Is the pendulum broken? Lieven thinks the jury is still out on this question, and this volume delivers a mixed verdict. On the one hand, it is clear that the Bush administration's second-term tilt toward diplomacy as a preferred mode of foreign policy seems to reflect a pullback from the "shock and awe" excesses of Operation Iraqi Freedom. On the other hand, the development of "global strike" capability and the recurrence of argument patterns used to prime audiences for war against Iraq (which resurfaced in discussions of Iran policy) suggest that the White House's audacious strategy of preventive warfare may have an extended shelf life.

If the White House does attempt to give first-strike force a second chance after the strategy's checkered debut in the 2003 Iraq War, a major determinant of policy success will likely be the degree to which key players remedy factors that contributed to "discourse failure" in 2002–2003. During that period, breakdown in the marketplace of ideas resulted in widespread support for a preventive war that was legitimated politically as an exercise in self-defense but turned out to be a straightforward instance of aggression against an exaggerated threat. Can US citizens learn from this episode and avoid unnecessary loss of blood and treasure in the future? One finds little basis for optimism in the results of a recent psychology study entitled "Memory for Fact, Fiction, and Misinformation: The Iraq War 2003."[111] That survey of American, German, and Australian audiences compared reactions to corrections and retractions of erroneous information about the war presented in major media publications. While German and Australian respondents adjusted their beliefs about Operation Iraqi Freedom when media sources retracted factually incorrect stories, their American counterparts "showed no sensitivity to corrections of misinformation, even when they knew that an event had been retracted."[112] In his study of public debate prior to the 2003 Iraq War, Kaufmann notes a similar phenomenon: "The authority of the White House allows even discredited claims to be repeated with some persuasive effect. Administration officials made use of this frequently during the prewar debate, and some continued to do so after the invasion."[113]

These findings are particularly disconcerting, given the crucial role that sound deliberation plays in countering what Goodnight (chapter 5) terms an "inbuilt impetus" within the NSS 2002 doctrine to exaggerate evidence in public debates where proposals to use preventive military force are vetted. What accounts for the inability of the American citizenry to take full advantage of public deliberation's corrective function? One explanation may be that American society is fragmenting into multiple public spheres that appear not to interact much with each other. Consider a remarkable poll conducted by political scientist Steven Kull in October 2003. Even after adjusting for viewership and political preference, Kull's survey found that viewers of Fox News were more likely to hold "misperceptions" such as the belief that "WMD" had been discovered in Iraq and that Saddam Hussein had been "personally involved in 9/11."[114] This same phenomenon was even more pronounced in another poll conducted by Kull just over one year later.[115] That survey found wide partisan splits in public opinion about factual issues relating to the 2003 Iraq War. For example, at the time of the survey (shortly after release of the Duelfer report certifying the dearth of unconventional weaponry in Iraq), 72 percent of Bush supporters believed that Iraq had "WMD" prior to war, but only 26 percent of Kerry supporters believed the same thing. Similarly, 75 percent of Bush supporters believed that Saddam Hussein was providing "substantial" support for al-Qaida, while just 30 percent of Kerry supporters held that view.

These wide gaps in public opinion on factual issues may reflect what legal scholar Cass Sunstein calls group polarization: "If certain people are deliberating with many like-minded others, views will not be reinforced, but instead will be shifted to more extreme points."[116] When groups engage in "enclave deliberation"—communicating exclusively with like-minded interlocutors, the polarization effect is heightened. This finding has major implications for the future of preventive warfare in US security strategy. Group polarization may seriously undercut the efficacy of public deliberation as a brake on unnecessary preventive warfare. Enclave deliberation, coupled with group polarization, "shrinks the argument pool" and creates a paradox:[117] as members of society communicate more, they grow farther apart and become less capable of coming to terms with unfamiliar viewpoints:

If the public is balkanized and if different groups are designing their own preferred communications packages, the consequence will be not merely the same but still more balkanization, as group members move one another toward more extreme points in line with their initial tendencies. At the same time, different deliberating groups, each consisting of like-minded people, will be driven increasingly far apart simply because most of their discussions are with one another.[118]

Sunstein posits that trends in Internet communication, especially the rapid growth of Weblogs (blogs), contribute to group polarization by encouraging in-group dialogue that shrinks argument pools. However, this sense of pessimistic technological determinism is not universally shared. Others point to the advent of Internet blog activity as a positive trend that facilitates new avenues of knowledge production. As Douglas Hart and Steven Simon argue, blog technology not only contributes to robust debate across lines of difference in public spheres of deliberation, it also has potential to cultivate for intelligence analysts argumentation and critical thinking skills. These unique skills may help analysts overcome structural aspects of intelligence tradecraft that invite bias and groupthink.

Blogs offer another form of software tool supporting the dual task of capturing diversity and encouraging consensus formation. . . . The adoption of blogging within the intelligence community could exploit this phenomenon in important ways. . . . Blogs can encourage critical thinking by placing bloggers in an informal and wide-reaching context of peer review that is not easily censored by management. Furthermore, a blog might be linked to structured arguments as evidence of the thought process that went into the argument. Alternatively, blogs, especially those espousing contrarian positions, could be linked to structured arguments as a means of safeguarding against analytical bias and its collective equivalent, groupthink. Blogs might also operate as digital dissent channels out of the glare of a stifling official context.[119]

A common refrain heard today is that the decision to invade Iraq in 2003 was the result of an intelligence failure—the inability of the official US IC to provide accurate information to Bush administration officials. Earlier chapters in this volume have brought the incompleteness of this conventional wisdom to light by elucidating the role of the White House in distorting public argument on Iraq and by showing how this distortion was facilitated by a public that was unwilling or unable to evaluate specious justifications for war. The dialogue strategies presented in this chapter are heuristic devices designed to illustrate what deliberators might say in future public debates regarding the proposed use of preventive military force. While such lines of argument have potential to help avert recurrence of the 2002–2003 "discourse failure" on Iraq, their impact is likely to be inconsequential without broader transformation of the US political terrain.[120]

On this front, there are encouraging signs, as well as some promising new ideas for change. As 2005 drew to a close, Michael Massing reported that among journalists, "there is much talk about the need to get back to the basic responsibility of reporters, to expose wrongdoing and the failures of the political system."[121] Can this newfound assertive journalism deliver the sort of information needed to check the American political system's proneness toward "discourse failure"? The outcome may hinge on the degree to which reporters, editors, and publishers successfully address some of the key "structural problems" that Massing says compromise media's watchdog function: a reliance on "access," an excessive striving for balance, an uncritical fascination with celebrities, and a tendency toward self-censorship, "shying away from the pursuit of truths that might prove unpopular, whether with official authorities or the public."[122]

The general phenomenon of American "group polarization" complicates even further constructive efforts to avert failures in implementation
of US security policy. Journalists can only produce the news; what citizens
do with the information is another matter. The rise of special-interest media "narrowcasting" and the preference of Americans for "enclave deliberation" with like-minded others are trends that create conditions ripe for
"opinion cascades," which tend to reproduce and reinforce extreme, often
uninformed, viewpoints.[123] Fortunately, as our understanding of this process
improves, new avenues for change emerge. For example, Jacob Hacker and
Paul Pierson's study shows how political gerrymandering facilitates enclave
deliberation by steadily shrinking the number of competitive House and Senate elections: "As recently as a decade ago, a quarter or more of congressional
seats genuinely were in play in any given election. Today, virtually none are.
. . . This leaves favored candidates to worry almost exclusively about pleasing
their partisans."[124] Hacker and Pierson's proposed remedies for recovering
the lost "middle" in American politics—making election day a national holi-
day, adopting the British tradition of parliamentary Question Time, opening primaries, and changing the rules governing congressional conference
committees—seem far removed from debates about US security policy. Yet
the complex dynamics of preventive force decision-making elucidated in this
volume indicate just how relevant proposals like theirs have become in the
daunting quest to secure a safer world.

NOTES

CHAPTER 1. PREEMPTION, PREVENTION, PREVARICATION

1. United States, White House Office of Homeland Security, "The National Security Strategy of the United States of America," September 2002, http://www.whitehouse.gov/nsc/nss.html, emphasis added.

2. US White House, "National Security Strategy."

3. Notable examples of early positive reactions to NSS 2002 include Joshua Muravchik, "The Bush Manifesto," *Commentary* (December 2002): 23–30; John Lewis Gaddis, "A Grand Strategy of Transformation," *Foreign Policy* (November/October 2002): 50–56; Norman Podhoretz, "In Praise of the Bush Doctrine," *Commentary* (September 2002): 19–28; and Richard H. Schultz and Andreas Vogt, "It's War! Fighting Post-11 September Global Terrorism through a Doctrine of Preemption," *Terrorism and Political Violence* 15 (Spring 2003): 1–30.

4. For early criticism of NSS 2002 along these lines, see G. John Ikenberry, "America's Imperial Ambition," *Foreign Affairs* 81 (September/October 2002): 44–60; Robert S. Litwak, "The New Calculus of Pre-emption," *Survival* 44 (Winter 2002): 53–79; Jeffrey Record, "The Bush Doctrine and War with Iraq," 33 *Parameters* (Spring 2003): 4–21; and John Steinbruner, "Confusing Ends and Means: The Doctrine of Coercive Pre-emption," *Arms Control Today* (January/February 2003): 3–6.

5. Condoleezza Rice, "A Balance of Power that Favors Freedom," *U.S. Foreign Policy Agenda* (December 2002), http://usinfo.state.gov/journals/itps/1202/ijpe/ijpe1202.pdfsid14901231.

6. See United Nations Charter, http://www.un.org/aboutun/charter/chapter7.htm.

7. See Robert E. Harkavy, "Preemption and Two-front Conventional Warfare," *Jerusalem Papers on Peace Problems* No. 23 (1977): 9.

8. This distinction is codified in the US Department of Defense's *Dictionary of Military and Associated Terms,* which defines a preemptive attack as one "initiated on the basis of incontrovertible evidence that an enemy attack is imminent" (415). A preventive war, on the other hand, is "initiated in the belief that military conflict, while not imminent, is inevitable, and that to delay would involve greater risk" (419). See United States, Department of Defense, *Dictionary of Military and Associated Terms,* Joint Publication I-02, April 2001, http://www.dtic.mil/doctrine/jel/new_pubs/jp1_02.pdf.

9. Arnel B. Enriquez, "The US National Security Strategy of 2002—A New Use-of-Force Doctrine?" *Air and Space Power Journal* (Fall 2004): 36; see also Melvyn P. Leffler, letter to the editor, *Foreign Policy* (January/February 2005): 11.

10. See Secretary Donald H. Rumsfeld, "Prepared Testimony of U.S. Secretary of Defense Donald H. Rumsfeld before the House and Senate Armed Services Committees Regarding Iraq," 18–19 September 2002, http://www.defenselink.mil/speeches/2002/s2002 0918-secdef.html.

11. United States, White House Office of Homeland Security, "National Strategy to Combat Weapons of Mass Destruction," December 2002, http://www.whitehouse.gov/ news/releases/2002/12/WMDStrategy.pdf.

12. Later, Bush administration press secretary Scott McClellan would explicitly eschew "imminent threat" terminology in lieu of characterization of Iraq as a "gathering" danger. See Scott McClellan, "Press Briefing by Scott McClellan," 27 January 2004, http://www .whitehouse.gov/news/releases/2004/01/20040127-6.html.

13. William Arkin, "Not Just a Last Resort? A Global Strike Plan, with a Nuclear Option," *Washington Post*, 15 May 2005; Andrew J. Bacevich, *The New American Militarism: How Americans Are Seduced by War* (New York: Oxford University Press, 2005); Daniel Benjamin and Steven Simon, *The Next Attack: The Failure of the War on Terror and a Strategy for Getting It Right* (New York: Henry Holt, 2005); Renato Cruz de Castro, "U.S. War on Terror in East Asia: The Perils of Preemptive Defense in Waging a War of the Third Kind," *Asian Affairs* 31 (Winter 2005): 212–32; Arnold A. Offner, "Rogue President, Rogue Nation: Bush and U.S. National Security," *Diplomatic History* 29 (June 2005): 433–35; Jeffrey Record, *Dark Victory: America's Second War Against Iraq* (Annapolis, Md.: Naval Institute Press, 2004); and Roger Speed and Michael May, "Dangerous Doctrine," *Bulletin of the Atomic Scientists* 61 (March/April 2005): 38–50.

14. John Lewis Gaddis, "After Containment," *New Republic*, 25 April 2005, 27–31; Newt Gingrich, *Winning the Future* (Washington, D.C.: Regnery, 2004); Stephen F. Hayes, "Sticking to His Guns," *Weekly Standard*, 14 February 2005, 10–12; Walter Russell Mead, *Power, Terror, Peace and War: America's Grand Strategy in a World at Risk* (New York: Knopf, 2004); Richard Miniter, *Shadow War: The Untold Story of How Bush Is Winning the War on Terror* (Washington, D.C.: Regnery, 2004); Robert J. Pauly Jr. and Tom Lansford, *Strategic Preemption: US Foreign Policy and the Second Iraq War* (Aldershot: Ashgate, 2004); Rowan Scarborough, *Rumsfeld's War: The Untold Story of America's Anti-Terrorist Commander* (Washington, D.C.: Regnery, 2004).

15. George Packer, *The Assassins' Gate: America in Iraq* (New York: Farrar, Strauss and Giroux, 2005), 63; James Mann, *The Rise of the Vulcans: The History of Bush's War Cabinet* (New York: Penguin Books), 317.

16. US White House, "National Security Strategy."

17. National Public Radio's informal sample of local public opinion revealed that NSS 2002's "plain English" resonated with residents of Lubbock, Texas: "In George W. Bush's blunt threats to Saddam Hussein to disarm or prepare for war, west Texans believe they recognize a streak of themselves." The White House could take heart in this finding, since "the president has long used the conservative city on the high Plains of west Texas as his political weather vane" (Jacki Lyden and John Burnett, "Support of the Bush Doctrine on Iraq by the People of the west Texas city of Lubbock," *All Things Considered*, National Public Radio broadcast, 24 October 2002, Lexis-Nexis news transcript database, http://www .lexis-nexis.com).

18. Condoleezza Rice, "Dr. Condoleezza Rice Discusses President's National Security Strategy," 1 October 2002, http://www.whitehouse.gov/news/releases/2002/10/20021001 -6.html.

19. For early examples of popular commentaries featuring the 9/11 = NSS 2002 formula, see Bob Deans, "Sept. 11 Jolted Bush's Stance on Security," *Atlanta Journal-Constitution*, 22 September 2002, Lexis-Nexis general news database, http://www.lexis-nexis.com; Roy Eccleston, "Bush's Rule of Fear for a Peaceful World," *Australian*, 30 September 2002, 14,

Lexis-Nexis general news database, http://www.lexis-nexis.com; and Muravchik, "Bush Manifesto."

20. George W. Bush, "The Second Gore-Bush Presidential Debate," 11 October 2000, http://www.debates.org/pages/trans2000b.html.

21. Bacevich, *New American Militarism*, 217. For additional commentary unpacking the rhetorical advantages afforded to Bush administration officials by their choice of 9/11 as the temporal starting point for discussions of terrorism policy, see Carol K. Winkler, *In the Name of Terrorism: Presidents on Political Violence in the Post-World War II Era* (Albany: State University of New York Press, 2006), 167–68.

22. "Excerpts from Pentagon's Plan: 'Prevent the Re-Emergence of a New Rival,'" *New York Times*, 8 March 1992. Useful context explaining the circumstances around which this document was leaked to the *Los Angeles Times* is provided in Patrick E. Tyler, "U.S. Strategy Plan Calls for Insuring No Rivals Develop," *New York Times*, 8 March 1992.

23. Richard Perle, Douglas Feith, and David Wurmser, "A Clean Break: A New Strategy for Securing the Realm," Institute for Advanced Strategic and Political Studies Paper, 8 July 1996, http://www.aaiusa.org/news/must_read_feith.htm.

24. Elliott Abrams et al., letter to Honorable William J. Clinton, 26 January 1998, http://www.newamericancentury.org/iraqclintonletter.htm.

25. Thomas Donnelly, Donald Kagan, and Gary Schmitt, "Rebuilding America's Defenses: Strategy, Forces and Resources for a New Century," Project for the New American Century Report, September 2000, http://www.newamericancentury.org/RebuildingAmericasDefenses.pdf.

26. For commentary placing these documents in an evolutionary trajectory culminating in NSS 2002, see Chris J. Dolan, "Foreign Policy on the Offensive," in *Striking First: The Preventive War Doctrine and the Reshaping of U.S. Foreign Policy*, ed. Betty Glad and Chris J. Dolan (London: Palgrave, 2004), 3–22; Stefan Halper and Jonathan Clarke, *America Alone: The Neo-Conservatives and the Global Order* (London: Cambridge University Press, 2004), 106–8; Chalmers Johnson, *Sorrows of Empire: Militarism, Secrecy and the End of the Republic* (New York: Metropolitan Books, 2004), 234–38; Mann, *Rise of the Vulcans*, 209–15, 238, 245; and Packer, *Assassins' Gate*, 30–32.

27. Donnelly, Kagan, and Schmitt, "Rebuilding America's Defenses," 2.

28. Donnelly, Kagan, and Schmitt, "Rebuilding America's Defenses," 51.

29. David Ray Griffin, *The New Pearl Harbor: Disturbing Questions about the Bush Administration and 9/11* (Northampton, Mass.: Interlink Press, 2004).

30. "The New Pearl Harbor: Disturbing Questions about the Bush Administration and 9/11," unsigned book review, *Publishers Weekly*, 31 March 2004, http://reviews.publishersweekly.com/bd.aspx?isbn=1566565529&pub=pw.

31. United States, National Commission on Terrorist Attacks upon the United States, *The 9/11 Commission Report* (Washington, D.C.: Government Printing Office, 2004), 335–36; Bob Woodward, *Plan of Attack* (New York: Simon and Schuster, 2004), 25; more generally, see Richard Clarke, *Against All Enemies* (New York: Free Press, 2004), 264–65.

32. Bob Woodward, *Bush at War* (New York: Simon and Schuster, 2002), 49.

33. Frank R. Baumgartner and Bryan D. Jones, *Agendas and Instability in American Politics* (Chicago: University of Chicago Press, 1993), 3–6; see also Carol Weissert, "Policy Entrepreneurs, Policy Opportunists, and Legislative Effectiveness," *American Politics Quarterly* 19 (1991): 262–74.

34. Chris Mackenzie, "Policy Entrepreneurship in Australia: A Conceptual Review and Application," *Australian Journal of Political Science* 39 (July 2004): 368.

35. Woodward, *Bush at War*, 84–85.

36. See Simon and Benjamin, *Next Attack*, 145–46.

37. Stephen Hadley, Remarks to the United States Institute of Peace on the President's National Security Strategy, U.S. Institute of Peace, Washington, D.C., 16 March 2006, http://www.whitehouse.gov/news/releases/2006/03/20060316-8.html.

38. This analytical approach fits with a broader body of scholarship that treats public discourse as a central object of study. Examples from political science that draw on public sphere theory to explain international relations include Neta C. Crawford, *Argument and Change in World Politics: Ethics, Decolonization, and Humanitarian Intervention* (London: Cambridge University Press, 2002); Jurgen Haacke, "Theory and Praxis in International Relations: Habermas, Self-Reflection and Rational Argumentation," *Millennium: Journal of International Studies* 25 (1996): 255–89; Marc Lynch, *State Interests and Public Spheres* (New York: Columbia University Press, 1999); Rodger A. Payne and Nayef H. Samhat, *Democratizing Global Politics: Discourse Norms, International Regimes and Political Community* (Albany: State University of New York Press, 2004); and Thomas Risse, "'Let's Argue!' Communicative Action in World Politics," *International Organization* 54 (2000): 1–39.

In the field of communication, notable studies of US foreign policy that elucidate dynamics of international security by analyzing rhetorical texts include Denise M. Bostdorff, *The Presidency and the Rhetoric of Foreign Crisis* (Columbia: University of South Carolina Press, 1994); Ronald H. Carpenter, *Rhetoric in Martial Deliberations and Decision Making* (Columbia: University of South Carolina Press, 2004); Cori Elizabeth Dauber, *Cold War Analytical Structures and the Post Post-War World* (Westport, Conn.: Praeger, 1993); Stephen A. Hartnett and Laura A. Stengrim, *Globalization and Empire: The U.S. Invasion of Iraq, Free Markets, and the Twilight of Democracy* (Tuscaloosa: University of Alabama Press, 2006); J. Michael Hogan, *The Nuclear Freeze Campaign* (East Lansing: Michigan State University Press, 1994); Robert L. Ivie, *Democracy and America's War on Terror* (Tuscaloosa: University of Alabama Press, 2005); Gordon R. Mitchell, *Strategic Deception: Rhetoric, Science, and Politics in Missile Defense Advocacy* (East Lansing: Michigan State University Press, 2000); Robert P. Newman, *Owen Lattimore and the "Loss" of China* (Berkeley: University of California Press, 1992); and Winkler, *In the Name of Terrorism*.

An illuminating collaborative effort that bridges political science and communication is *Post-Realism: The Rhetorical Turn in International Relations*, ed. Francis A. Beer and Robert Hariman (East Lansing: Michigan State University Press, 1994). Francis Beer, *Meanings of War and Peace* (College Station: Texas A&M University Press, 2001); and John Collins and Ross Glover, eds., *Collateral Language: A User's Guide to America's New War* (New York: New York University Press, 2002), feature similar collaborative work. For a review essay discussing recent multidisciplinary work in this area, see Gordon R. Mitchell, "Public Argument-Driven Security Studies," *Argumentation and Advocacy* 39 (Summer 2004): 57–71.

39. See George W. Bush, "President Bush Delivers Graduation Speech at West Point," 1 June 2002, http://222.whitehouse.gov/news/releases/2002/06/print/20020601-3.html; Richard Cheney, "Vice President Speaks at VFW 103rd National Convention," 26 August 2002, http://www.whitehouse.gov/news/releases/2002/08/print/20020826.html; and Colin Powell, "Remarks to the United Nations Security Council," 5 February 2003, http://www.state.gov/secretary/former/powell/remarks/2003/17300.htm.

40. Mohammed Ayoob, "The War against Iraq: Normative and Strategic Implications," *Middle East Policy* (Summer 2003): 27–34. See also Martha Finnemore, "Constructing Norms of Humanitarian Intervention," in *The Culture of National Security: Norms and Identity in World Politics*, ed. Peter J. Katzenstein (New York: Columbia University Press, 1996), 159.

41. For a concise history of the phrase, see Jacques E. C. Hymans, "Roots of the Washington Threat Consensus," in Glad and Dolan, *Striking First*, 37–39.

42. American Dialect Society, "2002 Words of the Year," http://www.americandialect
.org/index.php/amerdial/2002_words_of_the_y/.

43. Susan D. Moeller, "Media Coverage of Weapons of Mass Destruction," Center for
International and Security Studies Report (March 2004), http://www.cissm.umd.edu/doc
uments/WMDstudy_full.pdf.

44. Moeller, "Media Coverage."

45. See Wolfgang Panofsky, "Dismantling the Concept Of 'Weapons of Mass Destruction,'" *Arms Control Today* (April 1998), http://www.armscontrol.org/act/1998_04/wkhp
98.asp.

46. Panofsky, "Dismantling the Concept."

47. Gert G. Harigel, "Chemical and Biological Weapons: Use in Warfare, Impact on
Society and Environment," Carnegie Endowment for International Peace Report (2001),
http://www.ceip.org/files/Publications/Harigelreport.asp.

48. Moeller, "Media Coverage."

49. US DOD, *Dictionary of Military and Associated Terms.*

50. Anthony Clark Arend, "International Law and the Preemptive Use of Military
Force," *Washington Quarterly* 26 (Spring 2003): 89–103.

51. Here we use "prevaricate" in the narrow sense of the word: to "be deliberately
ambiguous or unclear in order to mislead or withhold information" (WordNet database,
http://wordnet.princeton.edu).

52. Arthur M. Schlesinger Jr., *War and the American Presidency* (New York: Norton,
2004), 23.

53. Henry S. Laver, "Preemption and the Evolution of America's Strategic Defense,"
Parameters 35 (Summer 2005): 114; see also Francois Heisbourg, "A Work in Progress: The
Bush Doctrine and Its Consequences," *Washington Quarterly* 26 (Spring 2003): 75–88.

54. Here it should be noted that, occasionally, contributors use the term "first-strike
force" to describe the overall set of military actions that include both preemptive and preventive use of force. In this sense, NSS 2002 can be described as a first-strike doctrine, because
it claims a prerogative to exercise preemptive and preventive use of force options.

55. Bill Yenne, *Attack of the Drones: A History of Unmanned Aerial Combat* (St. Paul,
Minn.: Zenith Press, 2004), 8–9; see also John B. Alexander, *Winning the War: Advanced
Weapons, Strategies and Concepts for the Post-9/11 World* (New York: St. Martin's Press,
2003), 49.

56. Seyom Brown, *The Illusion of Control: Force and Foreign Policy in the 21st Century*
(Washington, D.C.: Brookings Institution Press, 2003), 149.

57. Paul Friedman, "The Real-Time War; TV: A Missed Opportunity," *Columbia
Journalism Review* (May/June 2003): 29–31.

58. Mark Phillips, *The Early Show*, CBS News Transcripts, 9 April 2003, Lexis-Nexis
news transcripts database, http://www.lexis-nexis.com.

59. Matthew Gilbert and Suzanne C. Ryan, "Snap Judgments: Did Iconic Images from
Baghdad Reveal More about the Media than Iraq?" *Boston Globe*, 10 April 2003.

60. Katie Couric, *Today*, NBC News Transcripts, 9 April 2003, Lexis-Nexis news
transcripts database, http://www.lexis-nexis.com.

61. Tom Brokaw, *Today*, NBC News Transcripts, 9 April 2003, Lexis-Nexis news
transcripts database, http://www.lexis-nexis.com.

62. Robert Bianco, "Taking Down a Statue of Saddam Is Symbolic but Has Power All Its
Own," *USA Today*, 10 April 2003.

63. Ceci Connolly, "Fox Special Report with Brit Hume," 9 April 2003, Transcript
#040905cb.254, Lexis-Nexis news transcripts database, http://www.lexis-nexis.com.

64. Donald Rumsfeld and Richard Myers, "Defense Department Operational Briefing," 9
April 2003, Lexis-Nexis news transcripts database, http://www.lexis-nexis.com.

65. Joanne Ostrow, "Lasting Images: Tumbling Statue Immediately Burns into Memory," *Denver Post*, 10 April 2003.

66. Sheldon Rampton and John Stauber, *Weapons of Mass Deception: The Uses of Propaganda in Bush's War on Iraq* (New York: Center for Media and Democracy, 2003), 4.

67. Gregory Fontenot, E. J. Degen, and David Tohn, *On Point: The United States Army in Operation Iraqi Freedom* (Annapolis, Md.: Naval Institute Press, 2005), advance online copy available at http://onpoint.leavenworth.army.mil/.

68. Brian Plesic, interview with Lieutenant Colonel Dennis Cahill, 31 May 2003, in Fontenot, Degen, and Tohn, *On Point*.

69. Plesic, interview.

70. Christopher Simpson, quoted in Andrea McCarren, "Toppling of Saddam's Statue Staged?" WJLA-TV I-Team Report, 22 July 2004, http://www.wjla.com/news/stories/0704/161032.html.

71. Christopher Simpson, *National Security Directives of the Reagan and Bush Adminis-trations* (Boulder, Colo.: Westview Press, 1995), 366. For a one-page declassified "extract" of NSDD 138, see Simpson, *National Security*, 405. Discussion regarding implementation of the directive can be found in Charles Hill, Memorandum to Robert C. McFarlane, 19 June 1984, Folder "[Terrorism] [8404913]," Box 90761, files of D. Fortier, Ronald Reagan Library, Simi Valley, Calif.; and "Public Report of the Vice President's Task Force on Combating Terrorism," February 1986, Folder "[Terrorism] [OA/ID 14923]," Press Office, Bush Vice Presidential Records, George Bush Presidential Library, College Station, Tex. This archival research is presented and discussed in Winkler, *In the Name of Terrorism*, 93–95.

72. Dan Reiter, "Exploding the Powder Keg Myth: Preemptive Wars Almost Never Happen," *International Security* 20 (Fall 1995): 5–34.

73. The government of Denmark draws extensively from Reiter's survey to inform its recent study of preventive military force. See Danish Institute for International Studies, *New Threats and the Use of Force* (Copenhagen: Danish Institute for International Studies, 2005), 40–45, http://www.diis.dk/sw12399.asp.

74. Dan Reiter, letter to the editor, *Atlantic Monthly*, March 2005, 26–27; James Fallows, reply to letters, *Atlantic Monthly*, March 2005, 27–28. See also James Fallows, "Will Iran Be Next?" *Atlantic Monthly*, December 2004, 99–110; Dan Reiter, "The Osirak Myth and the Track Record of Preventive Military Attacks," Ridgway Center Policy Brief 04-2 (October 2004); James Fallows, "The Nuclear Power Beside Iraq," *Atlantic Monthly*, May 2006, 31-32.

75. Herman S. Wolk, "The Blueprint for Cold War Defense," *Air Force* 83 (2000), http://www.afa.org/magazine/march2000/0300coldwar.asp.

76. See Jean-Yves Haine and Gustav Lindström, "An Analysis of the National Security Strategy of the United States of America," Institute for Security Studies Analysis (January 2003), http://www.iss-eu.org/new/analysis/analy034.html; Melvyn P. Leffler, "9/11 and American Foreign Policy," *Diplomatic History* 29 (June 2005): 411–13; and John Shaw, "Bush National Security Strategy Drawing Both Praise and Criticism," *Washington Diplomat* (November 2002), http://washingtondiplomat.com/02-11/cl_02_11.html.

77. L. L. Lemnitzer, "Justification for US Military Intervention in Cuba (TS)," Memorandum for the Secretary of Defense, 13 March 1962, U.S. National Security Archive, http://www.gwu.edu/~nsarchiv/news/20010430/northwoods.pdf; see also James Bamford, *Body of Secrets* (New York: Doubleday, 2001), 81–89.

78. "The Secret Downing Street Memo," *Sunday Times* (London), 1 May 2005, http://www.timesonline.co.uk/article/0,,2087-1593607,00.html, emphasis added.

79. As John Steinbruner explains, "since the US military operates within a network of foreign basing rights and access agreements that require consent from host governments,

it would be difficult to organize a preemptive attack that did not enjoy general approval." Steinbruner, "Confusing Ends and Means," 3.

80. See Gregory R. Treverton, "Intelligence: The Achilles Heel of the Bush Doctrine," *Arms Control Today* (July/August 2003): 9–11.

81. Colin Powell, quoted in Bill Sammon, *Misunderestimated: The President Battles Terrorism, John Kerry, and the Bush Haters* (New York: HarperCollins, 2004): 145–46.

82. Hans Blix, "Report by the Chief Inspector for Biological and Chemical Arms," *New York Times*, 14 February 2003.

83. Sarah Lyall, "Britain Admits That Much of Its Report on Iraq Came from Magazines," *New York Times*, 8 February 2003.

84. David Albright, "The CIA's Aluminum Tubes' Assessment: Is the Nuclear Case Going Down the Tubes?" Institute for Science and International Security issue brief, 10 March 2003, http://www.isis-online.org/publications/iraq/al_tubes.html.

85. See United States, Senate Select Intelligence Committee, Report on the U.S. Intelligence Community's Prewar Assessments on Iraq, July 2004, 245–50, http://intelligence.senate.gov/iraqreport2.pdf; and Bob Drogin, "The Conflict in Iraq: Spy Work in Iraq Riddled with Failures," *Los Angeles Times*, 17 June 2004. For point-by-point analysis detailing the numerous claims in Secretary Powell's speech that stretched available intelligence data, see John Prados, *Hoodwinked: The Documents That Reveal How Bush Sold Us a War* (London: New Press, 2004), 207–36; and Charles J. Hanley, "Point by Point: A Look Back at a 'Thick' File," Associated Press Wire, 9 August 2003, Lexis-Nexis news wire database, http://www.lexis-nexis.com.

86. A *Newsweek* poll showed that Powell's address boosted overall public support for the war by 10 percent. Notably, the poll also found that "60 per cent of Americans now say they would support military action, even if the inspectors do not find any evidence for weapons of mass destruction, as long as the Bush administration says US intelligence indicates that the banned weapons are there" (David Rennie, "Powell Boosts Support in U.S.," *Daily Telegraph* [London], 10 February 2003, Lexis-Nexis general news database, http://www.lexis-nexis.com). On the positive reaction to Powell's address by opinion leaders, see Moeller, "Media Coverage"; and Prados, *Hoodwinked*, 258.

87. Stephen J. Hartnett and Laura A. Stengrim, "'The Whole Operation of Deception': Reconstructing President Bush's Rhetoric of Weapons of Mass Destruction," *Cultural Studies—Critical Methodologies* 4 (2004): 168.

88. See Charles Duelfer, *Comprehensive Report of the Special Advisor to the DCI on Iraq's WMD*, 30 September 2004, http://www.cia.gov/cia/reports/iraq_wmd_2004/; United States, Commission on the Intelligence Capabilities of the United States Regarding Weapons of Mass Destruction, *Report to the President*, March 2005, http://www.wmd.gov/report/; and US Senate Select Intelligence Committee, *Prewar Assessments*.

89. See Katherine Shrader, "Senate Iraq Intelligence Probe Nears End," Associated Press Wire, 10 March 2005, Lexis-Nexis news wire database, http://www.lexis-nexis.com.

90. Elsewhere in this volume, G. Thomas Goodnight quotes Antony J. Blinken's reference to the "Chicken Little effect." See Antony J. Blinken, "From Preemption to Engagement," *Survival* 45 (Winter 2003): 28.

91. Richard Cheney, "Vice President Dick Cheney Discusses a Possible War with Iraq," *Meet the Press*, 16 March 2003, NBC News Transcripts, Lexis-Nexis news wire database, http://www.lexis-nexis.org.

92. The "cakewalk" reference comes from Bush administration adviser Kenneth Adelman's op-ed, "Cakewalk in Iraq," *Washington Post*, 13 February 2002. For an exhaustive summary of the Bush administration's efforts to eschew prewar planning and punish those who disagreed with its rosy regime-change scenarios, see James Fallows, "Blind into

Baghdad," *Atlantic Monthly*, January/February 2004, 52–71. The most dramatic example of this tendency involved Pentagon reaction to congressional testimony by army chief of staff General Erik Shinseki, who suggested in February 2003 that "several hundred thousand troops" might be needed for Operation Iraqi Freedom. In response to this claim, senior Bush officials rebuked Shinseki and categorically dismissed his estimates out of hand. See Michael E. O'Hanlon, "Iraq without a Plan," *Policy Review* (December 2004/January 2005): 33–45; and Larry Diamond, "What Went Wrong in Iraq," *Foreign Affairs* 83 (September/October 2004): 34–57.

93. "Secret Downing Street Memo."

94. This bifurcation was mandated in the Intelligence Reform and Terrorism Prevention Act of 2004. See Congressional Record, 7 December 2004, H10930–H10993.

95. US White House, "National Security Strategy."

96. Condoleezza Rice, quoted in Steven R. Weisman, "Preemption: Idea with a Lineage Whose Time Has Come," *New York Times*, 23 March 2003.

CHAPTER 2. PREVENTIVE ATTACKS

1. US White House, "National Security Strategy."

2. Reiter, "Powder Keg," 5–34. Stephen Van Evera distinguished the two slightly differently, declaring that a state attacks preemptively if it believes that striking first offers a military advantage, whereas a state attacks preventively if its opponent is gaining in relative power. See Stephen Van Evera, *The Causes of War: Power and the Roots of Conflict* (Ithaca, N.Y.: Cornell University Press, 1999), 40n.

3. Quoted in Jack S. Levy, "Declining Power and the Preventive Motivation for War," *World Politics* 40 (October 1987): 103.

4. Reiter, "Powder Keg"; Douglas Lemke, "Investigating the Preventive Motive for War," *International Interactions* 29 (October–December 2003): 273–92. On the causes of preventive wars, see Robert Powell, *Bargaining in the Shadow of Power* (Princeton, N.J.: Princeton University Press, 1999); Van Evera, *Causes of War*; Dale C. Copeland, *The Origins of Major War* (Cornell, N.Y.: Cornell University Press, 2000); Levy, "Declining Power"; Jacek Kugler and Douglas Lemke, eds., *Parity and War* (Ann Arbor: University of Michigan Press, 1996); and Richard Ned Lebow, "Windows of Opportunity: Do States Jump through Them?" *International Security* 9 (Summer 1984): 147–86. For a formal model of the decision to launch a preventive strike against NBC programs, see Peter D. Feaver and Emerson M. S. Niou, "Managing Nuclear Proliferation: Condemn, Strike, or Assist?" *International Studies Quarterly* 40 (June 1996): 209–34.

5. Ivo Daalder and James M. Lindsay, *America Unbound: The Bush Revolution in Foreign Policy* (Washington, D.C.: Brookings Institution Press, 2003), 127; Noam Chomsky, *Hegemony or Survival: America's Quest for Global Dominance* (New York: Metropolitan Books, 2003), 12. See also the chapters by G. Thomas Goodnight and Tom Rockmore in this volume.

6. For a dissenting view, see John Lewis Gaddis, *Surprise, Security, and the American Experience* (Cambridge, Mass.: Harvard University Press, 2004). For a discussion of the Cold War roots of NSS 2002, see the chapter in this volume by Gordon Mitchell and Robert Newman.

7. For a partial list, see Robert S. Litwak, "The New Calculus of Pre-emption," *Survival* 44 (Winter 2002–3): 53–80.

8. Richard Rhodes, *The Making of the Atomic Bomb* (New York: Simon and Schuster, 1986), 455–57, 513–17; Thomas Powers, *Heisenberg's War: The Secret History of the German Bomb* (New York: Knopf, 1993), 211–12.

9. Powers, *Heisenberg's War*, esp. 263–69, 421–24.

10. Rhodes, *Making of the Atomic Bomb*, esp. 612.

11. Yuki Tanaka, *Hidden Horrors: Japanese War Crimes in World War II* (Boulder, Colo.: Westview Press, 1996), 139–40.

12. Khidhir Hamza with Jeff Stein, *Saddam's Bombmaker* (New York: Touchstone, 2000), 109, 129.

13. See Shai Feldman, *Nuclear Weapons and Arms Control in the Middle East* (Cambridge, Mass.: MIT Press, 1997), 109–10; see also Zeev Maoz, "The Mixed Blessing of Israel's Nuclear Policy," *International Security* 28 (Fall 2003): 64n.

14. Rebecca Grant, "Osirak and Beyond," *Air Force Magazine* 85 (August 2002), http://www.afa.org/magazine/aug2002/0802osirak.asp; Rodger W. Claire, *Raid on the Sun: Inside Israel's Secret Campaign That Denied Saddam the Bomb* (New York: Broadway Books, 2004), 119–20.

15. Mohammad-Mahmoud Mohamedou, *Iraq and the Second Gulf War: State Building and Regime Security* (San Francisco: Austin and Winfield, 1998), 159. There is only sketchy evidence that Dimona was targeted. Mohamedou appears to have drawn this conclusion on the basis of interviews with Iraqi government officials.

16. Thomas A. Keaney and Eliot A. Cohen, *Gulf War Air Power Survey Summary Report* (Washington, D.C.: Government Printing Office, 1993), 80.

17. Daniel L. Byman and Matthew C. Waxman, *Confronting Iraq: U.S. Policy and the Use of Force since the Gulf War* (Santa Monica, Calif.: RAND, 2000), 52.

18. Byman and Waxman, *Confronting Iraq*.

19. Woodward, *Plan of Attack*.

20. David Albright and Corey Hinderstein, "Iran, Player or Rogue?" *Bulletin of the Atomic Scientists* 59 (September/October 2003): 52–58; Andrew Koch and Jeannette Wolf, "Iran's Nuclear Facilities: A Profile," Center for Nonproliferation Studies Report, 1998, http://www.cns.miis.edu.; Anthony H. Cordesman, *Iran and Iraq: The Threat from the Northern Gulf* (Boulder, Colo.: Westview Press, 1993), 105.

21. James Risen, "Question of Evidence: A Special Report," *New York Times*, 27 October 1999; Peter L. Bergen, *Holy War Inc.: Inside the Secret World of Osama bin Laden* (New York: Free Press, 2001), esp. 123–25; Litwak, "New Calculus."

22. James Risen and Judith Miller, "Al Qaeda Site Points to Tests of Chemicals," *New York Times*, 11 November 2001.

23. Judith Miller, "Threats and Responses: Terrorist Weapons," *New York Times*, 13 September 2002; Jack Boureston, "Strategic Insight: Assessing al Qaeda's WMD Capabilities," Naval Security Affairs Department/Center for Contemporary Conflict, September 2002, http://www.ccc.nps.navy.mil/rsepResources/si/sept02/wmd.asp.

24. Woodward, *Plan of Attack*, 46.

25. Byman and Waxman, *Confronting Iraq*, 68–70.

26. United States, General Accounting Office (GAO), "Operation Desert Storm: Evaluation of the Air Campaign," GAO/NSIAD-97-134, June 1997, Appendix III 9.2.5, http://www.fas.org/man/gao/nsiad97134/index.html.

27. US GAO, "Operation Desert Storm"; Keaney and Cohen, *Gulf War*, 80–81.

28. United States, Department of Defense, "Proliferation: Threat and Response," April 1996, http://www.iraqwatch.org/government/US/Pentagon/dod-prolif-1996.htm. See also Keaney and Cohen, *Gulf War*, 82. This portrayal is confirmed by the testimony of Saddam's son-in-law, who defected to Jordan in 1995. See UNSCOM/IAEA, interview with General Hussein Kamal, Amman, Jordan, 22 August 1995, http://www.iraqwatch.org/un/UNSCOM/unmovic-kamalmeeting-082295.pdf.

29. Judith Miller, Stephen Engelberg, and William Broad, *Germs: Biological Weapons and America's Secret War* (New York: Simon and Schuster, 2001), esp. 187.

30. US GAO, "Operation Desert Storm," Appendix III 9.2.5; Hamza, *Saddam's Bombmaker*, 258; Barry D. Watts and Thomas A. Keaney, *Gulf War Air Power Survey*, vol. 2, *Operations and Effects and Effectiveness, Part II: Effects and Effectiveness* (Washington, D.C.: Government Printing Office, 1993), 345; Keaney and Cohen, *Gulf War*, 115; Feldman, *Nuclear Weapons*, 136.

31. Shlomo Nakdimon, *First Strike: The Exclusive Story of How Israel Foiled Iraq's Attempt to Get the Bomb*, trans. Peretz Kidron (New York: Summit Books, 1987), 336; United States, Central Intelligence Agency, "Prewar Status of Iraq's Weapons of Mass Destruction," March 1991, http://www.gwu.edu/~nsarchiv/NSAEBB/NSAEBB80/wmd04.pdf; Kenneth M. Pollack, *The Threatening Storm: The Case for Invading Iraq* (New York: Random House, 2002), 369; Jeremy Tamsett, "The Israeli Bombing of Osiraq Reconsidered: Successful Counterproliferation?" *Nonproliferation Review* 11 (Fall/Winter 2004): 70–85.

32. See Dan Reiter, "Preventive Attacks against Nuclear Programs and the 'Success' at Osiraq," *Nonproliferation Review* 12 (July 2005): 355–71.

33. Lucien S. Vandenbroucke, "The Israeli Strike against Osiraq," *Air University Review* 35 (September/October 1984): 35–47; Richard Wilson, "A Visit to the Bombed Nuclear Reactor at Tuwaitha, Iraq," *Nature*, 31 March 1983, 376.

34. David Albright and Khidhir Hamza, "Iraq's Reconstitution of its Nuclear Weapons Program," *Arms Control Today* (October 1998): 9–15. Saddam also planned to elude inspections by building a secret copy of the French-provided reactor, though whether such a facility could have been built and enough plutonium for a bomb produced by 1991, in secret, is unknown. Hamza, *Saddam's Bombmaker*, 120.

35. Hamza, *Saddam's Bombmaker*, 129–30.

36. Vandenbroucke, "Israeli Strike"; Anthony Fainberg, "Osirak and International Security," *Bulletin of the Atomic Scientists* 37 (October 1981): 34; H. Gruemm, "Safeguards and Tamuz: Setting the Record Straight," *IAEA Bulletin* 23 (December 1981): 10–14; Christopher Herzig, "Correspondence: IAEA Safeguards," *International Security* 7 (Spring 1983): 195–99.

37. Imad Khadduri, *Iraq's Nuclear Mirage: Memoirs and Delusions* (Toronto: Springhead, 2003), 81–82.

38. Nakdimon, *First Strike*, 53–55, 268, 335; Khadduri, *Iraq's Nuclear Mirage*, 74, 82; Wilson, "Visit," 376. See also Vandenbroucke, "Israeli Strike," who estimates that under the best of conditions, the Iraqis could have produced a kilogram of plutonium per year, enough for one or two bombs within a decade.

39. Michael Jansen, "Baghdad's Bomb—An Inside View," *Middle East International* 691 (10 January 2003): 11.

40. Hamza, *Saddam's Bombmaker*, 116.

41. Khadduri, *Iraq's Nuclear Mirage*, 78–79, 82. Feldman also believes that the Osiraq attack increased Saddam's commitment to acquiring nuclear weapons. Feldman, *Nuclear Weapons*, 136.

42. Khidir Hamza, quoted in "National Terrorism Alert Goes Up; Interview With Saddam's Bomb Maker," *CNN Crossfire*, 7 February 2003. http://transcripts.cnn.com/TRANSCRIPTS/0302/07/cf.00.html (22 November 2004).

43. Hamza, *Saddam's Bombmaker*, 131; Watts and Keaney, *Gulf War*.

44. Leon V. Sigal, *Disarming Strangers: Nuclear Diplomacy with North Korea* (Princeton, N.J.: Princeton University Press, 1998), 76; Joel S. Wit, Daniel B. Poneman, and Robert L. Gallucci, *Going Critical: The First North Korean Nuclear Crisis* (Washington, D.C.: Brookings Institution Press, 2004), 103–4.

45. Quoted in Ann Scott Tyson, "Use of Force in Korea Is Tricky Proposition," *Christian Science Monitor*, 12 February 2003.

46. Brenda Shaffer, "Iran at the Nuclear Threshold," *Arms Control Today* (November 2003): 7–12; Shahram Chubin and Robert S. Litwak, "Debating Iran's Nuclear Aspirations," *Washington Quarterly* 26 (Autumn 2003): 108; Michael Knights, "Iranian Nuclear Weapons, Part II: Operational Challenges," Policywatch No. 761, Washington Institute for Near East Policy, 29 May 2003, http://www.washingtoninstitute.org/watch/index.htm; Albright and Hinderstein, "Iran"; David E. Sanger, "Diplomacy Fails to Slow Advance of Nuclear Arms," *New York Times*, 8 August 2004; James Fallows, "Will Iran Be Next?" *Atlantic Monthly*, December 2004, 99–110.

47. Mark Hibbs, "Bushehr Construction Now Remote after Three Iraqi Air Strikes," *Nucleonics Week*, 26 November 1987, 5–6.

48. Anthony H. Cordesman, *Iran's Developing Military Capabilities* (Washington, D.C.: Center for Strategic and International Studies, 2005), 94.

49. Kenneth R. Timmerman, *Countdown to Crisis: The Coming Nuclear Showdown with Iran* (New York: Crown Forum, 2005), 66–67; Cordesman, *Iran's Developing Military Capabilities*, 95–121.

50. Wit, Poneman, and Gallucci, *Going Critical*, 211.

51. Boureston, "Strategic Insight."

52. See John W. Dower, "Lessons from Japan about War's Aftermath," *New York Times*, 27 October 2002; David M. Edelstein, "Occupational Hazards: Why Military Occupations Succeed or Fail," *International Security* 29 (Summer 2004): 49–91.

53. John W. Dower, *Embracing Defeat: Japan in the Wake of World War II* (New York: Norton, 1999).

54. Adam Przeworski, Michael E. Alvarez, José Antonio Cheibub, and Fernando Limongi, *Democracy and Development: Political Institutions and Well-Being in the World 1950–1990* (Cambridge: Cambridge University Press, 2000); Michael L. Ross, "Does Oil Hinder Democracy?" *World Politics* 53 April (2001): 325–61; Kristian S. Gleditsch, *All International Politics Is Local: The Diffusion of Conflict, Integration, and Democratization* (Ann Arbor: University of Michigan Press, 2002); Robert D. Putnam, *Making Democracy Work: Civic Traditions in Modern Italy* (Princeton, N.J.: Princeton University Press, 1993).

55. Joshua Muravchik, "Bringing Democracy to the Arab World," *Current History* 103 (January 2004): 8–11.

56. Anthony Smith, *America's Mission: The United States and the Worldwide Struggle for Democracy in the Twentieth Century* (Princeton, N.J.: Princeton University Press, 1994).

57. Roland Paris, *At War's End: Building Peace after Civil Conflict* (Cambridge: Cambridge University Press, 2004).

58. Marc Trachtenberg, *History and Strategy* (Princeton, N.J.: Princeton University Press, 1991); Heather A. Purcell and James K. Galbraith, "Did the U.S. Military Plan a Nuclear First Strike for 1963?" *American Prospect* 19 (Fall 1994): 89; William Burr and Jeffrey T. Richelson, "Whether to 'Strangle the Baby in the Cradle': The United States and the Chinese Nuclear Program, 1960–64," *International Security* 25 (Winter 2000/1): 54–99; Aleksandr Fursenko and Timothy Naftali, *"One Hell of a Gamble": Khrushchev, Castro, and Kennedy, 1958–1964* (New York: Norton, 1997); Sigal, *Disarming Strangers*, 33, 59–60, 75–76, 113, 121–23.

59. Scott D. Sagan and Kenneth N. Waltz, *The Spread of Nuclear Weapons: A Debate Renewed* (New York: Norton, 2003), 93–95; Elizabeth Wishnick, *Mending Fences: The Evolution of Moscow's China Policy from Brezhnev to Yeltsin* (Seattle: University of Washington Press, 2003), 34–36; Michael B. Oren, *Six Days of War: June 1967 and the Making of the Modern Middle East* (Oxford: Oxford University Press, 2002), 75–76; Avner Cohen, *Israel and the Bomb* (New York: Columbia University Press, 1998), 259–76; Feldman, *Nuclear Weapons*, 131.

60. Fursenko and Naftali, *"One Hell of a Gamble,"* 256.

61. Fursenko and Naftali, *"One Hell of a Gamble,"* 242–43.

62. See Robert S. Ross, "The 1995–96 Taiwan Strait Confrontation," *International Security* 25 (Fall 2000): 87–123.

63. Sigal, *Disarming Strangers*, 10, 211, 266n.

64. Wit, Poneman, and Gallucci, *Going Critical*, 104, 180; Nicholas D. Kristof, "Tunneling toward Disaster," *New York Times*, 21 January 2003.

65. Maoz, "Mixed Blessing."

66. George Perkovich, *India's Nuclear Bomb: The Impact on Global Proliferation* (Berkeley: University of California Press, 1999), 280; Robert Batcher, "The Consequences of an Indo-Pakistani Nuclear War," *International Studies Review* 6 (December 2004): 135–62.

67. Paul Lawrence Rose, *Heisenberg and the Nazi Atomic Bomb Project: A Study in German Culture* (Berkeley: University of California Press, 1998), 134–35.

68. Duelfer, *Comprehensive Report*.

69. For critical discussion, see Maoz, "Mixed Blessing," 55–59. See also Derek D. Smith, "Deterrence and Counterproliferation in an Age of Weapons of Mass Destruction," *Security Studies* 12 (Summer 2003): 152–97.

70. Byman and Waxman, *Confronting Iraq*; Dan Reiter, "Deterrence Has Worked in the Past: Use It with Iraq," *Atlanta Journal-Constitution*, 6 November 2002; John J. Mearsheimer and Stephen M. Walt, "An Unnecessary War," *Foreign Policy* 134 (January/February 2003): 50–59.

71. Ariel Levite, "Never Say Never Again: Nuclear Reversal Revisited," *International Security* 3 (Winter 2002/3): 59–88. Levite lists twenty-one nations (62), to which one should now add Libya. A possible twenty-third state would be Iraq, having essentially abandoned its NBC programs under sanctions and inspections in the late 1990s.

72. Flynt Leverett, "Why Libya Gave Up on the Bomb," *New York Times*, 23 January 2004; Geoff D. Porter, "The Faulty Premise of Pre-emption," *New York Times*, 31 July 2004; George A. Lopez and David Cortright, "Containing Iraq: Sanctions Worked," *Foreign Affairs* 83 (July/August 2004): 90–103.

73. *Imperial Hubris: Why the West Is Losing the War on Terror* (London: Brassey's, 2004); *Strategic Survey 2003/4* (London: International Institute for Strategic Studies, 2004), esp. 5–6, 169.

74. Jeffrey White, "Iranian Nuclear Weapons, Part III: How Might Iran Retaliate?" Policywatch No. 762, Washington Institute for Near East Policy, 29 May 2003, http://www.washingtoninstitute.org/watch/index.htm; Graham Allison, *Nuclear Terrorism: The Ultimate Preventable Catastrophe* (New York: Times Books, 2004), 35.

75. Michael Pan, Amanda Terkel, Robert Boorstin, P. J. Crowley, and Nigel Holmes, "Safety Second," *New York Times*, 8 August 2004.

CHAPTER 3. THE CURIOUS CASE OF KOFI ANNAN

1. For further details on the evolution of this debate within the UN and affiliated organizations, see Simon Reich, "Power, Institutions and Moral Entrepreneurs," ZEF-Discussion Paper on Development Policy No. 65, Center for Development Research (ZEF), Bonn, March 2003, http://www.mafhoum.com/press7/226P3.pdf.

2. Richard N. Haass, "Imperial America," Brookings Paper, November 2000, http://www.brook.edu/dybdocroot/views/articles/haass/2000imperial.htm. Haass most recently outlined an "integrationist" doctrine in Richard Haass, "Defining U.S. Foreign Policy in a Post-Post-Cold War World," 2002 Arthur Ross Lecture, Remarks to Foreign Policy Association, New York, 22 April 2002, http://www.state.gov/s/p/rem/9632.htm.

3. The literature on this issue is voluminous, needing no recapitulation here. But for notable examples, see the works of John O'Neal, John Owen, and Bruce Russett.

4. Stephen D. Krasner, in *Sovereignty: Organized Hypocrisy* (Princeton, N.J.: Princeton University Press, 1999), has, of course, argued that sovereignty is varied in character and was never as foundational as those who caricature realism have argued. For varied contrasting views, see Daniel Philpott, "Usurping the Sovereignty of Sovereignty," *World Politics* 53 (January 2001): 297–324; Daniel Philpott, *Revolutions in Sovereignty: How Ideas Shaped Modern International Relations* (Princeton, N.J.: Princeton University Press, 2001); Thomas J. Biersteker and Cynthia Weber, eds., *State Sovereignty as a Social Construct* (Cambridge: Cambridge University Press, 1996); and J. Samuel Barkin and Bruce Cronin, "The State and the Nation: Changing Norms and the Rules of International Relations," *International Organization* 48 (Winter 1994): 107–30.

5. For a discussion of the benchmark UN position on peacekeeping and intervention, see Commission on Global Governance, *Our Global Neighborhood* (New York: Oxford University Press, 1995), 85–93.

6. For a comprehensive statement, see I. William Zartman, *Ripe for Resolution* (New York: Oxford University Press, 1989); I. William Zartman, "Ripeness: The Hurting Stalemate and Beyond," in *International Conflict Resolution after the Cold War*, ed. Paul Stern and Daniel Druckman (Washington, D.C.: National Academy Press, 2000), 225–50; and, more recently, in a post-9/11 context, see the application of the concept in I. William Zartman, "The Attack on Humanity: Conflict and Management," Social Science Research Council Paper, http://www.ssrc.org/sept11/essays/zartman_text_only.htm.

7. For a concise but clear listing of these forces and their influences on intrastate conflict, see Fen Osler Hampson, Jean Daudelin, John B. Hay, Holly Reid, and Todd Martin, *Madness in the Multitude: Human Security and World Disorder* (New York: Oxford University Press, 2001).

8. For a summary statement of this position, see International Commission on Intervention and State Sovereignty, *The Responsibility to Protect* (Ottawa: International Development Research Center, 2001), xi.

9. For a concise justification of the principles legitimating intervention by just such a moral entrepreneur, see Kofi A. Annan, "Two Concepts of Sovereignty," *Economist*, 18 September 1999.

10. Martha Finnemore, *The Purpose of Intervention: Changing Beliefs about the Use of Force* (Ithaca, N.Y.: Cornell University Press, 2003), 11.

11. Finnemore, *Purpose of Intervention*.

12. Finnemore, *Purpose of Intervention*, 3 and ch. 2.

13. Finnemore, *Purpose of Intervention*, 6.

14. Michael Byers and Simon Chesterman, "Changing the Rules about Rules? Unilateral Humanitarian Intervention and the Future of International Law," in *Humanitarian Intervention: Ethical, Legal and Political Dilemmas*, ed. J. L. Holzgrefe and Robert O. Keohane (Cambridge: Cambridge University Press, 2003), 177–203.

15. Finnemore, Purpose of Intervention, 16–17.

16. On the influence of legitimacy on state action, see Thomas M. Franck, *The Power of Legitimacy among Nations* (New York: Oxford University Press, 1990).

17. Finnemore, *Purpose of Intervention*, 16–17. For the purposes of this essay, I adopt J. L. Holzgrefe's definition of "humanitarian intervention" as "the threat or use of force across state borders by a state (or group of states) aimed at preventing or ending widespread and grave violations of the fundamental human rights of individuals other than its own citizens, without the permission of the state within whose territory it is applied." See J. L. Holzgrefe, "The Humanitarian Intervention Debate," in Holzgrefe and Keohane, *Humanitarian Intervention*, 18.

18. John Gerard Ruggie, "The UN and the Collective Use of Force: Whither or Whether?" in *The UN, Peace and Force*, ed. Michael Pugh (London: Frank Cass, 1997), 1–2.

19. Ruggie, "UN," 5–7.

20. Mats Berdahl, "Whither UN Peacekeeping? An Analysis of the Changing Military Requirements of UN Peacekeeping with Proposals for Its Enhancement," *Adelphi Paper* 281 (1993): 3.

21. Conversation between author and Sir Marrack Goulding, Zentrum für Entwicklungs-forschung, Bonn, 5 July 2002.

22. Thomas G. Weiss, "Principles, Politics, and Humanitarian Action," *Ethics and International Affairs* 13 (1999): 1.

23. Weiss, "Principles," 3.

24. Bruce W. Jentleson, "Coercive Prevention: Normative, Political and Policy Dilemmas," Peaceworks No. 35 (Washington, D.C.: United States Institute of Peace, October 2000): 5. For a discussion of the conditions under which bilateral intervention might occur, see Patrick Regan, "Choosing to Intervene: Outside Intervention in Internal Conflicts," *Journal of Politics* 60 (August 1998): 754–79.

25. Jentleson, "Coercive Prevention," 18.

26. Ruggie, "UN," 6.

27. William Odom, "Intervention for the Long Run: Rethinking the Definition of War," *Harvard International Review* (Winter 2001): 50.

28. For a good example, see Paul F. Diehl, Daniel Druckman, and James Wall, "International Peacekeeping and Conflict Resolution: A Taxonomic Analysis with Implications," *Journal of Conflict Resolution* 42 (February 1998): 33–55.

29. Ruggie, "UN," 5. Note that Ruggie draws extensively from Boutros Boutros-Ghali, *An Agenda for Peace* (New York: United Nations, 1992), which I discuss later.

30. Donald C. F. Daniel and Bradd C. Hayes, with Chantal de Jonge Oudraat, *Coercive Inducement and the Containment of International Crises* (Washington, D.C.: U.S. Institute of Peace Press, 1999), 19.

31. Carnegie Commission on Preventing Deadly Conflict, *Preventing Deadly Conflict* (New York: Carnegie Corporation of New York, 1997), 28.

32. For such a list of factors, see, for example, Carnegie Commission, *Preventing Deadly Conflict*, 43–44.

33. See, for example, Kofi Annan, *Prevention of Armed Conflict: Report of the Secretary-General*, UN Document A/55/985-S/2001/574, 7 June 2001, 1.

34. Carnegie Commission, *Preventing Deadly Conflict*, xviii.

35. International Commission on Intervention, *Responsibility to Protect*, xi.

36. International Commission on Intervention, *Responsibility to Protect*, 8. For an academic analysis in support of this view tracing a broader historical element, see Bruce Cronin, "Changing Views of Sovereignty and Multilateral Intervention," in *Collective Conflict Management and Changing World Politics*, ed. Joseph Lepgold and Thomas G. Weiss (Albany: State University of New York Press), 159–60.

37. International Commission on Intervention, *Responsibility to Protect*, 13–14.

38. International Commission on Intervention, *Responsibility to Protect*, 32–34. This same point is also made in Jentleson, "Coercive Prevention," 19–20.

39. International Commission on Intervention, *Responsibility to Protect*, 15.

40. This distinction is discussed in Carnegie Commission, *Preventing Deadly Conflict*, 39; and amplified in Annan, *Prevention of Armed Conflict*, 7.

41. Again, this point is deliberated upon at length in Carnegie Commission, *Preventing Deadly Conflict*, 48–63. Daniel and Hayes focus on a variety of coercive aspects to extend the notion they developed of a "coercive inducement" option that judiciously employs forceful

persuasion to implement community norms or mediate in crisis, including but not limited to military force. See Daniel and Hayes, *Coercive Inducement*, 21–22.

42. Odom, "Intervention for the Long Run," 52.

43. Jentleson, "Coercive Prevention," 5.

44. Jentleson, "Coercive Prevention," 5.

45. Tom J. Farer, "Humanitarianism Intervention before and after 9/11: Legality and Legitimacy," in Holzgrefe and Keohane, *Humanitarian Intervention*, 59.

46. For an extended discussion of these events, see Reich, "Institutions and Moral Entrepreneurs."

47. Stephen John Stedman, "UN Intervention in Civil Wars: Imperatives of Choice and Strategy," in Daniel and Hayes, *Coercive Inducement*, 40–41.

48. See, for example, Alice Ackermann and Antonia Pala, "From Peacekeeping to Preventive Deployment," *European Security* 5 (Spring 1996): 83–97; Mats Berdahl, "United Nations Peacekeeping in the Former Yugoslavia," in *Beyond Traditional Peacekeeping*, ed. Donald C. F. Daniel and Bradd C. Hayes (London: Palgrave, 1995), 232; Carnegie Commission, *Preventing Deadly Conflict*, 64; and Jentleson, "Coercive Prevention," 6, 16.

49. For just one example of this oft-cited claim, see Annan, *Prevention of Armed Conflict*, 6.

50. Berdahl, "Whither UN," 18.

51. Edward C. Luck, "The Case for Engagement: American Interests in UN Peace Operations," in Daniel and Hayes, *Beyond Traditional Peacekeeping*, 69.

52. Daniel and Hayes, *Coercive Inducement*, 18–19.

53. Daniel and Hayes, *Coercive Inducement*, 23.

54. Daniel and Hayes, *Coercive Inducement*, 18–19.

55. Kofi Annan, "Peace Operations and the United Nations: Preparing for the Next Century," United Nations Working Paper, 1996, 15.

56. Stedman, "UN Intervention," 47.

57. Daniel and Hayes, *Coercive Inducement*, 84.

58. Daniel and Hayes, *Coercive Inducement*, 86

59. For examples of an extensive literature, see Mike Blakely, "Somalia," in *The Costs of Conflict: Prevention and Cure in the Global Arena*, ed. Michael E. Brown and Richard N. Rosecrance (New York: Rowman and Littlefield, 1999), 75–90; Carnegie Commission, *Preventing Deadly Conflict*, 75–90; Daniel and Hayes, *Coercive Inducement*, 73–112; and William J. Durch, "Introduction to Anarchy: Humanitarian Intervention and 'State Building' in Somalia," in *UN Peacekeeping, American Politics and the Uncivil Wars of the 1990s*, ed. William J. Durch (London: MacMillan Press, 1997), 311–66.

60. Stedman, "UN Intervention," 48.

61. This view is expressed in Daniel and Hayes, *Coercive Inducement*, 86.

62. Daniel and Hayes, *Coercive Inducement*, 90.

63. Daniel and Hayes, *Coercive Inducement*, 98.

64. Daniel and Hayes, *Coercive Inducement*, 99.

65. See Gary Anderson, "UNOSOM II: Not Failure, Not Success," in Daniel and Hayes, *Beyond Traditional Peacekeeping*, 273, 278–79.

66. Anderson, "UNOSOM II," 102.

67. Stedman, "UN Intervention," 69. Gary Anderson's comments are consistent with Stedman's assessment. See Anderson, "UNOSOM II," 273.

68. Luck, "Case for Engagement," 71.

69. Stanley Meisler, "Kofi Annan: The Soft Spoken Economist Who Runs UN Peacekeeping Forces," *Los Angeles Times*, 21 June 1994.

70. An outstanding case for examination is that of Bosnia. But doing so would support a comparable argument detailed in the Somalian case. Unlike in Somalia, UNPROFOR,

the force provided by the UN, preceded any US involvement. It initially proved inadequate in dealing with the aggression of the Bosnian Serbs. It was only when US policy changed course, and the US began air strikes against Bosnian Serb positions, that all antagonists were coerced into participating in the Dayton Peace Accords. See, for example, Joseph R. Biden, "Bosnia: Why the United States Should Finish the Job," *SAIS Review* 18 (Summer/Fall 1998): 1.

71. Luck, "Case for Engagement," 69.

72. For a perspective consistent with this, see, for example, Adam Garfinkle, "Strategy and Preventive Diplomacy: US Foreign Policy and Preventive Intervention," *Orbis* 45 (Fall 2001): 503.

73. Kofi A. Annan, *We the Peoples: The Role of the United Nations in the 21st Century* (New York: United Nations Department of Public Information, 2000), 43.

74. See, for example, Caroline Thomas, *Global Governance, Development and Human Security: The Challenge of Poverty and Inequality* (London: Pluto Press, 2000).

75. Although there are numerous examples of Annan offering this statement, for emphasis, see the first line of Annan, *Prevention of Armed Conflict*, 6.

76. See Jentleson, "Coercive Prevention," 20.

77. Annan, *Prevention of Armed Conflict*, 1.

78. Annan, *Prevention of Armed Conflict*, 3.

79. Annan, *Prevention of Armed Conflict*, 13–15.

80. Gareth Evans also serves as president of a Brussels-based NGO, the International Crisis Group, devoted to the issue of preventive intervention.

81. Jentleson, "Coercive Prevention."

82. See Bruce W. Jentleson and Rebecca L. Britton, "Still Pretty Prudent: Post–Cold War American Public Opinion on the Use of Military Force," *Journal of Conflict Resolution* 42 (August 1998): esp. 406.

83. See, for example, Julie Mertus, "Reconsidering the Legality of Humanitarian Intervention: Lessons from Kosovo," *William and Mary Law Review* 41 (May 2000): 1745. Mertus does argue, however, that the intervention may indeed be justifiable according to the UN Charter.

84. For a discussion of this issue, see Jeffrey C. Isaac and Suzanne Dovi, "Hypocrisy and the Limits of Debunking It," *Polity* 34 (Fall 2001): 31–40.

85. See, for example, Klinton W. Alexander, "NATO'S Intervention in Kosovo: The Legal Case for Violating Yugoslavia's National Sovereignty in the Absence of Security Council Approval," *Houston Journal of International Law* 22 (Spring 2000): 403. For a further variety of assessments by notable legal scholars, see "NATO's Kosovo Intervention," Editorial, *American Journal of International Law* 93 (1999), http://www.asil.org/kosovo.htm.

86. Cited in Garfinkle, "Strategy and Preventive Diplomacy," 507.

87. For a sympathetic statement of this perspective, see Charles Krauthammer, "The New Unilateralism," *Washington Post*, 8 June 2001.

88. George W. Bush to ABC News, 23 January 2000, quoted in Garfinkle, "Strategy and Preventive Diplomacy," 503. For supporting evidence, see Condoleezza Rice, "Promoting the National Interest," *Foreign Affairs* 79 (January/February 2000): 45–62.

89. For an expression of this position, see Christopher Layne, "Minding Our Own Business: The Case for American Non-Participation in International Peacekeeping/Peacemaking Operations," in Daniel and Hayes, *Beyond Traditional Peacekeeping*, 87–88.

90. Odom, "Intervention for the Long Run," 48–49.

91. George H. W. Bush had wanted to avoid either problem when initially engaging in Somalia, driven to act by a humanitarian impulse but keen to avoid the suggestion that

Americans were either there to govern or to assist in forming a new government. See Odom, "Intervention for the Long Run," 48–49.

92. See Haass, "Defining U.S. Foreign Policy."

93. Haass, "Defining U.S. Foreign Policy."

94. Haass, "Defining U.S. Foreign Policy."

95. Haass, "Defining U.S. Foreign Policy."

96. Support for Haass's views can be found in the work of some noted academics, particularly Michael Ignatieff, who argues for "a responsibility to protect, prevent and follow through." See Michael Ignatieff, "State Failure and Nation Building," in Holzgrefe and Keohane, *Humanitarian Intervention*, 320. It is a forceful liberalism in which Security Council authorization is preferred but not required and sovereignty has an instrumental value but is not absolute.

97. In effect, there appears to be little operational distinction employment of the two terms by the Bush administration. For the purpose of clarity, I therefore use the terms distinctly.

98. For a sympathetic statement of this perspective, see Krauthammer, "New Unilateralism."

99. Michael Mazarr, "Saved from Ourselves?" *Washington Quarterly* (Spring 2002): 228.

100. For an expression of this position, see Layne, "Minding Our Own Business," 87–88.

101. Odom, "Intervention for the Long Run," 48.

102. Weiss, "Principles," 17.

103. Weiss, "Principles," 51.

104. Bush, "Graduation Speech."

105. Cheney, "Vice President Speaks at VFW."

106. George W. Bush, "President Says Saddam Hussein Must Leave Iraq in 48 Hours," Address to the Nation by the President, 17 March 2003, http://www.whitehouse.gov/news/releases/2003/03/20030317-7.html.

107. Ken Roth, "War in Iraq: Not a Humanitarian Intervention," Human Rights Watch World Report 2004, http://www.hrw.org/wr2k4/3.htm.

CHAPTER 4. BY "ANY MEASURES" NECESSARY

1. Preface to "U.S. National Security Strategy: A New Era," *U.S. Foreign Policy Agenda* 7 (December 2002), http://usinfo.state.gov/journals/itps/1202/ijpe/ijpe1202.htm.

2. US White House, "National Security Strategy."

3. United States, National Security Council, "NSC 68: United States Objectives and Programs for National Security," 14 April 1950 (Top Secret, declassified 1975), http://www.fas.org/irp/offdocs/nsc-hst/nsc-68-9.htm.

4. George W. Bush, "Remarks by the President in Address to Faculty and Students of Warsaw University," 15 June 2001, http://www.whitehouse.gov/news/releases/2001/06/20010615-1.html.

5. Mark Joyce, Review of *Strategic Preemption: US Foreign Policy and the Second Iraq War*, by Robert Pauly and Tom Lansford, *Royal United Services Institute for Defence and Security Studies* 149 (October 2004), http://www.rusi.org/publications/journal/reviews/ref: B4174F50E9745A/; see also Jean-Yves Haine and Gustav Lindström, "An Analysis of the National Security Strategy of the United States of America," *Institute for Security Studies Analysis* (January 2003), http://www.iss-eu.org/new/analysis/analy034.html; and John Shaw, "Bush National Security Strategy Drawing Both Praise and Criticism," *Washington Diplomat* (November 2002), http://www.washdiplomat.com/02-11/c1_02_11.html.

6. George W. Bush, "President Discusses War on Terror at National Endowment for Democracy," 6 October 2005, http://www.whitehouse.gov/news/releases/2005/10/20051006

-3.html. Putting Bush's rhetoric in wider context, Carol Winkler observes that in the public debate over NSS 2002, "the fundamental tenets of the conventional Cold War narrative reemerged and provided rhetorical continuity for members of Bush's political base." Winkler, *In the Name of Terrorism*, 166; see also Carol Winkler, "Globalized Manifest Destiny: The Rhetoric of the Bush Administration in Response to the Attacks of September 11th," *Controversia: An International Journal of Debate and Democratic Renewal* 1 (2002): 85–105.

7. Herman S. Wolk, "The Blueprint for Cold War Defense," *Air Force* 83 (2000), http://www.afa.org/magazine/march2000/0300coldwar.asp.

8. Melvyn P. Leffler, "9/11 and American Foreign Policy," *Diplomatic History* 29 (June 2005): 395.

9. Leffler, "9/11," 411.

10. All references to American war plans in this period are from Steven T. Ross, *American War Plans 1945–1950* (London: Frank Cass, 1996).

11. Ross, *American War Plans*, 82.

12. Bushwacker also has the distinction of carrying the clearest recommendation for the use of biological warfare. This would be "supplemental" to atomic warfare, and it specified the troop levels necessary to "occupy the Soviet State and its satellites, allotting forty-four air groups and twenty-five divisions for the task." Ross, *American War Plans*, 85.

13. Ross, *American War Plans*, 97.

14. Although Secretary of State Dean Acheson was privy to the critical input Nitze was receiving, he did not pass it along to Truman. See Robert L. Beisner, "Patterns of Peril: Dean Acheson Joins the Cold Warriors," *Diplomatic History* 20 (Summer 1966): 321–56.

15. US NSC, "NSC-68."

16. US NSC, "NSC-68."

17. John Lewis Gaddis, *Strategies of Containment* (London: Oxford University Press, 1982), 92.

18. US NSC, "NSC-68."

19. Gaddis, *Strategies of Containment*, 95.

20. Harry S. Truman, *Public Papers*, 2 June 1950, http://www.trumanlibrary.org/public papers/index.php.

21. Dean Acheson, *Present at the Creation: My Years in the State Department* (New York: W. W. Norton, 1969), 374–75.

22. Steven Casey, "Selling NSC-68: The Truman Administration, Public Opinion, and the Politics of Mobilization, 1950–51," *Diplomatic History* 29 (September 2005): 655–90.

23. Edward Barrett, quoted in Casey, "Selling NSC-68," 656.

24. Acheson, *Present at the Creation*, 375.

25. "Significance of the H-Bomb, and America's Dilemma," *Newsweek*, 13 February 1950, 20.

26. *Christian Science Monitor*, 1 March 1950, review of "Is War with Russia Inevitable?" by George Kennan, *Reader's Digest*, March 1950, 1–9, quoted in Casey, "Selling NSC-68," 663.

27. Casey, "Selling NSC-68," 663.

28. Jerry W. Sanders, *Peddlers of Crisis* (Boston: South End Press, 1983), 60.

29. Sanders, *Peddlers of Crisis*, 95.

30. See Sanders, *Peddlers of Crisis*, 94.

31. Jeffrey T. Richelson, *A Century of Spies: Intelligence in the Twentieth Century* (New York: Oxford University Press, 1995), 249–50.

32. Stephen Kinzer, *All the Shah's Men: An American Coup and the Roots of Middle East Terror* (Hoboken, N.J.: John Wiley, 2003).

33. John Foran, "Discursive Subversions: Time Magazine, the CIA Overthrow of Musaddiq, and the Installation of the Shah," in *Cold War Constructions: The Political*

Culture of United States Imperialism, 1945–1966, ed. Christian G. Appy (Amherst: University of Massachusetts Press, 2000), 178–79.

34. Leffler, "9/11," 400–401.

35. James Bamford, *Body of Secrets* (New York, Doubleday, 2001), 81–89.

36. Lemnitzer, "Justification for US Military Intervention."

37. Lemnizter, "Justification for US Military Intervention," 8–10.

38. Lemnizter, "Justification for US Military Intervention," 8–10.

39. Bamford, *Body of Secrets*, 82. As Bamford details, Eisenhower "desperately wanted to invade Cuba in the weeks leading up to Kennedy's inauguration." The only problem was that Castro was not giving a good excuse to do so. With time growing short and his aides gathered in the White House Cabinet Room on 3 January 1962, "Eisenhower floated an idea. If Castro failed to provide that excuse, perhaps, he said, the United States 'could think of manufacturing something that would be generally acceptable.' . . . [T]he idea was not lost on General Lemnitzer." Bamford, *Body of Secrets*, 83.

40. Paul Nitze, Top Secret/Sensitive Memorandum to McGeorge Bundy, 10 May 1963, National Security Files, Meetings and Memoranda Series, Standing Group Meeting, John Fitzgerald Kennedy Presidential Library, Boston, quoted in Bamford, *Body of Secrets*, 89.

41. On competitive intelligence analysis, see Robert Reich, "Re-examining the Team A–Team B Exercise," *International Journal of Intelligence and Counterintelligence* 3 (Fall 1989): 383–403; and Kevin P. Stack, "A Negative View of Competitive Analysis," *International Journal of Intelligence and Counterintelligence* 10 (Winter 1997–98): 456–64.

42. Paul Nitze, *From Hiroshima to Glasnost: At the Center of Decision* (New York: Weidenfeld and Nicholson, 1989), 350.

43. In Nitze's words, "There was considerable pressure on the CIA to bring in an outside group to double-check the agency's findings and analytical methods." Nitze, *Hiroshima to Glasnost*, 351.

44. United States, Central Intelligence Agency, *Intelligence Community Experiment in Competitive Analysis: Soviet Strategic Objectives, an Alternate View: Report of Team "B"* (Washington, D.C.: Government Printing Office, 1976).

45. Anne Hessing Cahn and John Prados, "Team B: The Trillion Dollar Experiment," *Bulletin of the Atomic Scientists* 49 (1993): 22–31.

46. US CIA, *Intelligence Community Experiment*.

47. David Callahan, *Dangerous Capabilities: Paul Nitze and the Cold War* (New York: HarperCollins, 1990), 377.

48. Jay Kalner, quoted in Anne Hessing Cahn, *Killing Détente: The Right Attacks the CIA* (University Park: Pennsylvania State University Press, 1998), 158.

49. Sidney Graybeal, quoted in Cahn, *Killing Détente*, 158.

50. Callahan, *Dangerous Capabilities*, 379.

51. Donald P. Steury, ed., *Intentions and Capabilities: Estimates on Soviet Strategic Forces, 1950–1983* (Washington, D.C.: Central Intelligence Agency, 1996), 335.

52. Ray Cline, quoted in Willard C. Matthias, *America's Strategic Blunders* (University Park: Pennsylvania State University Press, 2001), 305–6.

53. Murray Marder, "Carter to Inherit Intense Dispute on Soviet Intentions," *Washington Post*, 2 January 1977.

54. Sanders, *Peddlers of Crisis*, 199–200.

55. Richard Lehman, quoted in Richard Kovar, "An Interview with Richard Lehman," *Studies in Intelligence* 9 (2000), http://www.cia.gov/csi/studies/summer00/art05.html.

56. Gary Hart, separate opinion, in United States, Senate Select Committee on Intelligence, Subcommittee on Collection, Production, and Quality, *The National Intelligence Estimates A–B Team Episode Concerning Soviet Strategic Capability & Objectives*, 95th

Cong., 2d sess, Committee Print (Washington, D.C.: Government Printing Office, 1978), 8; see also Cahn and Prados, "Million Dollar Experiment"; and Cahn, *Killing Détente*.

57. Hart, separate opinion, 7.

58. Fareed Zakaria, "Exaggerating the Threats," *Newsweek*, 16 June 2003, 33; see also Cahn, *Killing Détente*, 192–96.

59. Frank Gaffney, "Second Opinion on Defense," *Washington Times*, 8 May 1990.

60. William Safire, "Needed: A 'Team B,'" *New York Times*, 10 March 1994.

61. According to Wolfowitz, "The idea that somehow you are saving work for the policymaker by eliminating serious debate is wrong. Why not aim, instead, at a document that actually says there are two strongly argued positions on the issue? Here are the facts and evidence supporting one position, and here are the facts and evidence supporting the other, even though that might leave the poor policymakers to make a judgment as to which one they think is correct." Quoted in Jack Davis, "The Challenge of Managing Uncertainty: Paul Wolfowitz on Intelligence-Policy Relations," *Studies in Intelligence* 39 (1996), http://www .cia.gov/csi/studies/96unclass/davis.htm.

62. Quoted in Woodward, *Plan of Attack*, 25.

63. Mann, *Rise of the Vulcans*, 234–38; Clarke, *Against All Enemies*, 264–65; United States, National Commission on Terrorist Attacks upon the United States, *The 9/11 Commission Report* (Washington, D.C.: U.S. Government Printing Office, 2004), 335–36.

64. "Secret Downing Street Memo." According to National Security Archive senior fellow John Prados, the Dearlove memo makes apparent, "with stunning clarity," that "the goal of overthrowing Saddam Hussein was set at least a year in advance," and that "President Bush's repeated assertions that no decision had been made about attacking Iraq were plainly false." John Prados, "Iraq: When Was the Die Cast?" 3 May 2005, http://www.tompaine. com/articles/iraq_when_was_the_die_cast.php; see also Phillipe Sands, *Lawless World: America and the Making and Breaking of Global Rules from FDR's Atlantic Charter to George W. Bush's Illegal War* (New York: Viking, 2005): 182–85.

65. Quoted in US Senate Select Intelligence Committee, *Prewar Assessments*.

66. George Packer, *The Assassins' Gate: America in Iraq* (New York: Farrar, Strauss and Giroux, 2005), 106.

67. Richard Perle, Douglas Feith, and David Wurmser, "A Clean Break: A New Strategy for Securing the Realm," Institute for Advanced Strategic and Political Studies Paper, 8 July 1996, http://www.aaiusa.org/news/must_read_feith.htm. This plan for the overthrow of Saddam Hussein would later receive fuller treatment in David Wurmser, *Tyranny's Ally: America's Failure to Defeat Saddam Hussein* (Washington, D.C.: American Enterprise Institute Press, 1999) ("Defeating Saddam's regime in Iraq is critical for the United States. Our success affects both our international prestige and our strategic power in the Middle East," 116.)

68. Michael Maloof, quoted in James Risen, "How Pair's Finding on Terror Led to Clash on Shaping Intelligence," *New York Times*, 28 April 2004.

69. Quoted in US Senate Select Intelligence Committee, *Prewar Assessments*, 308, emphasis added.

70. Benjamin and Simon, *Next Attack*, 165.

71. Gordon R. Mitchell, "Team B Intelligence Coups," *Quarterly Journal of Speech* (forthcoming).

72. Quoted in US Senate Select Intelligence Committee, *Prewar Assessments*, 309.

73. See US Senate Select Intelligence Committee, *Prewar Assessments*, 307.

74. Bamford, *Pretext for War*, 290.

75. Benjamin and Simon, *Next Attack*, 170.

76. James E. Steiner, overview to "Challenging the Red Line between Intelligence and Policy," Georgetown University Institute for the Study of Diplomacy Report, 2004, 1, http://cfdev.georgetown.edu/sfs/programs/isd/redline.pdf.

77. US Senate Select Intelligence Committee, *Prewar Assessments*, 309.

78. US Senate Select Intelligence Committee, *Prewar Assessments*, 309.

79. Quoted in US Senate Select Intelligence Committee, *Prewar Assessments*, 309.

80. Carl Levin, "Report of an Inquiry into the Alternative Analysis of the Issue of an Iraq-al Qaeda Relationship," 21 October 2004, http://www.levin.senate.gov/newsroom/supporting/2004/102104inquiryreport.pdf.

81. US Senate Select Intelligence Committee, *Prewar Assessments*, 310.

82. Memorandum of the Deputy Assistant Secretary of Defense, quoted in US Senate Select Intelligence Committee, *Prewar Assessments*, 311. Senator Carl Levin spells out the upshot: "Administration officials relied on or cited these reports in their public statements about the Iraq–al Qaeda relationship and selectively used or cited questionable reports that went beyond the IC's judgments." Levin, "Alternative Analysis," 16.

83. See exchange between Senator Levin and DCI Tenet, United States, Senate Armed Services Committee, *Future Worldwide Threats to U.S. National Security*, Hearing of the Senate Armed Services Committee, 9 March 2004, Lexis-Nexis congressional database, http://www.lexis-nexis.com.

84. "Challenging the Red Line," 5.

85. Thielmann, personal communication with Gordon Mitchell, 16 July 2004.

86. Seymour Hersh, "The Stovepipe," *New Yorker*, 27 October 2003, 77–87.

87. Abram Shulsky and Gary Schmitt, *Silent Warfare: Understanding the World of Intelligence*, 2nd ed. (London: Brassey's, 1993), 80.

88. Bamford, *Pretext for War*, 307–31; Benjamin and Simon, *Next Attack*, 161–93; Seymour Hersh, *Chain of Command: The Road from 9/11 to Abu Ghraib* (New York: HarperCollins, 2004), 207–24; Levin, "Alternative Analysis"; Packer, *Assassins' Gate*, 104–10.

89. Thielmann, personal communication with Gordon Mitchell, 20 September 2004. For details on the efforts of Bolton's office to acquire control of Secure Compartmented Information Facilities in State Department offices, see Alex Bolton, "Report Could Hurt Bolton," Hill, 11 May 2005, http://www.thehill.com/thehill/export/TheHill/News/Frontpage/051105/report.html; Henry Waxman, letter to Christopher Shays, 1 March 2005, http://www.democrats.reform.house.gov/Documents/20050301112122-90349.pdf; and United States, Senate Foreign Relations Committee, "Interview of Ms. DeSutter with Regard to the Bolton Nomination," 5 May 2005, http://www.thewashingtonnote.com/archives/DeSutter%20Interview.pdf.

90. Kenneth M. Pollack, "Spies, Lies, and Weapons: What Went Wrong," *Atlantic Monthly*, January/February 2004, 88–90; see also Benjamin and Simon, *Next Attack*, 167–74; and W. Patrick Lang, "Drinking the Kool-Aid," *Middle East Policy* 11 (Summer 2004): 49–53. As the prewar public argument intensified, OSP's size and influence grew. According to Julian Borger, Shulsky hired "scores" of temporary "consultants" to help handle the surging workload: "They including [sic] like-minded lawyers, congressional staffers, and policy wonks from the numerous rightwing think tanks in the US capital. Few had experience in intelligence." Borger also quotes an unnamed intelligence source as saying that at one time, OSP had "over 100" of such employees on its payroll, working "off the books, on personal service contracts." Julian Borger, "The Spies Who Pushed for War," *Guardian* (London), 17 July 2003.

91. Pollack, "Spies, Lies and Weapons," 88. On the role played by the White House Information Group in systematically publicizing such B-teamed intelligence, see Bamford, *Pretext for War*, 317–31.

92. Bob Drogin, "The Conflict in Iraq," *Los Angeles Times*, 17 June 2004; Bob Drogin and John Goetz, "The Curveball Saga," *Los Angeles Times*, 20 November 2005, Lexis-Nexis general news database, http://www.lexis-nexis.com.

93. Niccolo Machiavelli, *The Discourses*, trans. Leslie J. Walker (New York: Penguin Books, 1970), 376–77.

94. Marquis Childs, contemplating the debacle of the Bay of Pigs invasion, wrote that "ever since the Russian Revolution of 1917 and increasingly in the past two decades exiles have influenced American policy and the American appraisal of critical situations. These are in most instances patriotic, dedicated, freedom-loving men and women. But by the very terms of exile they are more likely than not to be wrong in their estimates of what is happening in their former homeland. And quite understandably they want to believe that the forces of repression which drove them out can be overthrown." Marquis Childs, "Behind the Errors on Cuban Invasion," *Washington Post*, 26 April 1961.

95. Drogin, "Conflict in Iraq."

96. See US Senate Select Intelligence Committee, *Prewar Assessments*, 152–56; US, Commission on the Intelligence Capabilities of the United States Regarding Weapons of Mass Destruction, *Report to the President*, 81–111.

97. Paul Wolfowitz, prepared testimony, Joint Inquiry Hearing on Counterterrorist Center Customer Perspective, Senate Select Committee on Intelligence and House Permanent Select Committee on Intelligence, 19 September 2002, http://www.defenselink .mil/speeches/2002/s20020919-depsecdef1.html.

98. Quoted in Sidney Blumenthal, "There Was No Failure of Intelligence: U.S. Spies Were Ignored, or Worse, if They Failed to Make the Case for War," *Guardian* (London), 5 February 2004.

99. Bush, "President Discusses War on Terror."

100. Wolk, "Blueprint for Cold War Defense."

101. "Secret Downing Street Memo."

102. Packer, *Assassins' Gate*, 106; Benjamin and Simon, *Next Attack*, 165.

103. Committee on the Present Danger, "Our Mission," Committee on the Present Danger Web site, http://www.fightingterror.org/mission/index.cfm; see also Joe Lieberman and John Kyl, "The Present Danger," *Washington Post*, 20 July 2004.

104. Committee on the Present Danger, newsroom press release on publication of Kenneth R. Timmerman's *Countdown to Crisis*, http://www.fightingterror.org/newsroom/ press_050920.cfm.

105. William Van Cleave, member statement, Committee on the Present Danger Web site, http://www.fightingterror.org/members/index.cfm.

106. Casey, "Selling of NSC-68."

107. *Imperial Hubris*, 235.

108. George Bush, quoted in Woodward, *Bush at War*, 81.

109. See Robin Wright, "Postscript," in Robin Wright, *Sacred Rage: The Wrath of Militant Islam* (New York: Simon and Schuster, 2001), 287–90.

110. Winkler, *In the Name of Terrorism*, 184.

111. William Boykin, quoted in William Arkin, "Commentary: The Pentagon Unleashes a Holy Warrior," *Los Angeles Times*, 23 November 2003.

112. Benjamin and Simon, *Next Attack*, 275.

113. Johanna Neuman, "Bush's Inaction over General's Islam Remarks Riles Two Faiths," *Los Angeles Times*, 23 November 2003.

114. Benjamin and Simon, *Next Attack*, 278.

115. Ivan Eland, "Excessive U.S. Military Action Overseas Breeds Anti-U.S. Terrorism," 24 November 2002, 16, transcript of address available from Eland; see also Ivan Eland, *The Empire Has No Clothes: U.S. Foreign Policy Exposed* (Oakland, Calif.: Independent Institute, 2004).

116. Eland, "Excessive," 8–9. See also Leverett, "Why Libya Gave Up on the Bomb."

117. United States, Defense Science Board, *The Defense Science Board 1997 Summer Study Task Force on DoD Response to Transnational Threats*, vol. 1, *Final Report* (Washington, D.C.: Department of Defense, October 1997), 15.

118. See Fred Barnes, "They Still Blame America First," *Weekly Standard*, 4 July 2005, 16; David Frum and Richard Perle, *An End to Evil: How to Win the War on Terror* (New York: Random House, 2003); and Kenneth R. Timmerman, member statement, Committee on the Present Danger Web site, http://www.fightingterror.org/members/index.cfm.

119. On "shock and awe" military tactics, see Harlan K. Ullmann and James P. Wade, *Shock and Awe: Achieving Rapid Dominance* (Washington, D.C.: National Defense University, 1996). For discussion of how Ullmann and Wade's "shock and awe" approach shaped Iraq War planning, see Matt Walker, "Truth and Technology at War," *New Scientist*, 20 December 2003, 12–13. On "blowback terrorism," see Eland, *Empire Has No Clothes*, 197–208.

CHAPTER 5. STRATEGIC DOCTRINE

1. United States, Commission on National Security/21st Century, *Road Map for National Security: Imperative for Change*, 31 January 2001, http://www.cfr.org/content/publications/attachments/Hart-Rudman3.pdf.

2. Kenneth Burke, "War and Cultural Life," *American Journal of Sociology* 48 (1942): 404.

3. Michel Foucault, *The Archaeology of Knowledge* (New York: Pantheon, 1972). In this context, institutional discourse designed to persuade publics faces pressure to rationalize national and international justifications. See Erik Doxtader, "Learning Public Deliberation through the Critique of Institutional Argument," *Argumentation and Advocacy* 31 (1995): 163–84. On the linguistic turn in foreign policy studies, see Frank Beer and Robert Hariman, eds., *Post-Realism: The Rhetorical Turn in International Relations* (East Lansing: Michigan State University Press, 1996); and Mitchell, "Public Argument-Driven Security Studies," 57–72.

4. John T. Rourke, *Presidential Wars and American Democracy: Rally Round the Chief* (New York: Paragon House, 1993), 140; Cecil V. Crabb Jr. and Pat M. Holt, *Invitation to Struggle: Congress, the President, and Foreign Policy*, 3rd ed. (Washington, D.C.: Congressional Quarterly Press, 1989), 21.

5. J. Ceaser, G. E. Thurow, J. Tulis, and J. M. Besette, "The Rise of the Rhetorical Presidency," *Presidential Studies Quarterly* 11 (1981): 158–71.

6. Denise M. Bostdorff, *The Presidency and the Rhetoric of Foreign Crisis* (Columbia: University of South Carolina Press, 1993).

7. Samuel Kernell, *Going Public*, 3rd ed. (Washington, D.C.: Congressional Quarterly Press, 1997).

8. Kathryn M. Olson, "Constraining Open Deliberations in Times of War: Presidential War Justification for Grenada and the Persian Gulf," *Argumentation and Advocacy* 27 (1991): 64–97.

9. G. Thomas Goodnight, "Public Argument and the Study of Foreign Policy," *American Diplomacy* 3 (1998), http://www.unc.edu/depts/diplomat/. Critical studies are episodic and inquire into the use of discourse to structure expectations across time. The aim is to evaluate strengths and weaknesses when orientations used to persuade others meet with internal inconsistencies of development or are unable to come to terms with departures needed for justified adaptation. See Robert Ivie, "Metaphor and the Rhetorical Invention of Cold War 'Idealists,'" *Communication Monographs* 54 (1987): 165–82; and Robert Ivie, "Presidential Motives for War," *Quarterly Journal of Speech* 60 (1974): 337–45.

10. Thomas Kane, "Foreign Policy Suppositions and Commanding Ideas," *Argumentation and Advocacy* 28 (1991): 80–90.

11. Michael C. McGee, "The 'Ideograph': A Link between Rhetoric and Ideology," *Quarterly Journal of Speech* 66 (1980): 1–16.

12. Philip Wander, "The Rhetoric of American Foreign Policy," *Quarterly Journal of Speech* 70 (1984): 339–61; Shawn J. Parry-Giles, *The Rhetorical Presidency, Propaganda, and the Cold War, 1945–1955* (Westport, Conn.: Praeger, 2001); Martin J. Medhurst, "Rhetoric and Cold War: A Strategic Approach," in *Cold War Rhetoric: Strategy, Metaphor, and Ideology*, ed. Martin J. Medhurst, Robert L. Ivie, Philip Wander, and Robert L. Scott (East Lansing: Michigan State University Press, 1997), 19–28.

13. Kathryn M. Olson, "Democratic Enlargement's Value Hierarchy and Rhetorical Forms: An Analysis of Clinton's Use of Post–Cold War Symbolic Frame to Justify Military Interventions," *Presidential Studies Quarterly* 34 (2004): 307–40.

14. David Zarefsky, "President Johnson's War on Poverty: The Rhetoric of Three 'Establishment' Movements," *Communication Monographs* 44 (1977): 352–53.

15. Robert Asen, *Visions of Poverty: Welfare Policy and Political Imagination* (East Lansing: Michigan State University Press, 2002).

16. G. Thomas Goodnight, "Predicaments of Communication, Argument, and Power: Towards a Critical Theory of Controversy," *Informal Logic* 23 (2003): 119–38.

17. Leland M. Griffin, "When Dreams Collide: Rhetorical Trajectories in the Assassination of President Kennedy," *Quarterly Journal of Speech* 70 (1984): 111–31.

18. John Lewis Gaddis, "A Grand Strategy of Transformation," *Foreign Policy* (November/October 2002): 56.

19. Kenneth Burke, *Attitudes toward History*, 2nd ed. (Boston: Beacon Press, 1959), 216–338. Burke examines rhetorics as self-fashioning historical and cultural constructions. The entry point into analyzing such symbolic framing is through scrutiny of the work done by key "pivotal terms" in a rhetoric, that is, those terms that are characteristic of a complex of justifications, motivations, definitions, and equations deployed by proponents and opponents of action in policy advocacy.

20. Bush, "Graduation Speech."

21. Bush, "Graduation Speech."

22. Bush, "Graduation Speech."

23. Bush, "Graduation Speech."

24. Anthony Clark Arend, "International Law and the Preemptive Use of Military Force," *Washington Quarterly* 26 (Spring 2003): 89–103.

25. Cheney, "Vice President Speaks at VFW."

26. Cheney, "Vice President Speaks at VFW," emphasis added. See also Richard Cheney, "Vice President Honors Veterans of Korean War," 29 August 2002, http://www.whitehouse.gov/news/releases/2002/08/20020829-5.html.

27. Cheney, "Vice President Honors."

28. Cheney, "Vice President Honors," emphasis added.

29. Miriam Sapiro, "Iraq: The Shifting Sands of Preemptive Self-Defense," *American Journal of International Law* 97 (July 2003): 600, Lexis-Nexis legal research database, http://www.lexis-nexis.com.

30. Daniel Webster, letter to Lord Ashburton, 6 August 1842, quoted in John Bassett Moore, *A Digest of International Law* 412 (1906). Cited by Sapiro, "Shifting Sands," 600.

31. Arend, "International Law," 83.

32. Michael N. Schmitt, "Preemptive Strategies of International Law," *Michigan Journal of International Law* 24 (Winter 2003): 513–48; Richard A. Falk. "What Future for the UN Charter System of War Prevention?" *American Journal of International Law* 57 (July 2003): 592.

33. Lawrence Freedman, "Prevention, Not Preemption," *Washington Quarterly* 26 (Spring 2003), muse.jhu.edu/journals/washington_quarterly/vol262freedman.pdf.

34. Freedman, "Prevention."

35. Jeffery Record, "The Bush Doctrine and War with Iraq," *Parameters* (Spring 2003): 6.

36. Keir A. Lieber and Robert J. Lieber, "The Bush National Security Strategy," *U.S. Foreign Policy Agenda* (December 2002), http://usinfo.state.gov/journals/itps/1202/ijpe/pj7-4lieber.htm.

37. US White House, "National Security Strategy." Traditionally, there is a clear distinction between preemptive action as one "initiated on the basis of incontrovertible evidence that an enemy attack is imminent," and a preventive action, where war is "initiated in the belief that military conflict, while not imminent, is inevitable, and that to delay would involve greater risk." Michael Moore, "Truman Got it Right," *Bulletin of the Atomic Scientists* 59 (January/February 2003): 20.

38. US White House, "National Security Strategy," emphasis added.

39. US White House, "National Security Strategy."

40. Lieber and Lieber, "Bush National Security Strategy."

41. Michael J. Glennon, "Preempting Terrorism: The Case for Anticipatory Self-Defense," *Weekly Standard*, 28 January 2002, 24.

42. M. Elaine Bunn, "Preemptive Action: When, How, and to What Effect?" *Strategic Forum* 200 (July 2003): 4.

43. Condoleezza Rice, "Dr. Condoleezza Rice Discusses President's National Security Strategy," Waldorf Astoria Hotel, New York, 1 October 2002, http://www.whitehouse.gov/news/releases/2002/10/2002001-6.html.

44. Donald Rumsfeld and Peter Pace, "DOD News Briefing—Secretary Rumsfeld and Gen. Pace," Department of Defense News Transcript, 26 September 2002, http://222.defenselink.mil/news/Sep 2002/t09262002_t0926sd.html, emphasis added.

45. Donald Rumsfeld, quoted in Moore, "Truman Got It Right," 20.

46. Authorization for the Use of Military Force against Iraq Resolution of 2002, Pub. L. No. 107-243, 116 Stat. 1498, 1499 (2002), quoted in Michael N. Schmitt. "Preemptive Strategies of International Law," *Michigan Journal of International Law* 24 (Winter 2003): 529.

47. Sapiro, "Shifting Sands," 599.

48. Falk, "What Future."

49. George W. Bush, "President George Bush Discusses Iraq in National Press Conference," 6 March 2003, http://www.whitehouse.gov/news/releases/2003/03/20030306-8.html.

50. David Kay, testimony, *Hearings on Iraqi Weapons of Mass Destruction and Related Programs*, Hearing of the United States Armed Services Committee, 10 September 2002, Lexis-Nexis Congressional database, http://www.lexis-nexis.com.

51. Thomas M. Franck, "What Happens Now? The United Nations after Iraq," *American Journal of International Law* 97 (July 2003): 607–20, Lexis-Nexis legal research database, http://www.lexis-nexis.com.

52. George W. Bush, "State of the Union Address," 20 January 2004, www.whitehouse.gov/news/releases/2004/01/20040120-7.html.

53. John Warner, statement, *Hearing on Iraqi Weapons of Mass Destruction and Related Programs*, Senate Armed Services Committee Hearing, 28 January 2004, Lexis-Nexis congressional research database, http://www.lexis-nexis.com.

54. Carl Levin, statement, *Hearing on Iraqi Weapons of Mass Destruction.*

55. Mark Dayton and David Kay, statements, *Hearing on Iraqi Weapons of Mass Destruction.*

56. David Kay, statement, *Hearing on Iraqi Weapons of Mass Destruction.*

57. See Anderson Cooper, "Is 'Group Think' to Blame for Iraq WMD Intelligence Failure?" 12 July 2004, CNN Transcript #071200CN.V98, Lexis-Nexis news database, http://www.lexis-nexis.com.

58. In February 2004, President Bush announced the creation of a presidential commission to investigate the Iraq prewar intelligence failure, giving the commission a 31 March 2005 reporting deadline. See United States, White House, "Commission on the Intelligence Capabilities of the United States Regarding Weapons of Mass Destruction," Executive Order, 6 February 2004, http://www.whitehouse.gov/news/releases/2004/02/20040206 -10.html.

59. Jane Stromseth, "Law and Force after Iraq: A Transitional Moment," *American Journal of International Law* 97 (July 2003): 628–42, Lexis-Nexis legal research database, http://www.lexis-nexis.com.

60. William H. Taft IV and Todd F. Buchwald, "Preemption, Iraq, and International Law," *American Journal of International Law* 97 (July 2003): 557–85, Lexis-Nexis legal research database, http://www.lexis-nexis.com.

61. Antony J. Blinken, "From Preemption to Engagement," *Survival* 45 (Winter 2003): 28.

62. Francois Heisbourg. "A Work in Progress: The Bush Doctrine and Its Consequences," *Washington Quarterly* 26 (Spring 2003): 78–88.

63. Frank J. Gaffney, "God Save Us," *NRO* (*National Review Online*), 4 August 2005, Lexis-Nexis general news database, http://www.lexis-nexis.com.

64. George W. Bush, "President Discusses War on Terror at National Endowment for Democracy," 6 October 2005, http://www.whitehouse.gov/news/releases/2005/10/20051006-3.html.

65. Warren Vieth and Josh Meyer, "Bush Likens War on Terror to Cold War," *Los Angeles Times*, 7 October 2005.

CHAPTER 6. DELIBERATE BEFORE STRIKING FIRST?

1. George W. Bush, "Commencement Address at the United States Military Academy in West Point, New York, June 1, 2002," *Weekly Compilation of Presidential Documents* 38 (2002): 944–48.

2. US White House, "National Security Strategy."

3. Colin L. Powell, "A Strategy of Partnerships," *Foreign Affairs* 83 (January/February 2004): 23–24.

4. Scholars and policy analysts examining deterrence have long distinguished between declaratory and operational strategies. See Donald M. Snow, "Levels of Strategy and American Strategic Nuclear Policy," *Air University Review* 35 (November/December 1983), http://www.airpower.maxwell.af.mil/airchronicles/aureview/1983/Nov-Dec/snow.html.

5. US White House, "National Security Strategy," 15.

6. Even sympathetic voices make this point. See Robert Kagan, afterword to "American Power and the Crisis of Legitimacy," in Robert Kagan, *Of Paradise and Power* (New York: Vintage Books, 2004), 139n.

7. Paul W. Schroeder, "Iraq: The Case against Preemptive War," *American Conservative*, 10 October 2002, http://www.amconmag.com/2002_10_21/iraq.html.

8. John Mearsheimer, quoted in Marja Mills, "Waging a War of Euphemisms," *Chicago Tribune*, 10 October 2002, available in NewsBank, Record Number: CTR0210170003.

9. Secretary of State Powell noted on 8 January 2004 that he had "not seen smoking-gun, concrete evidence about the connection" between Iraq and al-Qaida. See Christopher

Marquis, "Powell Admits No Hard Proof in Linking Iraq to Al Qaeda," *New York Times*, 9 January 2004. In September 2003, President Bush declared, "We've had no evidence that Saddam Hussein was involved with September the 11th." See Terence Hunt, "Bush: No Proof of Saddam Role in 9-11," Associated Press Online, 17 September 2003, Lexis-Nexis news wire database, http://www.lexis-nexis.com.

10. George W. Bush, "Address before a Joint Session of the Congress on the State of the Union, January 29, 2002," *Weekly Compilation of Presidential Documents* 38 (2002): 133–39.

11. Bob Woodward and Dan Balz, "Combating Terrorism: 'It Starts Today,' " *Washington Post*, 1 February 2002. The president then apparently said, "I don't have the evidence at this point." The pundit Laurie Mylroie left out the caveat when discussing Bush's views. See Laurie Mylroie, "The Circle of Terror," NRO (National Review Online), 19 February 2003, http://www.nationalreview.com/comment/comment-mylroie021903.asp.

12. George W. Bush, "Address to the United Nations General Assembly in New York City, September 12, 2002," *Weekly Compilation of Presidential Documents* 38 (2002): 1531. Colin Powell suggested on several occasions that Iraq was not an example of preemptive attack. See United States, Department Of State, Office of the Spokesman, "Interview with Secretary of State Colin L. Powell by International Wire Services," 18 March 2003, http://usinfo.state.gov/mena/Archive/2004/Feb/05-814752.html.

13. George W. Bush, quoted in United States, White House Office of the Press Secretary, "Remarks Prior to Discussions with President Alvaro Uribe of Columbia and an Exchange with Reporters, September 27, 2002," *Weekly Compilation of Presidential Documents* 38 (2002): 1619.

14. George W. Bush, "Address to the Nation on Iraq, Cincinnati, Ohio, October 7, 2002," *Weekly Compilation of Presidential Documents* 38 (2002): 1718.

15. See Mitchell, *Strategic Deception*. See also Rodger A. Payne, "The Politics of Defense Policy Communication: The 'Threat' of Soviet Strategic Defense," *Policy Studies Review* 8 (1989): 505–26.

16. Chaim Kaufmann, "Threat Inflation and the Failure of the Marketplace of Ideas: The Selling of the Iraq War," *International Security* 29 (Summer 2004): 41.

17. For further elaboration of this point, see Payne and Samhat, *Democratizing Global Politics*.

18. Under certain circumstances, even preventive war might be necessary in a world of surprise terrorist attacks and nuclear proliferation. Elsewhere, I have argued that the Bush administration should work with domestic opponents and various other states to establish firm parameters for using force in certain circumstances. See Donald C. F. Daniel, Peter Dombrowski, and Rodger A. Payne, "The Bush Doctrine Is Dead; Long Live the Bush Doctrine?" *Orbis* 49 (Spring 2005): 199–212.

19. US White House, "National Security Strategy," 6.

20. US White House, "National Security Strategy," 15.

21. A more thorough version of this argument can be found in Peter Dombrowski and Rodger A. Payne, "Global Debate and the Limits of the Bush Doctrine," *International Studies Perspectives* 4 (November 2003): 395–408.

22. US White House, "National Security Strategy," 16.

23. US White House, "National Security Strategy," 15–16.

24. Condoleezza Rice, "A Balance of Power That Favors Freedom," 2002 Wriston Lecture, Manhattan Institute for Policy Research, New York City, 1 October 2002, http://www.manhattan-institute.org/html/wl2002.htm.

25. Dombrowski and Payne, "Global Debate."

26. United States, Department Of State, Office of the Spokesman, "Powell Says Time Is Running Out for Iraq to Comply with U.N." 19 January 2003, http://usinfo.state.gov/

xarchives/display.html?p=washfile-english&y=2003&m=January&x=20030119162306DDe
nny@pd.state.gov0.1734735&t=xarchives/xarchitem.html.

27. George W. Bush, "Bush Letter: 'America Intends to Lead,'" CNN, 4 September 2002, http://www.cnn.com/2002/ALLPOLITICS/09/04/bush.letter/.

28. George W. Bush, "Remarks at a Luncheon for Representative Anne M. Northup in Louisville, September 6, 2002," *Weekly Compilation of Presidential Documents* 38 (2002): 1498.

29. Donald H. Rumsfeld, quoted in George Gedda, "Bush: No Timetable for a Decision on Attacking Iraq," *Pittsburgh Post-Gazette*, 10 August 2002, http://www.post-gazette .com/nation/20020809iraqplannat2p2.asp.

30. Bush, "Bush Letter."

31. Lawrence Eagleburger, quoted in Ben Russell, "US Warns Syria Not to Provide Haven for Wanted Iraqis," *Independent* (UK), 14 April 2003, http://www.common dreams.org/headlines03/0414-01.htm. See also James Hardy, "Bush's Calls to Syrians," *Mirror* (UK), 14 April 2003, http://www.mirror.co.uk/news/allnews/page.cfm?objectid =12844873&method=full&siteid=50143&headline=BUSH%27S%20CALL%20TO% 20SYRIANS.

32. Paul Wolfowitz, Department of Defense transcript of Sam Tannenhaus interview with Deputy Secretary of Defense Wolfowitz, 9 May 2003, http://www.defenselink.mil/ transcripts/2003/tr20030510.

33. US, National Commission on Terrorist Attacks upon the United States, *The 9/11 Commission Report*, 66. At various times, however, al-Qaida sponsored antiregime forces within Iraq.

34. Wolfowitz, transcript of Tannenhaus interview.

35. Colin Powell, quoted in United States, Department of State, "Secretary of State Colin Powell on NBC's Meet the Press," 22 October 2002, http://usinfo.state.gov/xarchives /display.html?p=washfile-english&y=2002&m=October&x=20021021101237eichler@ pd.state.gov0.9141504&t=xarchives/xarchitem.html.

36. George W. Bush, quoted in United States, White House Office of the Press Secretary, "President George Bush Discusses Iraq in National Press Conference, March 6, 2003," *Weekly Compilation of Presidential Documents* 39 (2003): 304.

37. In July, the Senate Select Committee on Intelligence completed its investigation of prewar intelligence on Iraq. See US Senate Select Intelligence Committee, *Prewar Assessments*. However, the report focuses narrowly on the content of the intelligence assessments, rather than on the Bush administration's use of the intelligence.

38. Joseph Cirincione, Jessica T. Mathews, and George Perkovich, with Alexis Orton, *WMD in Iraq: Evidence and Implications* (Washington, D.C.: Carnegie Endowment for International Peace, 2004). See also David Isenberg and Ian Davis, *Unravelling the Known Unknowns: Why No Weapons of Mass Destruction Have Been Found in Iraq*, BASIC (British American Security Information Council) Special Report, January 2004, http://www.basic int.org/pubs/Research/2004WMD.pdf.

39. George W. Bush, "Address before a Joint Session of the Congress on the State of the Union, January 20, 2004," *Weekly Compilation of Presidential Documents* 40 (2004): 94–101.

40. David Kay, quoted in Tabassum Zakaria, "Give Up 'Delusional Hope' of Iraq WMD, Kay Says," ABC News, 28 July 2004, http://abcnews.go.com/wire/US/reuters20040728 _479.html.

41. Duelfer, *Comprehensive Report*.

42. Pollack, "Spies, Lies, and Weapons," 81.

43. Kaufmann, "Threat Inflation," 31.

44. Cheney, "Vice President Speaks at VFW." Cheney noted that the information was obtained from defectors.

45. Condoleezza Rice, quoted in "Interview with Condoleezza Rice," *CNN Late Edition with Wolf Blitzer*, 8 September 2002, CNN transcript #090800CN.V47, http://www.cnn.com/TRANSCRIPTS/0209/08/le.00.html.

46. George W. Bush, "The President's Radio Address, September 14, 2002," *Weekly Compilation of President Documents* 38 (2002): 1546.

47. Cheney, "Possible War with Iraq."

48. "News," USA Today/CNN/Gallup Poll, February 2003, http://www.usatoday.com/news/polls/tables/live/0203.htm. A Fox News Poll conducted by Opinion Dynamics Corporation on 8–9 September 2002 found that 69 percent of respondents believed "Iraq currently has nuclear weapons." The only choices were yes, no, or no opinion. See Dana Blanton, "Poll: Most Expect War with Iraq," Fox News Poll, 12 September 2002, http://www.foxnews.com/story/0,2933,62861,00.html.

49. Colin Powell, quoted in United States, Department of State, Office of the Spokesman, Colin Powell, "Press Remarks with Foreign Minister of Egypt Amre Moussa," 24 February 2001, http://www.state.gov/secretary/rm/2001/933.htm.

50. Condoleezza Rice, "Promoting the National Interest," *Foreign Affairs* 79 (January/February 2000): 61.

51. United States, National Intelligence Council, September 1999 National Intelligence Estimate, "Foreign Missile Developments and the Ballistic Missile Threat Through 2015," unclassified summary, December 2001, http://www.cia.gov/nic/PDF_GIF_otherprod/missilethreat2001.pdf.

52. See US Senate Select Intelligence Committee, *Prewar Assessments*, 19. The president has made several misleading comments about the status of international inspectors in Iraq. In his 2002 State of the Union address, he said: "This is a regime that agreed to international inspections—then kicked out the inspectors." In 1998, of course, they were withdrawn. After the American occupation began, the president claimed that arms inspectors had not been allowed into Iraq in 2002–3 after the UN sought them: "We gave him [Saddam] a chance to allow the inspectors in, and he wouldn't let them in. And, therefore, after a reasonable request, we decided to remove him from power." George W. Bush, quoted in United States, White House Office of the Press Secretary, "Remarks Following Discussions with Secretary General Kofi Annan of the United Nations and an Exchange with Reporters, July 14, 2003," *Weekly Compilation of Presidential Documents* 39 (2003): 917.

53. United Nations, International Atomic Energy Agency, "International Atomic Energy Agency Update Report for the Security Council Pursuant to Resolution 1441 (2002)," 20 January 2003, http://www.iaea.org/NewsCenter/Focus/IaeaIraq/unscreport_290103.html. All of the IAEA quotes in the paragraph are taken from this document.

54. US Senate Select Intelligence Committee, *Prewar Assessments*, 84.

55. Both quotes from the NIE are from US Senate Select Intelligence Committee, *Prewar Assessments*, 85, 126.

56. David Kay, "Statement by David Kay on the Interim Progress Report on the Activities of the Iraq Survey Group (ISG) before the House Permanent Select Committee on Intelligence, House Appropriations Subcommittee on Defense, and Senate Select Committee on Intelligence," 2 October 2003, http://www.cia.gov/cia/public_affairs/speeches/2003/david_kay_10022003.html.

57. David Kay, testimony, *Iraqi Weapons of Mass Destruction Programs*, Senate Armed Services Committee Hearing, 28 January 2004, Federal News Service Transcript, 14, http://www.ceip.org/files/projects/npp/pdf/Iraq/kaytestimony.pdf.

58. Duelfer, Comprehensive Report, 1.

59. Jay Rockefeller, Carl Levin, and Richard Durbin, "Additional Views," in US Senate Select Intelligence Committee, *Prewar Intelligence*, 452, 454. See also David Barstow, William J. Broad, and Jeff Gerth, "How the White House Embraced Disputed Iraqi Arms Intelligence," *New York Times*, 3 October 2004.

60. Quoted in US Senate Select Intelligence Committee, *Prewar Assessments*, 85–86, 126.

61. United States, National Intelligence Council, October 2002 National Intelligence Estimate, "Iraq's Continuing Programs for Weapons of Mass Destruction," declassified excerpts, 18 July 2003, http://www.fas.org/irp/cia/product/iraq-wmd.html.

62. Rockefeller, Levin, and Durbin, "Additional Views," 459.

63. Mohamed ElBaradei, "The Status of Nuclear Inspections in Iraq," 27 January 2003, http://www.iaea.org/NewsCenter/Statements/2003/ebsp2003n003.shtml.

64. Mohammed ElBaradei, "The Status of Nuclear Inspections in Iraq: An Update," 7 March 2003, http://www.iaea.org/NewsCenter/Statements/2003/ebsp2003n006.shtml.

65. Cheney, "Possible War with Iraq." In response to the IAEA findings the prior week, Cheney declared, "I think Mr. ElBaradei frankly is wrong. And I think if you look at the track record of the International Atomic Energy Agency and this kind of issue, especially where Iraq's concerned, they have consistently underestimated or missed what it was Saddam Hussein was doing. I don't have any reason to believe they're any more valid this time than they've been in the past."

66. Pollack, "Spies, Lies, and Weapons," 85.

67. Bush, "Address to the United Nations General Assembly," 1531.

68. Condoleezza Rice, quoted in Joby Warrick, "Evidence on Iraq Challenged," *Washington Post*, 19 September 2002. Rice later revealed that she knew of the debate about the tube's more benign uses. See Barstow, Broad, and Gerth, "How the White House Embraced."

69. Richard Cheney, "Vice President Dick Cheney Discusses 9/11 Anniversary, Iraq, Nation's Economy and Politics 2002," *Meet the Press*, NBC News transcripts, 8 September 2002, Lexis-Nexis news transcript database, http://www.lexis-nexis.com, emphasis added.

70. David Albright, quoted in Joby Warrick, "U.S. Claim on Iraqi Nuclear Program Is Called into Question," *Washington Post*, 24 January 2003.

71. US Senate Select Intelligence Committee, *Prewar Assessments*, 86. The "extensive dissenting opinions from both the DOE and INR" (96) were contained in an annex to the 2002 NIE. See also Barstow, Broad, and Gerth, "How the President Embraced."

72. ElBaradei, "Status of Nuclear Inspections."

73. US Senate Select Intelligence Committee, *Prewar Assessments*, 99. Though US intelligence services were provided complete information about IAEA inspections and tests, the CIA apparently prepared a brief circulated only to senior policy officials that "rejected the IAEA's conclusions" (119). The CIA thought that IAEA inspectors were "being fooled by Iraq" (20).

74. Kay, *Iraqi Weapons of Mass Destruction*, 13.

75. US Senate Select Intelligence Committee, *Prewar Assessments*, 241–42. Despite this attempted diligence, the Senate committee nonetheless concluded that because the speech relied upon the unsubstantiated NIE claims, "many of those [intelligence community] judgments that were included in Secretary Powell's speech, therefore, are also not substantiated by the intelligence source reporting." INR analysts were apparently granted less direct access to Secretary Powell during the briefing process. Ultimately, many of their suggested caveats were ignored.

76. The eventual Democratic nominee for president in 2004, Senator John Kerry, called the presentation "convincing" and based on evidence that "appears real and compelling." See Derrick Z. Jackson, "Kerry Still Needs to Explain War Vote," *Boston Globe*, 23 January

2004, http://www.boston.com/news/politics/debates/articles/2004/01/23/kerry_still
_needs_to_explain_war_vote/.

77. Ari Berman, "U.S. Iraq Policy Gains Support among Newspapers," *Editor &
Publisher*, 7 February 2003, http://www.editorandpublisher.com/eandp/news/article
_display.jsp?vnu_content_id=1812676.

78. Colin Powell, "Remarks to the United Nations Security Council," 5 February 2003,
http://www.state.gov/secretary/former/powell/remarks/2003/17300.htm.

79. US Senate Select Intelligence Committee, *Prewar Assessments*, 243.

80. Hanley, "Point by Point." The review surveyed a full array of flawed unconventional
weapons evidence, including the most important nuclear claims.

81. "Colin Powell on Iraq, Race, and Hurricane Relief," *ABC News*, 8 September 2005,
http://abcnews.go.com/2020/Politics/story?id=1105979&page=1.

82. George W. Bush, "Address before a Joint Session of the Congress on the State of the
Union, January 28, 2003," *Weekly Compilation of Presidential Documents* 38 (2003): 115.

83. Walter Pincus, "CIA Did Not Share Doubt on Iraq Data," *Washington Post*, 12 June
2003.

84. Walter Pincus and Dana Milbank, "Bush, Rice Blame CIA for Iraq Error," *Washington Post*, 12 July 2003.

85. Walter Pincus, "White House Backs Off Claim on Iraqi Buy," *Washington Post*, 8 July
2003.

86. ElBaradei, "Status of Nuclear Weapons."

87. United States, White House Office of the Press Secretary, "President Bush, Prime
Minister Blair Discuss Keeping the Peace, Camp David, MD, September 7, 2002," *Weekly
Compilation of Presidential Documents* 38 (2002): 1518.

88. Mark Gwozdecky, quoted in Joseph Curl, "Agency Disavows Report on Iraq Arms,"
Washington Times, 27 September 2002.

89. Cirincione, Mathews, and Perkovich, *WMD in Iraq*.

90. Rockefeller, Levin, and Durbin, "Additional Views," 463.

91. Greg Thielmann, quoted in Robert Dreyfuss and Jason Vest, "The Lie Factory,"
Mother Jones, January/February 2004, 40.

92. The Pentagon has concluded that very little security intelligence provided by the INC
was accurate. See Douglas Jehl, "Agency Belittles Information Given by Iraq Defectors,"
New York Times, 29 September 2003.

93. Pollack, "Spies, Lies, and Weapons," 88. See also Dreyfuss and Vest, "Lie Factory,"
34–41. This article includes on-the-record criticisms from air force lieutenant colonel Karen
Kwiatkowski, who served in the Pentagon's Near East and South Asia unit the year before
the invasion of Iraq.

94. "Transcript: David Kay on 'Fox News Sunday,'" Fox News, 1 February 2004,
http://www.foxnews.com/story/0,2933,109957,00.html.

95. Powell, "Strategy of Partnerships," 24. Powell argues that preemption "applies only
to the undeterrable threats that come from nonstate actors such as terrorist groups." This is
odd because President Bush has long argued that states that sponsor or harbor terrorists are
as guilty as the terrorists themselves, and many administration officials have openly worried
that such states, in possession of unconventional weapons, might not be deterred. The
National Security Strategy of 2002 discusses this problem on page 15.

96. Bush, "State of the Union Address 2004."

97. Nikolas Gvosdev, "Restoring American Credibility," *National Interest*, 25 June 2003,
http://www.inthenationalinterest.com/Articles/Vol2Issue25/Vol2Issue25Gvosdevpfv.html.
For a skeptical discussion of North Korea's nuclear program, see Selig S. Harrison, "Did
North Korea Cheat?" *Foreign Affairs* 84 (January/February 2005): 99–110.

CHAPTER 7. ON JUSTIFYING THE FIRST BLOW

1. For further discussion, see Robert Holmes, *On War and Morality* (Princeton, N.J.: Princeton University Press, 1989); Jenny Teichman, *Pacifism and the Just War* (Oxford: Oxford University Press, 1986); and Michael Walzer, *Just and Unjust Wars* (New York: Basic Books, 1977).

2. US White House, "National Security Strategy."

3. See Arthur Schlesinger Jr., "Eyeless in Iraq," *New York Review of Books*, 23 October 2003, http://www.nybooks.com/articles/article-preview?article_id=16677; Charles Knight, "First Strike Guidelines: The Case of Iraq," Project on Defense Alternatives Briefing Memo 25, 16 September 2002, revised and updated 10 March 2003; Neta Crawford, "The Best Defense: The Problem with Bush's 'Preemptive' War Doctrine," *Boston Review* (February/March 2003), http://www.bostonreview.net/BR28.1/crawford.html; and Charles Knight, "Essential Elements Missing in the National Security Strategy of 2002," Commonwealth Institute Project on Defense Alternatives Commentary (November 2002), http://www.comw.org/qdr/0210knight.html.

4. See Noam Chomsky, "Preventive War: 'The Supreme Crime,'" *ZNet*, 11 August 2003.

5. Noam Chomsky, *Hegemony or Survival* (New York: Metropolitan Books, 2003), 12.

6. See Volker Kröning, "Prevention or Preemption? Towards a Clarification of Terminology," Commonwealth Institute Project on Defense Alternatives Guest Commentary (March 2003), http://www.comw.org/pda/0303kroening.html.

7. See Lawrence Freedman, "Prevention, Not Preemption," *Washington Quarterly* (Spring 2003): 105–14.

8. US White House, "National Security Strategy."

9. Cited in Clarke, *Against All Enemies*, 266.

10. Clarke, *Against All Enemies*, 266.

11. Bush, "Saddam Hussein Must Leave Iraq."

12. This idea is specifically supported by Clarke in *Against All Enemies.*

13. See Ivo Daalder, James M. Lindsay, and James Steinberg, "The Bush National Security Strategy: An Evaluation," *Brookings Policy Brief* 109 (October 2002), http://www.brookings.edu/comm/policybriefs/pb109.htm.

14. According to Jürgen Habermas, the idea of mutual understanding rooted in language provides for the consensus about democratic will formation and law that undergird the modern state. See Jürgen Habermas, "Wahrheitstheorien," in *Wirklichkeit und Reflexion: Festschrift für Walter Schulz* (Pfullingen: Neske, 1973), 211–65; see also Jürgen Habermas, *Theory of Communicative Action*, vol. 2, trans. Thomas McCarthy (Boston: Beacon Press, 1984): 96; and Jürgen Habermas, *Philosophical Discourse of Modernity: Twelve Lectures*, trans. Frederick G. Lawrence (Cambridge, Mass.: MIT Press, 1987), 344–45.

15. See Noam Chomsky, "After Pinkville," *New York Review of Books*, 1 January 1970, http://www.nybooks.com/articles/article-preview?article_id=11087.

16. For the view that Christianity and war are compatible, not incompatible, since just war theory expresses the Christian view of moral and political responsibility, see Paul Ramsey, *The Just War: Force and Political Responsibility* (New York: Scribner's, 1968).

17. See Garry Wills, "The Tragedy of Bill Clinton," *New York Review of Books*, 12 August 2004, 64.

18. This practice was rejected by the U.S. Supreme Court. See Ronald Dworkin, "What the Court Really Said," *New York Review of Books*, 12 August 2004, 26–29.

19. See Chomsky, *Hegemony or Survival.*

20. Condoleezza Rice, "A Balance of Power that Favors Freedom," *U.S. Foreign Policy Agenda* (December 2002), http://usinfo.state.gov/journals/itps/1202/ijpe/ijpe1202.pdfsid 14901231.

CHAPTER 8. INTELLIGENCE IN PREVENTIVE MILITARY STRATEGY

1. Neither the nuclear-based defenses of the extensive and long-lasting Moscow ABM system nor the short-lived U.S. Safeguard/Sprint ABM system was considered capable of assuring that the offensive missiles of the other superpower would not penetrate their shields. There is so far little reason to believe that the untested developmental ABM system recently deployed in Alaska could reliably counter even the most rudimentary potential threat from North Korea.

2. See, for example, Harrison Salisbury, *War between Russia and China* (New York: Norton, 1969).

3. Bernard Brodie, *War and Strategy in the Missile Age* (Princeton, N.J.: Princeton University Press, 1959), 227–28.

4. Henry A. Kissinger, "Military Policy and the Defense of 'Gray Areas,'" *Foreign Affairs* 33 (April 1955): 416.

5. Brodie, *War and Strategy*, 228.

6. George W. Bush, "President Delivers 'State of the Union,'" 28 January 2003, 8, http://www.whitehouse.gov/news/releases/2003/01/20030128-19.html.

7. See, for example, Anatoli I. Gribkov and William Y. Smith, *Operation ANADYR: U.S. and Soviet Generals Recount the Cuban Missile Crisis* (Chicago: Edition Q, 1994).

8. Greg Thielmann, "Rumsfeld Reprise? The Missile Report That Foretold the Iraq Intelligence Controversy," *Arms Control Today* (July/August 2003): 3–9.

9. United States, National Intelligence Council, September 1999 National Intelligence Estimate, "Foreign Missile Developments and the Ballistic Missile Threat Through 2015," unclassified summary, December 2001, 9, http://www.cia.gov/nic/PDF_GIF_otherprod/missilethreat2001.pdf.

10. See Daniel Ellsberg, *Secrets: A Memoir of Vietnam and the Pentagon Papers* (New York: Viking, 2002), 7–20; *The Pentagon Papers* (New York: *New York Times*, 1971), 234–306.

11. See Ellsberg, *Secrets*, 7–20; *Pentagon Papers*, 234–306.

12. US Senate Select Committee on Intelligence, *Prewar Assessments*.

13. United States, Central Intelligence Agency, "Statement by David Kay on the Interim Progress Report on the Activities of the Iraq Survey Group (ISG) before the House Permanent Select Committee on Intelligence, the House Committee on Appropriations, Subcommittee on Defense, and the Senate Select Committee on Intelligence," 2 October 2003, http://www.cia.gov/cia/public_affairs/speeches/2003/david_kay_10022003.html; "Comprehensive Report of the Special Advisor to the DCI on Iraq's WMD," 30 September 2004, http://www.cia.gov/cia/reports/iraq_wmd_2004.

14. United States, National Intelligence Council, October 2002 National Intelligence Estimate, "Iraq's Continuing Programs for Weapons of Mass Destruction," declassified excerpts, 18 July 2003, 4, http://www.fas.org/irp/cia/product/iraq-wmd.html (hereafter cited as October 2002 NIE on Iraqi WMD).

15. US NIC, October 2002 NIE on Iraqi WMD, declassified excerpts, 1.

16. US Senate Select Intelligence Committee, *Prewar Assessments*, 14.

17. Paul Wolfowitz, "Deputy Secretary Wolfowitz Interview with Karen DeYoung, *Washington Post*, May 28, 2003," US Department of Defense News Transcript, http://www.defenselink.mil/cgi-bin/dlprin.cgi?.

18. See also Rodger Payne's description in chapter 6 in this volume of how inflation of the nuclear threat distorted the public debate.

19. US NIC, October 2002 NIE on Iraqi WMD, declassified excerpts, 1.

20. US NIC, October 2002 NIE on Iraqi WMD, declassified excerpts, 1, emphasis added.

21. George Tenet, "Transcript of Tenet Address on WMD Intelligence," 5 February 2004, 7, http://www.cnn.com/2004/US/02/05/tenet.transcript.ap/index.html.

22. Tenet, "Transcript," 8.

23. US NIC, October 2002 NIE on Iraqi WMD, declassified excerpts, 1.

24. US Senate Select Intelligence Committee, *Prewar Assessments*, 129.

25. US NIC, October 2002 NIE on Iraqi WMD, declassified excerpts, 2.

26. US Senate Select Intelligence Committee, *Prewar Assessments*, 217.

27. US Senate Select Intelligence Committee, *Prewar Assessments*, 218.

28. George Tenet, "The Worldwide Threat in 2003: Evolving Dangers in a Complex World," DCI's Worldwide Threat Briefing, 11 February 2003, 2, http://www.cia.gov/cia/public_affairs/speeches/dci_speech_02112003.html.

29. US NIC, October 2002 NIE on Iraqi WMD, declassified excerpts, 2, emphasis added.

30. US NIC, October 2002 NIE on Iraqi WMD, declassified excerpts, 2.

31. US Senate Select Intelligence Committee, *Prewar Assessments*, 230.

32. US NIC, October 2002 NIE on Iraqi WMD, declassified excerpts, 7.

33. US Senate Select Intelligence Committee, *Prewar Assessments*, 235.

34. US Senate Select Intelligence Committee, *Prewar Assessments*, 236.

35. US Senate Select Intelligence Committee, *Prewar Assessments*, 236.

36. US Senate Select Intelligence Committee, *Prewar Assessments*, 237.

37. US Senate Select Intelligence Committee, *Prewar Assessments*, 237.

38. Bill Nelson, statement, *Congressional Record*, 28 January 2004, S311.

39. Hans Blix, *Disarming Iraq* (New York: Pantheon Books, 2004), 265–66.

40. Paul Wolfowitz, Department of Defense transcript of Sam Tannenhaus interview with Deputy Secretary of Defense Wolfowitz, 9 May 2003, http://www.defenselink.mil/transcripts/2003/tr20030510.

41. United States, White House, "The National Security Strategy of the United States of America," September 2002, 16, http://www.whitehouse.gov/nsc/nss.pdf.

42. US White House, "National Security Strategy," 15.

43. US National Commission on Terrorist Attacks, *9/11 Commission Report*.

CHAPTER 9. MILITARY CAPABILITIES

1. John Lewis Gaddis, *Surprise, Security, and the American Experience* (Cambridge, Mass.: Harvard University Press, 2004), 86–88.

2. There is also a necessary and intimately related corollary question: does the United States have the intelligence capabilities necessary to sustain a doctrine of preemption over time? I will leave this question to other contributors given the limits of time and space.

3. For a firsthand account of the Kosovo campaign, see Wesley K. Clark, *Waging Modern War: Bosnia, Kosovo, and the Future of Combat* (New York: Public Affairs Press, 2001). On Iraq, see Williamson Murray and Robert H. Scales Jr., *The Iraq War: A Military History* (Cambridge, Mass.: Harvard University Press, 2003).

4. Donald C. F. Daniel, Peter Dombrowski, and Rodger A. Payne, "The Bush Doctrine: Rest in Peace?" *Defence Studies* 4 (Summer 2004): 18–39.

5. On why preemption will remain a policy option even as the "Bush Doctrine" per se is no longer tenable, see Daniel, Dombrowski, and Payne, "Bush Doctrine Is Dead," 199–212.

6. This chapter is not intended to support the doctrine of preventive military intervention or, in particular, a strategy of preventive war. Elsewhere and in forthcoming publications I have argued against the doctrine and its application as well as considered the negative global reaction to the idea of preemption. Yet as the attacks of 9/11 demonstrated, the dangers

faced by the United States are great. See Peter Dombrowski, "Against Pre-emptive Strikes," Information Technology, War and Peace Project Web site, 19 August 2002, http://www .watsoninstitute.org/infopeace/911/index.cfm?id=11#; and Dombrowski and Payne, "Global Debate."

7. Dombrowski and Payne, "Global Debate."

8. I leave discussion of intelligence capabilities to Greg Thielmann, whose chapter in this volume provides important context for my analysis, since to be blunt, military force is useless without information about what, where, and whom to target. For example, to implement preventive military action, the United States must know what regimes constitute "rogues," what terrorist groups have "global reach," and where both rogues and terrorists locate key facilities (for example, NBC research laboratories, terrorist training facilities, safe houses for key officials, and so on).

9. The term "rogue" state is controversial and not compatible with the perspectives of the volume editors and many other chapter authors. I prefer the term, however, even as I understand the intellectual and policy baggage it brings to our analysis. For better or worse, "rogue" state is the term of art among policy-makers and policy wonks. On the origins of the term, see Robert S. Litwak, *Rogue States and US Foreign Policy: Containment after the Cold War* (Washington, D.C.: Woodrow Wilson Center Press, 2000), 19–46.

10. Richard N. Haass, "Wars of Choice," *Washington Post*, 23 November 2003.

11. Steve Coll, *Ghost Wars: The Secret History of the CIA, Afghanistan, and Bin Laden, from the Soviet Invasion to September 10, 2001* (New York: Penguin Books, 2004); US National Commission on Terrorist Attacks, *9/11 Commission Report*.

12. For an official summary of Operation Northern Watch, see http://www.eucom.mil/ Directorates/ECPA/index.htm?http://www.eucom.mil/Directorates/ECPA/Operations/ onw/onw.htm&2.

13. Clark, *Waging Modern War*, 348.

14. For the theory underlying this approach, see Ullmann and Wade, *Shock and Awe*.

15. Robert Burns, "Peacekeeping Institute May Shut Down," Associated Press Wire, 11 March 2002, Lexis-Nexis news wire database, http://www.lexis-nexis.com.

16. James Jay Carafano, "Post-Conflict Operations from Europe to Iraq," Heritage Foundation Lecture (July 2004), http://www.heritage.org/Research/NationalSecurity/ loader.cfm?url=/commonspot/security/getfile.cfm&PageID=66346.

17. For a strong defense of this position emphasizing that militaries of other states might do operations other than war, but the United States as the sole superpower should not, see John Hillen, "Superpowers Don't Do Windows," in *America the Vulnerable: Our Military Problems and How To Fix Them*, ed. John Lehman and Harvey Sicherman (Philadelphia: Foreign Policy Research Institute, 2002), http://www.fpri.org/americavulnerable/03. SuperpowersDontDoWindows.Hillen.pdf.

18. For the best nearly contemporaneous accounts of preparations for the postwar period, see James Fallows, "The Fifty-first State?" *Atlantic Monthly*, November 2002, 53–64; and, after the war, James Fallows, "Blind into Baghdad," *Atlantic Monthly*, January/February 2004, 53–74.

19. David Reiff, "Blueprint for a Mess," *New York Times*, 2 November 2003.

20. Tommy Franks with Malcolm McConnell, *American Soldier* (New York: Regan-Books, 2004). On postwar planning, see esp. 351–52, 393, 419–24.

21. Dana Priest, *The Mission: Waging War and Keeping Peace with America's Military* (New York: W. W. Norton, 2003).

22. John R. Bolton, "Beyond the Axis of Evil: Additional Threats from Weapons of Mass Destruction," Remarks to the Heritage Foundation, Washington, D.C., 6 May 2002, http://www.state.gov/t/us/rm/9962.htm.

23. Paul Kerr, "Libya Vows to Dismantle WMD Program," *Arms Control Today* (January/February 2004): 29–30.

24. Paul Kerr, "IAEA: Questions Remain about Libya," *Arms Control Today* (July/August 2004): 28.

25. Kelly Wallace, "White House Repeats 'Concerns' about Cuba, Biological Weapons," CNN, 14 May 2002, http://www.cnn.com/2002/ALLPOLITICS/05/14/white.house.cuba/.

26. Kori N. Schake and Justin P. Bernier, "Dealing with Rogue States" in *The Global Century: Globalization and National Security*, vol. 1, ed. Richard L. Kugler and Ellen L. Frost (Washington, D.C.: National Defense University Press, 2002), 283–97, http://www.ndu.edu/inss/books/Books_2001/Global%20Century%20-%20June%202001/globcen cont.html.

27. See Robert A. Manning, "Triumph of the Periphery," *Washington Times*, 28 June 1999.

28. Kenneth M. Pollack, *Arabs at War: Military Effectiveness, 1948–1991* (Lincoln: University of Nebraska Press, 2002), 4.

29. Charles Krauthammer, "Axis of Evil, Part Two," *Washington Post*, 23 July 2004.

30. Krauthammer, "Axis of Evil."

31. By most accounts, Iraq drew the bile of neoconservative foreign policy analysts since President George H. W. Bush decided to stand down the American military rather than topple Hussein in 1991. See Mann, *Rise of the Vulcans*.

32. Steven Ekovich, "Iran and New Threats in the Persian Gulf and Middle East," *Orbis* 48 (Winter 2004): 71–87.

33. Sammy Salama and Karen Ruster, "A Preemptive Attack on Iran's Nuclear Forces: Possible Consequences," CNS Research Story, 12 August 2004, 3–4, http://cns.miis.edu/pubs/week/040812.htm.

34. "Syria in the Hot Seat," ABC News, 15 April 2004, http://abcnews.go.com.

35. Barry James, "Syria Warned—Perle Sees More 'Preemption' in Future," *International Herald Tribune*, 12 April 2003.

36. Pollack, *Arabs at War*, 549–51.

37. Michael M. Bennet, "The Syrian Military: A Primer," *Middle East Intelligence Bulletin* (August/September 2001), http://www.meib.org/articles/0108_s1.htm.

38. Anthony Cordesman, *The Military Balance in the Middle East* (Westport, Conn.: Praeger, 2004), 150–55.

39. Claudia Baumgart and Harald Müller, "Nuclear Weapons–Free Zone in the Middle East: A Pie in the Sky?" *Washington Quarterly* 28 (Winter 2005): 46.

40. Thomas Barnett of the Naval War College has been an unabashed proponent of the United States assuming the role of "global policeman." See Richard Salit, "Finally, His Vision Finds an Audience," *Providence (R.I.) Journal*, 2 March 2003, http://www.projo.com /news/content/projo_20030302_barnett2.c0fd3.html. For a more complete exposition of his views, see Thomas P. M. Barnett, *The Pentagon's New Map* (New York: Putnam, 2004).

41. Joseph Nye, *The Paradox of American Power* (London: Oxford University Press, 2000).

42. In particular, see Greg Theilmann, "Intelligence in Preventive Military Strategy," this volume.

43. Mary Kaldor, *New and Old Wars: Organized Violence in a Global Era* (Palo Alto, Calif.: Stanford University Press, 1999).

44. As to how and why, see James Dobbins et al., *America's Role in Nation-Building: From Germany to Iraq* (Santa Monica, Calif.: Rand, 2003).

45. Niall Ferguson, *Empire: The Rise and Decline of the British World Order and the Lessons for Global Power* (New York: Basic Books, 2003), see esp. 361–62, 367–70.

46. Niall Ferguson, "The Empire Slinks Back," *New York Times Magazine*, 27 April 2003, 52–57.

47. Thomas P. M. Barnett, "Mr. President, Here's How to Make Sense of Our Iraq Strategy," *Esquire*, June 2004, 148.

48. Peter Singer, "War, Profits and the Vacuum of Law: Privatized Military Firms and International Law," *Columbia Journal of Transnational Law* 42 (Spring 2004): 521–50.

49. Singer, "Vacuum of Law," 523.

50. Peter Singer, *Corporate Warriors: The Rise of the Privatized Military Industry* (Ithaca, N.Y.: Cornell University Press, 2003). On the history, see 19–39; on why, see 49–72.

51. David C. Gompert, Richard L. Kugler, and Marin C. Libicki, *Mind the Gap: Promoting a Transatlantic Revolution in Military Affairs* (Washington, D.C.: National Defense University Press, 1999).

52. Fallows, "Fifty-first State?" 53; Fallows, "Blind into Baghdad," 52.

CHAPTER 10: A SHEEP IN WOLF'S CLOTHING?

1. US White House, "National Security Strategy."

2. See, for instance, Madeleine Albright, "Bridges, Bombs, or Bluster?" *Foreign Affairs* 82 (September/October 2003): 2–19; Wesley Clark, "Broken Engagement," *Washington Monthly* 36 (May 2004): 26–33; Brent Scowcroft, "Don't Attack Saddam: It Would Undermine Our Anti-Terror Efforts," *Wall Street Journal*, 15 August 2002, http://www.opinionjournal.com/editorial/feature.html?id=110002133.

3. For instance, Thomas Friedman, "Take France Off the Security Council: India, the World's Largest Democracy, Deserves a Seat as a Permanent Member," *Guardian* (London), 11 February 2003.

4. For instance, Charles A. Kupchan, "Continental Rift," *Newark (N.J.) Star-Ledger*, 27 April 2003, http://www.cfr.org/pub5910/charles_a_kupchang/continental_rift.php.

5. Ulrich Krotz, "National Role Conceptions and Foreign Policies: France and Germany Compared," Program for the Study of Germany and Europe Working Paper 02.1, Minda de Gunzburg Center for European Studies, Harvard University, Cambridge, Mass., 2002, http://www.ces.fas.harvard.edu/working_papers/GermanSeries.html.

6. "Iraq Sanctions Cannot Be Forever," *New York Times*, 1 August 1994. For the French perspective, see Eric Rouleau, "America's Unyielding Policy toward Iraq," *Foreign Affairs* 74 (January/February 1995): 59–72.

7. See Philip H. Gordon and Jeremy Shapiro, *Allies at War: America, Europe, and the Crisis over Iraq* (New York: McGraw-Hill, 2004), 77–78.

8. Stanley Hoffmann, *Decline or Renewal? France since the 1930s* (New York: Viking Press, 1974), esp. ch. 11.

9. An appreciation of this French concept of the "political" underscores just how misguided are the attacks on the French state as simply the lapdog of French oil interests. The concept is well depicted in Bertrand Badie, "Le jeu triangulaire," in *Sociologie des nationalismes*, ed. Pierre Birnbaum (Paris: Presses Universitaires de France, 1997).

10. Jacques Beltran, "French Policy toward Iraq," US-France Analysis Series, Center for the United States and France, Brookings Institution, Washington, D.C., September 2002, http://www.brookings.edu/fp/cuse/analysis/beltran.htm.

11. On the importance of such "Cartesian" thinking in French foreign policy generally as well as in the specific case of French Iraq policy, see Charles Cogan, *French Negotiating Behavior: Dealing with La Grande Nation* (Washington, D.C.: United States Institute of Peace Press, 2003).

12. Russia scotched the first "smart sanctions" proposal with a veto threat in June 2001, but after further negotiations the UN Security Council approved the new sanctions formula in May 2002.

13. "Iraq: Bagdad s'en prend à la France," *Le Figaro*, 22 May 2001.

14. See Robert Holloway, "Revision improbable des sanctions contre l'Irak après le discours de M. Bush," *Agence France Presse*, 27 November 2001.

15. The beginning of their cave-in was their immediate embrace of Bush's call for a return of international inspectors to Iraq as a precondition for lifting the sanctions. "Paris soutient les propos de Bush sur les inspecteurs, souhaite un accord," *Agence France Presse*, 27 November 2001.

16. Dominique de Villepin did not help matters by publishing an adulatory, 600-page account of Napoleon's "hundred days" in 2001. See David A. Bell, "Dominique de Villepin's Idea of Glory: The Napoleon Complex," *New Republic*, 14 April 2003, http://jhunix.hcf.jhu.edu/~dabell/villepin.htm.

17. There is a parallel here with a broader loss of national self-confidence among French elites in the 1980s and 1990s. For a powerful account of this trend, see the two essays by Perry Anderson, "Dégringolade," *London Review of Books*, 2 September 2004, 3–9, and "Union Sucrée," *London Review of Books*, 23 September 2004, 10–17.

18. Krotz, "National Role Conceptions."

19. Jolyon Howorth, "La France, L'Otan et la sécurité Européenne: Statu quo ingérable, renouveau introuvable?" *Politique Etrangère* 4 (2002): 1001–6.

20. Jean-Marie Colombani, "Nous sommes tous Américains," *Le Monde*, 13 September 2001.

21. Tom Lansford, "Whither Lafayette? French Military Policy and the American Campaign in Afghanistan," *European Security* 11 (Fall 2002): 126–46.

22. Howorth, "La France."

23. See Cogan, *French Negotiating Behavior*, 197–205; Gordon and Shapiro, *Allies at War*, 108–14; and Woodward, *Plan of Attack*, 220–27.

24. French UN Ambassador Jean-David Levitte, cited in Cogan, *French Negotiating Behavior*, 199.

25. George W. Bush, quoted in Woodward, *Plan of Attack*, 227.

26. De Villepin, cited in Gordon and Shapiro, *Allies at War*, 104.

27. "Jacques Chirac: French Leader Offers America both Friendship and Criticism," interview excerpts published in the *New York Times*, 9 September 2002.

28. At a meeting in Washington, D.C., the day the Chirac interview was published, Deputy Secretary of State Richard Armitage noted what he termed the French evolution in the right direction. Patrick Jarreau, Sylvie Kauffmann, and Corinne Lesnes, "Paris-Washington: Les dessous d'une rupture," *Le Monde*, 27 March 2003.

29. Jarreau, Kauffmann, and Lesnes, "Paris-Washington."

30. Cogan, *French Negotiating Behavior*, 206–7.

31. Jarreau, Kauffmann, and Lesnes, "Paris-Washington."

32. Gordon and Shapiro, *Allies at War*, 120.

33. Much has been made of the bad British and American intelligence about the state of Saddam Hussein's illicit weapons programs; but equally bad was French intelligence about the state of British and American military preparations. Of course, these preparations had been intentionally dissimulated by the military and the administration through the summer and fall of 2002, but the deeper sources of the French failure lie in the continuing inability of French officials to get inside, or even to understand, the circles of power in Washington. See Stanley Hoffmann, *L'Amérique vraiment impériale? Entretiens sur le vif avec Frédéric Bozo* (Paris: Audibert, 2003), 18–25. On the dissimulation of the military preparations, see Woodward, *Plan of Attack*, 83–84.

34. Woodward, *Plan of Attack*, 284–85.

35. Marc Champion, Charles Fleming, Ian Johnson, and Carla Anne Robbins, "Allies at Odds: Behind US Rifts with Europeans," *Wall Street Journal*, 3 April 2003.

36. Hoffmann, *L'Amérique vraiment impériale?* 86–87.

37. See, for instance, William Safire, "Bad Herr Dye," *New York Times*, 23 January 2003.

38. Gordon and Shapiro, *Allies at War*, 173.

39. Quoted in John Kampfner, *Blair's Wars* (London: Free Press, 2003), 289.

40. This is not to suggest that the American stance was static during this period.

41. Karl Kaiser and Hans Maull, quoted in Anne-Marie le Gloannec, "Germany's Power and the Weakening of States in a Globalized World: Deconstructing a Paradox," *German Politics* 10 (April 2001): 118.

42. A penetrating and prescient article on this topic is Harald Mueller and Thomas Risse-Kappen, "Origins of Estrangement: The Peace Movement and the Changed Image of America in West Germany," *International Security* 12 (Summer 1987): 52–88.

43. Author's interview with a German journalist who was present for Schröder's private remarks, Cambridge, Mass., November 2003.

44. Gordon and Shapiro, *Allies at War*, 126.

45. Ulrich Krotz, "Structure as Process: The Regularized Intergovernmentalism of Franco-German Bilateralism," Program for the Study of Germany and Europe Working Paper 02.3, Minda de Gunzburg Center for European Studies, Harvard University, 2002.

46. Jeremi Suri, *Power and Protest: Global Revolution and the Rise of Détente* (Cambridge, Mass.: Harvard University Press, 2003), 60.

47. Krotz, "Structure as Process," 3.

48. Krotz, "Structure as Process," 17.

49. One might also invoke France's nuclear arsenal here, but it is highly unclear that the force de frappe confers any prestige today. Certainly it does not do so in Germany.

50. See Alex Macleod, "French Policy toward the War in the Former Yugoslavia: A Bid for International Leadership," *International Journal* 52 (Spring 1997): 243–64.

51. On 16 March, Chirac floated the idea of a thirty-day deadline for Iraqi compliance, which the Americans and British immediately shot down. Gordon and Shapiro, *Allies at War*, 154.

52. In Condoleezza Rice's notorious formulation, the US postwar policy has been to "forgive the Russians, ignore the Germans, and punish the French." Condoleezza Rice, quoted in "US-German Ties on the Mend," *Deutsche Welle*, 27 February 2004, http://www.dw-world.de/english/0,3367,1430_A_1124825,00.html.

53. Charles Grant, "Iraq War: Iraq Post-Mortem 1," *Prospect*, 19 May 2003. This story has been confirmed by France's UN ambassador of the period, Jean-David Levitte. See Cogan, *French Negotiating Behavior*, 210–11.

54. Woodward, *Plan of Attack*, 297.

55. Gordon and Shapiro, *Allies at War*, 148.

56. Hoffmann, *L'Amérique vraiment impériale?* 29–30.

57. Interview with Christopher Meyer (British ambassador to the US until February 2003) for *Frontline* program "Blair's War," http://www.pbs.org/wgbh/pages/frontline/shows/blair/interviews/meyer.html. This section was also enriched by off-the-record comments of Inocencio Arias, Spain's UN ambassador during this period, at the Minda de Gunzburg Center for European Studies, Harvard University, March 2004.

58. Grant, "Iraq War."

59. As could Bush and his allies, who coined the notorious term "freedom fries."

60. Woodward, *Plan of Attack*, 297, emphasis added.

61. Kampfner, *Blair's Wars*, 288.

62. Kampfner, *Blair's Wars*, 253.

63. Stefaan Walgrave, "Transnational Movements and National Opportunities: The Case of the Worldwide Anti-Iraqi War Protest on February 15th, 2003," paper presented at the Annual Meeting of the American Political Science Association, Chicago, September 2004.

64. It was also a dangerous game, for the street is fickle and often casts down its former idols—as de Gaulle himself experienced. Suri, *Power and Protest*, 194.

65. Kampfner, *Blair's Wars*, 254.

66. The first letter was signed by EU members or soon-to-be members Britain, the Czech Republic, Denmark, Hungary, Italy, Poland, Portugal, and Spain. The second was signed by NATO applicants Albania, Bulgaria, Croatia, Estonia, Latvia, Lithuania, Macedonia, Slovakia, Slovenia, and Romania.

67. Gordon and Shapiro, *Allies at War*, 134.

68. Attila Agh, "Smaller and Bigger States in the EU 25: The Eastern Enlargement and Decision-Making in the EU," *Perspectives: Central European Review of International Affairs* 21 (Winter 2003/4): esp. 5–6.

69. Kampfner, *Blair's Wars*, 12.

70. This was symbolized by their joint presentation of the "Third Way" document in June 1999, and by the subsequent success of "Third Way" ideas at the 2000 Lisbon European summit.

71. Britain's meteoric rise in Brussels can only be sustained by a continued demonstration of commitment to Europe, which in turn requires an American foreign policy that encourages rather than undermines the goal of integration, for the Franco-German "motor" still has some gas in it.

72. John Leicester, "Europe Remembers Rice's 'Punish France' Quip," Associated Press Online, 16 November 2004, Lexis-Nexis news wire database, http://www.lexis-nexis.com.

73. I made similar points with respect to Washington's misperceptions on the birth of the euro in "Raízes do eurocepticismo Americano: As consequências perceptivas da identidade nacional" (Roots of American Euroskepticism: The Perceptual Consequences of National Identity), *Estratégia: Revista de Estudos Internacionais*, No. 17 (Lisbon: Instituto de Estudos Estratégicos e Internacionais, 2002).

74. Anne-Marie Slaughter, *A New World Order* (Princeton, N.J.: Princeton University Press, 2004).

CHAPTER 11. PROMOTING PRACTICAL ALTERNATIVES

1. US White House, "National Security Strategy."

2. US White House, "National Security Strategy," 15.

3. George W. Bush, "President Bush Outlines Iraqi Threat," Remarks by President Bush on Iraq, Cincinnati Museum Center–Cincinnati Union Terminal, Cincinnati, Ohio, 7 October 2002, www.whitehouse.gov/news/releases/2002/10/20021007-8.html.

4. George W. Bush, "Excerpts from the State of the Union Regarding Iraq," 28 January 2003, www.whitehouse.gov/news/releases/2003/01/20030128-23.html.

5. Bush, " Saddam Hussein Must Leave Iraq."

6. Bush, "State of the Union Excerpts."

7. Thomas Powers, "The Vanishing Case for War," *New York Review of Books*, 4 December 2003, 5, http://www.nybooks.com/articles/16813.

8. Blix, *Disarming Iraq*, 69.

9. Charles Duelfer, *Comprehensive Report of the Special Advisor to the DCI on Iraq's WMD*, 30 September 2004, Key Findings, 11, 13, 17, http://www.cia.gov/cia/reports/iraq_wmd_2004/

10. "Bush: WMD Not the Issue," *St. Petersburg Times*, 8 October 2004; Warren P. Strobel and Matt Stearns, "No Weapons, No Matter; Saddam Aims Seen as Justifying War," *Seattle Times*, 8 October 2004; Kenneth Bazinet and Richard Sisk, "Prez: Wrong but Right; No WMD Then, but Woulda Been in Time," *New York Daily News*, 8 October 2004.

11. Thielmann, "Rumsfeld Reprise?" 6.

12. Dana Milbank and Walter Pincus, "As Rationales for War Erode, Issue of Blame Looms Large," *Washington Post*, 10 July 2004.

13. Thomas H. Kean and Lee H. Hamilton, *The 9/11 Commission Report: Final Report of the National Commission on Terrorist Attacks upon the United States* (New York: Norton, 2004), 228–29.

14. United States, Senate Select Committee on Intelligence, *Report on the US Intelligence Community's Prewar Intelligence Assessments on Iraq*, 7 July 2004, 345–47, www.intelligence .senate.gov/ iraqreport.pdf.

15. Richard W. Stevenson and David E. Sanger, "Stump Speech Re-tooled, Bush Goes on Attack," *New York Times*, 7 October 2004.

16. Daniel Benjamin, "Iraq and al Qaeda Are Not Allies," *New York Times*, 30 September 2002.

17. A copy of the letter is reproduced at www.newamericancentury.org/iraqclintonletter .htm.

18. Ron Suskind, *The Price of Loyalty: George W. Bush, the White House, and the Education of Paul O'Neill* (New York: Simon and Schuster, 2004), 86.

19. Suskind, *Price of Loyalty*, 86.

20. Suskind, *Price of Loyalty*, 72.

21. Cirincione, Mathews, and Perkovich, *WMD in Iraq*, 50–51.

22. Bradley Graham, *Hit to Kill: The New Battle Over Shielding America from Missile Attack* (New York: Public Affairs Press, 2001), 43–44.

23. Thielmann, "Rumsfeld Reprise?"

24. Cahn, *Killing Détente*.

25. "Secret Downing Street Memo."

26. Mark Danner, "The Secret Way to War," *New York Review of Books*, 9 June 2005, http://www.nybooks.com/articles/18034.

27. "Secret Downing Street Memo."

28. Suskind, *Price of Loyalty*; Clarke, *Against All Enemies*, 30–33; Woodward, *Plan of Attack*, 1–4.

29. Arthur Schlesinger Jr., "Unilateral Preventive War: Illegitimate and Immoral," *Los Angeles Times*, 21 August 2002.

30. Richard Perle, Douglas Feith, and David Wurmser, "A Clean Break: A New Strategy for Securing the Realm," Institute for Advanced Strategic and Political Studies Paper, 8 July 1996, http://www.aaiusa.org/news/must_read_feith.htm.

31. For a copy of the letter, see www.newamericancentury.org/iraqclintonletter.htm.

32. Steven Kull, Clay Ramsay, Stefan Subias, and Evan Lewis, "US Public Beliefs on Iraq and the Presidential Election," Program on International Policy Attitudes Report, University of Maryland, College Park, 22 April 2004, www.pipa.org/IraqReport4?22?04.pdf.

33. Kull, "US Public Beliefs on Iraq," 13.

34. Roger Cohen, "Kerry Must-Sell: A Tough Foreign Policy," *New York Times*, 28 July 2004.

35. Robin Toner and Marjorie Connelly, "Bush's Support Tumbles on Major Issues," *New York Times*, 17 June 2005.

36. Congressional Budget Office, "Estimated Costs of Continuing Operations in Iraq and Other Operations of the Global War on Terrorism," Washington, D.C., 25 June 2004, 1–3. The Congressional Budget Office estimates Iraq-related costs at $165 billion through the

end of Fiscal Year 2005; an $82 billion emergency war supplemental passed in early 2005, the vast bulk of which was for operations for Iraq, puts the costs at well over $200 billion.

37. "Iraq Casualty Count," www.icasualties.org.oif.

38. Douglas Jehl, "Iraq May Be Prime Place for Training of Militants, CIA Report Concludes," *New York Times*, 22 June 2005.

39. "Fact Sheet: Edwards' Strategy of Prevention, Not Preemption," 15 December 2003, www.johnedwards2004.compage.asp?id=445.

40. John Kerry, "Speech to the 2004 Democratic Convention," Boston, www.JohnKerry .com/pressroom/speeches/spc_2004?0729.html.

41. United States, Department of Energy, Secretary of Energy Advisory Board, "A Report Card on the Department of Energy's Non-Proliferation Programs with Russia," 10 January 2001, http://www.ceip.org/files/projects/npp/pdf/DOERussiaTaskForceRe port011001.pdf.

42. Matthew Bunn, Anthony Wier, and John P. Holdren, "Controlling Nuclear Warheads and Materials: A Report Card and Action Plan," Project on Managing the Atom, Belfer Center for Science and International Affairs. John F. Kennedy School of Government, Harvard University, March 2003, www.nti.org/cnwm.

43. Graham Allison, *Nuclear Terrorism: The Ultimate Preventable Catastrophe* (New York: Times Books, 2004).

44. Richard Lugar, "Next Steps in Non-Proliferation Policy," *Arms Control Today* (December 2002), http://www.armscontrol.org/act/2002_12/lugar_dec02.asp.

45. Lopez and Cortright, "Containing Iraq."

46. Leon V. Sigal, "North Korea Is No Iraq: Pyongyang's Negotiating Strategy," *Arms Control Today* (December 2002), http://www.armscontrol.org/act/2002_12/sigal_dec02. asp. For a history of the early years of U.S.–North Korean negotiations, see Leon V. Sigal, *Disarming Strangers* (Princeton, N.J.: Princeton University Press, 1998).

47. International Atomic Energy Agency, at www.iaea.org, under "budgets"; Julian Borger, "1625 U.N. and U.S. Inspectors Spent Two Years Searching for Weapons in Iraq," *Guardian* (London), 7 October 2004.

48. Bush, "Address before a Joint Session of the Congress on the State of the Union, January 20, 2004," 94–101.

49. Leverett, "Why Libya Gave Up on the Bomb."

50. Center for Strategic and International Studies, "Resuscitating the Bioweapons Ban: U.S. Industry Plans for Treaty Monitoring," Washington, D.C., November 2004, 11–13.

51. Marcus Corbin and Miriam Pemberton, "Report of the Task Force on a Unified Security Budget for the United States, 2006," Foreign Policy in Focus/Center for Defense Information, March 2004, 14.

52. Corbin and Pemberton, "Unified Security Budget," 22–41.

53. Frida Berrigan and William D. Hartung, "U.S. Weapons at War 2005: Promoting Democracy or Fueling Repression?" World Policy Institute Special Report, June 2005, http://www.worldpolicy.org/projects/arms/reports/wawjune2005.html; William D. Hartung and Frida Berrigan, "Hypocritical U.S. Fight for 'Freedom': Bush Arms Repressive Regimes, Sends Guns to Nations in Conflict, Ties Aid to Support of America's Terror War," *Newsday*, 13 June 2005.

54. See John Feffer, "Supporting the Arms Industry: US Government Subsidies for the Arms Trade," in *Challenging Conventional Wisdom: Debunking Myths and Exposing the Risks of Arms Export Reform*, ed. Tamar Gabelnick and Rachel Stohl (Washington, D.C.: Federation of American Scientists/Center for Defense Information, 2003), 25–52.

55. William D. Hartung, *And Weapons for All* (New York: HarperCollins, 1995), 224–49; Michael Dobbs, "US Had Key Role in Iraq Buildup: Trade in Chemical Arms Allowed Despite Their Use on Iranians, Kurds," *Washington Post*, 30 December 2002.

CHAPTER 12. PREVENTIVE FORCE

1. George W. Bush, "President Bush Announces Major Combat Operations in Iraq Have Ended," Remarks by the President from the USS Abraham Lincoln, at sea off the coast of San Diego, Calif., 1 May 2003, http://www.whitehouse.gov/news/releases/2003/05/iraq/20030501-15.html.

2. A giant banner stating "Mission Accomplished" hung as a backdrop for President Bush's 1 May 2003 speech on the USS *Abraham Lincoln*.

3. Senator Chuck Hagel (R-NE), quoted in Kevin Whitelaw, Ilana Ozernoy, and Terence Samuel, "Hit by Friendly Fire," *US News and World Report*, 27 June 2005, 26.

4. Marc Sandalow, "A Growing Challenge to Bush on Iraq War; His Ratings Drop as a Few GOP Leaders Ask for Exit Strategy," *San Francisco Chronicle*, 19 June 2005; see also "Not Whether, but How, to Withdraw," *Economist*, 26 November 2005.

5. US White House, "National Security Strategy."

6. Karl-Heinz Kamp, "Preemption: Far from Forsaken," *Bulletin of the Atomic Scientists* (March/April 2005): 26–27.

7. Condoleezza Rice, quoted in Steven R. Weisman, "Preemption: Idea with a Lineage Whose Time Has Come," *New York Times*, 23 March 2003.

8. Daniel, Dombrowski, and Payne, "Bush Doctrine Is Dead," 202.

9. Guillaume Parmentier, quoted in Howard LaFranchi, "Diplomacy's New Muscle under Rice," *Christian Science Monitor*, 29 June 2005.

10. Condoleezza Rice, interview with British foreign secretary Jack Straw on the Jonathan Dimbleby Programme, ITV1, 1 April 2006, http://www.state.gov/secretary/rm/2006/63993.htm.

11. For further commentary on this point, see Reiter, "Preventive Attacks."

12. See Reiter, "Preventive Attacks."

13. Chris Matthews used this terminology in posing a question to Madeleine Albright on Hardball, MSNBC Transcript #041700cb.461, 17 April 2003, Lexis-Nexis news transcripts database, http://www.lexis-nexis.com.

14. Donald Rumsfeld, transcript of Handelsblatt interview with Secretary of Defense Rumsfeld, 3 February 2006, http://www.dod.mil/transcripts/2006/tr20060203-12518.html; see also Richard Cheney, "Vice President's Remarks to the American Israel Public Affairs Committee 2006 Policy Conference," Washington, D.C., 7 March 2006, http://www.whitehouse.gov/news/releases/2006/03/20060307-1.html.

15. Richard Clarke and Steven Simon, "Bombs That Would Backfire," *New York Times*, 16 April 2006.

16. George W. Bush, "President Discusses War on Terror at National Endowment for Democracy," 6 October 2005, http://www.whitehouse.gov/news/releases/2005/10/20051006-3.html.

17. Hadley, Remarks to the United States Institute of Peace.

18. George W. Bush, "President Discusses War on Terror at Naval Academy Commencement," 27 May 2005, http://www.whitehouse.gov/news/releases/2005/05/20050527.html.

19. James Kitfield, "Coercion and Preemption," *National Journal*, 28 May 2005, 1618–25.

20. United States, Chairman of the Joint Chiefs of Staff, "Doctrine for Joint Nuclear Operations," 15 March 2005, draft of Joint Publication 3-12, http://www.globalsecurity.org/wmd/library/policy/dod/jp3_12fc2.pdf.

21. Hans M. Kristensen, "The Role of U.S. Nuclear Weapons: New Doctrine Falls Short of Bush Pledge," *Arms Control Today* (September 2005), http://www.armscontrol.org/act/2005_09/Kristensen.asp.

22. Jeffrey Lewis, "Doctrine for Joint Nuclear Operations (Joint Publication 3-12)," *ArmsControlWonk* Weblog, 4 April 2005, http://www.armscontrolwonk.com/512/doctrine -for-joint-nuclear-operations-joint-publication-3-12.

23. David Ruppe, "Democrats Object to Nuclear Pre-Emption Doctrine," Global Security Newswire, 6 December 2005, http://www.nti.org/d_newswire/issues/2005_12 _6.html#3C1EA569; see also Jeffrey Lewis, "A Nuclear Doctrine That Doesn't Deter," *ArmsControlWonk* Weblog, 7 December 2005, http://www.armscontrolwonk.com/891/ a-nuclear-doctrine-that-doesnt-deter.

24. Dianne Feinstein et al., letter to Hon. George W. Bush, 5 December 2005, http:// www.house.gov/tauscher/Press2005/12-05-05.htm; see also Walter Pincus, "Pentagon Revises Nuclear Strike Plan," *Washington Post*, 11 September 2005.

25. William Arkin, "Not Just a Last Resort? A Global Strike Plan, with a Nuclear Option," *Los Angeles Times*, 15 May 2005.

26. On "earth-penetrating weapons," see David Hambling, "Bunker-Busters Set to Go Nuclear," *New Scientist*, 9 November 2002, 6–8; Bryan L. Fearey, Paul C. White, John St. Ledger, and John D. Immele, "An Analysis of Reduced Collateral Damage Nuclear Weapons," *Comparative Strategy* 22 (October 2003): 305–25; Jonathan Medalia, "'Bunker Busters': Sources of Confusion in the Robust Nuclear Earth Penetrator Debate," Congressional Research Service Report for Congress, 22 September 2004; Robert W. Nelson, "Nuclear Bunker Busters, Mini-Nukes, and the US Nuclear Stockpile," *Physics Today* 56 (November 2003): 32–38; and Roger Speed and Michael May, "Dangerous Doctrine," *Bulletin of the Atomic Scientists* 61 (March/April 2005): 38–49. In late 2005, the fate of the Robust Nuclear Earth Penetrator (RNEP) remained unclear. After reports that Congress terminated funding for the RNEP program in November 2005, US Air Force official Billy Mullins indicated that the DOD would continue developing the 5,000-pound bomb as a nuclear weapon. See Jeffrey Lewis, "RNEP Raises Its Ugly Head Again," *ArmsControlWonk* Weblog, 6 December 2005, http://www.armscontrolwonk.com/889/rnep-raises-its-ugly-head-again.

27. Arkin, "Global Strike Plan."

28. Seymour M. Hersh, "The Iran Plans," *New Yorker*, 17 April 2006, http://www .newyorker.com/fact/content/articles/060417fa_fact; see also Peter Baker, Dafna Linzer, and Thomas E. Ricks, "U.S. Is Studying Military Strike Options on Iran," *Washington Post*, 9 April 2006.

29. James O. Ellis, testimony, in United States, Senate Armed Services Committee, *Army Transformation*, Senate Hearing, 12 March 2003, Federal Document Clearing House, Lexis-Nexis congressional database, http://www.lexis-nexis.com; see also United States, Air Force Space Command, *Strategic Master Plan, FY '04 and Beyond*, 5 November 2002, http://www.peterson.af.mil/hqafspc/library/AFSPCPAOffice/Final%2004%20SMP-- Signed!.pdf.

30. Richard B. Myers, "Change of Command/Retirement Ceremony," Offutt Air Force Base, Omaha, Neb., 9 July 2004, http://www.jcs.mil/chairman/speeches/STRAT COM_change_command.html.

31. United States, Strategic Command, Strategic Deterrence Joint Operating Concept, February 2004, http://www.dtic.mil/futurejointwarfare/concepts/sd_joc_v1.doc.

32. Jeffrey Lewis, "Lift-Off for Space Weapons? Implications of the Department of Defense's 2004 Budget Request for Space Weaponization," Center for International and Security Studies Paper, University of Maryland, College Park, 21 July 2003, http://www .cissm.umd.edu/documents/spaceweapons.pdf.

33. Brown, *Illusion of Control*. For a more general theory of how "positive illusions" contribute to overconfidence and inadvertent warfare, see Dominic D. P. Johnson, *Over- confidence and War: The Havoc and Glory of Positive Illusions* (Cambridge, Mass.: Harvard University Press, 2004).

34. Jeffrey Record, "The Limits and Temptations of America's Conventional Primacy," *Survival* 47 (Spring 2005): 44.

35. William Arkin, "Despite Denials, U.S. Plans for War," *Washington Post*, 13 April 2006.

36. Rice, quoted in Weisman, "Preemption."

37. See Ervand Abrahamian, "Empire Strikes Back: Iran in U.S. Sights," in *Inventing the Axis of Evil*, ed. Andre Schiffrin (New York: New Press, 2004), 93–156; and Jim VandeHei, "Cheney Warns of Iran as a Nuclear Threat," *Washington Post*, 21 January 2005.

38. Joseph Cirincione, "Fool Me Twice," *Foreign Policy*, 27 March 2006, Web exclusive, http://www.foreignpolicy.com/story/cms.php?story_id=3416.

39. See Laura Rozen, "The Report They Forgot," *American Prospect*, 19 October 2005, Web exclusive, http://www.prospect.org/web/page.ww?section=root&name=ViewlWeb&articleId=10446; and "Press Conference with Senator Jay Rockefeller (D-WV), Senator Carl Levin (D-MI); and Senator Dianne Feinstein (D-CA)—Subject: Phase 2 Review of Prewar Intelligence," 4 November 2005, Federal News Service, Lexis-Nexis congressional database, http://www.lexis-nexis.com.

40. Paul R. Pillar, "Intelligence, Policy, and the War in Iraq," *Foreign Affairs* 85 (March/April 2006), http://www.foreignaffairs.org/20060301faessay85202/paul-r-pillar/in telligence-policy-and-the-war-in-iraq.html. For details, see Paul Kerr, "Three Years Later, Iraq Investigations Continue," *Arms Control Today* (April 2006), http://www.armscontrol .org/act/2006_04/iraqinvestcont.asp.

41. John D. Rockefeller IV, Carl Levin, and Dianne Feinstein, letter to Bill Frist and Harry Reid, 14 November 2005, http://thinkprogress.org/wp-images/upload/Intel_Letter .pdf.

42. Jay Solomon, "Battle Looms over Use of Prewar Iraq Intelligence," *Wall Street Journal*, 24 March 2006.

43. Sarah Baxter, "Adwoman Leads the Global Battle for Hearts and Minds," *Sunday Times* (London), 5 January 2003.

44. See Brian D. Dailey and Patrick J. Parker, eds., *Soviet Strategic Deception* (Lexington, Mass.: D. C. Heath, 1987); Donald C. Daniel and Katherine Hebig, eds., *Strategic Military Deception* (New York: Pergamon Press, 1982); Michael I. Handel, "Intelligence and the Problem of Strategic Surprise," *Journal of Strategic Studies* 7 (1984): 229–81; Ronald Seth, *The Truth Benders: Psychological Warfare in the Second World War* (London: Leslie Frewin, 1969); and Barton Whaley, *Codeword Barbarossa* (Cambridge, Mass.: MIT Press, 1973).

45. William M. Arkin, "Defense Strategy: The Military's New War of Words," *Los Angeles Times*, 24 November 2002.

46. Arkin, "Defense Strategy."

47. On the psychological operations–CNN connection, see Rachel Coen, "Behind the Pentagon's Propaganda Plan," *Extra! Update* (April 2002), http://www.fair.org/extra/0204/ osi.html. For a description of the psychological operations mission at Firdos Square, see, in addition to the discussion in chapter 1 of this volume, Fontenot, Degen, and Tohn, *On Point*.

48. Secretary Donald H. Rumsfeld, Media Availability En Route to Chile, 18 November 2002, http://www.defenselink.mil/news/Nov2002/t11212002_t1118sd2.html.

49. Following Rumsfeld's comments, "the Pentagon increased spending on its psychological and influence operations and for the first time outsourced work to contractors. One beneficiary has been the Rendon Group, which won additional multimillion-dollar Pentagon contracts for media analysis and a media operations center in Baghdad, including 'damage control planning.' The new Lincoln Group was another winner." Jeff Gerth, "Military's Information War Is Vast and Often Secret," *New York Times*, 11 December 2005.

50. Jonathan S. Landay, "U.S. Military Pays Iraqis for Positive News Stories on War," Knight Ridder Newspapers, 30 November 2005, Lexis-Nexis news wire database, http://www.lexis-nexis.com; for related analysis, see James Bamford, "The Man Who Sold the War," *Rolling Stone*, 17 November 2005, 52–62.

51. Thomas E. Ricks, "Military Plays Up Role of Zarqawi," *Washington Post*, 10 April 2006. Ricks quotes army Colonel James A. Treadwell as saying that regarding the army's pursuit of domestic US propaganda: "We just don't do it." Yet Treadwell's further comment shows precisely how difficult it is to contain misinformation campaigns in the current global media environment: "With satellite television, e-mail and the Internet, it is impossible to prevent some carryover from propaganda campaigns overseas into the U.S. media. . . . [Such carryover is] not blowback, it's bleed-over. . . . There's always going to be a certain amount of bleed-over with the global information environment."

52. Lemnitzer, "Justification for US Military Intervention."

53. Don Van Natta Jr., "Bush Was Set on Path to War, Memo by British Adviser Says," *New York Times*, 27 March 2006.

54. Michael Handel, "A Runaway Deception: Soviet Disinformation and the Six-Day War, 1967," in *Deception Operations: Studies in the East-West Context*, ed. David A. Charters and Maurice A. J. Tugwell (London: Brassey's, 1990), 167.

55. Handel, "Runaway Deception," 167.

56. See Kamp, "Preemption," 27; Mann, *Rise of the Vulcans*, 406, 36n; Steve Andreason and Dennis Gormley, "Edging Ever Closer to a Nuclear Death Row," *Minneapolis Star-Tribune*, 29 March 2006.

57. Arthur M. Schlesinger Jr., *War and the American Presidency* (New York: W. W. Norton, 2004), 33; see also Bacevich, *New American Militarism*, 25–33.

58. Kaufmann, "Threat Inflation," 7; see also Chester A. Crocker, "A Dubious Template for US Foreign Policy," *Survival* 47 (Spring 2005): 51–70.

59. Peter R. Neumann and M.L.R. Smith, "Missing the Plot? Intelligence and Discourse Failure," *Orbis* (Winter 2005): 96.

60. Brown, *Illusion of Control*, 175–76.

61. See, for example, James S. Fishkin and Peter Laslett, eds., *Debating Deliberative Democracy* (London: Blackwell, 2003); John Forester, *The Deliberative Practitioner* (Cambridge, Mass.: MIT Press, 1999); and Charles Arthur Willard, *Liberalism and the Problem of Knowledge* (Chicago: University of Chicago Press, 1996).

62. Kaufmann, "Threat Inflation," 42–43.

63. On rhetorical invention in general, see Kendall R. Phillips, "Spaces of Invention: Dissension, Freedom and Thought in Foucault," *Philosophy and Rhetoric* 35 (2002): 328–44. For application of the concept "rhetorical invention" to a foreign policy context, see Jim A. Kuypers, "Hoyt Hopewell Hudson's Nuclear Rhetoric," in *Twentieth Century Roots of Rhetorical Studies*, ed. Jim A. Kuypers and Andrew King (New York: Praeger, 2001), 71–102.

64. Aristotle, *On Rhetoric: A Theory of Civic Discourse*, trans. George A. Kennedy (London: Oxford University Press, 1991), 188–89.

65. Eugene Garver, *Aristotle's Rhetoric: An Art of Character* (Chicago: University of Chicago Press, 1994), 79.

66. James Jasinski, *Sourcebook on Rhetoric: Key Concepts in Contemporary Rhetorical Studies* (Thousand Oaks, Calif.: Sage Publishing, 2001), 579. See also Ruth Anne Clark and Jesse Delia, "Topoi and Rhetorical Competence," *Quarterly Journal of Speech* 65 (April 1979): 195; and Richard E. Hughes, "The Contemporaneity of Classical Rhetoric," in *Landmark Essays on Rhetorical Invention in Writing*, ed. Richard E. Young and Yameng Liu (Davis, Calif.: Hermagoras Press, 1994), 39. For a contemporary effort to update the topoi,

see Karl R. Wallace, "Topoi and the Problem of Invention," *Quarterly Journal of Speech* 58 (December 1972): 387–96.

67. Aristotle, *On Rhetoric*, 53.

68. Brown, *Illusion of Control*, 154.

69. See Prados, *Hoodwinked*, 207–236; and Hanley, "Point by Point."

70. Kofi Annan, quoted in Colum Lynch, "Annan Warns U.S. Will Face Doubts," *Washington Post*, 7 February 2004.

71. Pillar, "Intelligence, Policy, and the War in Iraq."

72. Cheney, "Possible War with Iraq."

73. Lang, "Drinking the Kool-Aid," 42–48; Benjamin and Simon, *Next Attack*, 183; James Risen, *State of War: The Secret History of the CIA and the Bush Administration* (New York: Free Press, 2006): 75-76. For further discussion and explanation of the "stovepipe" metaphor, see Hersh, "Stovepipe."

74. George W. Bush, "President Discusses Freedom and Democracy in Iraq," George Washington University, Washington, D.C., 13 March 2006, http://www.whitehouse.gov/news/releases/2006/03/20060313-3.html.

75. Donald H. Rumsfeld and Peter Pace, "DOD News Briefing," Pentagon, Washington, D.C., 14 March 2006, http://www.defenselink.mil/transcripts/2006/tr20060314-12644.html.

76. US Commission on Intelligence Capabilities, *Report to the President*, 419.

77. Murray Waas, "What Bush Was Told about Iraq," *National Journal*, 2 March 2006, http://nationaljournal.com/about/njweekly/stories/2006/0302nj1.htm.

78. Patrick J. Fitzgerald, Government's Response to Defendant's Third Motion to Compel Discovery, *United States v. Libby*, filed 5 April 2006, U.S. District Court for the District of Columbia Case No. 05-394 (RBW); see also David E. Sanger and David Barstow, "Report Leaked by Cheney Aide Was in Dispute," *New York Times*, 9 April 2006; and Paul Pillar, "Great Expectations: Intelligence as Savior," *Harvard International Review* 27 (Winter 2006): 16-21.

79. See Prados, *Hoodwinked*, 93–104; Cirincione, Mathews, and Perkovich, *WMD in Iraq*; and US Senate Select Committee on Intelligence, *Prewar Assessments*.

80. Colin Powell, "Press Conference with Secretary of State Colin Powell Re: U.S. Reaction to Iraqi Arms Declaration," 19 December 2002, Federal News Service transcript, Lexis-Nexis news transcript database, http://www.lexis-nexis.com, emphasis added.

81. See Albright, "Iraq's Aluminum Tubes"; Cirincione, Mathews, and Perkovich, *WMD in Iraq*; and US Senate Select Committee, *Prewar Assessments*. One notable exception is Jonathan S. Landay, "CIA Report Reveals Analysts Split Over Extent of Iraqi Nuclear Threat," Knight Ridder Newspapers, 4 October 2002, Lexis-Nexis general news database, http://www.lexis-nexis.com. In key respects, this episode replays INR's role during the Vietnam War. A successful Freedom of Information Act request resulted in the 2004 release of documents showing that "INR's analysis on Vietnam stood out as tenaciously pessimistic from 1963 on, whether the question was the viability of the successive Saigon regimes, the Pentagon's statistical underestimation of enemy strength, the ultimate ineffectiveness of bombing the North, the persistence of the North Vietnamese and the Vietcong, or the danger of Chinese intervention." Former INR director Thomas Hughes contrasts INR's consistency with that "of leading actors who were hawks by day and doves by night." Hughes laments that "while we [in INR] were heeded, we were unable to persuade, sway, or prevail when it came to the ultimate decisions." Thomas L. Hughes, "INR's Vietnam Study in Context: A Retrospective Preface Thirty-five Years Later," National Security Archive, 2 May 2004, http://www.gwu.edu/~nsarchiv/NSAEBB/NSAEBB121/hughes.htm. On the exceptional role of the INR in resisting "communication pathologies" that plagued Vietnam War

intelligence analysis, see Robert P. Newman, "Communication Pathologies of Intelligence Systems," *Speech Monographs* 42 (1975): 279–80.

82. Pillar recommends one institutional reform that would bolster the proclivity of analysts to correct official mischaracterizations of intelligence reporting by political leaders: "On this point, the United States should emulate the United Kingdom, where discussion of this issue has been more forthright, by declaring once and for all that its intelligence services should not be part of public advocacy of policies still under debate. In the United Kingdom, Prime Minister Tony Blair accepted a commission of inquiry's conclusions that intelligence and policy had been improperly commingled in such exercises as the publication of the 'dodgy dossier,' the British counterpart to the United States' Iraqi WMD white paper, and that in the future there should be a clear delineation between intelligence and policy. An American declaration should take the form of a congressional resolution and be seconded by a statement from the White House. Although it would not have legal force, such a statement would discourage future administrations from attempting to pull the intelligence community into policy advocacy. It would also give some leverage to intelligence officers in resisting any such future attempts." Pillar, "Intelligence, Policy and the War."

83. See Douglas Jehl, "Report Warned Bush Team about Intelligence Suspicions," *New York Times*, 6 November 2005.

84. United States, Defense Intelligence Agency, DITSUM #044-02 (February 2002), declassified in Kathleen P. Turner, letter to Hon. John Rockefeller, 26 October 2005.

85. Michael Isikoff and Mark Hosenball, "Al Libi's Tall Tales," *Newsweek*, 10 November 2005, Web exclusive, http://www.msnbc.msn.com/id/9991919/site/newsweek/.

86. Walter Pincus, "Newly Released Data Undercut Prewar Claims Source Tying Baghdad, Al Qaeda Doubted," *Washington Post*, 6 November 2005.

87. George W. Bush, Interview by TVP, Poland, 29 May 2003, http://www.whitehouse.gov/g8/interview5.html.

88. Colin Powell, joint press availability with Italian foreign minister Franco Frattini, Rome, 2 June 2003, http://www.state.gov/secretary/former/powell/remarks/2003/21126.htm.

89. Joby Warrick, "Lacking Biolabs, Trailers Carried Case for War," *Washington Post*, 12 April 2006.

90. William Odom, *Fixing Intelligence: For a More Secure America* (New Haven, Conn.: Yale University Press, 2003), 186.

91. See Dana Milbank and Dana Priest, "Warning in Iraq Report Unread; Bush, Rice Did Not See State's Objection," *Washington Post*, 19 July 2003. Later in the same article, a White House source explained President Bush's decision not to delve into the details of IC disputes regarding the Iraqi threat by saying, "The president of the United States is not a fact-checker." Note how this account is difficult to square with reports that a one-page October 2002 President's Summary of the NIE, containing the INR and DOE dissents on aluminum tubes, was handed directly to President Bush and read by him in the presence of then CIA director George Tenet. See Waas, "What Bush Was Told."

92. See also Richards J. Heuer Jr., "Limits of Intelligence Analysis," *Orbis* (Winter 2005): 87–88.

93. US Commission on Intelligence Capabilities, *Report to the President*, 419.

94. For discussion of how a new approach to "words of estimative probability" might facilitate constructive intelligence reform, see Garrett Jones, "It's a Cultural Thing: Thoughts on a Troubled CIA," *Orbis* 50 (Winter 2006): 23–40.

95. For a searchable database of 237 "misleading" Bush administration statements regarding the 2003 Iraq War, see United States, House Government Reform Committee, "Iraq on the Record: The Bush Administration's Public Statements on Iraq," 16 March 2004, http://democrats.reform.house.gov/IraqOnTheRecord/.

96. Anatol Lieven, *America Right or Wrong: An Anatomy of American Nationalism* (London: Oxford University Press, 2004), 166.

97. George Tenet, letter to Hon. Bob Graham, 7 October 2002, *Congressional Record*, 9 October 2002, S10154, emphasis added.

98. Ray McGovern, "Bush, CIA Out of Synch on Iraq," *Hartford (Conn.) Courant*, 18 November 2002.

99. US NIC, October 2002 NIE on Iraqi WMD, declassified excerpts, emphasis added.

100. This point deserves special attention in future deliberations, since hindsight has shown that the combination of IAEA inspections and economic sanctions was far more effective in containing Iraq than Bush administration officials portrayed prior to Operation Iraqi Freedom. See Lopez and Cortright, "Containing Iraq"; and Blix, *Disarming Iraq*.

101. Dafna Linzer, "Iran Is Judged 10 Years from Nuclear Bomb," *New York Times*, 2 August 2005. Following disclosures that Iran resumed uranium enrichment in 2006, experts posited a "highly uncertain," worst-case timeline that estimates 2009 as the earliest date that Iran could conceivably acquire a nuclear weapon. David Albright and Corey Hinderstein, "Iran's Next Steps: Final Tests and the Construction of a Uranium Enrichment Plant," Institute for Science and International Security Issue Brief, 12 January 2006, http://www .isis-online.org/publications/iran/irancascade.pdf. For additional commentary on the technical obstacles likely to delay any Iranian effort to develop nuclear weapons, see the "Iran" issue section of Jeffrey Lewis and Paul Kerr's informative Web log at http://www .armscontrolwonk.com.

102. Curt Weldon, *Countdown to Terror* (Washington, D.C.: Regnery, 2005), 5.

103. Alexander H. Montgomery, "Ringing in Proliferation: How to Dismantle an Atomic Bomb Network," *International Security* 30 (2005): 153–87; see also Ashton Carter and Stephen A. LaMontagne, "A Fuel-Cycle Fix," *Bulletin of the Atomic Scientists* 62 (January/February 2006): 24–25; Colin Dueck, "Strategies for Managing Rogue States," *Orbis* 50 (Spring 2006): 223–41; and Abbas Maleki and Matthew Bunn, "Finding a Way Out of the Iranian Nuclear Crisis," Belfer Center for Science and International Affairs Paper (March 2006), http://bcsia.ksg.harvard.edu/whatsnew.cfm?program=STPP&nt=top&pb_id=523.

104. David Albright and Corey Hinderstein, "The Clock is Ticking, But How Fast?" Institute for Science and International Security Issue Brief, 27 March 2006, http://www .isis-online.org/publications/iran/clockticking.pdf.

105. Hersh, "Iran Plans."

106. Adelman, "Cakewalk in Iraq."

107. Abrahamian, "Empire Strikes Back," 147.

108. On the enduring significance of Operation Ajax in Iran's collective memory, see Kinzer, *All the Shah's Men*; Dan De Luce, "50 Years Later, Iranians Remember US-UK Coup," *Christian Science Monitor*, 22 August 2003.

109. Reza Pahlavi, Statement at the National Press Club, Washington, D.C., 1 March 2006, http://www.rezapahlavi.org/npc2006.html; see also Joseph Cirincione, "Controlling Iran's Nuclear Program," *Issues in Science and Technology* 22 (Spring 2006): 80.

110. Lieven, *America Right or Wrong*, 217.

111. Stephan Lewandowsky, G. K. Stritzke, Klaus Oberauer, and Michael Morales, "Memory for Fact, Fiction and Misinformation: The Iraq War 2003," *Psychological Science* 16 (2005): 190–95.

112. Lewandowsky et al., "Memory for Fact," 194.

113. Kaufmann, "Threat Inflation," 43.

114. Steven Kull, "Misperceptions, the Media and the Iraq War," Program on International Policy Attitudes/Knowledge Networks Poll, 2 October 2003, http://www.pipa .org/OnlineReports/Iraq/Media_10_02_03_Report.pdf.

115. Steven Kull, "The Separate Realities of Bush and Kerry Supporters," Program on International Policy Attitudes/Knowledge Networks Poll, 21 October 2004, http://www .pipa.org/OnlineReports/Pres_Election_04/Report10_21_04.pdf.

116. Cass Sunstein, *Republic.com* (New Haven, Conn.: Yale University Press, 2001), 101.

117. See Sunstein, *Republic.com*, 68.

118. Sunstein, *Republic.com*, 66.

119. Douglas Hart and Steven Simon, "Thinking Straight and Talking Straight: Problems of Intelligence Analysis," *Survival* 48 (Spring 2006): 54–55. On the promises and pitfalls of debate as a method of intelligence analysis, see Mitchell, "Team B Intelligence Coups"; Reich, "Team B Exercise"; and Stack, "Negative View of Competitive Analysis." For general discussion of argumentation as a method of decision-making, see Douglas Ehninger and Wayne Brockriede, *Decision by Debate* (New York: Dodd, Mead, 1963); Frans H. van Eemeren and Rob Grootendorst, *Speech Acts in Argumentative Discussions* (Dordrecht: Foris, 1984); and Chaim Perelman and Lucie Olbrechts-Tyteca, *The New Rhetoric: A Treatise on Argumentation* (South Bend, Ind.: Notre Dame University Press, 1969).

120. For commentary on a similar vector of analysis applied to the European context, see Hans Born and Heiner Hänggi, eds., *The "Double Democratic Deficit": Parliamentary Accountability and the Use of Force Under International Auspices* (Aldershot: Ashgate, 2004).

121. Michael Massing, "The Press: The Enemy Within," *New York Review of Books*, 15 December 2005, 36–41. An illuminating compilation of Massing's earlier commentary on the subject is Michael Massing, *Now They Tell Us: The American Press and Iraq* (New York: New York Review of Books, 2004).

122. Massing, "Press."

123. On the rise of "narrowcasting," see Chris Priestman, "Narrowcasting and the Dream of Radio's Great Global Conversation," *Radio Journal: International Studies in Broadcast & Audio Media* 2 (June 2004): 277–88; and Sut Jhally, *The Codes of Advertising: Fetishism and the Political Economy of Meaning in the Consumer Society* (London: Routledge, 1987), 90–92.

124. Jacob S. Hacker and Paul Pierson, *Off Center: The Republic Revolution and the Erosion of American Democracy* (New Haven, Conn.: Yale University Press, 2005), 9.

Abrahamian, Ervand. "Empire Strikes Back: Iran in U.S. Sights." In *Inventing the Axis of Evil,* edited by Andre Schiffrin, 93–156. New York: New Press, 2004.

Abrams, Elliott, et al. Letter to Honorable William J. Clinton. 26 January 1998. http://www .newamericancentury.org/iraqclintonletter.htm.

Acheson, Dean. *Present at the Creation: My Years in the State Department.* New York: W. W. Norton, 1969.

Ackermann, Alice, and Antonia Pala. "From Peacekeeping to Preventive Deployment." *European Security* 5 (Spring 1996): 83–97.

Adelman, Kenneth. "Cakewalk in Iraq." *Washington Post,* 13 February 2002.

Agh, Attila. "Smaller and Bigger States in the EU 25: The Eastern Enlargement and Decision-Making in the EU." *Perspectives: Central European Review of International Affairs* 21 (Winter 2003/4): 5–26.

Albright, David. "The CIA's Aluminum Tubes' Assessment: Is the Nuclear Case Going Down the Tubes?" Institute for Science and International Security Issue Brief. 10 March 2003. http://www.isis-online.org/publications/iraq/al_tubes.html.

———. "Iraq's Aluminum Tubes: Separating Fact from Fiction." Institute for Science and International Security Country Report. December 2003. http://www.isis-online .org/publications/iraq/IraqAluminumTubes12-5-03.pdf.

Albright, David, and Khidhir Hamza. "Iraq's Reconstitution of Its Nuclear Weapons Program." *Arms Control Today* (October 1998): 9–15.

Albright, David, and Corey Hinderstein. "Iran, Player or Rogue?" *Bulletin of the Atomic Scientists* 59 (September/October 2003): 52–58.

———. "Iran's Next Steps: Final Tests and the Construction of a Uranium Enrichment Plant." Institute for Science and International Security Issue Brief. 12 January 2006. http://www.isis-online.org/publications/iran/irancascade.pdf.

———. "The Clock Is Ticking, But How Fast?" Institute for Science and International Security Issue Brief. 27 March 2006. http://www.isis-online.org/publications/iran/ clockticking.pdf.

Albright, Madeleine. "Bridges, Bombs, or Bluster?" *Foreign Affairs* 82 (September/October 2003): 2–19.

Alexander, John B. *Winning the War: Advanced Weapons, Strategies and Concepts for the Post-9/11 World.* New York: St. Martin's Press, 2003.

Alexander, Klinton W. "NATO's Intervention in Kosovo: The Legal Case for Violating Yugoslavia's National Sovereignty in the Absence of Security Council Approval." *Houston Journal of International Law* 22 (Spring 2000): 403–49.

Allison, Graham. *Nuclear Terrorism: The Ultimate Preventable Catastrophe.* New York: Times Books, 2004.

Anderson, Gary. "UNOSOM II: Not Failure, Not Success." In *Beyond Traditional Peacekeeping,* edited by Donald C. F. Daniel and Bradd C. Hayes, 167–277. London: Palgrave, 1995.

Anderson, Perry. "Dégringolade." *London Review of Books,* 2 September 2004, 3–9.

———. "Union Sucrée." *London Review of Books,* 23 September 2004, 10–17.

Andreasen, Steve, and Dennis Gormley. "Edging Ever Closer to a Nuclear Death Row." *Minneapolis Star-Tribune,* 29 March 2006.

Annan, Kofi. "Peace Operations and the United Nations: Preparing for the Next Century." United Nations Working Paper, 1996.

———. *We the Peoples: The Role of The United Nations in the 21st Century.* New York: United Nations Department of Public Information, 2000.

———. *Prevention of Armed Conflict: Report of the Secretary-General.* UN Document A/55/985-S/2001/574. 7 June 2001.

Arend, Anthony Clark. "International Law and the Preemptive Use of Military Force." *Washington Quarterly* 26 (Spring 2003): 89–103.

Aristotle. *On Rhetoric: A Theory of Civic Discourse.* Translated by George A. Kennedy. London: Oxford University Press, 1991.

Arkin, William M. "Defense Strategy: The Military's New War of Words." *Los Angeles Times,* 24 November 2002.

———. "Commentary: The Pentagon Unleashes a Holy Warrior." *Los Angeles Times,* 23 November 2003.

———. "Not Just a Last Resort? A Global Strike Plan, with a Nuclear Option." *Los Angeles Times,* 15 May 2005.

———. "Despite Denials, U.S. Plans for War." *Washington Post,* 13 April 2006.

Asen, Robert. *Visions of Poverty: Welfare Policy and Political Imagination.* East Lansing: Michigan State University Press, 2002.

Ayoob, Mohammed. "The War against Iraq: Normative and Strategic Implications." *Middle East Policy* (Summer 2003): 27–39.

Bacevich, Andrew J. *The New American Militarism: How Americans Are Seduced by War.* New York: Oxford University Press, 2005.

Badie, Bertrand. "Le jeu triangulaire." In *Sociologie des Nationalismes,* edited by Pierre Birnbaum, 447–62. Paris: Presses Universitaires de France, 1997.

Baker, Peter, Dafna Linzer, and Thomas E. Ricks. "U.S. Is Studying Military Strike Options on Iran." *Washington Post,* 9 April 2006.

Bamford, James. *Body of Secrets.* New York, Doubleday, 2001.

———. *A Pretext for War.* New York: Doubleday, 2004.

———. "The Man Who Sold the War." *Rolling Stone,* 17 November 2005, 52–62.

Barkin, Samuel J., and Bruce Cronin. "The State and the Nation: Changing Norms and the Rules of International Relations." *International Organization* 48 (Winter 1994): 107–30.

Barnes, Fred. "They Still Blame America First." *Weekly Standard,* 4 July 2005, 16.

Barnett, Thomas P. M. *The Pentagon's New Map.* New York: Putnam, 2004.

———. "Mr. President, Here's How to Make Sense of Our Iraq Strategy." *Esquire,* June 2004, 148–54.

Barstow, David, William J. Broad, and Jeff Gerth. "How the White House Embraced Disputed Iraqi Arms Intelligence." *New York Times,* 3 October 2004.

Batcher, Robert. "The Consequences of an Indo-Pakistani Nuclear War." *International Studies Review* 6 (December 2004): 135–62.

Baumgart, Claudia, and Harald Müller. "Nuclear Weapons–Free Zone in the Middle East: A Pie in the Sky?" *Washington Quarterly* 28 (Winter 2005): 45–58.

Baumgartner Frank R., and Bryan D. Jones. *Agendas and Instability in American Politics.* Chicago: University of Chicago Press, 1993.

Baxter, Sarah. "Adwoman Leads the Global Battle for Hearts and Minds." *Sunday Times* (London), 5 January 2003.

Beer, Francis. *Meanings of War and Peace.* College Station: Texas A&M University Press, 2001.

Beer, Francis A., and Robert Hariman, eds. *Post-Realism: The Rhetorical Turn in International Relations.* East Lansing: Michigan State University Press, 1994.

Beisner, Robert L. "Patterns of Peril: Dean Acheson Joins the Cold Warriors." *Diplomatic History* 20 (Summer 1966): 321–56.

Bell, David A. "Dominique de Villepin's Idea of Glory: The Napoleon Complex." *New Republic,* 14 April 2003. http://jhunix.hcf.jhu.edu/~dabell/villepin.htm.

Beltran, Jacques. "French Policy toward Iraq." US-France Analysis Series, Center for the United States and France. Brookings Institution, Washington, D.C. September 2002. http://www.brookings.edu/fp/cuse/analysis/beltran.htm.

Benjamin, Daniel. "Iraq and al Qaeda Are Not Allies." *New York Times,* 30 September 2002.

Benjamin, Daniel, and Steven Simon. *The Next Attack: The Failure of the War on Terror and a Strategy for Getting It Right.* New York: Henry Holt, 2005.

Bennet, Michael M. "The Syrian Military: A Primer." *Middle East Intelligence Bulletin* (August/September 2001). http://www.meib.org/articles/0108_s1.htm.

Berdahl, Mats. "Whither UN Peacekeeping? An Analysis of the Changing Military Requirements of UN Peacekeeping with Proposals for its Enhancement." Adelphi Paper 281 (1993).

Bergen, Peter. *Holy War, Inc.: Inside the Secret World of Osama bin Laden.* New York: Free Press, 2001.

Berman, Ari. "U.S. Iraq Policy Gains Support among Newspapers." *Editor and Publisher,* 7 February 2003. http://www.editorandpublisher.com/eandp/news/article_display .jsp?vnu_content_id=1812676.

Berrigan, Frida, and William D. Hartung. "U.S. Weapons at War 2005: Promoting Democracy or Fueling Repression?" World Policy Institute Special Report. June 2005. http://www.worldpolicy.org/projects/arms/reports/wawjune2005.html.

Bianco, Robert. "Taking Down a Statue of Saddam Is Symbolic but Has Power All Its Own." *USA Today,* 10 April 2003.

Biden, Joseph R. "Bosnia: Why the United States Should Finish the Job." *SAIS Review* 18 (Summer/Fall 1998): 1–7.

Biersteker, Thomas J., and Cynthia Weber, eds. *State Sovereignty as a Social Construct.* Cambridge: Cambridge University Press, 1996.

Blakely, Mike. "Somalia." In *The Costs of Conflict: Prevention and Cure in the Global Arena,* edited by Michael E. Brown and Richard N. Rosecrance, 75–90. New York: Rowman and Littlefield, 1999.

Blanton, Dana. "Poll: Most Expect War with Iraq." Fox News Poll. 12 September 2002. http://www.foxnews.com/story/0,2933,62861,00.html.

Blinken, Antony J. "From Preemption to Engagement." *Survival* 45 (Winter 2003): 33–60.

Blix, Hans. "Report by the Chief Inspector for Biological and Chemical Arms." *New York Times,* 14 February 2003.

———. *Disarming Iraq.* New York: Pantheon Books, 2004.

Blumenthal, Sidney. "There Was No Failure of Intelligence: U.S. Spies Were Ignored, or Worse, if They Failed to Make the Case for War." *Guardian* (London), 5 February 2004.

Bolton, Alex. "Report Could Hurt Bolton." *Hill,* 11 May 2005. http://www.thehill.com/the hill/export/TheHill/News/Frontpage/051105/report.html.

Bolton, John R. "Beyond the Axis of Evil: Additional Threats from Weapons of Mass Destruction." Remarks to the Heritage Foundation, Washington, D.C. 6 May 2002. http://www.state.gov/t/us/rm/9962.htm.

Borger, Julian. "The Spies Who Pushed for War." *Guardian* (London), 17 July 2003.

———. "1625 U.N. and U.S. Inspectors Spent Two Years Searching for Weapons in Iraq." *Guardian* (London), 7 October 2004.

Born, Hans, and Heiner Hänggi, eds. *The "Double Democratic Deficit": Parliamentary Accountability and the Use of Force under International Auspices.* Aldershot: Ashgate, 2004.

Bostdorff, Denise M. *The Presidency and the Rhetoric of Foreign Crisis.* Columbia: University of South Carolina Press, 1994.

Boureston, Jack. "Strategic Insight: Assessing al Qaeda's WMD Capabilities." Naval Security Affairs Department/Center for Contemporary Conflict. September 2002. http://www.ccc.nps.navy.mil/rsepResources/si/sept02/wmd.asp.

Boutros-Ghali, Boutros. *An Agenda for Peace.* New York: United Nations, 1992.

Brodie, Bernard. *War and Strategy in the Missile Age.* Princeton, N.J.: Princeton University Press 1959.

Brokaw, Tom. *Today.* NBC News Transcripts, 9 April 2003. Lexis-Nexis news transcripts database. http://www.lexis-nexis.com.

Brown, Seyom. *The Illusion of Control: Force and Foreign Policy in the 21st Century.* Washington, D.C.: Brookings Institution Press, 2003.

Bunn, Elaine M. "Preemptive Action: When, How, and to What Effect?" *Strategic Forum* 200 (July 2003): 1–8.

Bunn, Matthew, Anthony Wier, and John P. Holdren. "Controlling Nuclear Warheads and Materials: A Report Card and Action Plan." Project on Managing the Atom. Belfer Center for Science and International Affairs. John F. Kennedy School of Government, Harvard University, Cambridge, Mass. March 2003. www.nti.org/cnwm.

Burke, Kenneth. "War and Cultural Life." *American Journal of Sociology* 48 (1942): 404–10.

———. *Attitudes toward History.* 2nd ed. Boston: Beacon Press, 1959.

Burns, Robert. "Peacekeeping Institute May Shut Down." Associated Press Wire, 11 March 2002. Lexis-Nexis news wire database. http://www.lexis-nexis.com.

Burr, William, and Jeffrey T. Richelson. "Whether to 'Strangle the Baby in the Cradle': The United States and the Chinese Nuclear Program, 1960–64." *International Security* 25 (Winter 2000/1): 54–99.

Bush, George W. "The Second Gore-Bush Presidential Debate." 11 October 2000. http://www.debates.org/pages/trans2000b.html.

———. "Remarks by the President in Address to Faculty and Students of Warsaw University." 15 June 2001. http://www.whitehouse.gov/news/releases/2001/06/20010615 -1.html.

———. "Address before a Joint Session of the Congress on the State of the Union, January 29, 2002." *Weekly Compilation of Presidential Documents* 38 (2002): 133–39.

———. "Commencement Address at the United States Military Academy in West Point, New York, June 1, 2002." *Weekly Compilation of Presidential Documents* 38 (2002): 944–48.

———. "President Bush Delivers Graduation Speech at West Point." 1 June 2002. http://222.whitehouse.gov/news/releases/2002/06/print/20020601-3.html.

———. "Bush Letter: 'America Intends to Lead.'" CNN, 4 September 2002. http://www .cnn.com/2002/ALLPOLITICS/09/04/bush.letter/.

———. "Remarks at a Luncheon for Representative Anne M. Northup in Louisville, September 6, 2002." *Weekly Compilation of Presidential Documents* 38 (2002): 1494–99.

————. "Address to the United Nations General Assembly in New York City, September 12, 2002." *Weekly Compilation of Presidential Documents* 38 (2002): 1529–33.

————. "The President's Radio Address, September 14, 2002." *Weekly Compilation of Presidential Documents* 38 (2002): 1545–46.

————. "Address to the Nation on Iraq, Cincinnati, Ohio, October 7, 2002." *Weekly Compilation of Presidential Documents* 38 (2002): 1716–20.

————. "Address before a Joint Session of the Congress on the State of the Union, January 28, 2003." *Weekly Compilation of Presidential Documents* 39 (2003): 109–16.

————. "Excerpts from the State of the Union Regarding Iraq." 28 January 2003. www .whitehouse.gov/news/releases/2003/01/20030128-23.html.

————. "President George Bush Discusses Iraq in National Press Conference." 6 March 2003. http://www.whitehouse.gov/news/releases/2003/03/20030306-8.html.

————. "President Says Saddam Hussein Must Leave Iraq in 48 Hours." Address to the Nation by the President. The Cross Hall. 17 March 2003. www.whitehouse. gov/2003/03/20030317-7.html.

————. "President Bush Announces Major Combat Operations in Iraq Have Ended." Remarks by the President from the USS *Abraham Lincoln*, at Sea off the Coast of San Diego, California. 1 May 2003. http://www.whitehouse.gov/news/releases/2003/05/ iraq/20030501-15.html.

————. Interview by TVP, Poland. 29 May 2003. http://www.whitehouse.gov/g8/interview 5.html.

————. "Address before a Joint Session of the Congress on the State of the Union, January 20, 2004." *Weekly Compilation of Presidential Documents* 40 (2004): 94–101.

————. "President Discusses War on Terror at Naval Academy Commencement." 27 May 2005. http://www.whitehouse.gov/news/releases/2005/05/20050527.html.

————. "President Discusses War on Terror at National Endowment for Democracy." 6 October 2005. http://www.whitehouse.gov/news/releases/2005/10/20051006-3.html.

————. "President Discusses Freedom and Democracy in Iraq." George Washington University, Washington, D.C. 13 March 2006. http://www.whitehouse.gov/news/ releases/2006/03/20060313-3.html.

Byers, Michael, and Simon Chesterman. "Changing the Rules about Rules? Unilateral Humanitarian Intervention and the Future of International Law." In *Humanitarian Intervention: Ethical, Legal and Political Dilemmas*, edited by J. L. Holzgrefe and Robert O. Keohane, 177–203. Cambridge: Cambridge University Press, 2003.

Byman, Daniel L., and Matthew C. Waxman. *Confronting Iraq: U.S. Policy and the Use of Force since the Gulf War*. Santa Monica, Calif.: RAND, 2000.

Cahn, Anne Hessing. *Killing Détente: The Right Attacks the CIA*. University Park: Pennsylvania State University Press, 1998.

Cahn, Anne Hessing, and John Prados. "Team B: The Trillion Dollar Experiment." *Bulletin of the Atomic Scientists* 49 (1993): 22–31.

Callahan, David. *Dangerous Capabilities: Paul Nitze and the Cold War*. New York: Harper-Collins, 1990.

Carafano, James Jay. "Post-Conflict Operations from Europe to Iraq." Heritage Foundation Lecture, July 2004. http://www.heritage.org/Research/NationalSecurity/loader.cfm ?url=/commonspot/security/getfile.cfm&PageID=66346.

Carnegie Commission on Preventing Deadly Conflict. *Preventing Deadly Conflict*. New York: Carnegie Corporation of New York, 1997.

Carpenter, Ronald H. *Rhetoric in Martial Deliberations and Decision Making*. Columbia: University of South Carolina Press, 2004.

Carter, Ashton, and Stephen A. LaMontagne. "A Fuel-Cycle Fix." *Bulletin of the Atomic Scientists* 62 (January/February 2006): 24–25.

Casey, Steven. "Selling NSC-68: The Truman Administration, Public Opinion, and the Politics of Mobilization, 1950–51." *Diplomatic History* 29 (September 2005): 655–90.

Ceaser, J., G. E. Thurow, J. Tulis, and J. M. Besette. "The Rise of the Rhetorical Presidency." *Presidential Studies Quarterly* 11 (1981): 158–71.

Champion, Marc, Charles Fleming, Ian Johnson, and Carla Anne Robbins. "Allies at Odds: Behind US Rifts with Europeans." *Wall Street Journal*, 3 April 2003.

Cheney, Richard. "Vice President Speaks at VFW 103rd National Convention." 26 August 2002. http://www.whitehouse.gov/news/releases/2002/08/print/20020826.html.

———. "Vice President Honors Veterans of Korean War." 29 August 2002. http://www.whitehouse.gov/news/releases/2002/08/20020829-5.html.

———. "Vice President Dick Cheney Discusses 9/11 Anniversary, Iraq, Nation's Economy and Politics 2002," *Meet the Press*, NBC News transcripts, 8 September 2002. Lexis-Nexis news transcript database, http://www.lexis-nexis.com.

———. "Vice President Dick Cheney Discusses a Possible War with Iraq." *Meet the Press*, NBC News Transcripts, 16 March 2003. Lexis-Nexis news wire database. http://www.lexis-nexis.org.

———. "Vice President's Remarks to the American Israel Public Affairs Committee 2006 Policy Conference." Washington, D.C. 7 March 2006. http://www.whitehouse.gov/news/releases/2006/03/20060307-1.html.

Childs, Marquis. "Behind the Errors on Cuban Invasion" *Washington Post,* 26 April 1961.

Chomsky, Noam. "After Pinkville." *New York Review of Books,* 1 January 1970. http://www.nybooks.com/articles/article-preview?article_id=11087.

———. "Preventive War: 'The Supreme Crime.'" *ZNet,* 11 August 2003.

———. *Hegemony or Survival: America's Quest for Global Dominance.* New York: Metropolitan Books, 2003.

Chubin, Shahram, and Robert S. Litwak. "Debating Iran's Nuclear Aspirations." *Washington Quarterly* 26 (Autumn 2003): 99–114.

Cirincione, Joseph. "Fool Me Twice." *Foreign Policy,* 27 March 2006. Web exclusive, http://www.foreignpolicy.com/story/cms.php?story_id=3416.

———. "Controlling Iran's Nuclear Program." *Issues in Science and Technology* 22 (Spring 2006): 80

Cirincione, Joseph, Jessica T. Mathews, and George Perkovich, with Alexis Orton. *WMD in Iraq: Evidence and Implications.* Washington, D.C.: Carnegie Endowment for International Peace, 2004.

Claire, Rodger W. *Raid on the Sun: Inside Israel's Secret Campaign That Denied Saddam the Bomb.* New York: Broadway Books, 2004.

Clark, Ruth Anne, and Jesse Delia. "Topoi and Rhetorical Competence." *Quarterly Journal of Speech* 65 (April 1979): 187–206.

Clark, Wesley K. *Waging Modern War: Bosnia, Kosovo, and the Future of Combat.* New York: Public Affairs Press, 2001.

———. "Broken Engagement." *Washington Monthly* 36 (May 2004): 26–33.

Clarke, Richard A. *Against All Enemies: Inside America's War on Terror.* New York: Free Press, 2004.

Clarke, Richard A., and Steven Simon. "Bombs That Would Backfire." *New York Times,* 16 April 2006.

Coen, Rachel. "Behind the Pentagon's Propaganda Plan." *Extra! Update* (April 2002). http://www.fair.org/extra/0204/osi.html.

Cogan, Charles. *French Negotiating Behavior: Dealing with La Grande Nation.* Washington, D.C.: United States Institute of Peace Press, 2003.

Cohen, Avner. *Israel and the Bomb.* New York: Columbia University Press, 1998.

Cohen, Roger. "Kerry Must-Sell: A Tough Foreign Policy." *New York Times*, 28 July 2004.

"Colin Powell on Iraq, Race, and Hurricane Relief." ABC News, 8 September 2005. http://abcnews.go.com/2020/Politics/story?id=1105979&page=1.

Coll, Steve. *Ghost Wars: The Secret History of the CIA, Afghanistan, and Bin Laden, from the Soviet Invasion to September 10, 2001.* New York: Penguin Books, 2004.

Collins, John, and Ross Glover, eds. *Collateral Language: A User's Guide to America's New War.* New York: New York University Press, 2002.

Colombani, Jean-Marie. "Nous sommes tous Américains." *Le Monde*, 13 September 2001.

Commission on Global Governance. *Our Global Neighborhood.* Oxford: Oxford University Press, 1995.

Committee on the Present Danger. "Our Mission." Committee on the Present Danger Web site. http://www.fightingterror.org/mission/index.cfm.

———. Newsroom press release on publication of Kenneth R. Timmerman's *Countdown to Crisis.* http://www.fightingterror.org/newsroom/press_050920.cfm.

Connolly, Ceci. "Fox Special Report with Brit Hume." 9 April 2003. Transcript #040905cb.254. Lexis-Nexis news transcripts database. http://www.lexis-nexis.com.

Cooper, Anderson. "Is 'Group Think' to Blame for Iraq WMD Intelligence Failure?" 12 July 2004. CNN Transcript #071200CN.V98. Lexis-Nexis news database. http://lexis-nexis.com.

Copeland, Dale C. *The Origins of Major War.* Ithaca, N.Y.: Cornell University Press, 2000.

Corbin, Marcus, and Miriam Pemberton. "Report of the Task Force on a Unified Security Budget for the United States." Washington, D.C.: Foreign Policy in Focus/Center for Defense Information, 2004.

Cordesman, Anthony. *Iran and Iraq: The Threat from the Northern Gulf.* Boulder, Colo.: Westview Press, 1993.

———. *The Military Balance in the Middle East.* Westport, Conn.: Preager, 2004.

———. *Iran's Developing Military Capabilities.* Washington, D.C.: Center for Strategic and International Studies, 2005.

Couric, Katie. *Today.* NBC News Transcripts, 9 April 2003. Lexis-Nexis news transcripts database. http://www.lexis-nexis.com.

Crabb, Cecil V., Jr., and Pat M. Holt. *Invitation to Struggle: Congress, the President, and Foreign Policy.* 3rd ed. Washington, D.C.: Congressional Quarterly Press, 1989.

Crawford, Neta C. *Argument and Change in World Politics: Ethics, Decolonization, and Humanitarian Intervention.* London: Cambridge University Press, 2002.

———. "The Best Defense: The Problem with Bush's 'Preemptive' War Doctrine." *Boston Review* (February/March 2003). http://www.bostonreview.net/BR28.1/crawford.html.

Crocker, Chester A. "A Dubious Template for US Foreign Policy." *Survival* 47 (Spring 2005): 51–70.

Cronin, Bruce. "Changing Views of Sovereignty and Multilateral Intervention." In *Collective Conflict Management and Changing World Politics,* ed. Joseph Lepgold and Thomas G. Weiss, 159–80. Albany: State University of New York Press.

Curl, Joseph. "Agency Disavows Report on Iraq Arms." *Washington Times*, 27 September 2002. Article ID: 200209271031520006. Lexis-Nexis news database. http://www.lexis-nexis.com.

Daalder, Ivo, and James M. Lindsay. *America Unbound: The Bush Revolution in Foreign Policy.* Washington, D.C.: Brookings Institution Press, 2003.

Daalder, Ivo, James M. Lindsay, and James Steinberg. "The Bush National Security Strategy: An Evaluation." Brookings Policy Brief 109 (October 2002). http://www.brookings.edu/comm/policybriefs/pb109.htm.

Dailey, Brian D., and Patrick J. Parker, eds. *Soviet Strategic Deception.* Lexington, Mass.: D. C. Heath, 1987.

Daniel, Donald C. F., Peter Dombrowski, and Rodger A. Payne. "The Bush Doctrine Is Dead: Long Live the Bush Doctrine?" *Orbis* (Spring 2005): 199–212.

———. "The Bush Doctrine: Rest in Peace?" *Defence Studies* 4 (Summer 2004): 18–39.

Daniel, Donald C. F., and Bradd C. Hayes, eds. *Beyond Traditional Peacekeeping.* London: Palgrave, 1995.

Daniel, Donald C. F., and Bradd C. Hayes, with Chantal de Jonge Oudraat. *Coercive Inducement and the Containment of International Crises.* Washington, D.C.: U.S. Institute of Peace Press, 1999.

Daniel, Donald C. F., and Katherine Hebig, eds. *Strategic Military Deception.* New York: Pergamon Press, 1982.

Danish Institute for International Studies. *New Threats and the Use of Force.* Copenhagen: Danish Institute for International Studies, 2005. http://www.diis.dk/sw12399.asp.

Danner, Mark. "The Secret Way to War." *New York Review of Books,* 9 June 2005. http://www.nybooks.com/articles/18034.

Dauber, Cori Elizabeth. *Cold War Analytical Structures and the Post Post-War World.* Westport, Conn.: Praeger, 1993.

Davis, Jack. "The Challenge of Managing Uncertainty: Paul Wolfowitz on Intelligence-Policy Relations." *Studies in Intelligence* 39 (1996). http://www.cia.gov/csi/studies/96unclass/davis.htm.

Deans, Bob. "Sept. 11 Jolted Bush's Stance on Security." *Atlanta Journal-Constitution,* 22 September 2002. Lexis-Nexis general news database. http://www.lexis-nexis.com.

De Castro, Renato Cruz. "U.S. War on Terror in East Asia: The Perils of Preemptive Defense in Waging a War of the Third Kind." *Asian Affairs* 31 (Winter 2005): 212–32.

De Luce, Dan. "50 Years Later, Iranians Remember US-UK Coup." *Christian Science Monitor,* 22 August 2003.

Diamond, Larry. "What Went Wrong in Iraq." *Foreign Affairs* 83 (September/October 2004): 34–57.

Diehl, Paul F., Daniel Druckman, and James Wall. "International Peacekeeping and Conflict Resolution: A Taxonomic Analysis with Implications." *Journal of Conflict Resolution* 42 (February 1998): 33–55.

Dobbins, James, John G. McGinn, Keith Crane, Seth G. Jones, Rollie Lal, Andrew Rathmell, Rachel M. Swanger, and Anga Timilsina. *America's Role in Nation-Building: From Germany to Iraq.* Santa Monica, Calif.: Rand, 2003.

Dobbs, Michael. "US Had Key Role in Iraq Buildup: Trade in Chemical Arms Allowed Despite Their Use on Iranians, Kurds." *Washington Post,* 30 December 2002.

Dolan, Chris J. "Foreign Policy on the Offensive." In *Striking First: The Preventive War Doctrine and the Reshaping of U.S. Foreign Policy,* edited by Betty Glad and Chris J. Dolan, 3–22. London: Palgrave, 2004.

Dombrowski, Peter. "Against Pre-emptive Strikes." Information Technology, War and Peace Project Web site. 19 August 2002. http://www.watsoninstitute.org/infopeace/911/index .cfm?id=11#.

Dombrowski, Peter, and Rodger A. Payne. "Global Debate and the Limits of the Bush Doctrine." *International Studies Perspectives* 4 (November 2003): 395–408.

Donnelly, Thomas, Donald Kagan, and Gary Schmitt. "Rebuilding America's Defenses: Strategy, Forces and Resources for a New Century." Project for the New American Century Report. September 2000. http://www.newamericancentury.org/Rebuilding AmericasDefenses.pdf.

Dower, John W. *Embracing Defeat: Japan in the Wake of World War II.* New York: Norton, 1999.

———. "Lessons from Japan about War's Aftermath." *New York Times*, 27 October 2002.

Doxtader, Erik. "Learning Public Deliberation through the Critique of Institutional Argument." *Argumentation and Advocacy* 31 (1995): 163–84.

Dreyfuss, Robert, and Jason Vest. "The Lie Factory." *Mother Jones* 29, January/February 2004, 34–41.

Drogin, Bob. "The Conflict in Iraq: Spy Work in Iraq Riddled with Failures." *Los Angeles Times*, 17 June 2004.

Drogin, Bob, and John Goetz. "The Curveball Saga." *Los Angeles Times*, 20 November 2005. Lexis-Nexis general news database. http://www.lexis-nexis.com.

Dueck, Colin. "Strategies for Managing Rogue States." *Orbis* 50 (Spring 2006): 223–41.

Duelfer, Charles. *Comprehensive Report of the Special Advisor to the DCI on Iraq's WMD*. 30 September 2004. http://www.cia.gov/cia/reports/iraq_wmd_2004/.

Durch, William J. "Introduction to Anarchy: Humanitarian Intervention and 'State Building' in Somalia." In *UN Peacekeeping, American Politics and the Uncivil Wars of the 1990s*, edited by William J. Durch, 311–66. London: MacMillan Press, 1997.

Dworkin, Ronald. "What the Court Really Said." *New York Review of Books*, 12 August 2004, 26–29.

Eccleston, Roy. "Bush's Rule of Fear for a Peaceful World." *Australian*, 30 September 2002. Lexis-Nexis general news database. http://www.lexis-nexis.com.

Edelstein, David M. "Occupational Hazards: Why Military Occupations Succeed or Fail." *International Security* 29 (Summer 2004): 49–91.

Ehninger, Douglas, and Wayne Brockriede. *Decision by Debate*. New York: Dodd, Mead, 1963.

Ekovich, Steven. "Iran and New Threats in the Persian Gulf and Middle East." *Orbis* 48 (Winter 2004): 71–87.

Eland, Ivan. *Protecting the Homeland: The Best Defense Is to Give No Offense*. Cato Institute Paper. Washington, D.C.: Cato Institute, 1998.

———. "Excessive U.S. Military Action Overseas Breeds Anti-U.S. Terrorism." 24 November 2002. Cato Institute presentation. Transcript of address available from Cato Institute, Washington, D.C.

———. *The Empire Has No Clothes: U.S. Foreign Policy Exposed*. Oakland, Calif.: Independent Institute, 2004.

ElBaradei, Mohamed. "The Status of Nuclear Inspections in Iraq." 27 January 2003. http://www.iaea.org/NewsCenter/Statements/2003/ebsp2003n003.shtml.

———. "The Status of Nuclear Inspections in Iraq: An Update." 7 March 2003. http://www.iaea.org/NewsCenter/Statements/2003/ebsp2003n006.shtml.

Ellis, James O. Testimony. In *Army Transformation*. Senate Hearing. 12 March 2003. Federal Document Clearing House. Lexis-Nexis congressional database. http://www.lexis-nexis.com.

Ellsberg, Daniel. *Secrets: A Memoir of Vietnam and the Pentagon Papers*. New York: Viking, 2002.

Enriquez, Arnel B. "The US National Security Strategy of 2002—A New Use-of-Force Doctrine?" *Air and Space Power Journal* (Fall 2004): 31–40.

"Excerpts from Pentagon's Plan: 'Prevent the Re-Emergence of a New Rival.'" *New York Times*, 8 March 1992.

Fainberg, Anthony. "Osirak and International Security." *Bulletin of the Atomic Scientists* 37 (October 1981): 33–36.

Falk, Richard A. "What Future for the UN Charter System of War Prevention?" *American Journal of International Law* 97 (July 2003): 590–98.

Fallows, James. "The Fifty-first State?" *Atlantic Monthly*, November 2002, 53–64.

———. "Blind into Baghdad." *Atlantic Monthly,* January/February 2004, 53–74.

———. "Will Iran Be Next?" *Atlantic Monthly,* December 2004, 99–110.

———. Reply to letters. *Atlantic Monthly,* March 2005, 27–28.

———. "The Nuclear Power beside Iraq." *Atlantic Monthly,* May 2006, 31–32.

Farer, Tom J. "The Prospect for International Law and Order of Iraq." *American Journal of International Law* 97 (July 2003): 621–28. Lexis-Nexis legal research database. http://www.lexis-nexis.com.

Fearey, Bryan L., Paul C. White, John St. Ledger, and John D. Immele. "An Analysis of Reduced Collateral Damage Nuclear Weapons." *Comparative Strategy* 22 (October 2003): 305–25.

Feaver, Peter D., and Emerson M. S. Niou. "Managing Nuclear Proliferation: Condemn, Strike, or Assist?" *International Studies Quarterly* 40 (June 1996): 209–34.

Feffer, John. "Supporting the Arms Industry: US Government Subsidies for the Arms Trade." In *Challenging Conventional Wisdom: Debunking Myths and Exposing the Risks of Arms Export Reform,* edited by Tamar Gabelnick and Rachel Stohl, 25–52. Washington, D.C.: Federation of American Scientists/Center for Defense Information, 2003.

Feinstein, Dianne, et al. Letter to Hon. George W. Bush, 5 December 2005. http://www.house.gov/tauscher/Press2005/12-05-05.htm.

Feldman, Shai. *Nuclear Weapons and Arms Control in the Middle East.* Cambridge, Mass.: MIT Press, 1997.

Ferguson, Niall. "The Empire Slinks Back." *New York Times Magazine,* 27 April 2003, 52–57.

———. *Empire: The Rise and Decline of the British World Order and the Lessons for Global Power.* New York: Basic Books, 2003.

Finnemore, Martha. "Constructing Norms of Humanitarian Intervention." In *The Culture of National Security: Norms and Identity in World Politics,* edited by Peter J. Katzenstein, 153–85. New York: Columbia University Press, 1996.

———. *The Purpose of Intervention: Changing Beliefs about the Use of Force.* Ithaca, N.Y.: Cornell University Press, 2003.

Fishkin, James S., and Peter Laslett, eds. *Debating Deliberative Democracy.* London: Blackwell, 2003.

Fitzgerald, Patrick J. Government's Response to Defendant's Third Motion to Compel Discovery. *United States v. Libby,* filed 5 April 2006. U.S. District Court for the District of Columbia. Case No. 05-394 (RBW).

Fontenot, Gregory, E. J. Degen, and David Tohn. *On Point: The United States Army in Operation Iraqi Freedom.* Annapolis, Md.: Naval Institute Press, 2005.

Foran, John. "Discursive Subversions: *Time* Magazine, the CIA Overthrow of Musaddiq, and the Installation of the Shah." In *Cold War Constructions: The Political Culture of United States Imperialism, 1945–1966,* edited by Christian G. Appy, 157–82. Amherst: University of Massachusetts Press, 2000.

Forester, John. *The Deliberative Practitioner.* Cambridge, Mass.: MIT Press, 1999.

Foucault, Michel. *The Archaeology of Knowledge.* New York: Pantheon, 1972.

Franck, Thomas M. *The Power of Legitimacy among Nations.* New York: Oxford University Press, 1990.

———. "What Happens Now? The United Nations after Iraq." *American Journal of International Law* 97 (July 2003): 607–20. Lexis-Nexis legal research database. http://www.lexis-nexis.com.

Franks, Tommy, with Malcolm McConnell. *American Soldier.* New York: ReganBooks, 2004.

Freedman, Lawrence. "Prevention, Not Preemption." *Washington Quarterly* (Spring 2003): 105–14.

Friedman, Paul. "The Real-Time War; TV: A Missed Opportunity." *Columbia Journalism Review* (May/June 2003): 29–31.

Friedman, Thomas. "Take France Off the Security Council: India, the World's Largest Democracy, Deserves a Seat as a Permanent Member." *Guardian* (London), 11 February 2003.

Frum, David, and Richard Perle. *An End to Evil: How to Win the War on Terror.* New York: Random House, 2003.

Fursenko, Aleksandr, and Timothy Naftali. *"One Hell of a Gamble": Khrushchev, Castro, and Kennedy, 1958–1964.* New York: Norton, 1997.

Gaddis, John Lewis. *Strategies of Containment.* London: Oxford University Press, 1982.

———. "A Grand Strategy of Transformation." *Foreign Policy* (November/October 2002): 50–56.

———. *Surprise, Security, and the American Experience.* Cambridge, Mass.: Harvard University Press, 2004.

———. "After Containment." *New Republic,* 25 April 2005, 27–31.

Gaffney, Frank. "Second Opinion on Defense." *Washington Times,* 8 May 1990.

———. "God Save Us." *NRO* (*National Review Online*), 4 August 2005. Lexis-Nexis general news database. http://www.lexis-nexis.com.

Garfinkle, Adam. "Strategy and Preventive Diplomacy: US Foreign Policy and Preventive Intervention." *Orbis* 45 (Fall 2001): 503–18.

Garver, Eugene. *Aristotle's Rhetoric: An Art of Character.* Chicago: University of Chicago Press, 1994.

Gedda, George. "Bush: No Timetable for a Decision on Attacking Iraq." *Pittsburgh Post-Gazette,* 10 August 2002. http://www.post-gazette.com/nation/20020809iraqplannat2p2.asp.

Gerth, Jeff. "Military's Information War Is Vast and Often Secret." *New York Times,* 11 December 2005.

Gilbert, Matthew, and Suzanne C. Ryan. "Snap Judgments: Did Iconic Images from Baghdad Reveal More about the Media than Iraq?" *Boston Globe,* 10 April 2003.

Gingrich, Newt. *Winning the Future.* Washington, D.C.: Regnery, 2004.

Gleditsch, Kristian S. *All International Politics Is Local: The Diffusion of Conflict, Integration, and Democratization.* Ann Arbor: University of Michigan Press, 2002.

Glennon, Michael J. "Preempting Terrorism: The Case for Anticipatory Self-Defense." *Weekly Standard,* 28 January 2002, 24.

Gloannec, Anne-Marie, le. "Germany's Power and the Weakening of States in a Globalized World: Deconstructing a Paradox." *German Politics* 10 (April 2001): 117–34.

Gompert, David C., Richard L. Kugler, and Marin C. Libicki. *Mind the Gap: Promoting a Transatlantic Revolution in Military Affairs.* Washington, D.C.: National Defense University Press, 1999.

Goodnight, G. Thomas. "Public Argument and the Study of Foreign Policy." *American Diplomacy* 3 (1998). http://www.unc.edu/depts/diplomat/.

———. "Predicaments of Communication, Argument, and Power: Towards a Critical Theory of Controversy." *Informal Logic* 23 (2003): 119–38.

Gordon, Philip H., and Jeremy Shapiro. *Allies at War: America, Europe, and the Crisis over Iraq.* New York: McGraw-Hill, 2004.

Grant, Charles. "Iraq War: Iraq Post-Mortem 1." *Prospect,* 19 May 2003.

Grant, Rebecca. "Osirak and Beyond." *Air Force Magazine* 85 (August 2002). http://www.afa.org/magazine/aug2002/0802osirak.asp.

Gribkov, Anatoli I., and William Y. Smith. *Operation ANADYR: U.S. and Soviet Generals Recount the Cuban Missile Crisis.* Chicago: Edition Q, 1994.

Griffin, David Ray. *The New Pearl Harbor: Disturbing Questions about the Bush Administra-tion and 9/11.* Northampton, Mass.: Interlink Press, 2004.

Griffin, Leland M. "When Dreams Collide: Rhetorical Trajectories in the Assassination of President Kennedy." *Quarterly Journal of Speech* 70 (1984): 111–31.

Gruemm, H. "Safeguards and Tamuz: Setting the Record Straight." *IAEA Bulletin* 23 (December 1981): 10–14.

Gvosdev, Nikolas. "Restoring American Credibility." *National Interest* 25 (June 2003). http://www.inthenationalinterest.com/Articles/Vol2Issue25/Vol2Issue25Gvosdevpfv .html.

Haacke, Jürgen. "Theory and Praxis in International Relations: Habermas, Self-Reflection and Rational Argumentation." *Millennium: Journal of International Studies* 25 (1996): 255–89.

Haass, Richard N. "Imperial America." Brookings Paper. 11 November 2000. http://www .brook.edu/dybdocroot/views/articles/haass/2000imperial.htm.

———. "Defining U.S. Foreign Policy in a Post-Post-Cold War World." 2002 Arthur Ross Lecture, Remarks to Foreign Policy Association, New York. 22 April 2002. http://www .state.gov/s/p/rem/9632.htm.

———. "Wars of Choice." *Washington Post,* 23 November 2003.

Habermas, Jürgen. "Wahrheitstheorien." In *Wirklichkeit und Reflexion: Festschrift für Walter Schulz,* 211–65. Pfullingen: Neske, 1973.

———. *Theory of Communicative Action.* Vol. 2. Translated by Thomas McCarthy. Boston: Beacon Press, 1984.

———. *Philosophical Discourse of Modernity: Twelve Lectures.* Translated by Frederick G. Lawrence. Cambridge, Mass.: MIT Press, 1987.

Hacker, Jacob S., and Paul Pierson. *Off Center: The Republic Revolution and the Erosion of American Democracy.* New Haven, Conn.: Yale University Press, 2005.

Hadley, Stephen. Remarks to the United States Institute of Peace on the President's National Security Strategy. U.S. Institute of Peace. Washington, D.C. 16 March 2006. http://www.whitehouse.gov/news/releases/2006/03/20060316-8.html.

Haine, Jean-Yves, and Gustav Lindström. "An Analysis of the National Security Strategy of the United States of America." Institute for Security Studies Analysis (January 2003). http://www.iss-eu.org/new/analysis/analy034.html.

Halper, Stefan, and Jonathan Clarke. *America Alone: The Neo-Conservatives and the Global Order.* London: Cambridge University Press, 2004.

Hambling, David. "Bunker-Busters Set to Go Nuclear." *New Scientist,* 9 November 2002, 6–8.

Hampson, Fen Osler, Jean Daudelin, John B. Hay, Holly Reid, and Todd Martin. *Madness in the Multitude: Human Security and World Disorder.* New York: Oxford University Press, 2001.

Hamza, Khidhir, with Jeff Stein. *Saddam's Bombmaker.* New York: Touchstone, 2000.

Handel, Michael I. "Intelligence and the Problem of Strategic Surprise." *Journal of Strategic Studies* 7 (1984): 229–81.

———. "A Runaway Deception: Soviet Disinformation and the Six-Day War, 1967." In *Deception Operations: Studies in the East-West Context,* edited by David A. Charters and Maurice A. J. Tugwell, 159–69. London: Brassey's, 1990.

Hanley, Charles J. "Point by Point: A Look Back at a 'Thick' File." Associated Press Online, 9 August 2003. Lexis-Nexis news wire database. http://www.lexis-nexis.com.

Hardy, James. "Bush's Calls to Syrians." *Mirror* (UK), 14 April 2003. http://www.mirror .co.uk/news/allnews/page.cfm?objectid=12844873&method=full&siteid=50143&head line=BUSH%27S%20CALL%20TO%20SYRIANS.

Harigel, Gert G. "Chemical and Biological Weapons: Use in Warfare, Impact on Society and Environment." Carnegie Endowment for International Peace Report (2001). http://www.ceip.org/files/Publications/Harigelreport.asp.

Harkavy, Robert E. "Preemption and Two-Front Conventional Warfare." Jerusalem Papers on Peace Problems No. 23 (1977).

Harrison, Selig S. "Did North Korea Cheat?" *Foreign Affairs* 84 (January/February 2005): 99–110.

Hart, Douglas, and Steven Simon. "Thinking Straight and Talking Straight: Problems of Intelligence Analysis." *Survival* 48 (Spring 2006): 35-60.

Hart, Gary. Separate Opinion. In United States Senate Select Committee on Intelligence, *The National Intelligence Estimates A–B Team Episode Concerning Soviet Strategic Capability and Objectives.* 95th Cong., 2d sess. Committee Print. Washington, D.C.: Government Printing Office, 1978.

Hartnett, Stephen A., and Laura A. Stengrim. "'The Whole Operation of Deception': Reconstructing President Bush's Rhetoric of Weapons of Mass Destruction." *Cultural Studies—Critical Methodologies* 4 (2004).

———. *Globalization and Empire: The U.S. Invasion of Iraq, Free Markets, and the Twilight of Democracy.* Tuscaloosa: University of Alabama Press, 2006.

Hartung, William D. *And Weapons for All.* New York: HarperCollins, 1995.

Hartung, William D., and Frida Berrigan. "Hypocritical U.S. Fight for 'Freedom': Bush Arms Repressive Regimes, Sends Guns to Nations in Conflict, Ties Aid to Support of America's Terror War." *Newsday,* 13 June 2005.

Hayes, Stephen F. "Sticking to His Guns." *Weekly Standard,* 14 February 2005, 10–12.

Heisbourg, Francois. "A Work in Progress: The Bush Doctrine and Its Consequences." *Washington Quarterly* 26 (Spring 2003): 75–88.

Hersh, Seymour. "The Stovepipe." *New Yorker,* 27 October 2003, 77–87.

———. *Chain of Command: The Road from 9/11 to Abu Ghraib.* New York: HarperCollins, 2004.

———. "The Iran Plans." *New Yorker,* 17 April 2006. http://www.newyorker.com/fact/content/articles/060417fa_fact.

Herzig, Christopher. "Correspondence: IAEA Safeguards." *International Security* 7 (Spring 1983): 195–99.

Heuer, Richards J., Jr. "Limits of Intelligence Analysis." *Orbis* (Winter 2005): 87–88.

Hibbs, Mark. "Bushehr Construction Now Remote after Three Iraqi Air Strikes." *Nucleonics Week,* 26 November 1987, 5-6.

Hill, Charles. Memorandum to Robert C. McFarlane. 19 June 1984. Folder "[Terrorism] [8404913]," Box 90761. Files of D. Fortier. Ronald Reagan Library, Simi Valley, Calif.

Hillen, John. "Superpowers Don't Do Windows." In *America the Vulnerable: Our Military Problems and How to Fix Them,* edited by John Lehman and Harvey Sicherman, 27–47. Philadelphia: Foreign Policy Research Institute, 2002. http://www.fpri.org/america vulnerable/03.SuperpowersDontDoWindows.Hillen.pdf.

Hoffmann, Stanley. *Decline or Renewal? France since the 1930s.* New York: Viking Press, 1974.

———. *L'Amérique vraiment impériale? Entretiens sur le vif avec Frédéric Bozo.* Paris: Audibert, 2003.

Hogan, J. Michael. *The Nuclear Freeze Campaign.* East Lansing: Michigan State University Press, 1994.

Holloway, Robert. "Revision improbable des sanctions contre l'Irak après le discours de M. Bush." *Agence France Presse,* 27 November 2001.

Holmes, Robert. *On War and Morality.* Princeton, N.J.: Princeton University Press, 1989.

Holzgrefe, J. L. "The Humanitarian Intervention Debate." In *Humanitarian Intervention: Ethical, Legal and Political Dilemmas*, edited by J. L. Holzgrefe and Robert O. Keohane, 15–52. Cambridge: Cambridge University Press, 2003.

Howorth, Jolyon. "La France, L'Otan et la sécurité Européenne: Statu quo ingérable, renouveau introuvable?" *Politique Etrangère* 4 (2002), 1001–6.

Hughes, Richard E. "The Contemporaneity of Classical Rhetoric." In *Landmark Essays on Rhetorical Invention in Writing*, edited by Richard E. Young and Yameng Liu, 37–40. Davis, Calif.: Hermagoras Press, 1994.

Hughes, Thomas L. "INR's Vietnam Study in Context: A Retrospective Preface Thirty-five Years Later." National Security Archive. 2 May 2004. http://www.gwu.edu/~nsarchiv/NSAEBB/NSAEBB121/hughes.htm.

Hunt, Terence. "Bush: No Proof of Saddam Role in 9-11." Associated Press Online, 17 September 2003. Lexis-Nexis news wire database. http://www.lexis-nexis.com.

Hymans, Jacques E. C. "Raízes do Eurocepticismo Americano: As Consequências Perceptivas da Identidade Nacional" (Roots of American Euroskepticism: The Perceptual Consequences of National Identity). *Estratégia: Revista de Estudos Internacionais* No. 17 (Lisbon: Instituto de Estudos Estratégicos e Internacionais, 2002).

———. "Roots of the Washington Threat Consensus." In *Striking First: The Preventive War Doctrine and the Reshaping of U.S. Foreign Policy*, edited by Betty Glad and Chris J. Dolan, 33–45. London: Palgrave, 2004.

Ignatieff, Michael. "State Failure and Nation Building." In *Humanitarian Intervention: Ethical, Legal and Political Dilemmas*, edited by J. L. Holzgrefe and Robert O. Keohane, 299–320. Cambridge: Cambridge University Press, 2003.

Ikenberry, G. John. "America's Imperial Ambition." *Foreign Affairs* 81 (September/October 2002): 44–60.

Imperial Hubris: Why the West Is Losing the War on Terror. London: Brassey's, 2004.

International Commission on Intervention and State Sovereignty. *The Responsibility to Protect.* Ottawa: International Development Research Center, 2001.

"Iraq: Bagdad s'en prend à la France." *Le Figaro*, 22 May 2001.

Isaac, Jeffrey C., and Suzanne Dovi. "Hypocrisy and the Limits of Debunking It." *Polity* 34 (Fall 2001): 31–40.

Isenburg, David, and Ian Davis. *Unravelling the Known Unknowns: Why No Weapons of Mass Destruction Have Been Found in Iraq.* BASIC (British American Security Information Council) Special Report. January 2004. http://www.basicint.org/pubs/Research/2004WMD.pdf.

Isikoff, Michael, and Mark Hosenball. "Al Libi's Tall Tales." *Newsweek*, 10 November 2005. Web exclusive, http://www.msnbc.msn.com/id/9991919/site/newsweek/.

Ivie, Robert. "Presidential Motives for War." *Quarterly Journal of Speech* 60 (1974): 337–45.

———. "Metaphor and the Rhetorical Invention of Cold War 'Idealists.'" *Communication Monographs* 54 (1987): 165–82.

———. *Democracy and America's War on Terror.* Tuscaloosa: University of Alabama Press, 2005.

Jackson, Derrick Z. "Kerry Still Needs to Explain War Vote." *Boston Globe*, 23 January 2004. http://www.boston.com/news/politics/debates/articles/2004/01/23/kerry_still_needs_to_explain_war_vote/.

James, Barry. "Syria Warned—Perle Sees More 'Preemption' in Future." *International Herald Tribune*, 12 April 2003.

Jansen, Michael. "Baghdad's Bomb–An Inside View." *Middle East International* 691 (10 January 2003): 11.

Jarreau, Patrick, Sylvie Kauffmann, and Corinne Lesnes. "Paris-Washington: Les dessous d'une rupture." *Le Monde*, 27 March 2003.

Jasinski, James. *Sourcebook on Rhetoric: Key Concepts in Contemporary Rhetorical Studies.* Thousand Oaks, Calif.: Sage, 2001.

Jehl, Douglas. "Agency Belittles Information Given by Iraq Defectors." *New York Times,* 29 September 2003.

———. "Iraq May Be Prime Place for Training of Militants, CIA Report Concludes." *New York Times,* 22 June 2005.

Jentleson, Bruce W. "Coercive Prevention: Normative, Political and Policy Dilemmas." *Peaceworks* No. 35. Washington, D.C.: United States Institute of Peace, October 2000.

Jentleson Bruce W., and Rebecca L. Britton. "Still Pretty Prudent: Post–Cold War American Public Opinion on the Use of Military Force." *Journal of Conflict Resolution* 42 (August 1998): 395–417.

Jhally, Sut. *The Codes of Advertising: Fetishism and the Political Economy of Meaning in the Consumer Society.* London: Routledge, 1987.

Johnson, Chalmers. *Sorrows of Empire: Militarism, Secrecy and the End of the Republic.* New York: Metropolitan Books, 2004.

Johnson, Dominic D. P. *Overconfidence and War: The Havoc and Glory of Positive Illusions.* Cambridge, Mass.: Harvard University Press, 2004.

Jones, Garrett. "It's a Cultural Thing: Thoughts on a Troubled CIA." *Orbis* 50 (Winter 2006): 23–40.

Joyce, Mark. Review of *Strategic Preemption: US Foreign Policy and the Second Iraq War,* by Robert Pauly and Tom Lansford. *Royal United Services Institute for Defence and Security Studies* 149 (October 2004). http://www.rusi.org/publications/journal/reviews/ref: B4174F50E9745A/.

Kagan, Robert. *Of Paradise and Power.* New York: Vintage Books, 2004.

Kaldor, Mary. *New and Old Wars: Organized Violence in a Global Era.* Palo Alto, Calif.: Stanford University Press, 1999.

Kamp, Karl-Heinz. "Preemption: Far from Forsaken." *Bulletin of the Atomic Scientists* (March/April 2005): 26–27.

Kampfner, John. *Blair's Wars.* London: Free Press, 2003.

Kane, Thomas. "Foreign Policy Suppositions and Commanding Ideas." *Argumentation and Advocacy* 28 (1991): 80–90.

Kaufmann, Chaim. "Threat Inflation and the Failure of the Marketplace of Ideas: The Selling of the Iraq War." *International Security* 29 (Summer 2004): 5–48.

Kay, David. "Statement by David Kay on the Interim Progress Report on the Activities of the Iraq Survey Group (ISG) before the House Permanent Select Committee on Intelligence, the House Committee on Appropriations, Subcommittee on Defense, and the Senate Select Committee on Intelligence." 2 October 2003. http://www.cia.gov/cia/public_affairs/speeches/2003/david_kay_10022003.html.

———. Testimony. *Iraqi Weapons of Mass Destruction Programs.* Senate Armed Services Committee Hearing, 28 January 2004. Federal News Service Transcript. http://www.ceip.org/files/projects/npp/pdf/Iraq/kaytestimony.pdf.

Kean Thomas H., and Lee H. Hamilton. *The 9/11 Commission Report: Final Report of the National Commission on Terrorist Attacks upon the United States.* New York: Norton, 2004.

Keaney, Thomas A., and Eliot A. Cohen. *Gulf War Air Power Survey Summary Report.* Washington, D.C.: Government Printing Office, 1993.

Kernell, Samuel. *Going Public.* 3rd ed. Washington, D.C.: Congressional Quarterly Press, 1997.

Kerr, Paul. "Libya Vows to Dismantle WMD Program." *Arms Control Today* (January/February 2004): 29–30.

————. "IAEA: Questions Remain about Libya." *Arms Control Today* (July/August 2004): 28.

————. "Three Years Later, Iraq Investigations Continue." *Arms Control Today* (April 2006). http://www.armscontrol.org/act/2006_04/iraqinvestcont.asp.

Kerry, John. "Speech to the 2004 Democratic Convention." Boston. http://www.JohnKerry.com/pressroom/speeches/spc_2004?0729.html.

Khadduri, Imad. *Iraq's Nuclear Mirage: Memoirs and Delusions.* Toronto: Springhead, 2003.

Kinzer, Stephen. *All the Shah's Men: An American Coup and the Roots of Middle East Terror.* Hoboken, N.J.: John Wiley, 2003.

Kissinger, Henry A. "Military Policy and the Defense of 'Gray Areas.'" *Foreign Affairs* 33 (April 1955): 416–28.

Kitfield, James. "Coercion and Preemption." *National Journal,* 28 May 2005, 1618–25.

Knight, Charles. "Essential Elements Missing in the National Security Strategy of 2002." Commonwealth Institute Project on Defense Alternatives Commentary (November 2002). http://www.comw.org/qdr/0210knight.html.

————. "First Strike Guidelines: The Case of Iraq." Project on Defense Alternatives Briefing Memo 25 (16 September 2002, revised and updated 10 March 2003). http://www.comw.org/pda/0209schneider.html.

————. "Iranian Nuclear Weapons, Part II: Operational Challenges." Policywatch No. 761. Washington Institute for Near East Policy. 29 May 2003. http://www.washingtoninstitute.org/watch/index.htm.

Koch, Andrew and Jeannette Wolf. "Iran's Nuclear Facilities: A Profile." Center for Nonproliferation Studies Report. 1998. http://www.cns.miis.edu.

Kovar, Richard. "An Interview with Richard Lehman." *Studies in Intelligence* 9 (2000). http://www.cia.gov/csi/studies/summer00/art05.html.

Krasner, Stephen D. *Sovereignty: Organized Hypocrisy.* Princeton, N.J.: Princeton University Press, 1999.

Krauthammer, Charles. "The New Unilateralism." *Washington Post,* 8 June 2001.

————. "Axis of Evil, Part Two." *Washington Post,* 23 July 2004.

Kristensen, Hans M. "The Role of U.S. Nuclear Weapons: New Doctrine Falls Short of Bush Pledge." *Arms Control Today* (September 2005). http://www.msnbc.msn.com/id/9991919/site/newsweek/.

Kröning, Volker. "Prevention or Preemption? Towards a Clarification of Terminology." Commonwealth Institute Project on Defense Alternatives Guest Commentary (March 2003). http://www.comw.org/pda/0303kroening.html.

Krotz, Ulrich. "National Role Conceptions and Foreign Policies: France and Germany Compared." Program for the Study of Germany and Europe Working Paper 02.1. Minda de Gunzburg Center for European Studies. Harvard University, Cambridge, Mass., 2002. http://www.ces.fas.harvard.edu/working_papers/GermanSeries.html.

————. "Structure as Process: The Regularized Intergovernmentalism of Franco-German Bilateralism." Program for the Study of Germany and Europe Working Paper 02.3. Minda de Gunzburg Center for European Studies. Harvard University, Cambridge, Mass., 2002.

Kugler, Jacek, and Douglas Lemke, eds. *Parity and War.* Ann Arbor: University of Michigan Press, 1996.

Kull, Steven. "Misperceptions, the Media and the Iraq War." Program on International Policy Attitudes/Knowledge Networks Poll. 2 October 2003. http://www.pipa.org/OnlineReports/Iraq/Media_10_02_03_Report.pdf.

————. "The Separate Realities of Bush and Kerry Supporters." Program on International Policy Attitudes/Knowledge Networks Poll. 21 October 2004. http://www.pipa.org/OnlineReports/Pres_Election_04/Report10_21_04.pdf.

Kull, Steven, Clay Ramsay, Stefan Subias, and Evan Lewis. "US Public Beliefs on Iraq and the Presidential Election." Program on International Policy Attitudes Report. University of Maryland, College Park. 22 April 2004. www.pipa.org/IraqReport4?22?04.pdf.

Kupchan, Charles A. "Continental Rift." *Newark (N.J.) Star-Ledger,* 27 April 2003. http://www.cfr.org/pub5910/charles_a_kupchang/continental_rift.php.

Kurth, James. "The Protestant Deformation and American Foreign Policy." *Orbis* 42 (Spring 1998): 221–26.

Kuypers, Jim A. "Hoyt Hopewell Hudson's Nuclear Rhetoric." In *Twentieth Century Roots of Rhetorical Studies,* edited by Jim A. Kuypers and Andrew King, 71–102. New York: Praeger, 2001.

LaFranchi, Howard. "Diplomacy's New Muscle Under Rice." *Christian Science Monitor,* 29 June 2005.

Landay, Jonathan S. "CIA Report Reveals Analysts Split Over Extent of Iraqi Nuclear Threat." Knight Ridder Newspapers, 4 October 2002. Lexis-Nexis general news database. http://www.lexis-nexis.com.

———. "U.S. Military Pays Iraqis for Positive News Stories on War." Knight Ridder Newspapers, 30 November 2005. Lexis-Nexis news wire database. http://www.lexis-nexis.com.

Lang, W. Patrick. "Drinking the Kool-Aid." *Middle East Policy* 11 (Summer 2004): 42–48.

Lansford, Tom. "Whither Lafayette? French Military Policy and the American Campaign in Afghanistan." *European Security* 11 (Fall 2002): 126–46.

Laver, Henry S. "Preemption and the Evolution of America's Strategic Defense." *Parameters* 35 (Summer 2005): 107–20.

Layne, Christopher. "Minding Our Own Business: The Case for American Non-Participation in International Peacekeeping/Peacemaking Operations." In *Beyond Traditional Peacekeeping,* edited by Donald C. F. Daniel and Bradd C. Hayes, 85–100. London: Palgrave, 1995.

Lebow, Richard Ned. "Windows of Opportunity: Do States Jump through Them?" *International Security* 9 (Summer 1984): 147–86.

Leffler, Melvyn P. Letter to the Editor. *Foreign Policy* (January/February 2005): 11.

———. "9/11 and American Foreign Policy." *Diplomatic History* 29 (June 2005): 395–413.

Leicester, John. "Europe Remembers Rice's 'Punish France' Quip." Associated Press Online, 16 November 2004. Lexis-Nexis news wire database. http://www.lexis-nexis.com.

Lemke, Douglas. "Investigating the Preventive Motive for War." *International Interactions* 29 (October–December 2003): 273–92.

Lemnitzer, L. L. "Justification for US Military Intervention in Cuba (TS)." Memorandum for the Secretary of Defense. 13 March 1962. U.S. National Security Archive. http://www.gwu.edu/~nsarchiv/news/20010430/northwoods.pdf.

Leverett, Flynt. "Why Libya Gave Up on the Bomb." *New York Times,* 23 January 2004.

Levin, Carl. "Report of an Inquiry into the Alternative Analysis of the Issue of an Iraq–al Qaeda Relationship." 21 October 2004. http://www.levin.senate.gov/newsroom/supporting/2004/102104inquiryreport.pdf.

Levy, Jack S. "Declining Power and the Preventive Motivation for War." *World Politics* 40 (October 1987): 82–107.

Lewandowsky, Stephan Werner, G. K. Stritzke, Klaus Oberauer, and Michael Morales. "Memory for Fact, Fiction and Misinformation: The Iraq War 2003." *Psychological Science* 16 (2005): 190–95.

Lewis, Jeffrey. "Lift-Off for Space Weapons? Implications of the Department of Defense's 2004 Budget Request for Space Weaponization." Center for International and Security

Studies Paper. University of Maryland, College Park. 21 July 2003. http://www.cissm
.umd.edu/documents/spaceweapons.pdf.

———. "Doctrine for Joint Nuclear Operations (Joint Publication 3–12)." *ArmsControl-
Wonk.com* Weblog, 4 April 2005. http://www.armscontrolwonk.com/512/doctrine-for
-joint-nuclear-operations-joint-publication-3-12.

———. "RNEP Raises Its Ugly Head Again." *ArmsControlWonk* Weblog, 6 December
2005. http://www.armscontrolwonk.com/889/rnep-raises-its-ugly-head-again.

———. "A Nuclear Doctrine That Doesn't Deter." *ArmsControlWonk.com* Weblog, 7
December 2005. http://www.armscontrolwonk.com/891/a-nuclear-doctrine-that
-doesnt-deter.

Lieber, Keir A., and Robert J. Lieber. "The Bush National Security Strategy." *U.S. Foreign
Policy Agenda* (December 2002). http://usinfo.state.gov/journals/itps/1202/ijpe/pj7
-4lieber.htm.

Lieberman, Joe, and John Kyl. "The Present Danger." *Washington Post,* 20 July 2004.

Lieven, Anatol. *America Right or Wrong: An Anatomy of American Nationalism.* London:
Oxford University Press, 2004.

Linzer, Dafna. "Iran Is Judged 10 Years from Nuclear Bomb." *New York Times,* 2 August
2005.

Litwak, Robert S. *Rogue States and US Foreign Policy: Containment after the Cold War.*
Washington, D.C.: Woodrow Wilson Center Press, 2000.

———. "The New Calculus of Pre-emption." *Survival* 44 (Winter 2002–3): 53–80.

Lopez, George A., and David Cortright. "Containing Iraq: Sanctions Worked." *Foreign
Affairs* 83 (July/August 2004): 90–103.

Lugar, Richard. "Next Steps in Non-Proliferation Policy." *Arms Control Today* (December
2002). http://www.armscontrol.org/act/2002_12/lugar_dec02.asp.

Lyall, Sarah. "Britain Admits That Much of Its Report on Iraq Came from Magazines."
New York Times, 8 February 2003.

Lyden, Jacki, and John Burnett. "Support of the Bush Doctrine on Iraq by the People of the
West Texas City of Lubbock." *All Things Considered.* National Public Radio broadcast.
24 October 2002. Lexis-Nexis news transcript database. http://www.lexis-nexis.com.

Lynch, Colum. "Annan Warns U.S. Will Face Doubts." *Washington Post,* 7 February 2004.

Lynch, Marc. *State Interests and Public Spheres.* New York: Columbia University Press, 1999.

Machiavilli, Niccolo. *The Discourses.* Translated by Leslie J. Walker. New York: Penguin
Books, 1970.

Mackenzie, Chris. "Policy Entrepreneurship in Australia: A Conceptual Review and
Application." *Australian Journal of Political Science* 39 (July 2004): 367–86.

Macleod, Alex. "French Policy toward the War in the Former Yugoslavia: A Bid for
International Leadership." *International Journal* 52 (Spring 1997): 243–64.

Makdisi, Ussami. "'Anti-Americanism' in the Arab World: An Interpretation of a Brief
History." *Journal of American History* 89 (September 2002): 538–57.

Maleki, Abbas, and Matthew Bunn. "Finding a Way Out of the Iranian Nuclear Crisis."
Belfer Center for Science and International Affairs Paper (March 2006). http://bcsia.ksg
.harvard.edu/whatsnew.cfm?program=STPP&nt=top&pb_id=523.

Mann, James. *The Rise of the Vulcans: The History of Bush's War Cabinet.* New York: Viking
Books, 2004.

Manning, Robert A. "Triumph of the Periphery." *Washington Times,* 28 June 1999.

Maoz, Zeev. "The Mixed Blessing of Israel's Nuclear Policy." *International Security* 28 (Fall
2003): 44–77.

Marder, Murray. "Carter to Inherit Intense Dispute on Soviet Intentions." *Washington Post,*
2 January 1977.

Marquis, Christopher. "Powell Admits No Hard Proof in Linking Iraq to Al Qaeda." *New York Times*, 9 January 2004.

Massing, Michael. *Now They Tell Us: The American Press and Iraq*. New York: New York Review of Books, 2004.

———. "The Press: The Enemy Within." *New York Review of Books*, 15 December 2005.

Matthews, Chris. *Hardball*. 17 April 2003. MSNBC Transcript #041700cb.461. Lexis-Nexis news transcripts database. http://www.lexis-nexis.com.

Matthias, Willard C. *America's Strategic Blunders*. University Park: Pennsylvania State University Press, 2001.

May, Ernest. *American Cold War Strategy: Interpreting NSC-68*. Boston: Bedford Books, 1993.

Mazarr, Michael. "Saved from Ourselves?" *Washington Quarterly* (Spring 2002): 221–32.

McCarren, Andrea. "Toppling of Saddam's Statue Staged?" WJLA-TV I-Team Report. 22 July 2004. http://www.wjla.com/news/stories/0704/161032.html.

McClellan, Scott. "Press Briefing by Scott McClellan." 27 January 2004. http://www.whitehouse.gov/news/releases/2004/01/20040127-6.html.

McGee, Michael C. "The 'Ideograph': A Link between Rhetoric and Ideology." *Quarterly Journal of Speech* 66 (1980): 1–16.

McGovern, Ray. "Bush, CIA Out of Synch on Iraq." *Hartford (Conn.) Courant*, 18 November 2002.

Mead, Walter Russell. *Power, Terror, Peace and War: America's Grand Strategy in a World at Risk*. New York: Knopf, 2004.

Mearsheimer, John J., and Stephen M. Walt. "An Unnecessary War." *Foreign Policy* 134 (January/February 2003): 50–59.

Medalia, Jonathan. "'Bunker Busters': Sources of Confusion in the Robust Nuclear Earth Penetrator Debate." Congressional Research Service Report for Congress, 22 September 2004.

Medhurst, Martin J. "Rhetoric and Cold War: A Strategic Approach." In *Cold War Rhetoric: Strategy, Metaphor, and Ideology*, edited by Martin J. Medhurst, Robert L. Ivie, Philip Wander, and Robert L. Scott, 19–28. East Lansing: Michigan State University Press, 1997.

Meisler, Stanley. "Kofi Annan: The Soft Spoken Economist Who Runs UN Peacekeeping Forces." *Los Angeles Times*, 21 June 1994.

Mertus, Julie. "Reconsidering the Legality of Humanitarian Intervention: Lessons from Kosovo." *William and Mary Law Review* 41 (May 2000): 1743–87.

Milbank, Dana, and Walter Pincus. "As Rationales for War Erode, Issue of Blame Looms Large." *Washington Post*, 10 July 2004.

Milbank, Dana, and Dana Priest. "Warning in Iraq Report Unread; Bush, Rice Did Not See State's Objection." *Washington Post*, 19 July 2003.

Miller, Judith. "Threats and Responses: Terrorist Weapons." *New York Times*, 13 September 2002.

Miller, Judith, Stephen Engelberg, and William Broad. *Germs: Biological Weapons and America's Secret War*. New York: Simon and Schuster, 2001.

Mills, Marja. "Waging a War of Euphemisms." *Chicago Tribune*, 17 October 2002. Available in NewsBank. Record Number: CTR0210170003.

Miniter, Richard. *Shadow War: The Untold Story of How Bush Is Winning the War on Terror*. Washington, D.C.: Regnery, 2004.

Mitchell, Gordon R. *Strategic Deception: Rhetoric, Science, and Politics in Missile Defense Advocacy*. East Lansing: Michigan State University Press, 2000.

———. "Public Argument-Driven Security Studies." *Argumentation and Advocacy* 39 (Summer 2004): 57–71.

———. "Team B Intelligence Coups." *Quarterly Journal of Speech* (forthcoming).

Moeller, Susan D. "Media Coverage of Weapons of Mass Destruction." Center for International and Security Studies Report. March 2004. http://www.cissm.umd.edu/documents/WMDstudy_full.pdf.

Mohamedou, Mohammad-Mahmoud. *Iraq and the Second Gulf War: State Building and Regime Security.* San Francisco: Austin and Winfield, 1998.

Montgomery, Alexander H. "Ringing in Proliferation: How to Dismantle an Atomic Bomb Network." *International Security* 30 (2005): 153–87.

Moore, Michael. "Truman Got It Right." *Bulletin of the Atomic Scientists* 59 (January/February 2003): 20–22.

Mueller, Harald, and Thomas Risse-Kappen. "Origins of Estrangement: The Peace Movement and the Changed Image of America in West Germany." *International Security* 12 (Summer 1987): 52–88.

Muravchik, Joshua. "The Bush Manifesto." *Commentary* (December 2002): 23–30.

———. "Bringing Democracy to the Arab World." *Current History* 103 (January 2004): 8–11.

Murray, Williamson, and Robert H. Scales Jr. *The Iraq War: A Military History.* Cambridge, Mass.: Harvard University Press, 2003.

Myers, Richard B. "Change of Command/Retirement Ceremony." Offutt Air Force Base, Omaha, Neb., 9 July 2004. http://www.jcs.mil/chairman/speeches/STRATCOM_change_command.html.

Mylroie, Laurie. "The Circle of Terror." *NRO* (National Review Online), 19 February 2003. http://www.nationalreview.com/comment/comment-mylroie021903.asp.

Nakdimon, Shlomo. *The Exclusive Story of How Israel Foiled Iraq's Attempt to Get the Bomb.* Translated by Peretz Kidron. New York: Summit Books, 1987.

"National Terrorism Alert Goes Up; Interview with Saddam's Bomb Maker." *CNN Crossfire.* 7 February 2003. http://transcripts.cnn.com/TRANSCRIPTS/0302/07/cf.00.html.

Nelson, Bill. Statement. *Congressional Record,* 28 January 2004, S311.

Nelson, Robert W. "Nuclear Bunker Busters, Mini-Nukes, and the US Nuclear Stockpile." *Physics Today* 56 (November 2003): 32–38.

Neuman, Johanna. "Bush's Inaction over General's Islam Remarks Riles Two Faiths." *Los Angeles Times,* 23 November 2003.

Neumann, Peter R., and M.L.R. Smith. "Missing the Plot? Intelligence and Discourse Failure." *Orbis* (Winter 2005): 95–107.

Newman, Robert P. "Communication Pathologies of Intelligence Systems." *Speech Monographs* 42 (1975): 273–90.

———. *Owen Lattimore and the "Loss" of China.* Berkeley: University of California Press, 1992.

"The New Pearl Harbor: Disturbing Questions about the Bush Administration and 9/11." Unsigned book review. *Publishers Weekly,* 22 March 2004. http://reviews.publishersweekly.com/bd.aspx?isbn=1566565529&pub=pw.

Nitze, Paul. Top Secret/Sensitive Memorandum to McGeorge Bundy. 10 May 1963. National Security Files, Meetings and Memoranda Series, Standing Group Meeting. John Fitzgerald Kennedy Presidential Library, Boston.

———. *From Hiroshima to Glasnost: At the Center of Decision.* New York: Weidenfeld and Nicholson, 1989.

"Not Whether, but How, to Withdraw." *Economist,* 26 November 2005.

Nye, Joseph. *The Paradox of American Power.* London: Oxford University Press, 2000.

Odom, William. "Intervention for the Long Run: Rethinking the Definition of War." *Harvard International Review* (Winter 2001): 48–52.

―――. *Fixing Intelligence: For a More Secure America*. New Haven, Conn.: Yale University Press, 2003.

Offner, Arnold A. "Rogue President, Rogue Nation: Bush and U.S. National Security." *Diplomatic History* 29 (June 2005): 433–35.

O'Hanlon, Michael E. "Iraq without a Plan." *Policy Review* (December 2004/January 2005): 33–45.

Olson, Kathryn M. "Constraining Open Deliberations in Times of War: Presidential War Justification for Grenada and the Persian Gulf." *Argumentation and Advocacy* 27 (1991): 64–97.

―――. "Democratic Enlargement's Value Hierarchy and Rhetorical Forms: An Analysis of Clinton's Use of Post–Cold War Symbolic Frame to Justify Military Interventions." *Presidential Studies Quarterly* 34 (2004): 307–40.

Oren, Michael B. *Six Days of War: June 1967 and the Making of the Modern Middle East*. Oxford: Oxford University Press, 2002.

Ostrow, Joanne. "Lasting Images: Tumbling Statue Immediately Burns into Memory." *Denver Post*, 10 April 2003.

Packer, George. *The Assassins' Gate: America in Iraq*. New York: Farrar, Strauss and Giroux, 2005.

Pahlavi, Reza. Statement at the National Press Club. Washington, D.C., 1 March 2006. http://www.rezapahlavi.org/npc2006.html.

Pan, Michael, Amanda Terkel, Robert Boorstin, P. J. Crowley, and Nigel Holmes. "Safety Second." *New York Times*, 8 August 2004.

Panofsky, Wolfgang. "Dismantling the Concept Of 'Weapons of Mass Destruction.'" *Arms Control Today* (April 1998). http://www.armscontrol.org/act/1998_04/wkhp98.asp.

Paris, Roland. *At War's End: Building Peace after Civil Conflict*. Cambridge: Cambridge University Press, 2004.

"Paris soutient les propos de Bush sur les inspecteurs, souhaite un accord." *Agence France Presse*, 27 November 2001.

Parry-Giles, Shawn J. *The Rhetorical Presidency, Propaganda, and the Cold War, 1945–1955*. Westport, Conn.: Praeger, 2001.

Pauly, Robert J., Jr., and Tom Lansford. *Strategic Preemption: U.S. Foreign Policy and the Second Iraq War*. Aldershot: Ashgate, 2004.

Payne, Rodger A. "The Politics of Defense Policy Communication: The 'Threat' of Soviet Strategic Defense." *Policy Studies Review* 8 (1989): 505–26.

Payne, Rodger A., and Nayef H. Samhat. *Democratizing Global Politics: Discourse Norms, International Regimes and Political Community*. Albany: State University of New York Press, 2004.

The Pentagon Papers. New York: *New York Times*, 1971.

Perelman, Chaim, and Lucie Olbrechts-Tyteca. *The New Rhetoric: A Treatise on Argumentation*. South Bend, Ind.: Notre Dame University Press, 1969.

Perkovich, George. *India's Nuclear Bomb: The Impact on Global Proliferation*. Berkeley: University of California Press, 1999.

Perle, Richard, Douglas Feith, and David Wurmser. "A Clean Break: A New Strategy for Securing the Realm." Institute for Advanced Strategic and Political Studies Paper. 8 July 1996. http://www.aaiusa.org/news/must_read_feith.htm.

Perlmutter, Amos. *The Life and Times of Menachem Begin*. Garden City, N.Y.: Doubleday, 1987.

Phillips, Kendall R. "Spaces of Invention: Dissension, Freedom and Thought in Foucault." *Philosophy and Rhetoric* 35 (2002): 328–44.

Phillips, Mark. *The Early Show*. CBS News Transcripts, 9 April 2003. Lexis-Nexis news transcripts database, http://www.lexis-nexis.com.

Philpott, Daniel. "Usurping the Sovereignty of Sovereignty." *World Politics* 53 (January 2001): 297–324.

———. *Revolutions in Sovereignty: How Ideas Shaped Modern International Relations.* Princeton, N.J.: Princeton University Press, 2001.

Pillar, Paul. "Intelligence, Policy, and the War in Iraq." *Foreign Affairs* 85 (March/April 2006). http://www.foreignaffairs.org/20060301faessay85202/paul-r-pillar/intelligence -policy-and-the-war-in-iraq.html.

———. "Great Expectations: Intelligence as Savior." *Harvard International Review* 27 (Winter 2006): 16-21.

Pincus, Walter. "CIA Did Not Share Doubt on Iraq Data." *Washington Post,* 12 June 2003.

———. "White House Backs Off Claim on Iraqi Buy." *Washington Post,* 8 July 2003.

———. "Pentagon Revises Nuclear Strike Plan." *Washington Post,* 11 September 2005.

———. "Newly Released Data Undercut Prewar Claims Source Tying Baghdad, Al Qaeda Doubted." *Washington Post,* 6 November 2005.

Pincus, Walter, and Dana Milbank. "Bush, Rice Blame CIA for Iraq Error." *Washington Post,* 12 July 2003.

Podhoretz, Norman. "In Praise of the Bush Doctrine." *Commentary* (September 2002): 19–28.

Pollack, Kenneth M. *Arabs at War: Military Effectiveness, 1948–1991.* Lincoln: University of Nebraska Press, 2002.

———. *The Threatening Storm: The Case for Invading Iraq.* New York: Random House, 2002.

———. "Spies, Lies, and Weapons: What Went Wrong." *Atlantic Monthly,* January/February 2004, 78–92.

Porter, Geoff D. "The Faulty Premise of Pre-emption." *New York Times,* 31 July 2004.

Powell, Colin. "Press Conference with Secretary of State Colin Powell Re: U.S. Reaction to Iraqi Arms Declaration." Federal News Service transcript, 19 December 2002. Lexis-Nexis news transcript database. http://www.lexis-nexis.com.

———. "Remarks to the United Nations Security Council." 5 February 2003. http://www .state.gov/secretary/former/powell/remarks/2003/17300.htm.

———. Joint Press Availability with Italian Foreign Minister Franco Frattini. Rome. 2 June 2003. http://www.state.gov/secretary/former/powell/remarks/2003/21126.htm.

———. "A Strategy of Partnerships." *Foreign Affairs* 83 (January/February 2004): 22–34.

Powell, Robert. *Bargaining in the Shadow of Power.* Princeton, N.J.: Princeton University Press, 1999.

Powers, Thomas. *Heisenberg's War: The Secret History of the German Bomb.* New York: Knopf, 1993.

———. "The Vanishing Case for War." *New York Review of Books,* 4 December 2003. http://www.nybooks.com/articles/16813.

Prados, John. *Hoodwinked: The Documents That Reveal How Bush Sold Us a War.* London: New Press, 2004.

———. "Iraq: When Was the Die Cast?" 3 May 2005. http://www.tompaine.com/articles/ iraq_when_was_the_die_cast.php.

"Press Conference with Senator Jay Rockefeller (D-WV), Senator Carl Levin (D-MI), and Senator Dianne Feinstein (D-CA)—Subject: Phase 2 Review of Prewar Intelligence." 4 November 2005. Federal News Service. Lexis-Nexis congressional database. http:// www.lexis-nexis.com.

Priest, Dana. *The Mission: Waging War and Keeping Peace with America's Military.* New York: W. W. Norton, 2003.

Priestman, Chris. "Narrowcasting and the Dream of Radio's Great Global Conversation." *Radio Journal: International Studies in Broadcast and Audio Media* 2 (June 2004): 277–88.

Przeworski, Adam, Michael E. Alvarez, José Antonio Cheibub, and Fernando Limongi. *Democracy and Development: Political Institutions and Well-Being in the World 1950–1990.* Cambridge: Cambridge University Press, 2000.

"Public Report of the Vice President's Task Force on Combatting Terrorism." February 1986. Folder "[Terrorism] [OA/ID 14923]." Press Office. Bush Vice Presidential Records. George Bush Presidential Library, College Station, Tex.

Purcell, Heather A., and James K. Galbraith, "Did the U.S. Military Plan a Nuclear First Strike for 1963?" *American Prospect* 19 (Fall 1994): 88–96.

Putnam, Robert D. *Making Democracy Work: Civic Traditions in Modern Italy.* Princeton, N.J.: Princeton University Press, 1993.

Rampton, Sheldon, and John Stauber. *Weapons of Mass Deception: The Uses of Propaganda in Bush's War on Iraq.* New York: Center for Media and Democracy, 2003.

Ramsey, Paul. *The Just War: Force and Political Responsibility.* New York: Scribner's, 1968.

Record, Jeffrey. "The Bush Doctrine and War with Iraq." *Parameters* 33 (Spring 2003): 4–21.

———. *Dark Victory: America's Second War against Iraq.* Annapolis, Md.: Naval Institute Press, 2004.

———. "The Limits and Temptations of America's Conventional Primacy." *Survival* 47 (Spring 2005): 33–49.

Regan, Patrick. "Choosing to Intervene: Outside Intervention in Internal Conflicts." *Journal of Politics* 60 (August 1998): 754–79.

Reich, Robert. "Re-examining the Team A–Team B Exercise." *International Journal of Intelligence and Counterintelligence* 3 (Fall 1989): 383–403.

Reich, Simon. "Power, Institutions and Moral Entrepreneurs." ZEF-Discussion Paper on Development Policy No. 65. Center for Development Research (ZEF). Bonn. March 2003. http://www.mafhoum.com/press7/226P3.pdf.

Reiff, David. "Blueprint for a Mess." *New York Times,* 2 November 2003.

Reiter, Dan. "Exploding the Powder Keg Myth: Preemptive Wars Almost Never Happen." *International Security* 20 (Fall 1995): 5–34.

———. "Deterrence Has Worked in the Past: Use It with Iraq." *Atlanta Journal-Constitution,* 6 November 2002.

———. "The Osirak Myth and the Track Record of Preventive Military Attacks." Ridgway Center Policy Brief 04-2 (October 2004). http://www.ridgway.pitt.edu/docs/policy_briefs/rcpb04-2_Reiter.pdf.

———. Letter to the Editor. *Atlantic Monthly,* March 2005, 26–27.

———. "Preventive Attacks against Nuclear Programs and the 'Success' at Osiraq." *Nonproliferation Review* 12 (July 2005): 355–71.

Rennie, David. "Powell Boosts Support in U.S." *Daily Telegraph* (London), 10 February 2003. Lexis-Nexis general news database. http://www.lexis-nexis.com.

Rhodes, Richard. *The Making of the Atomic Bomb.* New York: Simon and Schuster, 1986.

Rice, Condoleezza. "Promoting the National Interest." *Foreign Affairs* 79 (January/February 2000): 45–62.

———. "Dr. Condoleezza Rice Discusses President's National Security Strategy." 1 October 2002. http://www.whitehouse.gov/news/releases/2002/10/20021001-6.html.

———. "A Balance of Power that Favors Freedom." *U.S. Foreign Policy Agenda* (December 2002). http://usinfo.state.gov/journals/itps/1202/ijpe/ijpe1202.pdfsid14901231.

————. "Remarks by Condoleezza Rice Assistant to the President for National Security Affairs to the Chicago Council on Foreign Relations." 8 August 2003. http://www .whitehouse.gov/news/releases/2003/10/20031008-4.html.

————. Interview with British Foreign Secretary Jack Straw on the Jonathan Dimbleby Programme ITV1. 1 April 2006. http://www.state.gov/secretary/rm/2006/63993.htm.

Richelson, Jeffrey T. *A Century of Spies: Intelligence in the Twentieth Century.* New York: Oxford University Press, 1995.

Ricks, Thomas E. "Military Plays Up Role of Zarqawi." *Washington Post,* 10 April 2006.

Risen, James. "Question of Evidence: A Special Report." *New York Times,* 27 October 1999.

————. "How Pair's Finding on Terror Led to Clash on Shaping Intelligence." *New York Times,* 28 April 2004.

————. *State of War: The Secret History of the CIA and the Bush Administration.* New York: Free Press, 2006.

Risen, James, and Judith Miller. "Al Qaeda Site Points to Tests of Chemicals." *New York Times,* 11 November 2001.

Risse, Thomas. "'Let's Argue!' Communicative Action in World Politics." *International Organization* 54 (2000): 1–39.

Rockefeller John D., IV, Carl Levin, and Dianne Feinstein. Letter to Bill Frist and Harry Reid. 14 November 2005. http://thinkprogress.org/wp-images/upload/Intel_Letter.pdf.

Rose, Paul Lawrence. *Heisenberg and the Nazi Atomic Bomb Project: A Study in German Culture.* Berkeley: University of California Press, 1998.

Ross, Michael L. "Does Oil Hinder Democracy?" *World Politics* 53 (April 2001): 325–61.

Ross, Robert S. "The 1995–96 Taiwan Strait Confrontation." *International Security* 25 (Fall 2000): 87–123.

Ross, Steven T. *American War Plans 1945–1950.* London: Frank Cass, 1996.

Roth, Ken. "War in Iraq: Not a Humanitarian Intervention." Human Rights Watch World Report 2004. http://www.hrw.org/wr2k4/3.htm.

Rouleau, Eric. "America's Unyielding Policy toward Iraq." *Foreign Affairs* 74 (January/February 1995): 59–72.

Rourke, John T. *Presidential Wars and American Democracy: Rally 'Round the Chief.* New York: Paragon House, 1993.

Rozen, Laura. "The Report They Forgot." *American Prospect,* 19 October 2005. Web exclusive, http://www.prospect.org/web/page.ww?section=root&name=ViewlWeb&articleId=10446.

Ruggie, John Gerard. "The UN and the Collective Use of Force: Whither or Whether?" In *The UN, Peace and Force,* edited by Michael Pugh, 240–55. London: Frank Cass, 1997.

Rumsfeld, Donald H. Media Availability En Route to Chile. 18 November 2002. http:// www.defenselink.mil/news/Nov2002/t11212002_t1118sd2.html.

————. "Prepared Testimony of U.S. Secretary of Defense Donald H. Rumsfeld before the House and Senate Armed Services Committees Regarding Iraq." 18–19 September 2002. http://www.defenselink.mil/speeches/2002/s20020918-secdef.html.

————. Transcript of *Handelsblatt* Interview with Secretary of Defense Rumsfeld. 3 February 2006. http://www.dod.mil/transcripts/2006/tr20060203-12518.html.

Rumsfeld, Donald H., and Richard Myers. "Defense Department Operational Briefing." 9 April 2003. Lexis-Nexis news transcripts database. http://www.lexis-nexis.com.

Rumsfeld, Donald, and Peter Pace. "DOD News Briefing—Secretary Rumsfeld and Gen. Pace." Department of Defense News Transcript, 26 September 2002. http://222 .defenselink.mil/news/Sep 2002/t09262002_t0926sd.html.

————. "DOD News Briefing." Washington, D.C., 14 March 2006. http://www.defense link.mil/transcripts/2006/tr20060314-12644.html.

Ruppe, David. "Democrats Object to Nuclear Pre-Emption Doctrine." *Global Security Newswire*, 6 December 2005. http://www.nti.org/d_newswire/issues/2005_12_6.html #3C1EA569.

Russell, Ben. "US Warns Syria Not to Provide Haven for Wanted Iraqis." *Independent* (UK), 14 April 2003. http://www.commondreams.org/headlines03/0414-01.htm.

Safire, William. "Needed: A 'Team B.'" *New York Times*, 10 March 1994.

———. "Bad Herr Dye." *New York Times*, 23 January 2003.

Sagan, Scott D., and Kenneth N. Waltz. *The Spread of Nuclear Weapons: A Debate Renewed.* New York: Norton, 2003.

Salama, Sammy, and Karen Ruster. "A Preemptive Attack on Iran's Nuclear Forces: Possible Consequences." CNS Research Story, 12 August 2004. http://cns.miis.edu/pubs/week/040812.htm.

Salisbury, Harrison. *War between Russia and China.* New York: Norton, 1969.

Salit, Richard. "Finally, His Vision Finds an Audience." *Providence (R.I.) Journal*, 2 March 2003. http://www.projo.com/news/content/projo_20030302_barnett2.c0fd3.html.

Sammon, Bill. *Misunderestimated: The President Battles Terrorism, John Kerry, and the Bush Haters.* New York: HarperCollins, 2004.

Sandalow, Marc. "A Growing Challenge to Bush on Iraq War; His Ratings Drop as a Few GOP Leaders Ask for Exit Strategy." *San Francisco Chronicle*, 19 June 2005.

Sanders, Jerry W. *Peddlers of Crisis: The Committee on the Present Danger and the Politics of Containment.* Boston: South End Press, 1983.

Sands, Phillipe. *Lawless World: America and the Making and Breaking of Global Rules from FDR's Atlantic Charter to George W. Bush's Illegal War.* New York: Viking, 2005.

Sanger, David E. "Diplomacy Fails to Slow Advance of Nuclear Arms." *New York Times*, 8 August 2004.

Sanger, David E., and David Barstow. "Report Leaked by Cheney Aide Was in Dispute." *New York Times*, 9 April 2006.

Sapiro, Miriam. "Iraq: The Shifting Sands of Preemptive Self-Defense." *American Journal of International Law* 97 (July 2003). Lexis-Nexis legal research database. http://www.lexis-nexis.com.

Scarborough, Rowan. *Rumsfeld's War: The Untold Story of America's Anti-Terrorist Commander.* Washington, D.C.: Regnery, 2004.

Schake, Kori N., and Justin P. Bernier. "Dealing with Rogue States." In *The Global Century: Globalization and National Security*, Vol. 1, edited by Richard L. Kugler and Ellen L. Frost, 283–97. Washington, D.C.: National Defense University Press, 2002. http://www.ndu.edu/inss/books/Books_2001/Global%20Century%20-%20June%202001/globcencont.html.

Schlesinger, Arthur M., Jr. "Unilateral Preventive War: Illegitimate and Immoral." *Los Angeles Times*, 21 August 2002.

———. "Eyeless in Iraq." *New York Review of Books*, 23 October 2003. http://www.nybooks.com/articles/article-preview?article_id=16677.

———. *War and the American Presidency.* New York: W. W. Norton, 2004.

Schmitt, Michael N. "Preemptive Strategies of International Law." *Michigan Journal of International Law* 24 (Winter 2003): 513–48.

Schroeder, Paul W. "Iraq: The Case against Preemptive War." *American Conservative*, 10 October 2002. http://www.amconmag.com/2002_10_21/iraq.html.

Schultz, Richard H., and Andreas Vogt. "It's War! Fighting Post–11 September Global Terrorism through a Doctrine of Preemption." *Terrorism and Political Violence* 15 (Spring 2003): 1–30.

Scowcroft, Brent. "Don't Attack Saddam: It Would Undermine Our Anti-Terror Efforts."
    Wall Street Journal, 15 August 2002. http://www.opinionjournal.com/editorial/feature
    .html?id=110002133.
"The Secret Downing Street Memo." *Sunday Times* (London), 1 May 2005. http://www
    .timesonline.co.uk/article/0,,2087-1593607,00.html.
Seth, Ronald. *The Truth Benders: Psychological Warfare in the Second World War.* London:
    Leslie Frewin, 1969.
Shaffer, Brenda. "Iran at the Nuclear Threshold." *Arms Control Today* (November 2003):
    7–12.
Shaw, John. "Bush National Security Strategy Drawing Both Praise and Criticism."
    Washington Diplomat (November 2002). http://washingtondiplomat.com/02-11/
    c1_02_11.html.
Shrader, Katherine. "Senate Iraq Intelligence Probe Nears End." Associated Press Wire, 10
    March 2005. Lexis-Nexis news wire database. http://www.lexis-nexis.com.
Shulsky, Abram, and Gary Schmitt. *Silent Warfare: Understanding the World of Intelligence.*
    2nd ed. London: Brassey's, 1993.
Sigal, Leon V. *Disarming Strangers: Nuclear Diplomacy with North Korea.* Princeton, N.J.:
    Princeton University Press, 1998.
———. "North Korea Is No Iraq: Pyongyang's Negotiating Strategy." *Arms Control Today*
    (December 2002). http://www.armscontrol.org/act/2002_12/sigal_dec02.asp.
"Significance of the H-Bomb, and America's Dilemma." *Newsweek*, 13 February 1950, 20.
Simpson, Christopher. *National Security Directives of the Reagan and Bush Administrations.*
    Boulder, Colo.: Westview Press, 1995.
Singer, Peter. *Corporate Warriors: The Rise of the Privatized Military Industry.* Ithaca, N.Y.:
    Cornell University Press, 2003.
———. "War, Profits and the Vacuum of Law: Privatized Military Firms and International
    Law." *Columbia Journal of Transnational Law* 42 (Spring 2004): 521–50.
Slaughter, Anne-Marie. *A New World Order.* Princeton, N.J.: Princeton University Press,
    2004.
Smith, Anthony. *America's Mission: The United States and the Worldwide Struggle for
    Democracy in the Twentieth Century.* Princeton, N.J.: Princeton University Press, 1994.
Smith, Derek D. "Deterrence and Counterproliferation in an Age of Weapons of Mass
    Destruction." *Security Studies* 12 (Summer 2003): 152–97.
Snow, Donald M. "Levels of Strategy and American Strategic Nuclear Policy." *Air
    University Review* 35 (November/December 1983): 63–73. http://www.airpower
    .maxwell.af.mil/airchronicles/aureview/1983/Nov-Dec/snow.html.
Solomon, Jay. "Battle Looms over Use of Prewar Iraq Intelligence." *Wall Street Journal*, 24
    March 2006.
Speed Roger W., and Michael May. "Dangerous Doctrine." *Bulletin of the Atomic Scientists*
    61 (March/April 2005): 38–49.
Stack, Kevin P. "A Negative View of Competitive Analysis." *International Journal of
    Intelligence and Counterintelligence* 10 (Winter 1997–98): 456–64.
Steinbruner, John. "Confusing Ends and Means: The Doctrine of Coercive Pre-emption."
    Arms Control Today (January/February 2003): 3–6.
Steiner, James E. Overview to "Challenging the Red Line between Intelligence and Policy."
    Georgetown University Institute for the Study of Diplomacy Report, 2004. http://cfdev
    .georgetown.edu/sfs/programs/isd/redline.pdf.
Steury, Donald P., ed. *Intentions and Capabilities: Estimates on Soviet Strategic Forces,
    1950–1983.* Washington, D.C.: Central Intelligence Agency, 1996.
Strategic Survey 2003/4. London: International Institute for Strategic Studies, 2004.

Stromseth, Jane. "Law and Force after Iraq: A Transitional Moment." *American Journal of International Law* 97 (July 2003): 628–42. Lexis-Nexis legal research database. http://www.lexis-nexis.com.

Sunstein, Cass. *Republic.com.* New Haven, Conn.: Yale University Press, 2001.

Suri, Jeremi. *Power and Protest: Global Revolution and the Rise of Détente.* Cambridge, Mass.: Harvard University Press, 2003.

Suskind, Ron. *The Price of Loyalty: George W. Bush, the White House, and the Education of Paul O'Neill.* New York: Simon and Schuster, 2004.

Taft, William H., IV, and Todd F. Buchwald. "Preemption, Iraq, and International Law." *American Journal of International Law* 97 (July 2003): 557–85. Lexis-Nexis legal research database. http://www.lexis-nexis.com.

Tanaka, Yuki. *Hidden Horrors: Japanese War Crimes in World War II.* Boulder, Colo.: Westview Press, 1996.

Teichman, Jenny. *Pacifism and the Just War.* Oxford: Oxford University Press, 1986.

Tenet, George. Letter to Hon. Bob Graham. 7 October 2002. *Congressional Record,* 9 October 2002, S10154.

———. "The Worldwide Threat in 2003: Evolving Dangers in a Complex World." DCI's Worldwide Threat Briefing, 11 February 2003. http://www.cia.gov/cia/public_affairs/speeches/dci_speech_02112003.html.

———. "Transcript of Tenet Address on WMD Intelligence." 5 February 2004. http://www.cnn.com/2004/US/02/05/tenet.transcript.ap/index.html.

Thielmann, Greg. "Rumsfeld Reprise? The Missile Report That Foretold the Iraq Intelligence Controversy." *Arms Control Today* (July/August 2003): 3–9.

Thomas, Caroline. *Global Governance, Development and Human Security: The Challenge of Poverty and Inequality.* London: Pluto Press, 2000.

Timmerman, Kenneth R. Member Statement. Committee on the Present Danger Web site. http://www.fightingterror.org/members/index.cfm.

———. *Countdown to Crisis: The Coming Nuclear Showdown with Iran.* New York: Crown Forum, 2005.

Toland, John. *The Rising Sun: The Decline and Fall of the Japanese Empire 1936–1945.* New York: Random House, 1970.

Toner, Robin, and Marjorie Connelly. "Bush's Support Tumbles on Major Issues." *New York Times,* 17 June 2005.

Trachtenberg, Marc. *History and Strategy.* Princeton, N.J.: Princeton University Press, 1991.

Treverton, Gregory R. "Intelligence: The Achilles Heel of the Bush Doctrine." *Arms Control Today* (July/August 2003): 9–11.

Tyler, Patrick E. "U.S. Strategy Plan Calls for Insuring No Rivals Develop." *New York Times,* 8 March 1992.

Tyson, Ann Scott. "Use of Force in Korea Is Tricky Proposition." *Christian Science Monitor,* 12 February 2003.

Ullmann, Harlan, and James Wade Jr. *Shock and Awe: Achieving Rapid Dominance.* Washington, D.C.: National Defense University Press, 1996.

United Nations. International Atomic Energy Agency. "International Atomic Energy Agency Update Report for the Security Council Pursuant to Resolution 1441 (2002)." 20 January 2003. http://www.iaea.org/NewsCenter/Focus/IaeaIraq/unscreport_290103.html.

United States. Air Force Space Command. *Strategic Master Plan, FY '04 and Beyond.* 5 November 2002. http://www.peterson.af.mil/hqafspc/library/AFSPCPAOffice/Final%2004%20SMP--Signed!.pdf.

United States. Central Intelligence Agency. *Intelligence Community Experiment in Competitive Analysis: Soviet Strategic Objectives, an Alternate View: Report of Team 'B.'* Washington, D.C.: Government Printing Office, 1976.

————. "Prewar Status of Iraq's Weapons of Mass Destruction." March 1991. http://www
.gwu.edu/~nsarchiv/NSAEBB/NSAEBB80/wmd04.pdf.

————. *Iraq's Weapons of Mass Destruction Programs.* Washington, D.C.: Central Intelligence Agency, 2002.

United States. Chairman of the Joint Chiefs of Staff. "Doctrine for Joint Nuclear Operations." 15 March 2005 draft of Joint Publication 3-12. http://www.globalsecurity.org/
wmd/library/policy/dod/jp3_12fc2.pdf.

United States. Commission on National Security/21st Century. *Road Map for National
Security: Imperative for Change.* 31 January 2001. http://www.cfr.org/pdf/Hart-Rud
man3.pdf.

United States. Commission on the Intelligence Capabilities of the United States Regarding
Weapons of Mass Destruction. *Report to the President.* March 2005. http://www.wmd
.gov/report/.

United States. Defense Intelligence Agency. DITSUM #044-02. February 2002. Declassified in Kathleen P. Turner, Letter to Hon. John Rockefeller, 26 October 2005.

United States. Defense Science Board. *The Defense Science Board 1997 Summer Study Task
Force on DoD Response to Transnational Threats.* Vol. 1, *Final Report.* Washington, D.C.:
Department of Defense, 1997.

United States. Department of Defense. "Proliferation: Threat and Response." April 1996.
http://www.iraqwatch.org/government/US/Pentagon/dod-prolif-1996.htm.

————. *Dictionary of Military and Associated Terms.* Joint Publication I-02. April 2001.
http://www.dtic.mil/doctrine/jel/new_pubs/jp1_02.pdf.

United States. Department of Energy. Secretary of Energy Advisory Board. "A Report Card
on the Department of Energy's Non-Proliferation Programs with Russia." 10 January
2001. http://www.ceip.org/files/projects/npp/pdf/DOERussiaTaskForceReport011001.
pdf.

United States. Department of State. *Patterns of Global Terrorism 2001.* Washington, D.C.:
Department of State, 2002.

United States. Department of State. Office of the Spokesman, Colin Powell. "Press Remarks
with Foreign Minister of Egypt Amre Moussa." 24 February 2001. http://www.state
.gov/secretary/rm/2001/933.htm.

————. "Secretary of State Colin Powell on NBC's *Meet the Press.*" 22 October 2002.
http://usinfo.state.gov/xarchives/display.html?p=washfile-english&y=2002&m=Octo
ber&x=20021021101237eichler@pd.state.gov0.9141504&t=xarchives/xarchitem.html.

————. "Powell Says Time Is Running Out for Iraq to Comply with U.N." 19 January 2003.
http://usinfo.state.gov/xarchives/display.html?p=washfile-english&y=2003&m=Jan
uary&x=20030119162306DDenny@pd.state.gov0.1734735&t=xarchives/xarchitem.html.

————. "Interview with Secretary of State Colin L. Powell by International Wire Services."
18 March 2003. http://usinfo.state.gov/mena/Archive/2004/Feb/05-814752.html.

United States. General Accounting Office. "Operation Desert Storm: Evaluation of the
Air Campaign." GAO/NSIAD-97-134. June 1997. http://www.fas.org/man/gao/
nsiad97134/index.html.

United States. House Government Reform Committee. "Iraq on the Record: The Bush
Administration's Public Statements on Iraq." 16 March 2004. http://democrats.reform.
house.gov/IraqOnTheRecord/.

United States. National Commission on Terrorist Attacks upon the United States. *The 9/11
Commission Report.* Washington, D.C.: Government Printing Office, 2004.

United States. National Intelligence Council. National Intelligence Estimate. "Foreign
Missile Developments and the Ballistic Missile Threat Through 2015." Unclassified
summary. December 2001. http://www.cia.gov/nic/PDF_GIF_otherprod/missile
threat2001.pdf.

————. National Intelligence Estimate. "Iraq's Continuing Programs for Weapons of Mass Destruction." Declassified excerpts. 18 July 2003. http://www.fas.org/irp/cia/product/iraq-wmd.html.

United States. National Security Council. "NSC 68: United States Objectives and Programs for National Security." 14 April 1950. (Top Secret, declassified 1975.) http://www.fas .org/irp/offdocs/nsc-hst/nsc-68-9.htm.

United States. Senate Armed Services Committee. *Hearings on Iraqi Weapons of Mass Destruction and Related Programs.* 10 September 2002. Lexis-Nexis congressional research database. http://www.lexis-nexis.com.

————. *Hearing on Iraqi Weapons of Mass Destruction and Related Programs.* 28 January 2004. Lexis-Nexis congressional research database. http://www.lexis-nexis.com.

————. *Future Worldwide Threats to U.S. National Security.* Hearing of the Senate Armed Services Committee. 9 March 2004. Lexis-Nexis congressional research database. http://www.lexis-nexis.com.

United States. Senate Foreign Relations Committee. "Interview of Ms. DeSutter with Regard to the Bolton Nomination." 5 May 2005. http://www.thewashingtonnote.com/archives/DeSutter%20Interview.pdf.

United States. Senate Select Committee on Intelligence. *Report on the US Intelligence Community's Prewar Intelligence Assessments on Iraq.* 7 July 2004. http://www.intel ligence.senate.gov/ iraqreport.pdf.

United States. Strategic Command. *Strategic Deterrence Joint Operating Concept.* February 2004. http://www.dtic.mil/futurejointwarfare/concepts/sd_joc_v1.doc.

United States. White House. "Commission on the Intelligence Capabilities of the United States Regarding Weapons of Mass Destruction." Executive Order. 6 February 2004. http://www.whitehouse.gov/news/releases/2004/02/20040206-10.html.

United States. White House Office of Homeland Security. "The National Security Strategy of the United States of America." September 2002. http://www.whitehouse.gov/nsc/nss .html.

————. "National Strategy to Combat Weapons of Mass Destruction." December 2002. http://www.whitehouse.gov/news/releases/2002/12/WMDStrategy.pdff.

United States. White House Office of the Press Secretary. "President Bush, Prime Minister Blair Discuss Keeping the Peace, Camp David, MD, September 7, 2002." *Weekly Compilation of Presidential Documents* 38 (2002): 1518–20.

————. "Remarks Prior to Discussions with President Alvaro Uribe of Columbia and an Exchange With Reporters, September 27, 2002." *Weekly Compilation of Presidential Documents* 38 (2002): 1618–20.

————. "President George Bush Discusses Iraq in National Press Conference, March 6, 2003." *Weekly Compilation of Presidential Documents* 39 (2003): 295–305.

————. "Remarks Following Discussions with Secretary General Kofi Annan of the United Nations and an Exchange with Reporters July 14, 2003." *Weekly Compilation of Presidential Documents* 39 (2003): 914–17.

Van Cleave, William. Member statement. Committee on the Present Danger Web site. http://www.fightingterror.org/members/index.cfm.

VandeHei, Jim. "Cheney Warns of Iran as a Nuclear Threat." *Washington Post,* 21 January 2005.

Vandenbroucke, Lucien S. "The Israeli Strike against Osiraq." *Air University Review* 35 (September/October 1984): 35–47.

Van Eemeren, Frans, and Rob Grootendorst. *Speech Acts in Argumentative Discussions.* Dordrecht: Foris, 1984.

Van Evera, Stephen. *The Causes of War: Power and the Roots of Conflict.* Ithaca, N.Y.: Cornell University Press, 1999.

Van Natta, Don, Jr. "Bush Was Set on Path to War, Memo by British Adviser Says." *New York Times,* 27 March 2006.

"Vice President Dick Cheney Discusses a Possible War with Iraq." *Meet the Press.* NBC News Transcripts, 16 March 2003. Lexis-Nexis news wire database. http://www.lexis -nexis.org.

Vieth, Warren, and Josh Meyer. "Bush Likens War on Terror to Cold War." *Los Angeles Times,* 7 October 2005.

Waas, Murray. "What Bush Was Told about Iraq." *National Journal,* 2 March 2006. http://nationaljournal.com/about/njweekly/stories/2006/0302nj1.htm.

Walgrave, Stefan. "Transnational Movements and National Opportunities: The Case of the Worldwide Anti–Iraqi War Protest on February 15th, 2003." Paper presented at the Annual Meeting of the American Political Science Association, Chicago, September 2004.

Walker, Matt. "Truth and Technology at War." *New Scientist,* 20 December 2003, 12–13.

Wallace, Karl R. "Topoi and the Problem of Invention." *Quarterly Journal of Speech* 58 (December 1972): 387–96.

Wallace, Kelly. "White House Repeats 'Concerns' about Cuba, Biological Weapons." CNN, 14 May 2002. http://www.cnn.com/2002/ALLPOLITICS/05/14/white.house.cuba/.

Walzer, Michael. *Just and Unjust Wars.* New York: Basic Books, 1977.

Wander, Philip. "The Rhetoric of American Foreign Policy." *Quarterly Journal of Speech* 70 (1984): 339–61.

Warrick, Joby. "Evidence on Iraq Challenged." *Washington Post,* 19 September 2002.

———. "U.S. Claim on Iraqi Nuclear Program Is Called Into Question." *Washington Post,* 24 January 2003.

———. "Lacking Biolabs, Trailers Carried Case for War." *Washington Post,* 12 April 2006.

Watts, Barry D., and Thomas A. Keaney. *Gulf War Air Power Survey.* Vol. 2, *Operations and Effects and Effectiveness, Part II: Effects and Effectiveness.* Washington, D.C.: Government Printing Office, 1993.

Waxman, Henry. Letter to Christopher Shays. 1 March 2005. http://www.democrats.reform .house.gov/Documents/20050301112122-90349.pdf.

Weisman, Steven R. "Preemption: Idea With a Lineage Whose Time Has Come." *New York Times,* 23 March 2003.

Weiss, Thomas G. "Principles, Politics, and Humanitarian Action." *Ethics and International Affairs* 13 (1999): 1–22.

Weissert, Carol. "Policy Entrepreneurs, Policy Opportunists, and Legislative Effectiveness." *American Politics Quarterly* 19 (1991): 262–74.

Weldon, Curt. *Countdown to Terror.* Washington, D.C.: Regnery, 2005.

Whaley, Barton. *Codeword Barbarossa.* Cambridge, Mass.: MIT Press, 1973.

White, Jeffrey. "Iranian Nuclear Weapons, Part III: How Might Iran Retaliate?" Policywatch No. 762. Washington Institute for Near East Policy. 29 May 2003. http://www .washingtoninstitute.org/watch/index.htm.

Whitelaw, Kevin, Ilana Ozernoy, and Terence Samuel. "Hit by Friendly Fire." *U.S. News and World Report,* 27 June 2005, 26.

Willard, Charles Arthur. *Liberalism and the Problem of Knowledge.* Chicago: University of Chicago Press, 1996.

Wills, Garry. "The Tragedy of Bill Clinton." *New York Review of Books,* 12 August 2004, 64.

Wilson, Richard. "A Visit to the Bombed Nuclear Reactor at Tuwaitha, Iraq." *Nature,* 31 March 1983, 373–76.

Winkler, Carol. "Globalized Manifest Destiny: The Rhetoric of the Bush Administration in Response to the Attacks of September 11th." *Controversia: An Internatonal Journal of Debate and Democratic Renewal* 1 (2002): 85–105.

————. *In the Name of Terrorism: Presidents on Political Violence in the Post–World War II Era.* Albany: State University of New York Press, 2006.

Wishnick, Elizabeth. *Mending Fences: The Evolution of Moscow's China Policy from Brezhnev to Yeltsin.* Seattle: University of Washington Press, 2003.

Wit, Joel S., Daniel B. Poneman, and Robert L. Gallucci. *Going Critical: The First North Korean Nuclear Crisis.* Washington, D.C.: Brookings Institution Press, 2004.

Wolfowitz, Paul. Prepared Testimony. *Joint Inquiry Hearing on Counterterrorist Center Customer Perspective.* Senate Select Committee on Intelligence and House Permanent Select Committee on Intelligence. 19 September 2002. http://www.defenselink. mil/speeches/2002/s20020919-depsecdef1.html.

————. Department of Defense Transcript of Sam Tannenhaus Interview with Deputy Secretary of Defense Wolfowitz. 9 May 2003. http://www.defenselink.mil/transcripts/ 2003/tr20030510.

————. "Deputy Secretary Wolfowitz Interview with Karen DeYoung, *Washington Post,* May 28, 2003." U.S. Department of Defense News Transcript. http://www.defenselink .mil/cgi-bin/dlprin.cgi?.

Wolk, Herman S. "The Blueprint for Cold War Defense." *Air Force* 83 (2000). http://www .afa.org/magazine/march2000/0300coldwar.asp.

Woodward, Bob. *Bush at War.* New York: Simon and Schuster, 2002.

————. *Plan of Attack.* New York: Simon and Schuster, 2004.

Wright, Robin. *Sacred Rage: The Wrath of Militant Islam.* New York: Simon and Schuster, 2001.

Wurmser, David. *Tyranny's Ally: America's Failure to Defeat Saddam Hussein.* Washington, D.C.: American Enterprise Institute Press, 1999.

Yaqub, Salim. "Imperious Doctrines; U.S.-Arab Relations from Dwight D. Eisenhower to George W. Bush." *Diplomatic History* 26 (Fall 2002): 579–90.

Yenne, Bill. *Attack of the Drones: A History of Unmanned Aerial Combat.* St. Paul, Minn.: Zenith Press, 2004.

Yoo, John. "International Law and the War in Iraq." *American Journal of International Law* 97 (July 2003): 563–75. Lexis-Nexis legal research database. http://www.lexis-nexis.com.

Zakaria, Fareed. "Exaggerating the Threats." *Newsweek,* 16 June 2003, 33.

Zakaria, Tabassum. "Give Up 'Delusional Hope' of Iraq WMD, Kay Says." ABC News, 28 July 2004. http://abcnews.go.com/wire/US/reuters20040728_479.html.

Zarefsky, David. "President Johnson's War on Poverty: The Rhetoric of Three 'Establishment' Movements." *Communication Monographs* 44 (1977): 352–53.

Zartman, I. William. *Ripe for Resolution.* New York: Oxford University Press, 1989.

————. "Ripeness: The Hurting Stalemate and Beyond." In *International Conflict Resolution after the Cold War,* edited by Paul Stern and Daniel Druckman, 225–50. Washington, D.C.: National Academy Press, 2000.

————. "The Attack on Humanity: Conflict and Management." Social Science Research Council Paper. http://www.ssrc.org/sept11/essays/zartman_text_only.htm.

CONTRIBUTORS

PETER DOMBROWSKI is Associate Professor in the Strategic Research Department of the Center for Naval Warfare Studies, U.S. Naval War College. Dombrowski's research specializes in international relations, global finance, foreign economic policy-making, and international assistance to the post-Communist transition. He is author of *Policy Responses to the Globalization of American Banking* (University of Pittsburgh Press, 1996), and his articles have appeared in journals such as *Policy Studies Review, Nationalism and Ethnic Politics, International Studies Perspectives*, and *Policy Studies Journal*. Dombrowski currently serves as coeditor of the journal *International Studies Quarterly*.

G. THOMAS GOODNIGHT is Professor at the Annenberg School for Communication, University of Southern California. Goodnight's research interests include deliberation and postwar society, science communication, argument and aesthetics, public discourse studies, and communicative reason in controversy. His articles on Cold War rhetoric, crisis management, and communicative dimensions of diplomacy have appeared in journals such as *American Diplomacy, International Journal of Public Opinion Research, Quarterly Journal of Speech, Argumentation and Advocacy*, and *Communication Monographs*.

WILLIAM HARTUNG is President's Fellow and Director of the Arms Trade Resource Center of the World Policy Institute, New School for Social Research. Hartung's research focuses on the arms trade, missile defense, and military spending. He is the author or coauthor of numerous books and studies, including *The Economic Consequences of a Nuclear Freeze* (Council on Economic Priorities, 1983), *And Weapons for All* (HarperCollins, 1985), *Star Wars* (Ballinger Press, 1987), and *Peddling Influence* (World Policy Institute, 1997). His articles have appeared in the *New York Times, Washington Post,*

347

Newsday, USA Today, Christian Science Monitor, Nation, Harper's, Bulletin of the Atomic Scientists, and *World Policy Journal.*

JACQUES E. C. HYMANS is Assistant Professor of Government at Smith College. Hymans received his Ph.D. in political science from Harvard University in 2001. He has held residential fellowships at the Mershon Center at the Ohio State University, the Olin Institute for Strategic Studies at Harvard University, the Center for International Security and Cooperation at Stanford University, and the École Normale Supérieure in Paris. His research focuses on international relations and foreign policy, with an emphasis on the growth and impact of collective identities, and his work has appeared in journals such as the *European Journal of International Relations, Security Studies,* and *Nonproliferation Review.* Hymans is author of *The Psychology of Nuclear Proliferation: Identity, Emotions, and Foreign Policy* (New York: Cambridge University Press, 2006).

WILLIAM W. KELLER is the Wesley W. Posvar Professor of International Security Studies and Director of the Ridgway Center for International Security Studies, University of Pittsburgh. Keller's primary fields of research include terrorism, weapons of mass destruction, Asian innovation, multinational corporations, internal security and the FBI, the arms trade, and international security theory and practice. He is author of *The Liberals and J. Edgar Hoover* (Princeton University Press, 1989) and *Arm-in-Arm* (Basic Books, 1995) and coauthor of *The Myth of the Global Corporation* (Princeton University Press, 1998) and *Crisis and Innovation in Asian Technology* (Cambridge University Press, 2002). Keller formerly worked as executive director of the Center for International Studies at the Massachusetts Institute of Technology (MIT) and research director of MIT's Japan Program. From 1987 to 1995, he was project director and senior analyst for the US Congress's Office of Technology Assessment in Washington, D.C.

GORDON R. MITCHELL is Associate Professor of Communication and Director of Debate at the University of Pittsburgh, and Chair of the Working Group on Preemptive and Preventive Military Intervention at the Ridgway Center for International Security Studies. Mitchell's research concentrates on public argument and rhetoric of science. His book *Strategic Deception* (Michigan State University Press, 2000) won the National Communication Association's Winans-Wichelns Award for Distinguished Scholarship in Rhetoric and Public Address. His articles on missile defense have appeared in journals such as the *Bulletin of the Atomic Scientists; Fletcher Forum of World Affairs; Science, Technology, and Human Values;* and *Quarterly Journal of Speech.* Mitchell's briefing papers have been published by numerous organizations, including the Federation of American Scientists, the International Security Information Service (UK and Europe), and the Peace Research Institute Frankfurt.

ROBERT P. NEWMAN is Professor Emeritus of Communication at the University of Pittsburgh. Newman's research focuses on Asian–US relationships, American foreign interventions, NSC–68, and other official doctrines relating to US foreign policy. He is author of *Recognition of Communist China?* (Macmillan, 1961), *The Cold War Romance of Lillian Hellman and John Melby* (University of North Carolina Press, 1990), *Owen Lattimore and the "Loss" of China* (University of California Press, 1992), *Truman and the Hiroshima Cult* (Michigan State University Press, 1995), and *Enola Gay in the Court of History* (Peter Lang, 2004). His books have won the National Communication Association's (NCA) Winans-Wichelns Award for Distinguished Scholarship in Rhetoric and Public Address, and the NCA's Diamond Anniversary Book Award. Newman is a decorated World War II veteran, having served in the Saar, Rhein, and Central European Campaigns with the 70th Cavalry Reconnaissance Troop.

RODGER A. PAYNE is Professor of Political Science at the University of Louisville. Payne is the coauthor of *Democratizing Global Politics: Discourse Norms, International Regimes and Political Community* (State University of New York Press, 2004). He has also authored a large number of articles and book chapters on global environmental politics, international security, and political communication. His work as appeared in journals such as the *European Journal of International Relations, Journal of Democracy, Journal of Peace Research,* and *Political Communication.* Since 1994, Payne has served as the director of the Grawemeyer Award for Ideas Improving World Order, an endowed $200,000 annual prize. In 2005, Payne was a Fellow at the Belfer Center for Science and International Affairs at Harvard University. He was previously the recipient of an SSRC-MacArthur Foundation fellowship.

SIMON REICH is Professor of Political Science and Public and International Affairs (joint appointment), Director of the Ford Institute for Human Security, and Research Associate of the Ridgway Center for International Security Studies, University of Pittsburgh. Reich is author and coauthor of several books, including of *The Fruits of Fascism* (Cornell University Press, 1990), *The German Predicament* (Cornell University Press, 1997), and *The Myth of the Global Corporation* (Princeton University Press, 1998). He has been awarded a numerous fellowships, including those from the Ford Foundation, the Sloan Foundation, and the Kellogg Institute, and was an International Affairs Fellow at the Council on Foreign Relations. Reich formerly worked at the US Congressional Office of Technology Assessment and has served as Director of Research and Analysis at the Royal Institute of International Affairs, Chatham House.

DAN REITER is the Winship Research Professor of Political Science, Emory University. Reiter's research specializations include international conflict, foreign policy decision-making, national security policy, and international alliances. He is author of *Crucible of Beliefs* (Cornell University Press, 1996) and coauthor of *Democracies at War* (Princeton University Press, 2002). Reiter's articles have appeared in journals such as *International Security, Journal of Conflict Resolution, International Studies Quarterly, Journal of Politics, Political Science Review,* and *World Politics.*

TOM ROCKMORE is Professor of Philosophy at Duquesne University. Rockmore specializes in continental philosophy. He is coeditor of *The Philosophical Challenge of September 11* (Blackwell, 2004) and author of numerous other books, including *Hegel, Idealism and Analytical Philosophy* (Yale University Press, 2005), *Cognition: An Introduction to Hegel's Phenomenology of Spirit* (University of California Press, 1997), and *Habermas on Historical Materialism* (Indiana University Press, 1989).

GREG THIELMANN is the former Director of the Office of Strategic Proliferation and Military Affairs, U.S. State Department, and a retired US Foreign Service officer. In addition to tours abroad as a political officer (in Brazil, Germany, and the Soviet Union), he participated in the opening round of the Geneva negotiations on Intermediate-Range Nuclear Forces and served in a number of domestic State Department positions, including Officer-in-Charge of German Affairs, Special Assistant to Ambassador Paul Nitze (then special adviser to the president and secretary of state for arms control affairs), and Congressional Fellow in the Office of Senator Tom Harkin. His last position was Office Director for Strategic, Proliferation, and Military Issues in the Bureau of Intelligence and Research.

INDEX

214; and Iran, 252; and Iraq War, 7, 13, 15,
80–81, 83, 86, 121, 143, 164, 182, 198, 222;
and nuclear first strikes, 241; and planning
documents, 6, 222, 226; on preventive
force, 4, 19, 45, 104, 241; and psychological
operations, 246; and Team B, 224
Rumsfeld Commission, 157, 224
Russert, Tim, 125
Russia: and Chechen terror groups, 229; and
Kosovo bombing campaign, 60; nuclear
weapons in, 231, 232. *See also* Union of
Soviet Socialist Republics (USSR)
Rwanda, 54–55
Rycroft, Matthew, 225

Saddam Hussein. *See* Hussein, Saddam
Safire, William, 80
Sahnoun, Mohamed, 45, 60
sanctions, against Iraq, 201–3, 233
Sapiro, Miriam, 106
Sawyer, Diane, 142
Schake, Kori, 184
Scheuer, Michael, 88
Schlesinger, Arthur M., Jr., 10, 140, 225, 248
Schröder, Gerhard, 204–7, 212
Schroeder, Paul, 116
Schultz, George, 104
self-defense, as justification for war, 98–101,
138, 140, 146, 149
Senate Select Intelligence Committee, 20, 110,
123, 125, 126, 128, 131, 134, 159, 161, 163,
171–72, 222
September 11, 2001, attacks: conspiracy
theories about, 7; French diplomacy after,
202–4; impact of, 94; Iraq War and, 80;
NSS 2002 as response to, 5–6; security
policy shifts after, 105–11, 114
Serbia, 209
Shulsky, Abram, 6, 85, 285n90
Sierra Leone, 60
Silberman-Robb Commission, 172, 252, 255
Simon, Steven, 82, 87, 89, 241, 261–62
Simpson, Christopher, 15
Six Days' War, 149, 247
Slovenia, 209
Smith, M. L. R., 248
Somali National Alliance, 58
Somalia, 55, 56–58, 65, 93
South Africa, 43
South Korea, 235
sovereignty: dilution of, 47–49, 66, 69;
peacekeeping and, 16–17, 47–51; preventive
intervention and, 52, 61; and responsibility,
52, 59, 63; traditional concept of, 47, 50–51
Soviet Union. *See* Union of Soviet Socialist
Republics (USSR)
spectrum of force, 11–12

Stalin, Joseph, 73
State Department Bureau of Intelligence and
Research (INR), 128–30, 161, 165, 166, 221,
253, 311n31
Stedman, Stephen John, 56, 58
Steiner, James, 82
Stengrim, Laura, 19
Steury, Donald, 79
Stevenson, Adlai, 18
stovepiping, 84–86, 134, 251
STRATCOM (US Strategic Command), 242,
243
Strategic Arms Reduction Treaty, 159
strategic doctrine: consequences of, 94;
formation of post–September 11, 102–5;
purpose of, 95–96; rhetoric of, 96
Strategic Offensive Reductions Treaty, 232
Stromseth, Jane, 111
Sudan, 32, 33, 56
Sun (newspaper), 211
Sunstein, Cass, 261
Sutton, Willie, 231
Syria, 121, 184, 188–90, 247

Taft, William, IV, 111
Team B, 17, 78–86, 224
technology: preventive force and, 243, 248; and
public discourse, 261–62
Teller, Edward, 78
Tenet, George, 83–84, 132, 161, 162, 172, 223,
253, 257
terrorism: attitude toward, pre–September 11,
94; deterrence ineffective against, 42, 233;
and nuclear weapons, 230–32; organizational
relationships in, 81; preventive diplomacy
and, 235–36; preventive war strategy and,
97–102, 116, 169–71, 192, 217, 228–29;
rhetorical use of, 106. *See also* al-Qaida; war
on terrorism
Themistocles of Athens, 85
Thielmann, Greg, 10, 21–23, 41, 84–86, 134,
221, 244, 250, 252, 253, 257
Thompson, Llewellyn, 73
threats: evidence of, 20; exaggeration of, 22–23,
124–29, 156–59, 165, 219–24; imminence of,
11, 19, 97, 100–101, 103–4, 139, 141
Thucydides, 148
Tonkin Gulf affair, 158–59
topoi, 249
Trojan, 72, 75
Truman, Harry S., and administration, 73–75,
95
truth, consensus versus, 144
Turner Foundation, 232
two-war standard, for military force evaluation,
178–79